Rationality, Rules, and Ideals

Critical Essays on Bernard Gert's Moral Theory

edited by
WALTER SINNOTT-ARMSTRONG
AND
ROBERT AUDI

ROWMAN & LITTLEFIELD PUBLISHERS, INC.
Lanham • Boulder • New York • Oxford

ROWMAN & LITTLEFIELD PUBLISHERS, INC.

Published in the United States of America
by Rowman & Littlefield Publishers, Inc.
An Imprint of the Rowman & Littlefield Publishing Group
4720 Boston Way, Lanham, Maryland 20706
www.rowmanlittlefield.com

12 Hid's Copse Road
Cumnor Hill, Oxford OX2 9JJ, England

British Library Cataloguing in Publication Information Available

Library of Congress Cataloging in Publication Data

Rationality, rules, and ideals : critical essays on Bernard Gert's moral theory / edited by Walter Sinnott-Armstrong and Robert Audi.
p. cm.
Includes bibliographical references and index.
ISBN 0-7425-1316-5 (cloth : alk. paper)—ISBN 0-7425-1317-3 (pbk. : alk. paper)
1. Gert, Bernard, 1934—Ethics. 2. Ethics, Modern—20th century. I. Sinnott-Armstrong, Walter, 1955– II. Audi, Robert, 1941–

BJ354.G473 R38 2002
171'.2—dc21

2002024822

Printed in the United States of America

™ The paper used in this publication meets the minimum requirements of American National Standard for Information Sciences—Permanence of Paper for Printed Library Materials, ANSI/NISO Z39.48-1992.

Contents

Part IV: Ideals and Goods

Part V: Virtue and Character

Part VI: Reply

Preface

Bernard Gert's *Morality* is the culmination of forty years of development of an original moral theory. In every version in which Gert has stated the theory, it has struck readers as a comprehensive and bold expression of a position that provokes reflection and strong reactions independently of whether one agrees. The theory is built on distinctive accounts of rationality and impartiality; it yields a set of concrete moral rules for human life; and it ranges over moral ideals, moral virtues, and many other major topics in ethics. This collection provides rigorous responses to Gert's work by leading moral philosophers who offer both stimulating critiques of Gert and their own positions on many of the major issues.

The first book-length statement of Gert's theory, *The Moral Rules,* appeared in 1970. Since then the view has had a far-reaching influence in applied ethics, including medical ethics, business ethics, engineering ethics, and the ethics of scientific research. Gert has served as a consultant on professional codes of ethics for the American Anthropological Association and the Geological Society of America, and also as a consultant for the Third Edition, Revised, of the *Diagnostic and Statistical Manual, Revised* (DSM-III-R) of the American Psychiatric Association. Gert was a member of the Panel on Scientific Responsibility and the Conduct of Research of the National Academy of Sciences, and he was the first philosopher to receive a grant from the Ethical, Legal, and Social Implications of the Human Genome Project (ELSI). His work on this project led to *Morality and the New Genetics* (1996). He is also the lead author of *Bioethics: A Return to Fundamentals* (1997), which applies his moral theory to a wide range of moral problems in medicine.

The growing recognition of the importance of Gert's moral theory has generated many discussions in books and a number of articles in journals, including a lively interchange in recent issues of *Ethics*. A recent conference at the Kulturwissenschaftliches Institut in Germany and a book symposium on Gert's work in *Philosophy and Phenomenological Research* are further indications of his importance. Nonetheless, there remain unexplored or inadequately studied aspects of his position. This volume fills the need to examine its potential as the comprehensive, lucidly justified, universally acceptable account of morality he intends it to be, and it does so in a way that fruitfully compares his position with other major views on the contemporary scene.

To ensure that the theory would receive critical evaluation by a wide range of leading ethical theorists, we held an international conference at Dartmouth in 1999, with contributors from Australia, Canada, and Germany as well as the United States. Their papers were circulated to all participants in advance of the conference. The authors have sought not only to evaluate major elements in Gert's theory, but to make a number of points of independent interest. In many cases the papers will be useful to readers as contributions by leading moral philosophers even apart from their value in appraising important elements in Gert's position.

Of special value is Gert's detailed reply to the other contributors. He clarifies his views, shows that they incorporate more subtlety and qualifications than their usually simple formulations suggest, and brings his theory to bear on some problems not previously raised for it. Taking this major paper together with the other contributions, the book presents the first stage in what will be a fruitful debate among the several competing theories represented in the volume.

Both in preparing for the conference and in the revisions that followed, authors sought to write with a clarity that makes their papers accessible to general readers in ethics. The conference was attended by students and nonphilosophers, and selected Dartmouth students were asked to provide comments on the papers, with special attention to any passages they found difficult. The papers were presented in extended sessions in which commentaries were provided by other theorists, and criticisms and ideas were exchanged among participants. The result is a set of papers that meet high professional standards but are readily intelligible to students and professionals outside philosophy.

For contributing to the conference and to discussions of the papers we thank the sessions chairs, Dan Brock, Ruth Chang, David Cummiskey, Ron Green, Virginia Held, Bob Ladenson, Paul McNamara, Stephen Nathanson, David Phillips, Fred Schauer, Jim Sterba, and Kathleen Wallace. We are also grateful to Barbara Hillinger and Bonnie Bergeron at Dartmouth's Institute for Applied and Professional Ethics for magnificent office support; to Dan Bush, who provided research assistance and comments on all of the papers; and to Kier Olsen DeVries, who helped us put together the camera-ready copy. Financial support was provided by Eunice and Julian Cohen, as well as by Ed Berger, Dean of the Faculty at Dartmouth College. We gratefully acknowledge their help. It need hardly be said that the other contributors deserve our thanks for their work over a period of some two years.

Finally, we should say that this volume is only one among many tributes to the value of Bernard Gert's writings in moral philosophy. Without his provocative and comprehensive theorizing as a stimulus, the original essays appearing here and a multitude of other contributions to the field would not exist. It is with both appreciation and pleasure that we dedicate this volume to him.

The Scope and Structure of the Essays: A Short Introduction

Robert Audi and Walter Sinnott-Armstrong

Gert's *Morality*, like his earlier statements of his position, has many important virtues. First, it is among the clearest and most comprehensive moral theories on the contemporary scene. Second, it is bold and provocative: whether or not readers agree with him, Gert's forceful and straightforward formulations challenge one to grapple with his arguments. Third, in contrast with the relatively few competing comprehensive theories, Gert's moral theory is far more detailed and more concretely worked out, with numerous illustrations of each major point. By contrast with the much more common narrowly focused treatments of individual moral issues, Gert's position is far more systematic.

Because of these virtues, Gert's moral theory provides what many people are looking for. In recent years philosophers and others have expressed much dissatisfaction concerning the dominant orientations in ethics, particularly utilitarianism, Kantianism, contractarianism, and, more recently, virtue ethics. Gert's theory has affinities with each of these but does not fall neatly into any of these categories, because Gert tries to preserve the insights but avoid the problems in each of the traditional approaches. Also, Gert's theory is set forth, not with an overarching principle, but with a set of moral rules and ideals that are each applicable to everyday life; so it fits better with the way that most common people think about morality.

The overall structure of Gert's theory contains three interconnected elements: rationality, impartiality, and morality. Gert provides an original account of each of these concepts: a hybrid list theory of rationality, an analysis of impartiality as elliptical, and a definition of morality as public and universal. Morality is conceived as constituted not only by moral rules—including standards and procedures for making reasonable exceptions to basic rules—but also by moral ideals and virtues. Gert's précis and the papers in this volume range over all of these topics. What follows is an indication of the scope of the papers in each part of the book.

Part I, Justification and Method, contains general papers by Ernst Tugendhat, Matthias Kettner, and Geoffrey Sayre-McCord. Tugendhat traces the development of Gert's claims for his justification of the moral rules and then argues that Gert conceded too much to his critics when he modified his views. Kettner argues that, while Gert provides a "value esperanto" that can be accepted by philosophers with widely disparate viewpoints, Gert's theory still needs to be supplemented by some insights from discourse ethics in order to achieve its practical goals. Sayre-McCord then contrasts Gert's "dumb bastard" theory with ideal observer theories and argues that moral theory need not be restricted to beliefs accepted by every rational person. Even if agents should not be held responsible for unavoidable ignorance when they act, fundamental moral theory still may employ facts about human nature or society which only some rational persons know.

Part II, Rationality and Reasons, begins with a paper by Robert Audi in which Audi supports the basic thrust of Gert's approach to rationality but argues for three ideas that a theory of rationality, including Gert's, needs to incorporate. First, rationality might be a positive status; hence it is not simply the absence of irrationality. Second, rationality is comparative; hence it admits of greater and lesser degrees in persons or actions. Third, even when a type of a thing is rational *for* a person to *do*, the person's doing it (the concrete token of that deed) may be done for a reason having nothing to do with the reason why it is the right thing to do; and then it might not be rational. Next, David Copp, after contrasting Gert's theory of rationality with more traditional theories in ways that commend Gert's theory, goes on to question whether any list theory of rationality can be helpful theoretically without being unified (such as by a concept of harm), whether it is sometimes irrational not to seek goods (as opposed to not avoiding losses of goods), and whether our desires, values, and life plans can provide reasons that can affect what it is rational for us to do. Michael Smith closes this section by defending his subjective desire-satisfaction theory of rationality against Gert's criticisms of subjective theories. Smith argues that his subjective theory can accommodate the main aspects of Gert's theory that make it so intuitively attractive.

In part III, Consequences and Rules, Shelly Kagan argues forcefully that Gert has failed to show that we are not both morally and rationally required to aid others. Walter Sinnott-Armstrong then interprets Gert as a special kind of rule consequentialist and defends a sophisticated version of act consequentialism against Gert's objections. In the end, Sinnott-Armstrong argues, the force of Gert's objections depends on the purpose of a moral theory, so Gert's criticisms fail to touch theories, including act consequentialism, that are supposed to serve purposes other than those of Gert's own theory. Susan Wolf defends Gert by lucidly presenting several practical and theoretical advantages of moral theories, like Gert's, that emphasize general rules instead of particular acts and their consequences.

This leads right into part IV, Ideals and Goods. John Deigh begins by separating several ways in which Gert distinguishes between moral rules and ideals and showing how some of Gert's claims depend upon conflating these distinctions. In particular, Deigh challenges Gert's use of impartiality to distinguish rules from ideals. Then Deigh proposes his own alternative account of moral ideals. Doug MacLean follows by characterizing Gert as a Hobbesian and revealing important advantages of a Hobbesian approach to morality, with its emphasis on avoiding evils. Frances Kamm responds by revealing some ways in which Gert deviates from Hobbes and falls more in line with common sense morality, with its emphasis on the separateness of persons. Ted Bond closes this section by arguing that morality is not exclusively concerned with avoiding and preventing evils, but aims instead to "create and maintain the good relations among people which enable individual persons to live rich and fulfilling self-directed lives."

Part V, Virtue and Character, includes papers by Julia Driver and Marcia Baron. Driver claims that Gert's views on moral virtue are distorted by his definition of morality as necessarily universal, public, and rational so that his account of moral virtues is further from commonsense morality in this area than Gert acknowledges. Baron, while agreeing with Gert's moderate impartialism, argues that Gert's view of morality is too restricted because of his emphasis on punishment, which leaves Gert unable to recognize several kinds of moral wrongness that do not warrant explicit punishment of the kind that Gert has in mind. In particular, according to Baron, the moral importance of character and feelings is underestimated by Gert.

In part VI, Reply, Gert responds to the major objections raised by the other contributors. Although he admits that the critical papers have shown him several ways in which details of his theory need to be reformulated, Gert argues that the core of his theory remains intact. Overall, his response shows that his view is more nuanced and resilient than many critics have thought. This response by itself constitutes a major contribution to moral theory that should help focus future debates on these important issues.

It will be obvious that this book, together with Gert's *Morality*, constitutes ample material for a wide-ranging course in ethics. What is perhaps less obvious is that such a course can be offered at several different curricular levels, depending on the amount of material to be covered, the level of detail in which it is treated, and the character of the institution and students in question. The collection is also designed to serve as material for a segment of a course. Each part can serve as a segment with a corresponding selection from *Morality*. Gert criticizes utilitarianism, Kantianism, and aspects of virtue ethics, and some of the papers respond in their defense; so the volume is eminently useful as a supplement to course sections on those topics. The same use could be made of the chapters in *Morality* on rationality and reason together with the corresponding section of this book.

Given the philosophical value of the papers, especially in the context of Gert's replies, we are confident that both professionals working in ethics and students of the subject will find much to work with here, whether in relation to teaching or in connection with research in the field. Each paper—particularly in the context of the admirably broad but concise précis of *Morality* Gert has provided—is essentially self-contained. The discussions at the conference made it plain that, both in philosophy and in other fields, there is a receptivity to the kinds of debates into which these papers enter. They contribute not only to understanding Gert's wide-ranging theory but to a number of important topics in ethical theory, the theory of rationality, and applied ethics.

Précis of *Morality: Its Nature and Justification*

Bernard Gert

This book provides an account of morality which explains and justifies the thoughtful moral decisions and judgments of moral agents, including all of the readers of this book. The accounts of impartiality and rationality are also accounts of these concepts that explain their central and coherent use by thoughtful people in everyday life. The point is to describe these concepts, not to revise them. These descriptions of the concepts of impartiality, morality, and rationality also show the close but complex relationship between them. It is the actual coherent employment of these concepts, not what philosophers say about them, that is important. This is a book about common morality, not about philosophers' concepts of morality.

Morality's close relationship with impartiality and rationality becomes apparent only when a rational person uses only those beliefs that are shared by all rational persons (rationally required beliefs). Even with this limitation to rationally required beliefs, not all impartial rational persons will agree on all of their moral decisions and judgments, but they will all agree on the general moral system or framework that they use in making these moral decisions and judgments. However, if an impartial rational person uses idiosyncratic beliefs, e.g., religious beliefs, there may be no way to reach agreement about morality. Any claim about all rational persons agreeing should be understood as a claim that all rational persons who use only rationally required beliefs agree.

Given this limitation on beliefs, the relationship between rationality, impartiality, and morality can be formulated in several different ways. (1) All rational persons who seek agreement with other rational persons about whom they know only that they also have the rationally required beliefs must take the appropriate moral attitude toward the basic general moral rules, i.e., that they be impartially obeyed with regard to rational persons. (2) All rational persons who view morality as an informal public system that applies to all rational persons must also take the attitude toward the basic general moral rules that they be impartially obeyed with regard to all rational persons. (3) All rational persons who are impartial with regard to all rational persons with respect to obeying the moral rules favor adopting morality as an informal public guide for all rational persons, including themselves.

Morality is not derived from the concepts of rationality and impartiality; rather the close relationship between these three concepts constitutes a justification of morality.

Rationality and Irrationality

"Rationality" and "irrationality" are used in a number of different ways, but their most important philosophical use is as the fundamental normative terms. No moral agent, that is, no one who is responsible for his actions, would ever seriously ask, "Why should I act rationally?" when this is taken as asking, "Why shouldn't I act irrationally?"

This fundamental sense of "rationality" is captured by my account, which has three distinctive features.

The first is the explicit recognition that acting rationally requires no more than avoiding acting irrationally. Irrational actions rather than rational actions are fundamental; rational actions share no distinctive common feature except not being irrational, and so a detailed account of an irrational action is provided. This way of defining a rational action has the desirable result that the importance of the category of rationally allowed actions is apparent. It explains what everyone knows, namely, that in many situations it is rationally allowed to act in any of several different incompatible ways. What is of particular philosophical interest is that in cases of conflict between morality and self-interest, it always will be rationally allowed to act in either way. But, surprisingly, it can also be rationally allowed to act both immorally and against one's self-interest, if doing so benefits some persons or groups for whom one is concerned, such as one's children, colleagues, members of one's religion, or fellow citizens.

The second feature is the hybrid character of rationality. An action can count as irrational in the basic sense only if it causes, or significantly increases the risks of, some harm to oneself. However, the reasons that can justify harming oneself, that is, that can make harming oneself rational, are not limited to beliefs about harms and benefits to oneself. Beliefs about harms and benefits to others can be better or stronger reasons than beliefs about harms and benefits to oneself. The strength of a reason is completely determined by which otherwise irrational actions it can make rational. This depends completely upon the degree and kind of harm (evil) prevented or benefit (good) gained, and not by who suffers that harm or gains that good, oneself or someone else. The strength of a reason is completely distinct from the strength of a motive. The strength of a reason does not depend at all on how strongly it motivates, but is determined completely by which otherwise irrational actions that it can make rational. This hybrid character reinforces the conclusion that in cases of conflict between morality and self-interest, it is rationally allowed to act in either way.

The third feature is that, when functioning as the fundamental normative concepts, reasons, rationality, and irrationality are identified by their content rather than by means of some formula, e.g., conflicting with maximizing the satisfaction of one's desires, that does not specify the content. This content is given by means of the following lists. An action is irrational in the basic sense only if it causes, or significantly increases the risks of (avoidable) death, pain, disability, loss of freedom, or loss of pleasure for oneself, and there is not an adequate reason for doing that action. A belief is a reason only if it involves avoiding one or more of the items on the previous list, or gaining greater consciousness, ability, freedom, or pleasure for anyone. The adequacy of the reason is determined in a particular case by determining if the harms avoided or goods gained compensate for the harm suffered. Since rational persons may rank the items on the list differently, they may sometimes disagree about which action they would advocate to someone for whom they are concerned. These lists provide objectivity to the concept of rationality, but this objectivity does not rule out any of the disagreements that rational persons actually have.

The account of an irrational action must account for both the normative function of irrationality and its content. Children are told that an action is irrational and should not be done because they will burn themselves, or break the toy they love, etc. Later, when they can handle the complexity, it is pointed out that sometimes it may not be irrational to act in these ways and that in these situations they may sometimes do such actions. With varying degrees of success, we try to make clear how irrational kinds of actions can sometimes become rational in a particular situation, for example, when doing them helps someone else avoid a serious harm. The function and content are intimately related; our tone of voice and accompanying actions make clear that irrational actions are to be avoided, and at the same time make clear what kinds of actions are irrational. We explain when doing one of these kinds of actions is not irrational, that is, when there is an adequate reason for doing it.

Similarly, the account of reasons must provide not only the function of reasons, but also their content. It is because the primary function of reasons is to make otherwise irrational actions rational that reasons must have a specific content. If a child is going to act in a way that significantly increases the risk that he will harm himself, we demand that he provide us with reasons for acting in that way and only accept as reasons those that have a specific content. Reasons must have the specified content in order to perform the function of justifying actions, that is, making it allowable to do an otherwise irrational action. The account of a reason must provide both its function and its content; neither one without the other is adequate.

This account of rationality is formulated so that the question "Why act rationally?" understood as "Why not act irrationally?" makes no sense. If rationality, or rather irrationality, is to play the philosophically significant role that it plays in ordinary life as well as in most philosophical theories, rational persons cannot ever favor acting irrationally. Were they ever to do so, irrationality would not be the basic normative concept, a role that, explicitly recognized or not, it has in ordinary life as well as in the works of all nonskeptical philosophers. To guarantee the fundamental normative status of irrationality, the critical test of all accounts of rationality must be whether they allow any moral agent to ever advise anyone for whom they care, including themselves, to act irrationally. If any account of rationality would ever allow this, it is an inadequate account.

This account of rationality enables one to derive objective concepts of goods and evils, while still remaining dependent on the attitudes of rational persons. In the absence of reasons, evils or harms are what all rational persons avoid, and goods or benefits are what no rational person gives up or avoids. It follows that nothing can be both a good and an evil and that most things are neither goods nor evils. The content of irrationality and reasons is determined by the two lists of basic evils and goods that were given above. Everything that is universally regarded as a good, e.g., health and wealth, and as an evil, disease and punishment, can be derived from these lists of basic goods and evils. This account also explains how a person may be in a situation where it is rational to choose the lesser of two evils. Since rational persons may rank the items on the list differently, there can be disagreement about what is better and worse without challenging the objectivity of the goods and evils.

Impartiality

The definition of the concept of impartiality is intended to capture what everyone means by saying that a person is acting impartially. "*A* is impartial in respect *R* with regard to group *G* if and only if *A*'s actions in respect *R* are not influenced by which member(s) of *G* benefit or are harmed by these actions." What is distinctive about this account is its explicit recognition that talk about impartiality is elliptical, that there is no such thing as simply being impartial. Impartiality must be specified both with respect to the kind of action and with regard to the group toward whom one is impartial in this respect.

Distinguishing between impartiality and consistency shows that the widely accepted truism "impartiality requires treating like cases alike" is not true. A referee can be erratic in his refereeing without ceasing to be impartial, as long as his decisions are not influenced by who is benefited or harmed by them. However, in most cases where impartiality is required, e.g., in judges, referees, and umpires, consistency is also required.

Recognizing that impartiality must always be specified with regard to group and respect has important consequences for morality. Although almost everyone agrees that morality requires impartiality, there has been significant disagreement both about the group with regard to which morality requires impartiality and the respect in which morality requires impartiality with regard to this group. *Moral impartiality* is the kind of impartiality required by morality.

Kant and his followers claim that morality requires impartiality only with regard to moral agents, i.e., only with regard to those who are themselves required to act morally. Bentham and his followers claim that morality requires impartiality with regard to all sentient beings. The latter hold that basic moral judgments are appropriately made about the way moral agents treat any sentient beings, including nonhuman animals. The former hold that basic moral judgments are appropriately made only about the way moral agents treat other moral agents.

Common morality accepts neither Kant nor Bentham. Rational persons need not agree on any unique determination of the group toward which morality requires impartiality. Although all agree that the minimal group must include all present moral agents and all former moral agents who are still sentient, some might want the group to include all potential sentient beings. But if the group toward which a person is impartial is smaller than the minimal group, e.g., includes only members of his race, religion, or nationality, then he is not acting morally. Disagreement among rational persons about the scope of morality, that is, about the size of the group toward which morality requires impartiality, is responsible for one class of unresolvable moral disagreements.

On the other hand, disagreement about the respect in which morality requires impartiality is resolvable. The differing views are exemplified in the writings of a single philosopher. In the second chapter of *Utilitarianism*, Mill says, "As between his own happiness and that of others, utilitarianism requires him to be as strictly impartial as a disinterested and benevolent spectator." Here, Mill seems to be holding that morality requires impartiality with respect to all of our actions that have any bearing on anyone's happiness. But in the fifth chapter, Mill says, "Impartiality . . . does not seem to be regarded as a duty in itself, but rather as instrumental to some other duty." Here, Mill can be taken as holding that morality requires impartiality only when one is considering the violation of a moral rule. This latter view is much closer to an adequate account of the respect in which morality requires impartiality.

To say that morality requires doing something means that all impartial rational persons hold that a person should be liable to punishment for not doing that kind of action. Morality requires impartiality only with respect to obeying the basic general moral rules; it does not require impartiality with respect to following the basic general moral ideals. This account of moral impartiality explains the following facts: (1) All rational persons agree that a moral agent should be liable to punishment for violating a moral rule with regard to some person when everyone knows that violating the rule with regard to that person is not acting impartially with regard to everyone in the group impartially protected by morality. (2) When no moral rule is being violated, no rational person favors liability to punishment for not following a moral ideal with regard to some person even when everyone knows that not following the ideal with regard to that person is not acting impartially with regard to everyone in the group impartially protected by morality.

Morality

"Morality" is sometimes used in such a wide sense that any decision about how to live one's life may count as a moral decision and any judgment about how one should act may count as a moral judgment. However, the concern of my book is with that concept of morality such that it provides all moral agents with a public guide that is known by all normal adults. Moral judgments are limited to those made about the actions (intentions, motives, and character) of persons who know what this guide prohibits, requires, discourages, encourages, and allows. This account of morality is not an attempt to invent a new moral system, but simply an attempt to describe that concept of morality which is relevant to its central use.

What is true of reasons and irrationality, namely, that both function and content are required for an adequate account, is also true of the concept of an immoral action. All of these concepts are taught not merely by pointing out their function but also by means of their content. For example, we teach children that it is immoral to hurt someone, to break a promise, or to deceive, and that they should not do these kinds of actions. When they can handle the complexity, we make it clear that sometimes it is not immoral to do these kinds of actions. Then, with varying degrees of success, we try to make clear that these actions are not immoral when they are done in circumstances such that one would be willing for everyone to know that they are allowed to do them. The Golden Rule and Kant's Categorical Imperative are among the better inadequate ways in which we try to make this point.

Morality differs from law and religion in that morality can be used to judge only the behavior of those who are not legitimately ignorant of what the moral system prohibits, etc. Also, unlike law and religion, it is never irrational to act as morality encourages or requires. Incorporating all of the central features of morality leads to the following definition of morality. "Morality is an informal public system applying to all rational persons, governing behavior that affects others, and includes what are commonly known as the moral rules, ideals, and virtues and has the lessening of evil or harm as its goal."

The phrase "public system" is used to refer to a guide to conduct that has the following two features: (1) All persons to whom it applies, all those whose behavior is to be guided and judged by that system, understand it and know what kind of behavior the system prohibits, requires, discourages, encourages, and allows. (2) It is not irrational for any of these persons to accept being guided and judged by that system.

The first of these features guarantees that no moral judgment is appropriately made about the behavior of anyone who is legitimately ignorant of what morality prohibits, etc. Sometimes there may be disputes about whether a person is legitimately ignorant of what morality prohibits, etc., but determining that someone is legitimately ignorant entails that it is inappropriate to make moral judgments concerning his behavior. This is why moral judgments are never made about the actions of nonhuman animals, infants, or those who are severely retarded.

The second feature of a public system, its relationship to rationality, is intimately related to the justification of morality. Only if morality has this second feature can morality be justified. If it were ever irrational to accept being guided or judged by morality, morality could not even be a public system, let alone one that all rational persons would favor adopting as the public system that applies to all of them. Although it is not irrational to act immorally, it is never irrational to act as morality encourages or requires. This justification of acting morally shows only that it is always rationally allowed to act morally, not that it is rationally required.

The paradigm cases of public systems, namely, games, can be formal or informal. Formal public systems have a procedure for settling all disputes, informal public systems do not. Defining morality as an *informal* public system makes clear that there is no decision procedure that will settle all moral disagreements. Saying that this system applies to all rational persons is another way of saying that morality is universal, i.e., that it is sometimes appropriate to make moral judgments about people in all societies at all times and places. All normal adult human beings have sufficient knowledge that they are not legitimately ignorant of the kinds of actions that morality prohibits, etc.

That everyone knows the kinds of actions that morality prohibits, etc., is an essential element of what is often called natural law theory. This account of morality could be classified as a version of natural law theory except for the fact that most natural law theories now seem to involve some theological foundation. However, Hobbes holds a secular natural law theory, and my theory is in that tradition. This version of natural law theory is closely related to various versions of social contract theories of morality as well as to various consequentialist and Kantian theories, so that it is not surprising that this theory has been characterized as a kind of social contract theory, as a Kantian theory, or as a kind of rule consequentialism.

Even though morality is an informal public system, that it is a public system that applies to all rational persons guarantees that there is overwhelming agreement concerning what the moral system prohibits, etc. The philosophical description of the moral system is based on this overwhelming agreement about moral matters. This moral theory explains both why there is such overwhelming agreement and why there are limited but important areas of disagreement.

Talk about the general moral rules is equivalent to talk about those simple kinds of actions that all rational persons agree would count as immoral unless the person doing the action has an adequate moral justification for doing that kind of action. These simple kinds of actions are killing, causing pain (both physical and mental), disabling, depriving of freedom, depriving of pleasure, deceiving, breaking promises, cheating, breaking the law, and failing to do one's duty. If all that is known about an action is that it is one of these kinds of actions, all impartial rational persons are against doing it. Unless a person has an adequate justification, all impartial rational people favor requiring him not to do these kinds of actions, that is, favor making him liable to punishment if he does them.

Talk about general moral ideals is equivalent to talk about those simple kinds of actions that all rational persons agree would count as morally good actions unless there were a moral rule prohibiting that action or a competing moral ideal. Examples of such simple kinds of actions are relieving pain and suffering, helping the needy, and encouraging people to avoid immoral actions. If all that one knows about an action is that it is one of these kinds of actions, all impartial rational persons would favor its being done. All impartial rational persons would favor encouraging people to do these kinds of actions, but they would not require such actions. That is, they would not make someone liable to punishment for not doing them. When following a moral ideal conflicts with a moral rule or another moral ideal, rational persons may disagree about whether the action is morally good.

In addition to the general moral rules and ideals, morality also consists of a two-step decision procedure to be used when one is considering violating a moral rule. It involves, as the first step, describing the violation by means of its morally relevant features. These features include (1) what rule is being violated, (2) the harms caused, avoided (not caused), and prevented, (3) the relevant beliefs and desires of the person toward whom the rule is being violated, (4) the relationship between that person and the person violating the rule, (5) the goods being promoted, (6) whether a moral rule violation is being prevented or (7) punished, (8) what alternatives are available, (9) whether the violation is being done intentionally or only knowingly, and (10) whether it is an emergency situation.

The second step of the procedure is estimating the effects of everyone knowing that this kind of violation is allowed (publicly allowed) and comparing that to one's estimate of the effects of this kind of violation not being publicly allowed. If all rational persons would estimate that the former would result in less harm than the latter, the violation is strongly justified; if all rational persons would estimate that the latter would result in less harm than the former, the violation is unjustified; if rational persons disagree in their estimates of which would result in the least harm, then the violation is weakly justified. Since weakly justified violations may be justifiably punished, to call a violation weakly justified is to make a very weak claim.

This description of common morality shows that all of our moral judgments can be accounted for by regarding them as being derived from applying this coherent moral system to the facts. It is unlikely that people have this moral system consciously in mind when they make their moral decisions and judgments. However, if they use their own rankings of the evils and their own estimates of the consequences of a kind of action being publicly allowed, their explicitly use of this moral system would result in moral decisions and judgments virtually identical to the thoughtful moral decisions and judgments that they already make. (There is a strong analogy between knowing common morality and knowing the grammar of one's language.)

Common morality is essentially a systematic guide to moral behavior, and all evaluative moral judgments are judgments about the extent to which a moral agent abides by this guide. It is this moral system that explains the coherent moral decisions and judgments of rational persons. Any moral decision or judgment that is not accounted for by this description of the moral system can be shown to be incompatible with the vast majority of a person's other moral decisions and judgments. Common morality or the moral system is justified by showing that all rational persons, if they seek agreement among all moral agents, favor adopting common morality as a public system that applies to all rational persons.

Given the goal of reaching agreement among all moral agents, morality can be strongly justified, that is, all moral agents would favor each other adopting morality as a public guide for their behavior. However, only a weak justification for acting morally can be provided. Moreover, neither of these justifications can be provided unless the only beliefs used are those that are shared by all rational persons. Given this limitation on beliefs, it can be shown that it is rationally required to endorse morality as a public system that applies to all rational persons. Given this same limitation, it can be shown only that it is always rationally allowed to act morally.

Virtues

Although moral virtues are mentioned in the definition of morality, they are not basic features of the informal public system that is common morality; rather they are derived from the basic features of common morality. However, that the virtues can be so derived confirms the correctness of the account of common morality. As a practical matter, the moral virtues are extremely important and morality could be discussed solely in terms of these virtues. Moral virtues are those traits of character that all impartial rational persons want everyone to have. All of these virtues are closely related to the moral rules and moral ideals. To want people to have the moral virtues is to want them to obey the moral rules and to follow the moral ideals as an impartial rational person would. But since impartial rational persons can disagree, this does not provide a unique answer about how one should behave. A representative list of moral virtues would contain truthfulness, trustworthiness, fairness, law-abidingness, dependability, and kindness.

Moral virtues are not the only kind of virtues; there are also personal virtues, those traits of character that all rational persons want to have themselves. The most commonly discussed personal virtues are courage, prudence, and temperance. These virtues are not opposed to the moral virtues. On the contrary, it may be impossible for a person to have the moral virtues without having these personal virtues as well. Unfortunately, it is possible for one to have the personal virtues without having the moral virtues. Like the moral virtues, the personal virtues not only involve acting in certain ways, they also involve being motivated to act in these ways and even to enjoy acting in these ways. Raising children so that they have both the moral and the personal virtues is one of the most important tasks a person can perform.

Summary

This account of common morality has all of the features that most people take morality to have. It not only has the content that people normally take morality to have, it is related to impartiality and rationality in the way that most people think. This relationship is much weaker than many philosophers have wanted, but it is as strong as one can make it without significantly distorting one or more of the concepts involved. Chapters devoted to explaining why one should be moral and to clarifying the relationship of morality to law and government show that this account of morality satisfies most of what people realistically expect of morality.

This account of morality could probably be stated more clearly and precisely, and there are probably still some mistakes in it. The papers in this volume have helped me to clarify this account, to make it more precise, and to correct some mistakes in its details. I thank their authors for their help.

Part I: Justification and Method

1

Justification in Bernard Gert's Moral Theory

Ernst Tugendhat

It does not seem obvious what it means "to justify" morality. Some people think it cannot be justified at all. Bernard Gert gives, right at the beginning of his book, an explanation of what, for him, justification in morality means: "morality is justified" if "with the appropriate qualifications, all rational persons would favor adopting it" (3, cf. also 7, 128). The reader may of course ask: how can anybody without discussion just start out with such a definition? Now the definition just cited is not so tight as to leave no space open, and in fact Gert later expands on it a bit (cf. 153, 158, 168-71). The intent of my paper is to show that there is a tension within the account which Gert gives of the justification of morality, in particular of the moral rules in chapter 7—a tension which, I think, can be better appreciated when we compare the conception as presented in its newest edition[1] with the original version of the book that had been published under the title *The Moral Rules*.[2] I think that the new edition contains a change in the concept of moral justification that is not made explicit.

Even though the reference to the moral rules is dropped in the title of the book, the central part of the theory remains, as it had been in the old version, the characterization and justification of the moral rules (cf. 158). The general characterization of these rules in the new version is essentially the same as it had been in the first edition. But before proceeding to "justifying the moral rules" in chapters 7 and 8, which correspond to chapters 5 and 6 of the old version, the author now inserts a chapter on "impartiality." The reason why this new chapter had become necessary seems to be that Gert had come to believe that the justification of the moral rules that he had given in the old version in chapter 5 had been unsuccessful.

Gert does not say this explicitly, but at an important juncture in chapter 7 he says: "In a very important sense this problem cannot be solved" (167), and the problem to which he is here referring seems to be the old account he had given of the justification of the moral rules. There follow four new pages (167-71) which I find unusually obscure in this otherwise so lucid book. But so much seems certain, that the author is trying to substitute the argument of the old version with a new argument in which he replaces the weaker phrase "all rational persons" with the stronger premise that in order to advocate or favor the moral rules persons must not only be rational, as he had said before, but impartial. This seems to be the reason why the chapter on impartiality had to be inserted, but it is noteworthy that in this chapter Gert does not try to justify why we must be impartial in morality; he only gives a description of this concept. I shall argue that thus presupposing impartiality for the justification of the moral rules has two unhappy consequences: first, the place that impartiality has in morality seems to be missed, since impartiality would have to be justified together with the moral rules; and second, the idea of a justification of the moral rules is being changed so fundamentally that one might ask whether it does not lose its very point.

I must first show how Gert proceeded in the old version. The justification of a moral rule, he says there in chapter 5, must consist in showing that it is rationally required for every person to want it to be followed by everybody. At the beginning of the chapter, Gert said: "This discussion does not depend in any way upon the meaning of the word 'moral'" (76). This sentence significantly no longer appears in the new edition. I might paraphrase its intent by saying: the word "moral" is after all only a word (and, I might add, a very ambiguous word at that); what is to be justified is not that these rules are to be called "moral rules" but that their acceptance is being advocated universally. This implies that what the author had said in the preliminary chapters on morality was not definitory but provisional for what is to be understood as morality. In all of this Gert has changed his opinion in the new version. He now introduces in the first chapter a conception of morality—what he calls "common morality"—which is not provisional but definitive and which will count even as the criterion of any justification. What has to be justified no longer is, as it had been in the old version, that certain rules are to be adopted, but that they are to be adopted if we want to accept moral rules (cf. 167-69).

In the old version he had proceeded in two steps. The first is that it seems rationally required for everybody to adopt toward certain rules (the rules that then may be called the moral rules) a certain attitude that he called the egocentric attitude. It is to consist in the following: "all other people are to obey the rule with regard to me and to everybody for whom I am concerned," with exceptions of course (86). This first step Gert maintained unchanged in the new edition (161). It is the second step of the old version that is being dropped in the new version.

This second step had been introduced by the statement: "The egocentricity of the attitude must be eliminated" (88). That this is what must be done is also maintained in the new version (167), but Gert now rejects the answer he had given to this problem. This answer had been as follows: the only way to get all other people to observe these rules toward me is that I agree that everybody should observe them toward everybody, and so for everybody else. "If one wishes to reach agreement among all rational men, he must advocate that the rule be obeyed with regard to all" (88). "When an attitude is being advocated in order to reach agreement among all rational men," Gert called this "public advocacy" (89). Not to advocate such an agreement concerning these rules of reciprocal protection would be "irrational," since it would increase one's "chances of suffering evil" (90). To publicly advocate that everybody agree to these rules is therefore required by reason. It is on the basis of this argument that the old version gave at the end of the chapter its definition of "justification": "Showing that reason publicly requires the moral attitude toward a moral rule is what I call justifying that moral rule" (101).

This argument of the old version might appear very plausible, but it is precisely here where Gert claims in the new edition that "this problem cannot be solved" (167). Rationality, he now says, is not enough: "No adequate account of rationality . . . can require of all rational persons to favor impartial obedience to these . . . rules" (167).

Why not? I have not been able to find any very explicitly definite argument for this assertion in the pages that follow. In one place, in the summary to this chapter, Gert says that it cannot be shown "that rationality requires acting" according to these rules (182). Now this is of course true but beside the point. What Gert had claimed in the old version was not that it would be irrational not to act according to these rules but not to publicly advocate them, and "public advocacy need not (even) be sincere" (89).

The explanations that Gert gives why the argument of the old version is insufficient are scattered in the fourth paragraph of page 169 and in the first paragraph of page 170. Some things he says here lead me to suggest the following reconstruction of why he came to believe that the argument of the first version had been unsound. Although it is irrational for a person not to want others not to inflict harm on her, she might prefer, instead of getting universal rules that prohibit doing harm, a life of war of everybody against everybody or, more realistically, to restrict the scope of the rules in question to her own group. This seems to be what in fact happened in large measure in history. (Gert remarks on 119: "it is very likely that most societies do enforce obedience to all of the moral rules, at least with regard to members of their own society.") So we may assume that Gert came to believe in the new edition that in the old version he had presented a solution that had been too ambitious: it consisted in claiming that "there is a conceptual or analytic relationship between a person being rational and his having a certain attitude toward a particular set of rules" (first edition, 77). To be rational had been defined in the second chapter of the old version in a way that not taking this attitude of universal advocacy had to seem to be irrational. But, as Gert says in the new edition, it is not, because even if it is irrational to want an evil, there are different possibilities of how to protect ourselves against these evils. Thus the sweeping justification that Gert had given in the old version is now seen to lead into an impasse.

How could this impasse have been overcome? I believe that there actually would have been two possibilities. The one not mentioned by Gert would have been to hold on to the notion of justification of the old version as an intersubjective enterprise of publicly advocating an agreement but giving up the claim that a person would necessarily be irrational if she did not adopt this attitude. In this case Gert would have had to give up the analytic claim; the moral attitude would have been seen to be a plausible attitude to take, but it would not have been necessary. And why, I would ask as a comment, must morality and its justification be a matter of necessity, and why is there only one possible solution, to see this in a universal frame?

The other possibility is the one that Gert presents in the new version. It consists in dropping the idea of an intersubjective justification altogether, thus holding on to the idea that justification must mean necessary justification but giving up the conception that the justification consists in advocating an agreement. Gert believes now that we have to introduce, besides rationality, impartiality as an additional "constraint." So he seems to suggest: only if we already presuppose impartiality as an additional constraint can the claim that it is necessary to adopt what he calls the moral attitude toward these rules be justified. He thus can hold on to the idea of a conceptual necessity in his claim for universal justification, but at the price of having to presuppose impartiality as an additional constraint instead of letting it be generated by the agreement which had been the object of public advocacy. This explains why the new chapter on impartiality had to be inserted between the chapter that contains the general description of moral rules and the chapter on their justification.

But the consequences of this change for the idea of what it means to justify the moral rules are much deeper. As I mentioned before, Gert now introduces already in the first chapter a more or less definitive conception of morality which he calls "common morality". This term is not yet contained in the old version. Gert gives no precise definition of it. In part it stands for the conviction that morality is something objective and universal, in part it implies that contemporary intuitions are definitive of what morality is, and finally this assumption tends to turn the obligation of justification upside down. It is this that I meant when I spoke at the beginning of a tension in Gert's conception of justification. On the one hand he says, in agreement with the old version, that all parts of common morality have to be justified by showing that the items contained in it "are such that all rational persons could favor adopting them" (3, 13). On the other hand common morality is now understood not as something that *needs* justification but that *gives* justification. So Gert says that it would "not count as justifying *morality* unless the code of conduct being justified was virtually identical to the moral system that is now implicitly used" (7). Thus the introductory chapter on morality acquires a weight of its own which it did not have (or did not have quite to this extent) in the old version, and what I have called a tension in Gert's conception of justification is that on the one hand he continues to accept the old concept of justification—that an item of morality can only be justified by relating it to what everybody would universally advocate or, as he now says, "favor"—but, on the other hand, justifying an item of morality now seems to mean to show that it really belongs to (our preconceived notion of) morality.

Another new concept not yet found in the old version which Gert introduces in the first chapter and which he claims is an essential characteristic of common morality (and it continues to be, in the following chapters, a criterion of anything that can be called moral) is that it must be what he calls a "public system" (10). No precise definitory conditions of this concept are stated. "The clearest example of a public system," he says, "is a game such as baseball or bridge" (10). One clear condition of such a system is that everybody who takes part in it must "know what behavior the system prohibits, requires, encourages and allows" (10). He then continues: "Morality is the one public system that a person cannot quit," and adds: "Morality is a public system that applies to all rational persons." But why to *all* rational persons? Is not a public system conceivable that is moral but applies only to a group that does not include all rational persons? Is Gert not taking here intuitively two steps at once, first that morality is different from a game, but second that morality must be universal? Must not the application to all rational persons be justified in turn? If this is not the case for Gert, the reason obviously is that he had already taken universality to be a characteristic of common morality. But does this not mean that universality is an aspect that is not to be justified but is simply presupposed in what is being called common morality?

Again, is impartiality a necessary condition of a public system? This seems to be maintained in the section of chapter 7 which I find so obscure. He there says: "It has now been shown that if a person is considering these rules as moral rules, that is, as rules in a public system that applies to all moral agents, the attitude he will adopt will be an impartial" one (169). Now if this is so, we could drop the constraint of impartiality as an independent constraint and replace it by the constraint that what is to be justified must fit into common morality. Thus instead of attempting to justify the contents of common morality and of a public system, these concepts are themselves being used for the justification of the moral rules, and with this the idea of justification may seem to lose much of its significance.

It is the very item of impartiality that can best exemplify the problem. I must confess that I do not find Gert's discussion of impartiality in chapter 6 as illuminating as he thinks it is. The real problem concerning impartiality would seem to me to consist in showing why in certain intersubjective contexts we *must* be impartial for certain definite reasons that we should be able to spell out. For example, it is insufficient just to say that public systems such as social games are governed by impartial rules; the question is *why* are they? In the case of games the answer obviously is that without impartiality a game would lose its function of competition; it seems, in the case of games, essential that everyone of the players wants the game to be impartial for the reason that otherwise playing it could not show that one player is better than the other. Now in morality too we should not be content to say, as Gert seems to be, that it is, as a matter of fact, impartial, but rather ask why it is. Here too we seem to have a reason to be impartial, but a very different one from games. In morality, impartiality may seem to be generated because it results from the concession which the individuals have to make to each other when they want to arrive at a formulation of the rules on which they can mutually agree, or it may result from the necessity to have to justify the rules to each other. It is here where, in morality, impartiality seems to have its place, and only now the exciting problems of the justification of impartiality come up: first, what is it that makes people agree on general impartiality in contrast to incomplete and fragmented impartiality as in a caste society? And second, is universality something rational persons necessarily want (as Gert simply presupposes in his idea of common morality and as he indeed also presupposed in the account of justification that he had given in the old version) or can they also prefer a more restricted scope of impartiality? They certainly have done so in the past, as Gert admits (191), so universal morality cannot be universal in the sense of being the common morality of everybody. And there are also obvious contemporary tendencies, of which Gert is also aware (317), in nationalism and ethnicism, to revert to more provincial conceptions of the scope of moral responsibility.

Can we really struggle against these tendencies by just proclaiming that what we believe morality to be is as a matter of fact universally impartial? Will our opponents not ask us to give arguments that can convince them, and must we not, to achieve this, try to show that the mutual agreement between rational persons contains factors that lead to unrestricted impartiality and universality? But which are these factors? If we do not try to identify them, our opponents could suggest that the reason why so many today believe that morality is universal is only that we stand in the Christian tradition. Or it could be said that under conditions of modernization and globalization we are merely pragmatically motivated to understand the rules as universal. Could this latter suggestion not indeed be true? If our moral beliefs are based on a generalization of the egocentric attitude, the scope in which we find it rational to generalize the egocentric attitude may depend on such empirical matters as whether there is more to gain if we extend the impartiality of the moral rules or not. That in today's "common morality" universality seems to be presupposed so naturally might depend on such factors as greater mobility and general interdependence.

When I first read Gert's book in its old version more than twenty years ago, I wondered why he so confidently asserted that morality must be universal. Why could one not rationally advocate these rules to a more narrow community? Confronted with the new edition I can now see that Gert himself admits that the argument had not been compelling, but instead of improving the argument he simply abandons the question how a universal impartial moral stance can be generated and is content in asserting that the morality that is generally accepted today simply contains universal impartiality as a matter of fact. At any rate he is certainly misinterpreting the project of the old version when he writes, in note 2 to chapter 6, that he had there used the concept of public advocacy "as a substitute [!] for the kind of impartiality required of morality" (153, note 2; cf. also note 10). With the term "public advocacy" the old version had not simply been *referring* to moral impartiality; it had rather been an attempt to show how impartiality *enters* into morality, how it is being generated, and this had been an enterprise which Gert now seems to have lost sight of.

In what remains, I want to ask what effect Gert's vacillation between the two conceptions of justification has on the method on which he proceeds in the rest of the book. How, for example, does he justify his method of justification of exceptions to the moral rules? How does he justify what he says on moral ideals and their delimitation from utilitarian ideals? How does he, in the last chapter, justify what he says about the duties of government? Both conceptions that he has of justification seem to play a role. Thus he says in the first chapter that all items of morality have to be justified by showing "that all rational persons could favor adopting them as parts of a public system" (13). On the other hand, in most questions Gert no longer is concerned to show this. Often an item is being justified simply by stating that common morality calls for it (124, 252); quite often Gert insists that at least "all readers of this book" would see it that way (4 and *passim*), and in most places Gert simply states the way he thinks things are, obviously relying on his intuitions concerning common morality, sometimes adding that "everybody would agree" where we are left in the dark who is meant by "everybody." Now Gert's intuition is excellent and perhaps he means to say that in all such cases a more elaborate argument which would take us back to the situation of universal advocacy would lead to the same result, but the reader may find it disconcerting that he does not say so. Let me try to point out a few difficulties that are the consequences.

First, the moral ideals: here I only want to point out that most of the distinctions Gert makes, though intuitively plausible, are not explicitly supported by reasons. Why is it, in the first instance, that moral ideals are being morally encouraged? Second, why can moral ideals justify a violation of a moral rule? What is it that makes it possible that something that is only being encouraged can justify breaking a rule that is required? And, third, why can the same not be said of utilitarian ideals? There does seem to be an answer that Gert gives to the first question, why preventing evil is encouraged at all, but this answer I find strange. He says several times that "the point of morality" is "lessening evil" (253); this only creates a new puzzle. On what conception of morality—common morality or universal advocacy—is the lessening of evil its very point? At the beginning of the book Gert had a more cautious statement, "that morality is concerned with the lessening of evil" (16). Only in this latter form can the statement be seen to fit the kind of justification that Gert had in mind in the first edition. The moral rules are justified because it is not rational for anybody to want to be harmed, and therefore "most everybody" (as I would prefer to say instead of "all rational people") will favor an agreement according to which nobody is allowed to harm anybody. It appears only natural that this agreement be supplemented with mutually agreeing to prevent harm wherever possible. This then would seem to me to be a simple way of continuing the justification of the moral rules to include the support for the moral ideals. To follow the rules and ideals thus generated will indeed also have the consequence of lessening the evil in the world, but it is not the intention of the moral person to do so. She is not directed at diminishing the net amount of evil; she will rather see herself face to face in relation to those to whom she feels responsible on account of the moral agreement. Gert seems to be correctly identifying the virtue of such a person as kindness, but kindness is directed at persons, not at lessening the amount of evil in the world.

An important point which Gert makes is that in general it is impossible to be kind impartially (in general, I say, since it would seem to be unjust for a mother or a teacher to be kind partially). But how are we to visualize the kind person? There seems to be a tendency in Gert to see the person who is following the moral ideals as picking out a random group somewhere in the world that is especially deprived, for example, by joining the Peace Corps, and in this way to contribute to lessening the amount of evil in the world. This is indeed what you would think of when you hear that the point of morality is to lessen evil. But if we take as point of departure the implicit agreement which individuals enter to avoid evil, a picture emerges that is closer to the Parable of the Samaritan: a kind person is one who is sensitive to the needs of people around her and willing to go out of her way for their sake. Of course she can be as little impartial as the person who chooses helping somewhere as a profession, but the way of not being impartial is different. It is not she who picks out at random some evil far from home but she will be responsive if it so happens that it is the situation of suffering of somebody that picks her out.

Gert correctly points out that there is not much sense in an individual trying to be impartial in relation to the moral ideals. But does this imply that this part of morality is inaccessible to impartiality? Once again it is not from the point of view of intersubjective justification that Gert contemplates this matter. If this perspective were taken, I think the following would have to be said: the first layer of morality that presents itself in the public advocacy of an agreement to spare each other evils would be the moral rules, and this in impartiality, because otherwise an agreement would not be forthcoming; second, the moral ideals would follow, necessarily, I think, because once the moral community is created by moral rules, it would not be rational not to demand more. But if impartiality is necessary for mutuality of demands, would not impartiality be demanded here likewise? But this is impossible, says Gert, since "it is humanly impossible to be following" these maxims "with regard to everyone" (123), much less impartially. He is certainly right as far as he goes. He repeats the old Kantian principle "if no one can, no one can be required to" (126). But is there not an obvious way out of this dilemma? Why should we not say: if, on the one hand, the agreement calls for impartiality, and for individuals impartiality in regard of the moral ideals is impossible, the moral ideals require that we join hands? As a political community we may be able to do what as individuals we are not.

This idea leads, of course, to the problem of the moral duties of government, which Gert treats in his last chapter, but he treats them as if that were a separate problem. My complaint is the same as before. Gert makes no attempt to link what he says about what the government may or must do morally with his concept of justification, but instead proceeds in a purely intuitive way. From the point of view of justification, it would seem natural that we would have to say: a government must be, in the first place, democratic. And must we not, second, also see the duties of government from the point of view of an original agreement? And does this not lead to justice as what must be one of the foremost moral criteria of governmental action?

Gert's chapter on government makes a small step in this direction, but confines itself to allow the government to tax for utilitarian ideals (and thus violate a moral rule which individuals are not allowed in the same way), but Gert is very restrictive in enumerating the purposes. He says: governments may do so to promote "medical research," "the arts, parks or better schools" (367). He clearly evades speaking of redistributive taxation. The only ideals must be lessening harm and promoting good, not justice, but again the reader may ask why. Gert says: "equality is not needed for this kind of action, lessening harm is sufficient" (255). Let me recall that Gert had given, in the chapter on ideals, as the only reason for not requiring impartiality of individuals when they try to prevent evil, that this is, for individuals, impossible. But why then must a democratic government not have this goal, since now such a goal can be at least approached? And is it not also in fact a general point of complaint against governmental action if its aid measures do not have a tendency toward impartiality? The ultimate reason for this is of course the idea of impartiality contained in moral agreement. This same point of departure leads now not only to impartial observation of rules, but to impartial concern for people and thus to justice. I find it difficult to understand Gert's aversion to this ideal. He calls egalitarianism "the politics of envy" (376). But to treat unjustly—or refuse justice—creates humiliation, and to humiliate could be considered to be the primary moral vice which cannot just be subsumed, as it would have to be in Gert's system, under causing pain.

Why should anybody publicly advocate obedience to the moral rules if he cannot at the same time advocate that everybody join hands to promote justice? That we should not separate these two aspects of morality can, I think, be visualized by the question how a destitute person should be convinced that theft is wrong. Morality is a system based on symmetry, on symmetrical obligations, and where the preconditions of symmetry are not given, the obligations lose their sense. If we had to counsel a destitute street child, we should, I suggest, dissuade the child from stealing, not because it is immoral, but only because of the danger of being caught. Should one in such cases not say that it is the society that is immoral, because it makes it irrational for some people to freely agree on some of the moral rules?

In our society the imperative of more justice gains an additional weight because of the relations of power and dependence created by the economic system. In Gert the view seems to be that deprived persons only exist out there; deprivation appears as something given by God or by chance, but other people think that in large measure it is the human institution of the economic system that is responsible for some being born in circumstances without opportunities and others with. The word "power" is as absent in Gert's book as the word "justice". With these comments I do not want to advocate any specific alternative; I only wanted to mention aspects that should at least not be dismissed without argument. In fact, Gert does seem to imply in his last chapter a minimum consideration for justice. Otherwise how could he advocate taxation for "better schools for all"? Why not leave schools to those who can afford them? The same could be said for the health system, of which Gert speaks at the end of this chapter. However, Gert says that a good health system would not be one that provides for equal opportunities of treatment, but one that would result in the least amount of harm being suffered (378).

I continue to be baffled by this conception of least amount. How did Gert arrive at it? For it certainly does not seem to be the consequence of anything like an agreement. In an agreement, the demand of equality of consideration would be the first item of public advocacy, and the idea of a maximum or minimum, without consideration of distribution, could come up only as a marginal consideration. Should we then look for the origin of this concern for the least amount to the other justificatory basis of Gert's theory, to what he calls "common morality"? But is not the goal of justice at least as well rooted in "common morality" as the goal of least amount of evil? If anything, this shows that common morality is an unreliable guide. My guess is that we are confronted here with a third source of Gert's moral intuitions: besides appealing, on the one hand, to what can be impartially favored, and, on the other, to common morality, he also seems to be drawing on a specific philosophical tradition, utilitarianism. In spite of his demolishing criticism of positive utilitarianism and in spite of his rejection of negative consequentialism, he may have remained at his heart a utilitarian, but it remains unclear what the justification of these utilitarian remainders are.

I must come to an end. Perhaps, it may be said, the idea of agreement which has guided my criticism is itself misbegotten. The explanation that I gave why Gert rejects in his new edition his earlier version of justification of the moral rules may have been insufficient. An additional reason may be that he now seems to reject the idea of agreement altogether. But the only explanation that I have found for this radical step is the strong displeasure that Gert expresses in the new edition toward contractarianism (128, note 3). Once again he does not give much of an explanation. But I suppose that the reason is his proposition that the moral rules are "discovered rather than invented" (113). This proposition, which is to be found already in the old version (67), is of course closely connected with Gert's conception of morality as universal: the contents of the moral rules are in some way necessary, and even if, as I suggested, we should have to relax this condition and speak instead of something approaching necessity, Gert would be correct in claiming that there is no place here for the kind of arbitrariness that is characteristic of a contract. ("Any account of general moral rules that makes them subject to human decision must be mistaken." 114) Gert goes so far as to claim that the moral rules "have a status similar to the laws of logic" (114). He adds, of course, that there is a difference, but he does not spell it out.

Let me try to do this. The laws of logic are necessary in the sense that they are the necessary rules of valid inference. They are justified in the sense that we would otherwise contradict ourselves. If the moral rules are similarly necessary or nearly necessary rules, what is it that they are necessary for? I suggest, in keeping with the original version of Gert's conception of justification: they are the rules that emerge in an agreement of everybody with everybody not to harm each other. (At this moment I am only concerned with the terms of the agreement, not its scope. I have already voiced my doubts about the justification of scope being necessarily universal.) This agreement is not arbitrary because it is based only on what everybody or nearly everybody acknowledges to be evils. The rules are justified because they and no other rules emerge in this kind of agreement, and not, as might be suggested by the line taken by the new edition, because they follow necessarily from "common morality". The agreement, being necessary or nearly necessary, should not be called a contract because it is not open to any arbitrary suggestions of the contracting parties. Up to this point I can follow Gert. It is an agreement, nevertheless, because if we did not reciprocally agree on these rules, they would not come about and certainly not be justified. They and the other aspects of morality, including impartiality, are justified because they are what rational persons under suitable conditions necessarily (or nearly necessarily) agree upon. Thus I believe that Gert's plausible proposition that these rules are "discovered, not invented" does not exclude that the rules of morality are generated in an agreement. It is the terms of this agreement that are being "discovered, not invented".

Postscript

Gert pointed out to me that in the passage that I had thought was obscure he did not just introduce, as I had claimed, impartiality as an "additional constraint" but had clearly stated that "one can replace the egocentric attitude toward the rules by an appropriate moral attitude, *either* by adding the constraint that the person also be impartial, *or* the constraint that the attitude be one that would be acceptable to all rational persons" (170). Hence I seem to have been mistaken in assuming that Gert had dropped in the new version the idea of the old version that the justification of the moral rules is an intersubjective affair ("publicly advocating an agreement"). Rather, this idea is being retained in speaking of an "attitude" that is to be "acceptable to all rational persons." The only change, Gert told me, consists in denying that merely by restricting oneself to only required beliefs a person would be irrational if she did not endorse the moral rules.

I accept this correction, but let me point out that I had not denied that Gert had retained in the new version his old idea of what justification means in morality alongside the new one; I said he "vacillated" between the two. It now seems to me that I have not succeeded in making the difference between the conceptions of justification of the two versions (or what I take them to be) sufficiently clear.

The difference is more subtle than I had thought. It may look like hairsplitting, but to my eyes it is important. What Gert had meant by "justifying" morality in the old version (or at least part of what he had meant) was explaining what *motivates* people to embrace morality: you must "publicly advocate" an agreement that everybody is to obey certain rules if you want to avoid being harmed, and it is irrational not to want that. In the new version, Gert says it is an exaggeration to claim that what motivates us to embrace the moral rules is simply rationality, but this leads him to drop the question of motivation (justification in *this* sense) altogether. Instead, he now gives conditions that must be added in order to endorse these rules "*as* moral rules" (171, second paragraph). The repeated insistence in the "obscure" passage (167-71)—I continue to consider it obscure because neither the criticism of the old version nor the new position are exposed in a straightforward argument—that without accepting either one of the "constraints" we cannot arrive at morality shows how decisive here the presupposition is of wanting to arrive at "morality" as introduced in the first chapter, whereas in the old version Gert had said that the justification of these rules does not depend on the word "morality". There Gert was concerned to justify that we are motivated to endorse these rules; in the new edition he is concerned to justify that what we endorse can only be called moral if certain requirements are fulfilled, but he now neither tells us why we should be motivated to endorse morality in the first place nor why we should be motivated to want either one of the alternative "constraints".[3] I think I was right in saying in my paper that Gert is primarily concerned to give a definitive answer; so, when he saw that he no longer could give a definitive answer to the question of motivation, instead of giving a less definitive answer to this question, he switched the question: the question now is what are "necessary and sufficient" conditions for considering "rules as moral rules" (168, first paragraph). These constraints are to be understood as criteria, as "tests" "of one's considering these rules as moral rules" (170, second paragraph).

One indication for the difference of what had been the question in the old version and of what it is in the new version is that Gert says in the new version that it "makes no difference" whether one adds the constraint of impartiality or the constraint that "the attitude be one that would be acceptable to all rational persons" (170, 171). It indeed makes no difference if the question is what is a criterion of the moral attitude. But if the question had been what can motivate a person to embrace these constraints, why should anybody want to be impartial if he or she did not have some further reason for this? On the other side, everybody does have a strong reason to convert what had been the egocentric attitude into an imperative that is "acceptable to all," since otherwise he or she would not arrive at an agreement. We have to be impartial *in order* to arrive at an imperative that is acceptable to the others, and certainly not the other way around, so if this is the question, it makes all the difference in the world which of the two constraints has priority.

Indeed, if we formulate the requirement of acceptability as weakly as I just did, speaking of acceptability to *others* or *the* others (of a group) instead of acceptability to "all rational persons", the position of the old version of Gert's book—that it is irrational not to endorse these rules—becomes much less susceptible to the criticisms which Gert brings in the new version, since without the common adoption of such rules people will not be able to get along with each other at all.

So, a bit of impartiality seems to be required by what may be seen as the pragmatic basis of even a rudimentary "morality" (such as the morality of thieves of which Mackie speaks),[4] but this impartiality may be, as I said in my paper, fragmented: there may be a distinction between privileged and underprivileged people within the group morality, and besides "everybody" may be just "everybody of the group." How is one to be convinced that impartiality must be general and universal (universal in the sense of what Gert calls (141) the "minimal group")? In the old version of his book Gert had not confronted the problem of impartiality at all; he simply presupposed that morality is related to "all rational people", as indeed "all the readers of his book" do, but what are the reasons? The way justification was understood in the old version, this problem would have had to be faced. The way justification is understood in the new version does not have to be faced since justification is from the start being defined as acceptability to "all rational persons" (e.g., 3, 7, 10) and morality too is from the beginning being understood as "common or universal morality" (3). If Gert were to be questioned why the "constraint of (universal) impartiality" must be accepted, he would answer: because otherwise you cannot arrive at the moral attitude. But is not "morality", the questioner would resume, only a word? You must, Gert would say, distinguish between morality in the wide, sociological sense and "those moral rules that can be justified" (341, second paragraph). All moralities, the questioner might answer, have been justified in some way; what makes your sense of justification nonarbitrary? Here we seem to arrive at a circle. Gert would simply repeat his definitions. This dead end would not have to worry the author of the new version, but it would have been a worry for the old version, and I think it had been the better for remaining open to this problem. My own view is as follows:

First, we need, I think, a formal, sociological concept of morality from where to start out, e.g., morality as a system of rules sustained by social pressure or as a system of reciprocal imperatives.[5] These systems have not always but mostly been held for some sort of reasons or justifications. It now would have to be shown in which sense the reasons for "common or universal morality" are superior to any other justification.

Second, the reasoning which leads to universal morality seems to me to have to proceed in two steps. In both of them we give reasons for why we have to be impartial. In the first step, the reasoning is pragmatical: we get no agreement without some impartiality. This reasoning does not get us beyond a scope of the rules that is useful for the contracting parties. What is it that makes us go farther? This is the second step, and since it is difficult, some contemporary moral philosophers deny it and are happy with a contractualism in the sense of David Gauthier, whereas others skip it and, as Gert does, just define morality in the required way. But, I think, as we make the first, pragmatic step, we learn a new concept, the concept of justifiability-to-x. So, although a fragmented impartiality or an impartiality limited in scope may be more useful to us, a new question arises: is this *justifiable to* those we are excluding or putting at a disadvantage? This is the question of justice. "They" are going to ask us to give reasons that are justifiable *to them*. To speak of the justification *of* a moral rule or of morality seems to me to be derivative: being justifiable-to-x is a more primitive concept, in morality, than being justified. You cannot justify a rule as you can justify a proposition. Being justified in morality can be said to *mean* being justifiable *to* everybody equally.

If I now were to resume the dialogue with the questioner of Gert that I introduced a moment ago, I would tell him: you have to go beyond pragmatical impartiality if you want to arrive at a system of norms that is justifiable to the others (and, in the last resort, to everybody). But if (a) you do not care about being able to justify the rules to some of the others and if (b) you have the power to impose the rules on those others or to exclude them by force, this is your other option. Now this may appear as much of a dead end as the one we were left with in the dialogue with Gert. Of course any practical reasoning must leave us at an end, but it is not a dead end, I think, if it does not consist merely in a certain definition and if it tells the questioner what other option he has.

Notes

1. Bernard Gert, *Morality: Its Nature and Justification* (New York: Oxford University Press, 1998).

2. Bernard Gert, *The Moral Rules* (New York: Harper & Row, 1970). I cite *The Moral Rules* according to the Harper Torchbook edition of 1973.

3. The word "motivation" can be easily misunderstood in this connection: I am clearly not speaking here of the motivation to *act* morally (the "why be moral?" in the sense of Gert's thirteenth chapter) but of the motivation to *endorse* the moral rules. Most people want *this* but few want *that*. Gert himself has kept the two questions clearly apart except in one place: the summary to chapter 7, 182.

4. J. L. Mackie, *Ethics: Inventing Right and Wrong* (Harmondsworth, Eng.: Penguin Books, 1977), 10.

5. You don't have to start with this definition (call it $morality_1$); you could start with another one (call it $morality_2$). But what you should not do, in my opinion, is give just

one definition and leave its relationship to other understandings of the word open, calling them merely "false" (cf. ch. 1, notes 1 and 15).

2

Gert's Moral Theory and Discourse Ethics*

Matthias Kettner

Morality and Argumentative Discourse: Two Informal Universal Public Systems

The argument that I set out in what follows is very straightforward. I look at Gert's theory of the common moral system in order to locate a number of places where this theory requires reference to a theory of practices of consensus-building.

Admittedly, there are many different theoretical approaches to consensus and consensus-formation, both in ethics, traditional or applied, and in political philosophy. Notions of consensus are notoriously controversial.[1] Sometimes the term "consensus" is meant to express a strong requirement of unanimity. But often "consensus" means something weaker, namely "a state of agreement, which varies in intensity and scope over time, incorporating the goals for society, the procedures for decision making, and the particular policies."[2] Consensus-building can be understood to aim at a number of different goals, such as making people assent, agree, acquiesce, or give permission. However, the bare fact that many people have come to be of one mind about the moral worth of a certain way of acting, say, is certainly no good warrant for thinking that their verdict is right.[3]

The theory of practices of consensus-building that we are looking for must answer specifically to the needs that are identified within one's moral theory. So what are the goals of the latter? Gert holds that a "moral theory should make explicit, explain, and, if possible, justify morality and relate morality to human nature, impartiality and rationality."[4] Gert's theory is normative in that it is concerned with establishing and vindicating the validity of common morality. Yet not all of its concerns are normative; some are descriptive. For instance, he claims that a moral theory should "describe the procedures involved in moral reasoning" (M, 6). Whether the theory of practices of consensus-building that is required to fill certain lacunae in Gert's moral theory will have to be a normative one depends centrally on which of the goals of the moral theory the proposed supplementation is meant to advance or modify. I presume that if the central goal of Gert's moral theory is to "provide a limit to genuine moral disputes" (M, 239), then it will not be sufficient to merely *describe* the procedures involved in moral reasoning. Moral reasoning is what lands us in genuine moral disputes, and what else if not moral reasoning should guide us in our attempts to deal as unobjectionably as we can with those disputes (e.g., by determining their limits)? I take it that a moral theory should advance our goal of so dealing with controversial moral decisions and judgments.[5] In order to do so the theory must establish and *justify* the *right* procedures involved in moral reasoning.[6]

My aim is to push this concern further than Gert (at present) does. I hold that the theory of consensus-building that we seek must be normative and must permit us to consider consensus-building to be an intersubjective vehicle for moral reasoning. We need an approach to consensus-building practices that focuses on the sense(s) in which these practices can be understood to embody standards closely related either to *rationality,* or to *morality,* or to both. If Gert's theory can be extended from within in order to fill the gaps, then so much the better. If not—and I shall argue that his moral theory cannot fill the gaps by itself—then whence the supplementation?

I suggest that what is needed is a theory that focuses on practices of consensus-building specifically about debatable claims to validity, i.e., claims that we recognize (and think relevant others ought likewise to recognize) when we make judgments which we think are warranted by the reasons we think we have for so judging. That a claim to validity for a judgment is debatable means, roughly, that it makes sense for us to be on the lookout for reasons that should weigh with us either pro or contra, treating the judgment in a determinate sense of validity that is our concern. Any shared beliefs about how our reasons should weigh with us (concerning the acceptability of validity-claims in our judgments) reflects a normative consensus. Such a normative consensus depends on argumentative discourse in that there is no nonargumentative way of comparing, tracking, or modifying "intersubjectively"[7] any occurring differences in how given reasons do in fact, and how we think they rationally should, weigh with us.

Moral controversies involve *moral* validity-claims (for moral judgments). Sure, how far consensus-building can go will often depend on how far we can agree on the facts, i.e., on the kind of validity-claim that is our concern specifically when we argue about assertions of fact ("truth-claims"). Yet even where coming to agree on all the relevant facts would prompt a consensus, if the controversy is a moral one, then the normative commitments which we associate with such a consensus do not boil down to those we associate with a consensus about truth-claims regarding matters of fact. Precisely in what sense do validity-claims for moral judgments and those for factual judgments differ? This is a large theoretical question. Without rushing to an answer, it is safe to say that claims to truth (for judgments regarding matters of fact) and claims to rightness (for judgments regarding moral matters) both are determinables that are to be determined in argumentative discourse. The gaps in Gert's moral theory call for a normative theory of that kind of argumentative discourse through which we determine the latter claims. Approaches known as "discourse ethics" are promising in this respect.

What do I mean by argumentation? A discursive practice of argumentation is a common rational procedure (generally recognized as such within some real or potential community of interlocutors) and a common medium of public communication. Although identifying a pervasive or unifying operation that accounts for the rational pretensions of various forms and domains of argumentation is controversial, I take it as a premise this unifying operation is the evaluation of reasons that are perceived as more controversial in light of reasons that are perceived as less controversial. When participants in argumentation so defined use this operation to build consensus in a public that is not divided into groups separated by unjustifiable boundaries, I call this "argumentative discourse."[8] Clearly, whenever argumentation is harnessed in order to determine truth-claims or truthlike validity-claims (if there are other validity-claims similar to truth in that they concern prima facie *all* rational beings capable of evaluating those claims), then the corresponding consensus-building must be aimed at a public whose boundaries are justifiable, as opposed to arbitrary or otherwise rationally unwarranted.

Moral Judgments (1): Narrative, Comparative, List-Based

Moral judgments can be backed by reasons. So, whenever a moral judgment is challenged, argument can ensue about whether or not one is justified in claiming that the judgment is right (or wrong). Notwithstanding important differences between the rationality judgments of an action and moral judgments, there is an essential parallel between the two kinds of judgments in that they are justified in a similar way. Gert characterizes moral justification as

> similar to rational justification in that only those actions that would be immoral if one did not have a reason, that is, that are violations of the moral rules, need to be morally justified. . . . When all impartial rational persons would publicly allow a violation, it is a *strongly justified* violation. . . . When impartial rational persons differ on whether or not they would publicly allow a violation, it is a *weakly justified* violation. . . . When no impartial rational person would publicly allow a violation, it is a morally unjustified violation. (M, 222f.)

I take it that these distinctions in justificatory status ("strongly," "weakly," "unjustified") will not be assigned on the basis of a head count or opinion poll. Rather, they are normative distinctions in justificatory status that must be based on the rational evaluation of better or worse reasons. To "test" for "public allowability" (as Gert says) must mean to *probe* better or worse reasons. Understood monologically, the notion of "testing", as one might test a fluid for alcoholic content, is completely misleading. To be sure, Gert holds that the object of what he refers to as testing is the determination of whether something (e.g., a certain violation of a moral rule) can be "publicly allowed" (M, 150f). Yet he does not guard against reading into this notion the fact that the test (for *public* allowability) can be performed monologically rather than in a fashion akin to its own publicness (see Conclusion, later). Argumentative discourse between real people is the only medium in which allegedly good enough reasons for claiming a moral judgment's rightness (or wrongness) can get a hearing and can be probed for their rational merit.[9]

Gert holds that all adequate reasons are comparative considerations of goods and harms that are either sufficiently convincing to members of some particular community or that can back moral judgments for the community of all who have the moral system in common. Such comparative considerations must be sufficiently convincing to exempt agents from those censorious judgments made by their moral peers that they would otherwise incur for acting irrationally, or immorally, or both. Whenever Gert's theory deals with questions of justification,[10] the suggestion is that *weighing benefits, weighing harms, and trading the one against the other* constitute the essence of both coming to have a reason for acting and of moral reasoning, which turns on the relative rational strength of such reasons.

But what about such weighing and comparing when the outcomes of several exercises of practical reasoning by different people or by someone whose mind is divided on the matter do not coincide? Can they be brought to converge, at least to the extent to which it is rational to expect them to converge? Disagreement, it is true, cannot be entirely avoided. But should we simply let disagreement be? Should we adopt as a rationally advisable default position that whenever we *find* people disagreeing about moral judgments that each of their underlying moral positions is *justified* (albeit *weakly*).[11]

One reason why the latter does not appear to be an unqualifiedly rational option is that common morality is a *public* system. Gert even makes universality part of the definition of common morality, suggesting that common morality is *one all-encompassing* public system. Then everyone must regard it as the norm, i.e., as normatively normal, that everyone should know the same moral system, and that everyone should apply it to everyone. However, simply letting disagreement be or adopting as a default position that the fact of disagreement attests to the weakly justified status of the judgments in question would license, and cause, a fragmentation of the public to whom the demands of the moral system are salient into as many subgroups ("we" and "they") as lines of disagreement happen to crop up. This would eventually destroy our valuable and perhaps indispensable practice of using the moral judgments we make to criticize, and thereby reshape, albeit indirectly, how people do in fact behave and how they think *anyone* (not merely moral peers or our intimates) should behave.

I define a moral community as one linked by expectations that others will agree to assess each others' actions on the basis of the same public system of morality. I am not suggesting that disagreement *as such* is fragmenting for a moral community. Rather, it is brute disagreement, as distinct from what one might call reflective disagreement, that fragments. Disagreement is *brute* if it is unconstrained by any reason-giving aimed at reaching a common understanding of the reasonableness or unreasonableness of a disagreement in light of other factual, evaluative, and normative beliefs on which there is currently less or no disagreement. Conversely, disagreement so constrained is *reflective* disagreement.

Given that disagreement cannot be avoided and assuming that, in general, we have reason to try to cope reflectively with it, where reaching agreement is better than ending in brute disagreement, how are we to deal reflectively with disagreement, specifically, in the practice of moral judgment? If by consensus-building about discrepancies in the products of the exercises of moral reasoning, *how* is moral reasoning to be exercised in such consensus-building? I now look at what is involved, on Gert's theory, in dealing rationally with reasons relating to moral judgments:

For any particular moral judgment *j* that I make, the validity-claim of which is up for debate, an attempt to assess how convincing[12] *j* is to others must begin by my making plausible to others (to whom this may initially not appear plausible, given what I anticipate of their views) how I weigh the benefits and harms that I take to be salient regarding the controversial validity-claim raised for my judgment. Consider, e.g., the judgment that it is morally wrong of the medical profession to revise its Helsinky declaration so that the former distinction between experimental treatments and medical experiments on patients is blurred. In justifying that claim, I would begin by making it plausible that the protection of patients' bodily integrity is important, that the autonomy of medical science to progress as it seems fit to do is important, and that the former is more important than the latter.

Rarely, if ever, will the weighing of benefits and harms be a straightforwardly deductive matter. Instead, such weighing will often, if not always, require a narrative articulation of collateral reasons from contextual or background beliefs. In my example, I would perhaps have to recount my convictions about the scandalous history of medical science.

I am inclined to say that weighing benefits and harms requires in all nontrivial cases a mode of reasoning that is open to narratively embedded reasons.[13] For if I have to make plausible to *S1* how a certain reason *R* weighs with me in certain judgments that I hold, then it probably does not make sense to repeat or simply paraphrase *R*. However, provided that *S1* and I have sufficient communicative rapport, it makes sense for me to try (in order to make *S1* see *R*'s point) to reveal to *S1* by analogies and examples more and more of the experiential background that makes *R* the good reason it is, in my view.

Gert's general views about moral justification imply that such narratively open reasoning, no matter how complex or simple, has to involve comparisons across what I would call "benefiting and harming scenarios." *All* such scenarios have to map onto Gert's list of basic personal evils and goods. To see why, consider how Gert defines the concepts (i) of an evil or a good, (ii) the concept of rationality (as attributed to persons), (iii) the concept of morality, and (iv) the concept of anyone's having an adequate reason for her action. I look at (i)-(iii) here and then, in the next section, at (iv).

Gert defines an evil or harm as "that which all rational persons avoid unless they have an adequate reason not to" (M, 90). Similarly, "a good is that which no rational person will give up or avoid without an adequate reason" (M, 92). Treating the concept of personal rationality or irrationality as already fixed yields the items death, pain, disability, loss of freedom, and loss of pleasure as uncontroversially evil and consciousness, ability, freedom, and pleasure as good,[14] provided everyone wants to eschew any controversy about purportedly adequate reasons. Conversely, treating the concept of a basic personal evil or harm as already fixed by the entries in the list yields content for an uncontroversial concept of rationality or irrationality (M, 94). It seems to me that the list is an attempt to articulate with utmost generality a common normative self-understanding. That is, it is an account of what we normally regard as irrational for people whom we take to be people *like us* either not to avoid or not to give up, pending good enough ("adequate") justifying reasons for making any deviation from the norm one that is justified for people like us ("rational"), i.e., one which we need not regard as irrational. The list adumbrates a consensus on the part of people like us about what "we" normally have reason to avoid, or not to give up, *without* further reason. Thus, on Gert's theory, the basic personal goods and evils (which are *materially* defined by the entries in the list) *formally* function for people like us to mark off that which we normally have reason to be able to justify to people like us *with* further reasons (which have to be commonly recognized as "adequate" for this justificatory task) on the one hand, and that which people like us take not to stand in need of justification.

It is now easy to articulate how the first three definitions are related. For Gert, the very purpose of morality is "the lessening of evil or harm being suffered."[15] Let us presume that this is true. Then it is part of our common normative self-understanding that the point of morality is the lessening of what the negative entries in the list adumbrate, provided that we assume agreement on (or indifference to) what constitutes an adequate reason. Morality maps onto the list because we understand the very point of morality (or, why morality is important to us) in terms of what is on the list. Moral judgments map onto the list because we understand morally right action as action that is in accord with, and morally wrong action as action that runs against, the very point of morality. When these judgments become more complicated, we must tap, and work from inside, our elementary grasp of harms or evils on the list and imagine our way into more or less complex scenarios and types of harming.

So far I have argued that Gert's notion of moral reasoning is intimately connected with the list of basic personal evils and have suggested that this linkage calls for an openness to narrative scenarios of evil or harm. I have not yet argued that this involves *comparisons* between evils (harms) and goods (benefits). This claim is particularly relevant in light of Gert's assigning to any adequate reason the structure of a (positive) comparison between evils avoided or goods gained and evils suffered or goods forgone.

Gert on Adequate Reasons and Significant Groups

For Gert, an "adequate" reason can justify the claim that some conceptually suitable object *x* (e.g., a person's action) is rational, or conversely, can defeat apparently good reasons on strength of which it is claimed that *x* is irrational. In the preceding section I paid homage to Gert's distinction between "basic" and nonbasic evils and goods with the qualifying condition that there is no need to debate what counts as an adequate reason. I now drop this methodologically simplifying condition. So how do Gert's definitions of good and evil, morality, personal (ir)rationality, and one's justifying one's action to someone work when we *are* (and have reason to be) in dispute about the adequacy of proffered reasons?

Gert's notion of an adequate reason is indexed to groups in at least two ways: to the group of all those whom one recognizes as justified in expecting that one justify one's action to anyone of them, and to the group of those who regard one's reason as adequate, or who one thinks should so regard one's reason.

Concerning the first index, if there were no others expecting one's action to be justifiable, then one could always act as one found fit without worrying about the adequacy of one's reasons in the judgment of others. In such a world, the concept of a good enough justifying reason for acting would presumably have no hold at all.

Concerning the second index, Gert counts "any reason as adequate if any significant group of otherwise rational people regard that reason as adequate, *that is*, if they regard the harm avoided or benefit gained to compensate for the harm suffered."[16]

Call this last kind of group "rational evaluators." Why are good reasons indexed to groups of rational evaluators? Gert holds that a person's acting rationally does not require acting on stronger or better reasons (M, 79). It often does not require acting on any reasons at all. This is a controversial point.[17] But suppose that Gert is right. Even then, Gert should at least include the criterion that rationality requires a *competence* to act on better rather than worse reasons. Possession of this competence includes the ability to distinguish good from better reasons and a concern for doing this reliably and in ways that express recognition of the fact that others are, as rational evaluators, on equal footing with oneself. The fact that rational evaluators are so situated need not be interpreted morally (e.g., as a status of equal respect for moral personhood or for personal autonomy). Rather, it mirrors how a reason's normative status as an adequate reason *R* is constituted by *intersubjective recognition* of *R* (as a good enough answer to a certain question about justification). *R* has to be "regarded" as adequate. Such regarding has to be mutually shared; it could not be so shared but for the premise that it is no more or less in one person's power to bring about that *R* be so regarded than it is in another's.

The notions of "acting for a reason" and of "evaluating reasons as better or worse" can be seen to be interrelated if it is granted that rational agents (1) are able to aim at doing what they have better reasons to do, and (2) are able and willing to scrutinize available reasons in order to find out what (given their situation) their better or worse reasons are, and (3) are able to aim at employing, in these efforts, only those procedures that cannot be faulted for irrationality.

The fact that these three abilities belong to the self-conception of rational agents can be seen by considering our common concept of what is for something[18] to be given or taken as a reason for doing something. To say of someone's action that it is done for good reasons is to attribute to the actor a reason that not only the actor himself appreciates as good but that others too can appreciate. *Someone's* good reason is first of all *a* reason the appreciation of which *someone else* can be trusted to share. Neither reasons nor the points of view from which they can be found to be arguably better or worse are private property. We might say that good reasons, i.e., reasons and generally accepted evaluative viewpoints, are "community property"—property, that is, of a community of argumentation.

Whether it is the case that rationality cannot be defined short of invoking a list of contents over and above any rationality formula, as Gert claims, is a cardinal question. However, regardless of one's answer to this question, it remains true that if one cannot apply the rational/irrational distinction unless one can secure a sense for the distinction between reasons that are better or worse in relation to each other and good enough or not good enough in relation to a way of acting that they purportedly rationalize, then rationality cannot be defined short of invoking a community of argumentation.

This holds because the distinctions regarding better, worse, and good enough reasons, to the extent that they are determinable at all, cannot be determined all on one's own but must be determined by a community of argumentation. Since Gert characterizes rationality as the rationalization *by adequate reasons* of what would otherwise be irrational, it is clear that Gert's integrated theory of rationality and morality does secure a sense for the distinction between reasons that are better or worse in relation to each other and good enough or not good enough in relation to what they purportedly rationalize. Also, Gert's theory includes the claim that those distinctions do not make sense short of a community in which it is possible that how anyone in particular employs those distinctions vis-à-vis certain reasons can be compared with how others employ them. My claim goes beyond what Gert's theory says, however, in that I contend that the requisite community must be a community of argumentation, and more precisely of argumentative discourse. To justify this claim is one thing; to show how this claim relates to Gert's theory is another.

I begin with the latter by raising objections to how Gert fleshes out the reference to a community in his notion of an adequate reason. My own claim (that a satisfactory account of rationality requires reference to a community of argumentation) is not thereby already vindicated. Nor would it be vindicated if one showed that reference to a community of argumentation, specifically, avoids objections to which Gert's notion of a significant community is vulnerable. Instead, my own claim has to be vindicated independently. Here, I can merely offer a definition. A "community of argumentation," in the sense in which I shall use this term, is a network of communication in which a commitment to building consensus about the goodness of reasons has caught on as a settled procedure in at least one particular domain of judgment (e.g., of propositions as either truc or false). Moreover, this commitment, amongst the people who undertake or attribute it, warrants building consensus even about those reasons that one regards as fixing the line between that which counts as susceptible and that which counts as nonsusceptible to argumentation.[19]

Gert's definition relativizes the adequacy of a reason to a "significant group," thereby acknowledging the constitutive role of community in the use of basic normative distinctions (better, worse, good enough) regarding reasons. However, Gert fails to clarify in what the significance of a "significant group" consists.

Surely, significance cannot merely signify large numbers, since that would make the category an arbitrary one. Leaving the line between significant and insignificant groups up for grabs engenders a nightmarish communitarianism with regard to adequate reasons since any and every ad-hoc group interested in insulating against criticism what they regard as adequate reason for conducting their affairs could rightly claim to be a significant group, or declare other groups to be insignificant groups whose allegedly rational evaluations of reasons should not be taken seriously. A second unsatisfactory reading of "significance" is suggested by Gert's formulation that a reason is adequate "if any significant group . . . *regards* that reason as adequate."[20] Here, significance might be taken to consist in sharing a significantly close and rich interpretation of Gert's list of basic personal evils and goods and repertoire of benefiting and harming scenarios. This closed consensus of interlocking interpretations of evils, goods, and tradeoffs, and of judgments as to when it is worthwhile to forgo some good or not to avoid some evil could amount to something like a well-ordered, secluded community (e.g., a monastery of world-renouncing monks). Reflective governance of claims to adequacy of reasons would be suspended in such a community owing to a consensus that is always already closed.[21] If the significance of the reference group that figures in Gert's definition of an adequate reason were to boil down to the mere *fact* of a closed consensus, then such "adequacy" (of a reason) loses the rational potential it possesses when being treated as an open claim inviting certain forms of criticism and permitting corresponding modifications of the intersubjectively recognized authority that is part and parcel of a reason's adequacy. The significance-defining group would be locked in, so to speak, in the significance of that group to itself.

The Significance of Shareable Controversiality

I do not know how a more satisfactory reading of significance in the crucial notion of a significant group can be culled from Gert's theory. Therefore, I suggest interpret significance not in terms of uncontroversiality (common in some group) but in terms of *shareable controversiality* (across individuals).

Let us call two discrepant evaluations of the same reason "shareably controversial" if the respective evaluators have a way of articulating the discrepancy in their evaluations, if they wish, so that the discrepancy becomes a reflective disagreement (i.e., a disagreement constrained by reason giving aimed at reaching a common understanding of the reasonableness or unreasonableness of the disagreement in light of other factual, evaluative, and normative beliefs on which there is occurently less or no disagreement).

On any of the suggested interpretations of Gert's account of a group's significance for a reason's adequacy, if *S1-3* are rational individuals[22] and *S1* and *S2* agree that some reason *R* has rational merits that *S1* and *S2* think redeem a certain validity-claim associated with a certain judgment, but *S3* regards *R* as inadequate in the same respect, *S1* and *S2* are at any rate more of a significant group whose regarding *R* as adequate eventually constitutes *R*'s being adequate, than is *S3*. But why should we think that this is so?

Suppose *S1* and *S2* just happen to find themselves in agreement regarding *R* but have never been confronted with how *S3* thinks regarding *R*. *R* goes unchallenged by dispute. Or suppose *S1* and *S2* have never confronted how each regards *R* with how each regards, or with how the other regards, many other reasons for many other judgment-related validity-claims. *R* goes unchallenged by coherence. Or suppose *S1* and *S2* live in different corners of the globe unconnected by communication.[23] In all of these constellations common uncontroversiality (for the group consisting of *S1* and *S2*) is present, while shareable controversiality is absent. Imagine someone (*S4*) as yet completely in doubt regarding *R* but also knowing about any of these constellations. Should this knowledge make a significant difference in how *S4* rationally evaluates *R*? I doubt it. In contrast, it should certainly make a significant difference if, through argumentative discourse (either actually—in on-line communication—or virtually—in thinking), *S4* could understand what *S1*, *S2*, and *S3* (among them or together with *S4*) find controversial in how they regard R. If anyone's (say, *S3*'s) rational evaluation of *R* could make a difference in someone else's rational evaluation of *R*, then the former person is a *significant* rational evaluator for the latter.

It is the rule rather than the exception that, when judgments are made about interesting issues, the difference between significant and insignificant persons as rational evaluators cannot be fixed a priori. Usually, issues that are interesting from a practical point of view will be experience laden as will the reasons given to support claims about such issues owing to their interestingly different experiences pertinent to the issue. This is a partial (and very simplified) explanation of why no particular community of argumentation, as constituted by the intersubjective relation of shareable controversiality, is *the* definite community of argumentation. Rather, any particular community of argumentation is a particular closure within the essentially open community of argumentation.

Although in any real episode of argumentation the community of those who exchange, evaluate, or modify their reasons may be small, there is no *outwardly* determined limit to the community of rational evaluators short of a complete incapacity to argue at all. If I believe of *S1* that *S1* is completely incapable of arguing, then I suppose that this belief, if true, is for any rational evaluator a good enough reason to justify stopping to treat *S1* in ways that it is proper to treat specifically rational co evaluators. But short of this belief of zero status there is no uncontroversially good enough reason for excluding any *potential* member. *Inwardly* determined limits include willingness to enter into an argument, as well as competence and willingness to avoid those types of inconsistency (like pragmatic self-contradictions and logical contradictions) the nonavoidance of which would give *S1*'s interlocutor *S2* good enough reason to stop presupposing that *S1* intends to raise or assess validity-claims for judgments like anyone else in the role of a rational evaluator.

This is part of what I mean by characterizing a community of argumentation as an essentially open community. This openness also extends through time: no reason can be unconditionally removed from scrutiny in light of other, perhaps novel, reasons or rational evaluators. This is because once some reason's rational merits have been determined in a particular community of argumentation, removing this reason from further reevaluation is itself a determinate action that stands in need of justification. The removed reason would have to be removed for some (other) supposedly good enough reason, which in turn cannot be removed from scrutiny except for some further supposedly good enough reason, and so on. So even "best" reasons are best not in an absolute sense but only relative to a determinate range of reasons, namely, relative to all reasons that have so far been advanced in the matter in question and that have been revealed in the ongoing process of argumentatively-governed consensus-building to be comparatively worse.

So much for the significance of shareable controversiality. To sum up the critical import of this discussion: Gert's *formal* definition of adequate reasons is either completely unclear or implausibly relativistic unless the significance of community in this definition is spelled out as an account of a maximally inclusive virtual community of rational evaluators that are capable of governing their consensus-building by argumentation.

Does my criticism of Gert's definition of adequacy for reasons carry over to Gert's general account of a reason?[24] I think it does, since the latter account defines a reason as any belief that can make, through shared recognition by a "significant group," some otherwise irrational action rational; this account seems to imply that every reason must at least sometimes be adequate to make something rational.

Basic Personal Evil and Harms: Value-Esperanto Requiring Interpretation

I now turn to Gert's *material* account of rationality. Gert regards the sense of irrationality and rationality that is captured in his harm-avoidance account of rationality as *basic*. On Gert's account, all practical reason*ing* (in the sense of rationally evaluating reasons for acting in a certain way) consists in asking for, giving, and taking reasons that serve to put into doubt or to convincingly remove from doubt a belief that someone is giving up or is avoiding what we think people like us *basically* should not give up or avoid unless there is a benefit for someone involved in such a way as to compensate for what is given up or avoided.[25]

Similarly, reasoning about the merits (moral and nonmoral) of acting in a certain way consists in asking for, giving, and taking reasons that represent items on a list of basic personal evils and goods and are to be compared across different individuals or within one and the same individual to other reasons that represent, once again, items on the same list of basic personal evils and goods. Gert's method is to put only the most uncontroversial items on this list. It is therefore bound to contain only very few and very general items, as compared with the myriad of different reasons in terms of which human action makes sense for us (as being the appropriate thing to do) and in terms of which we can defend our own conduct and that of others against criticism.

How can a short list of highly abstract value terms match the richness of the space of reasons in terms of which people really justify or criticize their actions? Against this obvious objection to the list of basic personal evils and goods—call it the objection of expressive poverty—Gert claims that "any other belief that counts as a reason whatever must involve these basic reasons" (M, 61). How is this relation of involvement to be construed?

Let's take a simple case. Nontrivial pain is an item on the list of basic evils. Suffering a severe sunburn is painful; hence, it causally involves a basic evil. The sunburn causes an instance of something (nontrivial pain) that among rational persons, other things being equal, counts uncontroversially as something one should avoid in the absence of a good enough reason. The belief that one should avoid sunburn counts as a belief that can justify acting in certain ways (e.g., buying and applying sunblock before going to the beach on a sunny day) to the extent that this belief counts as involving another belief: that one should avoid nontrivial pain.

However, the involvement of pain in a sunburn is different from the involvement of the reason that pain is an evil in the reason that a sunburn is a bad thing. The former involvement relation is causal, the latter, interpretative. By "interpretative" I mean that which determines which ways of acting can be rationalized, i.e., made to count as proper, by representing them as done for a certain reason. For example, *that a sunburn is a bad thing* does not simply represent somebody's or even everybody's recognition that this reason brings into play something as uncontroversial as *that pain is something anyone should avoid unless for some good reason.* Rather, the extension of the given reason's power to rationalize action, or defend action from certain reasoned criticisms, is determined by how sunburns and their avoidance fit into a great many other beliefs of evaluative significance for people living lives similar to ours, or who are at least ready to imagine ours in sufficiently concrete detail. What does the determining is not an "objective" theory (i.e., a scientific authority) or some individual's whimsical subjective preferences, but processes of (re)interpreting and thereby perhaps modifying the intersubjectively recognizable reasons that have gained currency with regard to the matter. The more common the subject matter, the more distributed are such processes across communities of communication who share similar forms of life.

Imagine that the reason *R1 that a sunburn is a bad thing* attracts some attention in this process of interpretation.[26] Note that how *R1* is interpreted as rationalizing in that context certain ways of acting and failing to rationalize certain others will somehow be oriented by the reason *R2* (provided *R2* is "involved" in *R1*) *that pain is something anyone should avoid unless for some good reason*; however, it will not be wholly determined by that reason. We can acknowledge that *R1* would not have the currency it has if *R1* did not involve *R2*. But this does not take us to any determinate interpretation of what currency *R1* should actually have for us.

The fact that the significance of *R1* for rational evaluators is underdetermined by a basic reason *R2* that is involved in *R1* cannot be equated with the fact (readily acknowledged by Gert) that rational people may rank basic personal evils and goods differently. Rather, underdetermination is accounted for by those relevant collateral beliefs and background experiences that go into making a sunburn a bad thing, as it is intersubjectively construed when people give currency to *R1*. People may of course differ in their ranking of how bad sunburns are in comparison to many other bad things. But the underdetermination cannot be accounted for by considering how they differ in their ranking of how bad basic pain is in comparison to the other items on the list of basic personal harms.

Consider an example. At the beach *A*'s three-year-old child *C* wants to play unencumbered by cap and shirt, but *A* insists that *C* wear a cap and shirt "because the sun is so strong." *B* objects that "it is more fun for *C* to feel the wind in one's hair and the sun on one's body." Assuming that *A* cares to respond to *B* in a way that involves reason-giving in defense of *A*'s original proposal, *A* will articulate reasons for which *A* thinks it right that *C* dress properly and for which *A* thinks that *B*'s objection should not make a difference in this claim. Among the sundry reasons that *A* can articulate in this situation, we should expect to find that risking sunburn or putting someone for whom one cares at risk of sunburn is a bad thing since sunburn causes pain.

Note that this fact cannot be reduced to causal knowledge about the effects of radiation. The fact that *A* will urge *B* to consider and that what *A* thinks ought to carry some weight with *B* cannot be represented as a bit of causal knowledge about the effects of strong radiation on human tissue. Rather, what we think *A* should think ought to be taken into account here is this: *C* needs proper protection against something painful that *C* is likely to suffer otherwise. "Pain" is one of a number of terms in which we articulate an order of evaluative significance for us within the space of the reasons that we give and take when reflecting on our actions. We are confident about the presence of this order no matter who is reflecting on which actions. This confidence gives sense to the calling of reasons that saliently and exclusively turn around pain-avoidance "basic". *A*'s initial reason for insisting that C wear a cap and shirt ("because the sun is so strong") involves a basic reason in that, when pressed to point out the intended justificatory force of that remark, *A* will express the belief that *C* is likely to suffer pain and the belief that the importance of avoiding avoidable pain ought to be salient from anyone's point of view.

Justificatory considerations are "nonbasic" either (1) when they turn around things of evaluative significance of an order that we do not confidently think is there no matter who is reflecting on which actions, or (2) when they turn on an interlocking variety of things of some evaluative significance or other so that nothing in the overall complex can without distortion be factored out as that about which the significance of the complex saliently and exclusively turns. As an example of the former, consider shame and pride. An example of the latter can be drawn from the beach scenario by reimagining it as a story in which, say, someone's fear of appearing malevolently neglectful about childcare in the eyes of one's former spouse has strong evaluative significance.

With this in mind, let us return to Gert's list of basic personal evils and goods. The point I want to make is that such a list does not facilitate agreement about comparisons by making them more objective (or, less dependent on how things look from one's own point of view), like the Celsius and the Fahrenheit scales as different but equivalent metrics for measuring temperature. Rather, the list of evils and goods primarily facilitates "reason-able" (i.e., possible to be made the object of reasoning) disagreement, namely, by providing a universally accessible space of articulation for discordant value judgments. This is probably not the case for all kinds of value judgments, but it surely applies to some very important kinds, for instance, value judgments expressing perceived "moral costs" of certain ways of acting. Far from a groundfloor metric for moral space, Gert's list is an unconcrete (abstract, unsatisfied) common language: *esperanto* for expressing some universally intelligible axes of "moral space," i.e., evaluative dimensions in how people take seriously how the outcome of our conduct affects similar sentient beings for good or ill.

The problem, however, is this: I agree that the list, or some such list, can be called basic in that we have no good reason not to expect that every human community of communication will have, or be able to establish, some quite uncontroversial—and, in that sense, paradigmatic—semantic interpretations of open linguistic formats from the list, like "This is a case of radical loss of freedom" or "This is a case of great pleasure." The trouble is that such basic cases are *merely* basic cases. The nonbasic value judgments that underlie complex moral judgments, like the judgment that abortion should be illegal, cannot be reduced to basic cases or decomposed into spin-offs of basic cases. In the face of disagreement concerning complex value judgments (including moral judgments), basic cases can serve merely as a fall-back position for prompting agreement on some simple value judgments. But it is a long interpretative route for us to travel from clear consensus about abstract value judgments framed in axiological esperanto (e.g., that unwanted death is an evil and that taking someone's life is morally wrong) to our sorting out reasons for qualified agreement or disagreement about complex value judgments (e.g., whether risking one's life in a holy war is worth the pain) or to our sorting out reasons for complex moral judgments (e.g., whether risking one's life in a *jihad* is, in a certain context, morally worse than staying home and caring for one's sick wife or child).

It is far from clear that a set of uncontroversially shared basic value judgments (the list of basic personal evils and goods), basic irrationality judgments (the list of irrational beliefs and desires), or basic moral judgments (the list of moral rules) can provide an overarching framework for achieving reflective disagreement about complex matters. Judgments from the basic set may not be relevant when some complex judgment is argumentatively challenged. That some judgments are basic does not imply that they amount to anything like the essential core or the robust foundation of all judgments. If basic judgments are to serve as sources of analogies for complex ones, these basic judgments have to be *interpreted,* claims of intersubjective validity for such interpretations have to be *determined,* and these validity-claims have to be *geared to reasons* that are considered good enough justifiers. Is there a framework that can help us render reflective the disagreements in all of these critical dimensions?

I conclude that such a framework can only emerge out of constitutive constraints within the very activity of argumentative consensus-building. Perhaps Gert can concede this point. However, the depth of the problem for Gert's theory is not exhausted by the observation that common morality requires validity-determining practices of argumentation if it is to live up to the rational pretension that he attributes to it. Rather, the deeper problem is that the practices of argumentation required for the rationality of common morality must be appropriate. What is required is practices of argumentation of the right kind, or with the right kind of constraints for the reflective governance of consensus-building about moral judgments. My claim is that the (moral and rational) normative content of Gert's theory does not reach, or does not have specific and well-grounded normative implications for, the collective activity of such argumentative consensus-building. These normative implications are precisely what a *discourse ethics* should be able to articulate (see Conclusion, later).

Moral Judgments (2): Handling the Public Allowability Test

The problem that I have raised—that, being list-based, moral rules and adequate reasons depend on interpretations with validity-claims, the final arbiter of which is a collective activity of specifically argumentative consensus-building—is not merely a problem in the first step of moral judgments. The problem recurs at still other areas in Gert's theory. One particularly dramatic example is the second step of the two-step structure of moral reasoning, the public allowability test. For Gert, this test is the final arbiter of moral validity.[27]

Moral judgments are made about moral matters on the basis of a moral system. Moral matters are "actions by moral agents affecting beings that are protected by morality and that are covered by some moral rule or ideal" (M, 314). For moral systems with a universal claim to validity, any "moral judgment must be believed, at least when challenged, to be one that could be made by an impartial rational person on the basis of a public system that applies to all rational persons. Either it must be a judgment that itself is understood and could be accepted by all impartial rational persons"—what Gert calls a "*basic* moral judgment"—"or it must be related to a basic moral judgment in an appropriate way."[28] Gert's claim that there is an "appropriate way" in which basic (moral) judgments must be related to not so basic (moral) judgments is the next aspect of his theory that I want to claim requires supplementation by a normative theory of argumentation.

Presumably, appropriateness implies a normative concern for doing justice to claims concerning the validity of any (moral) judgment in as far as it is a *judgment.* However, practices of judgment are rational to the extent to which they are mediated by argumentative discourse. Putting a gloss on Gert's terminology, if morality is an "informal public system applying to all rational persons" (M, 13), then so is argumentative discourse; and to the extent that the normative framework of the moral system (the moral rules and ideals) or any particular moral judgments made within this normative framework can be said to be rational or rationally justifiable, the informal, universal public system that is morality partakes in the informal, universal public system that is argumentative discourse.

I want to relate this point specifically to the public allowability test, i.e., the practice of moral judgment that Gert claims is essential for contextualizing the moral rules by determining valid (strongly/weakly justified) violations of them. The first step in this test is discourse-dependent in that we must determine kinds of violation by reference to their "morally relevant features," which are based on the moral rules and on list-based scenarios of benefits and harms. This list, as I showed above, is axiological esperanto requiring interpretation governed by argumentative discourse.

The second step of the test consists in settling the question of the relative acceptability of the trade-off insofar as the consequences of publicly allowing or disallowing the particular kind of violation can be foreseen (M, 236f.). Here Gert's crucial distinction between moral judgments (as to particular violations of the moral rules) that could be accepted by all impartial rational persons and those that are acceptable only to some can be appropriately handled only in a medium in which it is possible for some impartial rational persons (1) to project counterfactually some of their own moral judgments onto the set of moral judgments that all impartial rational persons would accept, and (2) to find out whether they have been mistaken in this counterfactual universal projection. I will first argue that this medium has to be dialogical, and then, more specifically, that it has to be argumentative discourse.

Suppose that one tries to complete the second step of the test monologically, say, by some kind of observation. Suppose, e.g., that I project onto every impartial rational person my moral judgment,

> *j*: that it is morally right to substantiate (e.g., by suitable legislation) women's freedom to determine what kind of life they want to live even with regard to aborting a fetus.

For me, *j* seems valid in virtue of certain reasons pertinent to *j* that I accept. Imagine that I submit *j* in the fashion of a yes or no choice to large numbers of people whom I presume to be neither aberrantly socialized nor irrational. Surprisingly for me, many of those confronted with my judgment respond negatively. Here is where monological resources for suitably revising my judgment run out. Would it be rational to begin to think of my moral judgment as non-basic? (This implies that I qualify my initial assumption that others will assent to my judgment.) Or that perhaps all negative responses are (contrary to appearance) due to failures of impartiality or rationality, or both, on the part of my respondents? (This implies that I redraw the border of the community of those whose judgment I am prepared to take seriously.) Or that my initial judgment was wrong and that the converse judgment is right? (This implies revising my belief about being right in my judgment.) Or those assenting to my judgment are right in some respect (namely, in that they see *j* as flowing from a presumably basic moral judgment *j'*) and that those dissenting are right in some other respect (namely, in that they see *j*'s negation as flowing from a presumably basic moral judgment *j''*)? Perhaps *j'* and *j''* are even equivalent moral judgments[29] and those who assent differ from those who dissent only in how they link up the basic judgment to certain collateral judgments or beliefs?

The upshot of this is that without getting at the reasons that back the "yes" or "no" in a way that permits me to assess their weight as compared with the reasons that back my own judgment, I cannot be said to be situated rationally well enough to make up my mind.

Monological resources of judgment run out where revising one's judgment *j* requires, in order to eschew charges of irrationality, that any reason perceived as good enough for supporting (or defeating) *j* be inspectable as such across different rational evaluators. This condition requires (3) intersubjective comparisons of assessments of reasons, or the public uptake and reevaluation of such reasoning. This third feature makes it definitive: argumentative discourse should serve as the medium for the second step of Gert's public allowability test.

This medium cannot be substituted in a "reflective equilibrium" in the sense of a cognitive process occurring in an individual's thinking that is sealed off from any real confrontation in the give-and-take of reasons with real others.[30] Nor can it be reduced to a counting of votes, as it well could if the question were what to jointly decide to do from amongst a set of already agreed-upon alternative options, and not what to think concerning the validity of a moral judgment.

What Gert says about the justification of judgments in the face of moral controversy falls short of the conjunction of features (1)-(3) as outlined above. This makes the concept of the public allowability test useless. In the face of real controversies, the test is either so vague as to settle no disagreement at all or so generous as to leave all parties to the controversy "weakly justified", a normative label that is reassuring at best and devoid of any reflective disagreement at worst.

In step two of the test, we are to estimate whether impartial rational persons, when comparing the consequences of everyone's allowing everyone to act in a certain way with the differential consequences of everyone's disallowing everyone to act in that way, can prefer one over the other. Note the subjectivist and monological tone of Gert's description of the operation of the public allowability test. What common ground of appeal would remain for us if you simply "prefer" (M, 237) to have some identifiable violation of a moral rule generally allowed, whereas I simply "decide" (M, 239) to have it generally not allowed? How else if not by articulating and suitably modifying our "preferences" and "decisions" through challenges and defenses based on the informal public system of argumentative discourse are we to do the "comparing," assuming that the testing procedure itself aspires to operate on public reason and hence be a public procedure?

Drawing also on points made in previous sections, my diagnosis of a discourse lacuna in Gert's most important device in practices of moral reasoning for rendering the abstract moral system concrete, the public allowability test, can be summarized in three points: (1) the moral rules must be interpreted before they can be regarded impartially. How are we to handle validity-claims with regard to such interpretations? (2) Properly handling the distinctions between rationally required, allowed, and prohibited beliefs or reasons in discourse depends on interpreting reasons as adequate. But there are two horns of a dilemma in interpreting adequacy. The first horn is dogmatism. The opposite extreme, and the second horn to be avoided, is an overly tolerant attitude based on nothing more than acknowledgment of the widely attested fact that rational people disagree. How to reduce the arbitrariness of consensus? (3) Can the public allowability test be handled monologically? If so, odd and arbitrary results are to be expected for want of reflective checks. If not, and if the test requires something like dialogical checks and balances, how are we to distinguish, in proceeding with the test, between discourses that are appropriately argumentative and other communicative exchanges which, albeit superficially conducted as a give-and-take of reasons, are structured more by unequal powers of negotiation and persuasion than by fairly distributed powers of autonomous insight?

In Conclusion: Discourse Ethics and the Moral System

Questions like those raised in the preceding paragraph are addressed by what has come to be labeled "discourse ethics." Although there is a common theoretical core that unifies the approach, its elaboration over more than twenty years has introduced nontrivially different versions. In this section, I can merely state some results.[31]

The original insight that makes the elaboration of a discourse ethics a worthwhile pursuit in normative ethics must be credited to Karl-Otto Apel,[32] who argued that anyone who takes part in an argument implicitly acknowledges, at least potentially, all the claims of all the members of the communication community, as long as they can be justified by rational arguments.[33]

Any version of a discourse ethics must provide an account of its general contention that validity-claims, at least insofar as they are rational, depend on rationally qualified consensus-building. For both Apel and Habermas the term "discourse" means, roughly, that argumentation is carried on under conditions of free and open dialogue. In Apel's transcendental-pragmatic version, discourse ethics is rooted in the fact that there are some morally normative proprieties in the practice of argumentation. Habermas has suggested that a rational discourse is a moral one if participants adopt as the decisive validity-determining question whether "the foreseeable consequences and side effects of [a norm's] general observance for the interests and value-orientations of *each individual* could be freely accepted *jointly* by *all* concerned."[34]

The moral content of discourse concerns how anyone with whom we would, or who would with us, use (and think it rational to use) argumentation as the sole arbiter of the validity-claims that we associate with our reason-backed judgments, should treat anyone else who could so use argumentation. Thus, each participant rationally should want certain proprieties of mutual recognition and symmetrical situatedness, which ideally regulate discursive commitments, to be the norm for everyone actually (and possibly) involved.[35]

Apel explicates these (moral) proprieties in terms of a moral co-responsibility (between actual as well as possible participants) to ensure that all action in discourse is in accordance with a generic deontic status of free and equal co-subjects.[36] Habermas articulates them in terms of rules, as follows: "that nobody who could make a relevant contribution may be excluded"; "that all participants are afforded an equal opportunity to make contributions"; "that the participants must mean what they say: only truthful utterances are admissible"; "that communication must be freed from external and internal compulsion so that the *yes/no* stances that participants adopt on criticizable validity-claims are motivated solely by the rational force of the better reasons."[37] I prefer conceptualizing them in terms of five parameters of idealization that shape a discourse into a specifically moral discourse.[38]

This is not the occasion to discuss how my construal of discourse ethics goes beyond Apel and Habermas. My principal aim here has been to trace how much space is left for moral discourse in Gert's theory. I hope to have shown not only that there is a lot of space but that this space needs filling out—and that the discourse ethics approach is a good candidate for the job.

My punch line, then, is that Gert's theory should, but cannot, say more about the reflective governance of both controversy and indeterminacy in the moral system that we can achieve via consensus-building of the right kind. I made this point with regard to brute disagreement about (1) the weighing of evils and goods ("Moral Judgments (1)"), (2) a reason's adequacy ("Gert on Adequate Reasons. . ." and "The Significance of Shareable Controversiality"), (3) the involvement of basic reasons in real reasons ("Basic Personal Evil and Harms"), and (4) the public allowability test for particular violations of the moral rules ("Moral Judgments (2)"). This critique could easily be extended to what Gert says about (5) causation (of death, pain, and disability) on a socially entrenched interpretation, and (6) law as a partial determiner of moral costs.[39] The critique is independent of the specific remedy that I propose, discourse ethics. But the diagnosis makes it more difficult for Gert to downplay issues of dissidence, moral controversy, and difference by the two theoretical strategies of either methodologically abstracting from whatever might be the object of controversy or delegating such questions to decision-making procedures of a political rather than moral nature.

On the other hand, I have made no attempt to gloss over notorious problems with discourse ethics. One such problem—call it the inclusion problem—is how to spell out suitable constraints on the concept of "everyone affected" (e.g., by the adoption of a norm). Here some theoretical equivalent of what Gert calls the "morally relevant features" is required within discourse ethics. Also, Gert's notion of irrationality appears to be an undeniable negative constraint on the "interests" or "need-claims" that define the scope of moral concerns, according to discourse ethics.

The most important topic for further debate about the theoretical benefits of viewing Gert's theory through the lens of discourse ethics is probably how thick or how thin a conception of rationality should be in order to power a normatively universal morality. Discourse ethics presupposes a type of rationality—call it discursive rationality—that is theoretically irreducible both to rationality concepts of Humean derivation (stringently criticized by Gert) and to Gert's own harm-avoidance account of rationality. The vindication of this presupposition will have to await another occasion.

Notes

* In revising this paper I have received valuable support from Bernard Gert, Walter Sinnott-Armstrong, Kier Olsen DeVries, Robert Audi, and, especially, my commentator Kathleen Wallace. I also want to thank Joshua Gert, Michael Smith, Virginia Held, and students from Bernie's class, in particular Jay Bregman, for important points.

1. Cf. H. A. M. J. ten Have and Hans-Martin Sass, eds., *Consensus Formation in Healthcare Ethics* (Dordrecht, Neth.: Kluwer Academic Publishers, 1988).

2. George J. Graham, "Consensus," in *Social Science Concepts: A Systematic Analysis*, ed. G. Sartori (Beverly Hills, Calif.: SAGE, 1984), 89-124, 94.

3. Sidney Lumet's 1957 classic movie "The Twelfth Man" illuminates the vagaries of consensus brilliantly.

4. Bernard Gert, *Morality. Its Nature and Justification* (New York: Oxford University Press, 1998), 6 (henceforth: M).

5. In what follows I will speak of moral judgments rather than "moral decisions" since a morally valid decision is parallel to the singular moral judgment that this decision is morally right.

6. In a somewhat surprising passage, Gert proclaims that a "moral theory cannot and should not be used to settle controversial moral questions" (M, 379). I presume he means that no moral theory should aspire to decide *in theory all* controversial moral questions. However, the theory should speak to the question of how *we* should *best* go about settling controversial moral questions.

7. That is, presumed by different persons to be the same for each one.

8. For a discussion of the notion of an argumentative discourse as the locus of what Apel and Habermas have termed "communicative rationality", see Matthias Kettner, "Second Thoughts about Argumentative Discourse, Good Reasons, and 'Communicative Rationality,'" in *i foerste, andre og tredje person. Festskrift til Audun Oefsti*, ed. S. Boe, B. Molander, and B. Strandhagen (Trondheim, Nor.: NTNU Filosofisk Institutt, 1999), 223-34.

9. Of course, it is possible for an individual person to *think* in terms of an argumentative discourse with, or between, *anticipated* or *specificable* people. Call this "hypothetical discourse." Hypothetical discourse can correct real discourse, and vice versa. Yet there is an asymmetry: where a thinker invokes hypothetical discourse for correcting real discourse, a burden of proof is incurred that has to be discharged (if it can be discharged at all) in further *real* discourse. So there is a methodological primacy of real discourse over hypothetical discourse.

10. Cf. M, 13, 103, 157-85, 186ff., 221-46, 248f., 346.

11. This is a reading of Gert's theory suggested by formulations like the following (M, 239): "Applying the justification procedure [what Gert calls the public allowability test] to controversial cases will almost always result in the violation being weakly justified, that is, with impartial rational persons disagreeing about whether it should be publicly allowed." I wonder how best to understand the idea that a justificatory status *results*. It would be highly uncharitable to interpret Gert's statement on the model of a prediction, as in "repeatedly throwing a dice will normally result in an even distribution of the values one to six." But how, then, is one to understand it in terms of a rational procedure?

12. By convincingness I mean to include mere acceptability. If *S1*'s judgment *j* is an acceptable one for *S2* then *S2* must find *j* at least not entirely unconvincing even though *S2* might fail to be convinced of *j* enough to assent to it.

13. I use the term "narrative" to characterize this mode of practical reasoning at the suggestion of my colleague Martin Loew-Beer.

14. M, 31f. Gert claims that "[t]here is no significant disagreement about what belongs on the list, even if there are some disagreements on the best way to formulate it" (M, 106). The list "coincides with almost everyone's view of what counts as an evil or harm and as a good or benefit" (M, 107).

15. M, 247; cf. 107.

16. M, 57, italics mine. Note again Gert's identification of adequacy-probing reasoning with comparative assessments of evils and harms.

17. Cf. M, 60. Gert breaks up the term "reason" into one sense that is merely explanatory, having "nothing to do with rationality" (M, 63), and another that is justificatory and is supposed to exhaust what reasons for acting have to do with rationality, namely, being able to make some otherwise irrational action rational. I disagree. In my view, the concept of a reason should allow for a sense in which a reason can make some otherwise intersubjectively objectionable action unobjectionable, without reducing the sense of intersubjective (un)objectionableness to the (Gertian) irrational-rational axis.

18. For Gert, reasons must be beliefs. For my argument, it is immaterial whether one holds reasons to be beliefs, thoughts, or considerations of facts.

19. Of course, this definition does not establish my crucial assumption that in determining the goodness of a reason there is *nothing over and beyond* what a community of argumentation that is not unjustifiably exclusive would be able to determine.

20. M, 57, my italics.

21. I call a consensus "open" if the content of the consensus is actually accepted by some and not outright unacceptable to anyone (where "everyone" and "anyone" range over those people whose accepting or rejecting makes a difference to the rational merits of the consensus). In contrast, the content of a "closed" consensus is actually accepted by everyone.

22. In the minimal and universalist sense of rationality that must be attributable to any individual *S* if *S* is to be taken as a moral actor, cf. M, 33f.

23. "S1 and S2" here may be taken to stand for large numbers of people dispersed in geographical space or historical time.

24. I owe this question to Walter Sinnott-Armstrong.

25. Cf. the definition of a reason for acting in a certain way as a belief "about anyone benefiting anyone" (M, 81) and the claim that "[n]o beliefs unrelated to avoiding harm or gaining benefits are basic reasons" (M, 74). Although Gert nowhere explicitly discusses reason*ing*, I take it that reasoning is implied when we determine whether this or that reason justifies this or that action standing in need of justification.

26. Imagine, e.g., that sunbathing in Australia is thought to cause skin cancer.

27. By "moral validity" I mean claims about the validity of the deontic content of a moral judgment. For instance, when I judge that *Heinz should steal the only drug that can save his wife's life*, I thereby claim that it is a morally right thing to do for anyone in such a situation.

28. M, 315f. The notion of "could be accepted by" in this quotation is a normative modality meaning "by rational standards ought to be acceptable for."

29. The equivalent judgment might be the judgment that we think it morally right that human life should be cherished. This is Dworkin's claim. See Ronald Dworkin, *Life's Dominion* (New York: Knopf, 1993).

30. I agree with Gert's criticism of using the Rawlsian concept of a (narrow or wide) reflective equilibrium as a justificatory method (cf. M, 379f.).

31. For a more detailed exposition, see Matthias Kettner, "Discourse Ethics: A Novel Approach to Moral Decision Making," *International Journal of Bioethics* 10, no. 3 (1999).

32. Discourse ethics, though in the American philosophical context usually associated with Habermas, has its *locus classicus* in Karl-Otto Apel, "The A Priori of the Communication Community and the Foundations of Ethics," in *Towards a Transformation of Philosophy* (London: Routledge, 1980), 225-300. This paper dates back to a lecture given in 1967. For an overview of Apel's philosophical position, see Matthias Kettner, "Karl-Otto Apel's Contribution to Critical Theory," in *Handbook of Critical Theory*, ed. David Rasmussen (London: Basil Blackwell, 1996), 258-86.

33. Cf. Apel, "The A Priori of the Communication Community and the Foundations of Ethics," 277. It is against this background that Habermas later proclaimed as "the distinctive idea of an ethics of discourse" the "discourse principle" (D) that "only those norms can claim to be valid that meet (or could meet) with the approval of all affected in their capacity as participants in a *practical* discourse." See Jürgen Habermas, "Discourse Ethics: Notes on a Program of Philosophical Justification," in *Moral Consciousness and Communicative Action* (Cambridge, Mass.: MIT Press, 1990), 43-115, 66.

34. See Jürgen Habermas, "Eine genealogische Betrachtung zum kognitiven Gehalt der Moral," in *Die Einbeziehung des Anderen. Studien zur politischen Theorie* (Frankfurt, Ger.: Suhrkamp, 1996), 11-64. Habermas refers to this question as "the principle of universalization 'U.'" Cf. Habermas, "Discourse Ethics: Notes on a Program of Philosophical Justification," 65.

35. For rational evaluators, this content is always already recognized since it is *implicit* in argumentation and irrefutable since it is implicit in *argumentation*.

36. Cf. Karl-Otto Apel, "The Problem of a Universalistic Macroethics of Coresponsibility," in *What Right Does Ethics Have?: Public Philosophy in a Pluralistic Culture*, ed. S. Griffioen (Amsterdam: VU University Press, 1990), 23-40, and Karl-Otto Apel, "Der Begriff der primordialen Mit-Verantwortung," in *Angewandte Ethik als Politikum*, ed. M. Kettner (Frankfurt: Suhrkamp, 2000).

37. Cf. Habermas, "Eine genealogische Betrachtung zum kognitiven Gehalt der Moral," and Habermas, "Discourse Ethics: Notes on a Program of Philosophical Justification," 89.

38. The parameters are: *Reasonable Articulation of Need Claims*: all participants in a discourse should be capable of reasonably articulating any need claim they take to be morally significant. *Bracketing of Power Differentials*: differences in (all forms of) power that exist between participants (both within and outside of argumentation) should not be any participant's good reason in discourse for endorsing any moral judgment. *Nonstrategic Transparency*: all participants should be able articulate morally significant need claims truthfully, without strategical reservations. *Fusion of Moral Horizons*: all participants should be able to sufficiently understand articulated need claims in the corresponding moral horizons of whoever articulates them. *Comprehensive Inclusion*: participants should make the following a constraint on what their community of discourse can accept as good reasons: that participants must anticipate whether their reasons can be rehearsed by all nonparticipant others who figure in any moral judgment that may result from their discourse. For the derivation, in some detail, see Matthias Kettner, "Neue Perspektiven der Diskursethik," in *Ethik technischen Handelns. Praktische Relevanz und Legitimation*, ed. A. Grunwald and S. Saupe (Heidelberg: Springer Verlag, 1999), 153-96.

39. Cf. M, 172-77. For reasons of space I cannot follow Sinnott-Armstrong's suggestion to develop this point at length.

3

On the Relevance of Ignorance to the Demands of Morality*

Geoffrey Sayre-McCord

"It is impossible to overestimate the amount of stupidity in the world."
Bernard Gert[1]

Introduction

In *Morality*, Bernard Gert argues that the fundamental demands of morality are well articulated by ten distinct, and relatively simple, rules. These rules, he holds, are such that any person, no matter what her circumstances or interests, would be rational in accepting, and guiding her choices by, them. The rules themselves are comfortably familiar (e.g., "Do not kill," "Do not deceive," "Keep your promises") and sit well as intuitively plausible. Yet the rules are not, Gert argues, to be accepted merely because they are intuitively attractive, nor because they are already widely recognized, but because they stand as the only set of rules that can qualify as appropriately acceptable to all rational beings.

Two questions naturally arise when confronted with a proposed account of morality's standards. The first question is: why believe the account is true? The second question is: supposing it is true, what reason do people have to accept those standards as guides either for themselves or others?

Before turning directly to the details of Gert's defense of the rules and the accompanying answers he offers to these two questions, it is worth highlighting the different attitudes people have taken toward these questions and the relation answers to them might bear to one another.

A fair number of people think that the two questions are completely independent. One question focuses on what morality demands while the other focuses on the apparently distinct issue of whether, and why, one might rationally accept morality's demands either as a standard for oneself or for others. In general, it seems just a matter of being clear-headed to recognize these as different issues. After all, it is one thing to identify what a particular legal system might demand, for instance, and something else entirely to decide whether it is rational to obey those demands. Similarly, isn't it one thing to identify what morality might demand and something else entirely to decide whether it is rational to obey those demands? It seems pretty clear that what is demanded, and what one might rationally do, can come apart quite radically.

Still, at least when it comes to the demands of morality, there are also a fair number of people who think that once one has established demands as the demands *of morality* there is no real question as to whether it is rational to accept or obey them. Morality's demands, they argue, set an ultimate standard and enjoy an authority that provides decisive reason to act. That one has a moral (as opposed to a legal, or professional, or even prudential) duty to act in some way, they hold, settles the issue of whether one has adequate and even decisive reason to do it. So in determining that some set of standards are in fact those of morality, one has settled whether or not people should accept them as guides to their own and other people's behavior. The two questions are not really distinct, so they are not independent either.

Not surprisingly, there are people who fall in between these two extremes, people who hold that while both questions stand as distinct, an answer to one of the questions depends, in some interesting way, on the answer to the other. Determining what might be rationally accepted, some of them suggest, requires first determining what morality demands, permits, and forbids. Flipping the dependence around, others suggest that figuring out what morality demands requires first figuring out what might be rationally accepted. Either way, the idea is that successfully defending an answer to one of the questions will require grappling with the other.

Fitting squarely into this third group, Gert sees the two questions as distinct but not independent. He holds that no proposed account of morality is even in the running unless its rules or standards are such that those to whom they apply can rationally accept them. As a result, successfully defending his own account as true, and so answering the first question, involves answering the second.

Gert takes this position because he thinks morality is essentially "an informal public system," where a set of standards counts as an informal public system only if it is both known by,[2] and rationally acceptable to, all to whom it applies.[3] And he argues that, since moral judgments may be made about any and all rational agents, the rules or standards on offer must constitute an informal public system that applies to all rational beings, so "every feature of morality must be known to and rationally chosen by any rational person."[4] As a result, if not all rational agents could rationally accept some proposed moral system, the system would be (according to Gert) a nonstarter.

One thing to ask, then, about any proposed moral system, Gert's included, is whether it satisfies the second condition on being an informal public system—whether it is rational for people to accept its rules as setting a standard for themselves and others. It is important, that is, to pursue an answer to the second question I mentioned at the beginning.[5]

In pursuing it, Gert offers a particular account of when and why a system would count as rationally acceptable and argues that his account—and any plausible account—must prove rationally acceptable to all to whom it applies (which is all rational agents). I am skeptical, for reasons I will try to bring out, concerning both his account of rational acceptability and his contention that an account of morality, to be plausible, must be an account of a system that is rationally acceptable to all to whom it applies.

Rational Acceptance

When is a system of rules such that all rational beings could rationally accept it? Gert's answer to this question falls within a familiar framework of justification. The framework is one in which someone is taken to be rational in accepting (or choosing, or doing) something if and only if a fully rational person, appropriately situated, would favor accepting (or choosing, or doing) it.[6] Real people, of course, are often irrational, woefully ignorant, horridly biased, etc. What real people might approve of frequently carries pitifully little justificatory weight. Yet those same people, cured of their ills, appropriately informed, freed of partiality, would, it seems, set a perfect standard. What grounds could there be for discounting their approval? Seemingly: none. If none, then, the thought goes, what such people—made fully rational and appropriately situated—would favor should set the standard for what we might rationally accept.[7]

This general line of thought, and the resulting framework for thinking about justification, has informed a number of otherwise quite different approaches to moral theory—Ideal Observer theories[8], informed desire theories,[9] and theories that appeal to what rational beings would agree to in a suitably described contract situation.[10] All of these views set out to link the rational acceptability of a set of rules or standards to the approval of rational beings appropriately situated. Different versions of each view advance different characterizations of what goes into being a rational being, of what sort of approval is relevant, and of what is involved in these rational beings being appropriately situated, when it comes to setting the standard for real people. Some think that the rational beings whose approval matters to the justification of moral standards are those—and only those—who are fully informed. Ignorance, on this view, disqualifies. Others, John Harsanyi and John Rawls, for instance, agree that all general knowledge is required, but hold that the sort of impartiality important to the justification of moral standards requires some ignorance, specifically ignorance of one's identity.

Gert goes further by requiring (in effect) almost total ignorance—to the point where those whose approval sets the standard for rational acceptability of a proposed set of moral rules are to rely *solely* on the beliefs it would be "irrational not to hold."[11] All and only such "rationally required beliefs" are supposed to figure in determining the approvals that matter, according to Gert.[12] Otherwise, he points out, the acceptability of the proposed rules would turn on considerations available not to all rational beings, but only to those who are better informed than rationality itself requires.[13] The need to show that the rules are acceptable to all rational agents thus imposes a striking constraint, in Gert's hands, on what might be appealed to in determining the acceptability of a proposed set of rules as the rules of morality.

Among rational agents, those who possess only rationally required beliefs fall at the very bottom of the heap. Any belief that some rational agent or other might lack without irrationality, they lack. Consequently, they know extraordinarily little about themselves, about others, and about the world they inhabit.[14] It would not be unfair to say that, among rational agents, they constitute the lowest common denominator. Of course, in some ways they might still be better off than many real people who fail to be rational. But even compared to such real people, these rational agents know amazingly little. And if we compare these rational agents (who hold only rationally required beliefs) with others who have learned more about how the world around them works, they will look poorly off indeed. Nonetheless, Gert argues, the fact that morality is meant to apply, as an informal public system, to all rational agents means that the acceptability of the rules that constitute the system cannot depend on anything not shared by all rational agents.[15]

On Gert's view, then, a proposed moral system is rationally acceptable, in the relevant sense, if, but only if, those who are extraordinarily ignorant—and others relying solely on rationally required beliefs even the ignorant would have—would favor that system. Only then, he maintains, would the system have a claim to being such that *all* rational beings, and so all to whom the system applies, could rationally accept it.

Yet, as Gert notes, even the system of rules he defends can be shown to secure the approval he thinks necessary only if, in addition to constricting the relevant beliefs to those that are shared by all rational beings, some assumption is made concerning the desires that might influence the attitudes of the people in question. What rational beings might favor, in light of their beliefs, will turn on what they happen to value or care about. Whether any, let alone all, rational agents who rely solely on rationally required beliefs might favor something or not is up in the air until their desires, values, and concerns, are specified.

Just as there are certain rationally required beliefs, Gert holds that there are some desires that are rationally required, for example, the desire to avoid pain, and some that are irrational (i.e., irrational to act on absent adequate reason), for example, the desire to die.[16] And just as hope for securing a consensus among all rational beings appropriately situated involved seeing the appropriate situation as involving a reliance solely on rationally required beliefs, so too it might seem that the appropriate situation would likewise require that only rationally required desires be allowed to have sway. As it turns out, though, limiting the approval that matters to approval prompted solely by rational desires will still not secure unanimous approval for the system of rules Gert proposes. Indeed, as he notes, a rational person may consistently be an egoist, and in being an egoist will favor rules that constrain others, but not herself, whereas the rules Gert proposes are rules that are to constrain all.[17]

"The problem," as Gert sees it, "is how to replace the egocentric attitude . . . with the appropriate moral attitude while at the same time keeping it an attitude that would be taken by all rational persons."[18] It is, he recognizes, not a solvable problem. There is no such attitude. Gert admits that, given certain commitments that are rationally permitted, a rational person will not adopt anything like the sort of attitude that Gert needs to suppose is shared in order to secure the relevant approval for the rules he recommends. In fact, as he recognizes, some rational beings might, without irrationality, acquire convictions, say religious convictions, that lead them to reject not only the rules as applied to themselves but also as applied as egoistically motivated constraints on others. "A rational person," he notes, "might hold some religious belief that was in conflict with taking the egocentric attitude toward these rules, and he might give priority to the religious belief."[19]

Still, while there is no attitude all rational persons must take, the fact that we are considering the rules as proposed moral rules—as part of an informal public system that applies to all rational beings—means, Gert maintains, "that a rational person cannot adopt any attitude toward the rules, except one like that which would be adopted by a rational person who has an impartial concern for all persons."[20] Considering the rules as moral rules constrains us, that is, to relying only on attitudes that all other rational beings might share. In one sense, of course, they might share an egoistic attitude, but the upshot of that attitude is for them each in effect to differ, sometimes radically, in what they actually favor. But they can really only share an attitude that makes no egocentric reference, either implicitly or explicitly. In other words, considering the rules as moral rules leads one inevitably to adopt both an impartial attitude and a commitment to mutual acceptability.

If we can stipulate, as this argument suggests, EITHER that the rational beings in question are concerned to favor moral rules OR, what turns out to be functionally equivalent, that they are committed to impartiality, OR, functionally equivalent again, that they are willing to favor only what could be favored by all rational beings, the argument for Gert's proposed system seems to go through.[21] For any one of these concerns, in contrast with an egoistic attitude, will lead someone relying solely on rationally required beliefs to favor the rules Gert recommends.

At the same time, only with one or another of these additional commitments on board will the system of rules Gert endorses be favored by those who rely only on rationally required beliefs. Accordingly, Gert ends up arguing that a candidate moral system is justified in the relevant way—is such that all to whom it applies could rationally accept it—if and only if all rational people who rely only on rationally required beliefs (and suffer no irrational desires) would, if considering the system as a moral system, or if committed to impartiality, or favoring only what could be favored by all, all favor it. Showing that a system enjoys this sort of justification—showing that it would be favored by *all* rational beings appropriately situated—is establishing that the system in question is (in Gert's terms) strongly justified.[22]

As it happens, Gert holds that any one of these three commitments—to morality, or impartiality, or mutually acceptability—is sufficient to secure the favor of all appropriately situated rational beings. And he takes the fact that each commitment will, independently of the others, secure the relevant approval reveals the deep sense in which the justification of a moral system is tied both to its being impartial and to its being acceptable to all. If the arguments work, one gets a lovely convergence.

I am not here going to spend any time on the question of whether the arguments work. For the sake of this discussion, we can simply grant that all who rely solely on rationally required beliefs and are concerned either with morality, or with impartiality, or with what all could favor, would favor the set of rules Gert advances.

Leaving these claims in place, I am instead going to focus primarily on Gert's contention that the rational acceptability of a set of rules that are to apply to all rational beings depends upon their being favored by those who are influenced solely by rationally required beliefs in a way that leaves out of account whatever might be known to some but not all. In other words, my interest is in Gert's view that the appropriate standard of justification is set by what the lowest common denominator might approve.

Why Only Rationally Required Beliefs?

Why accept this view? Why take what people who are woefully ignorant would approve of as setting the standard for whether a system is rationally acceptable in the appropriate way? Why think that what they might favor has any implications whatsoever for what people like us might rationally accept?

One might think that an appeal to their approval works as a kind of argumentative *tour de force*. After all, if even those who are pitifully ignorant would favor the system of rules Gert advocates—if even those who know very little and care not at all about others would endorse rules that constrain everyone from inflicting harm on others—that would seem a strikingly impressive discovery. Moreover, one might think, if even the ignorant and uncaring would favor the rules, then surely all other rational beings would as well. So, by limiting the premises of the argument to claims about what even the worst among us might favor, it may seem the argument avoids appealing to anything either morally or rationally controversial. In relying on the shared subset of beliefs that are rationally required we seem to have what is sufficient to ensure the favoring of the rules (assuming either a concern for morality, or for impartiality, or for securing the favor of all), so the argument apparently needs to rely on nothing more.

Now this is not Gert's strategy, and for good reason. To understand why, it is important to note that reasoning in a practical sphere is nonmonotonic (i.e., defeasible)—adding premises to what was, initially, a good argument can undermine the conclusion. For this reason, given an initial inference that is acceptable, it is a mistake to assume that adding information will leave the inference untainted. If all I know of someone is that she is your beloved sister, I might reasonably trust her . . . until I learn that you do not trust her yourself, in which case I might reasonably be suspicious of her . . . until I discover that you trust no one, under any circumstance, in which case it would be unreasonable for me to suspect her . . . until I learn that she has lied to you. . . . Similarly, what people might favor if they rely on certain beliefs (e.g., concerning your sister's trustworthiness) may well be something they quickly come to oppose in the face of new information. People who have more than the beliefs that are rationally required may well not favor things that they would have favored had they not acquired extra information.

Indeed, as Gert notes explicitly in *Morality*, what people limited to rationally required beliefs would favor are things that people who rely on other rationally permitted beliefs—say scientifically founded beliefs, or various moral or religious beliefs—would firmly oppose.[23]

This fact about how beliefs might influence what rational people favor means that limiting the argument to the attitudes of those relying solely on rationally required beliefs is a seriously *nontrivial* assumption. Far from ensuring the power of the argument by bringing all rational beings within its scope (which is what it may have initially seemed to be doing in relying on rationally required beliefs), the limitation dramatically constricts its appeal. For what such people would favor would be rationally rejected by others who are more informed. Most significantly, actual people (virtually all of whom have more than the beliefs rationally required of all) will often be among those who will rationally not favor what those who are less informed would.[24] Actual people who are rational and informed about the world might well find themselves committed to standards that require people to help others in need—a requirement rejected by Gert. Alternatively, they might come to reject (perfectly rationally, it seems) standards that require obeying the civil law—a requirement imposed by Gert.

As far as I can tell, for all Gert argues, actual people may come to have certain beliefs that are rational for them to hold and *in light of which* accepting the standards he defends as guides to their own behavior and the behavior of others would be positively irrational. In the cases I am imagining, people have, without irrationality, come to hold standards that differ in some significant way from the ones Gert proposes. The standards might, on these people's view, have their source in reason, or in religion, or in nature. Whatever the supposed source, given that the people actually have the convictions, and assuming that, given their evidence, they have positive grounds for embracing the convictions, if their standards conflict with the rules Gert advocates, they may well be in a situation in which obeying the rules he proposes goes against all that they reasonably see themselves as having reason to do. This is true regardless of whether their views are actually correct, as long as the views are rationally held and provide the people with reason to accept the standards they do.

There are two kinds of cases to keep in mind here, I think. In some cases, the people in question might find themselves with convictions that require them to accept standards—say requiring benevolence or self-sacrifice—that go beyond Gert's. In others, they might find themselves with reason to reject one or another of the rules Gert advocates.

Cases of the first kind are interesting because Gert is committed to rejecting any rules that would not be favored by *all* rational beings who rely solely on rationally required beliefs and a concern for establishing rules all could accept. To the extent a requirement of benevolence (for instance) would be grounded in reflections that go beyond what such people would engage in, Gert would reject the requirement as one of morality. In requiring more than what rational beings situated in the way he specifies would favor, the rule goes beyond morality. That is not to say, of course, that Gert is committed to opposing beneficence, nor is it to say that he is committed to thinking that beneficence is not valuable. It is to say, though, that he is committed to rejecting it as required by morality. Thus he is at odds, in a deep and interesting way, not only with utilitarians, but also with Kantians and with many others who see having a concern for the welfare of others as a fundamental moral requirement.

Cases of the second kind, in which people are rationally required to reject (as opposed to add on to) Gert's rules, introduce some nice complexities. The rules Gert proposes are all very general and each allows exceptions. So there is some reason to wonder whether a plausible view could reject any of them without, in effect, mobilizing the sort of considerations the rules, in Gert's hands, already recognize as justifying exceptions. Thus, for instance, while Gert thinks that among the fundamental rules is a requirement that one obey the law, he does not suppose that people are never justified in violating the law. Under certain circumstances, he notes, they clearly are.[25] In a similar way, the prohibitions against lying and stealing and killing and adultery are all prohibitions that admit of exceptions.

To get a case in which people might rationally reject the rules Gert advocates, one needs a case in which the people's convictions would require them to reject the rules, taking into account the rules' ability to accommodate exceptions.

According to Gert all the exceptions come under the same broad rubric—they are all such that an impartial rational person can publicly allow their violation. Thus, for instance, the general rule that one should obey the law does admit of exceptions—exactly when, and only if, "an impartial rational person can publicly allow the law to be ignored or broken."[26] This means that the alternative view to focus on is one in which the legitimacy of an exception to one of the general rules is not seen as dependent upon its being publicly allowable. Various consequentialist views come to mind as candidates that recommend, in the world as it is, that we promulgate and follow rules that largely coincide with Gert's, even as it holds that exceptions are legitimately made whenever in fact (or in prospect) the consequences are better—whether or not the exceptions might be publicly allowed.

There are familiar problems with such a view, but it does not seem right to think that a person who accepted consequentialism would thereby be irrational.

And it does seem right to think that under some circumstances, in the face of certain bits of evidence and with a certain background in place, it would be positively irrational for someone to reject her consequentialism just because those who know little and do not care about the welfare of others would not favor its requirements.

Even as the limitation to rationally required beliefs is nontrivial, it is also *indispensable* for Gert's defense of his system. For that defense goes through, if it goes through at all, only if a whole slew of rationally permissible beliefs are put aside—among them beliefs many people would be irrational to reject, given their evidence. If additional beliefs were allowed in, there would be no grounds at all for thinking all rational agents would approve of what they would approve if they knew much less. Indeed, there is good reason to think they would not, as Gert himself acknowledges: "All rational persons have rationally allowed beliefs, based on some combination of their present circumstances and their training or education, such that it would not be irrational for them not to favor impartial obedience to these rules."[27] It is worth noting that the beliefs that count here as (merely) rationally allowed might be such that, given "their present circumstances and their training or education," people would have to be irrational not to hold them. Thus, in context, the beliefs might be rationally required of the person in question. And in light of those beliefs, it might also turn out that the person would be irrational to favor impartial obedience to the rules, as when, for instance, favoring such obedience would require failing to do something they rationally believe to be required.

There are, then, two different contexts in which additional information could influence what someone might rationally favor and so influence the arguments. One context is that in which real people find themselves, the other is the context in which those who are supposed to set the standard for actual people find themselves.

In the first context, actual people who hold beliefs that go beyond those that count as rationally required might well find themselves with beliefs that would make it irrational for them to constrain themselves by the rules Gert proposes. Even if they would favor the rules were they to be influenced solely by rationally required beliefs and a commitment to impartiality, they are in fact influenced—and seemingly appropriately—by other beliefs and commitments that stand in the way of their accepting the rules. Of course, supposing their failure to accept the rules, under the circumstances, is appropriate is to reject the view that the standard of rational acceptability for them is set by the approval of those who constitute the lowest common denominator of rational agents. For the problem emerges precisely because what real people might rationally do, or accept, seems to be highly sensitive to what they, in their context, actually believe and have evidence concerning. So responding to this sort of worry requires showing, somehow, that actual people all have reason to believe or accept that the rules of morality (at least) are exactly those rules that would be approved of by people responding solely in light of rationally required beliefs and a concern with impartiality.

In the second context, whether the people who are supposed to set the standard for actual people would approve of just the rules Gert defends turns crucially on what beliefs and commitments are genuinely rationally required. Even if the standard of rational acceptability, when it comes to proposed rules of morality, is set by what would be approved of by people influenced solely by rationally required beliefs and a concern for impartiality, that standard is highly sensitive to what goes into the set of beliefs that count as rationally required.

The fact that these considerations are nonmonotonic means that discovering that an additional belief is rationally required can make a dramatic difference to whether a set of rules would secure the relevant approval. One cannot assume that, having been favored in light of some beliefs, a set of rules will continue to be favored as more beliefs are added in.

In both contexts, the threat to Gert's arguments is most clearly posed by moral and religious commitments people might rationally acquire that would lead them to approve of sets of rules Gert rejects or disapprove of the set of rules Gert advances. Such commitments most clearly have direct implications for whether a person might rationally approve of some set of rules advanced as standards for behavior.[28] For instance, on Gert's view, neither beneficence nor self-sacrifice are morally required, since rules requiring them would not be favored by those relying only on the beliefs and desires that are rationally required. Yet people might, so it seems, rationally accept utilitarianism (even if it is not, after all, the right moral standard). Such people will (rationally, though perhaps not correctly) see beneficence and self-sacrifice as morally required. At the same time, they will (again rationally) see rules Gert endorses, for instance, the one requiring that promises be kept, as not setting an independent standard of behavior but as only capturing the general fact that breaking a promise usually has comparatively bad consequences.[29] Similarly, one might rationally accept a theological view in light of which certain kinds of acts—of devotion, or atonement, or obedience—are morally required. If these acts are incompatible with rules of the sort Gert advances, then a person who held such a view would find herself with a commitment not to accept those rules as authoritative.

One might argue, of course, that when we are trying to determine the correct standards for morality it is a mistake to give weight, in the first instance, to people's current evaluative commitments. After all, these are precisely what are at issue. We need, instead, to bracket such commitments. What would people rationally accept (in the first context) or rationally favor (in the second) were they to leave out of account their prior evaluative commitments concerning morality? This looks to be the relevant question, and it would clear away the problematic cases that appeal to those who already, as it were, accept utilitarianism, or Kantianism, or some other substantive normative view. In order to decide for ourselves which, if any, of these views are correct we need to ask, it seems, which such view would gain the appropriate approval.

This is reasonable enough, but no real help with the problems at hand. For the problems arise not on the assumption that people hold distinctively moral commitments that clash with the rules Gert is defending. Rather they emerge once we recognize that people might, for various reasons, or no reason at all, have commitments—say to the welfare of others or the significance of a deity—that make it irrational for them to accept a proposed set of rules and that influence what rules they might rationally favor. These commitments need neither be, nor be held to be, *true or correct* for them to have the relevant impact. So, the question of whether the commitments are true or correct is not, at this stage, at issue. Instead, when focusing on the first context, where we are considering whether actual people might be rationally required to reject Gert's proposed rules, the question is whether it is always irrational for actual people to have the commitments that would make their accepting Gert's rules irrational. If it is not always irrational to have such commitments, then actual people will sometimes find themselves rationally required to reject the rules Gert proposes (despite their supposedly being acceptable by all rational beings). And when focusing on the second context, where we are considering what those who set the standard for rational acceptability might favor, the question is whether they are appropriately situated only if they lack the commitments that would lead them not to favor the rules Gert proposes. If those who set the standard might be influenced by these commitments, then they might find themselves not favoring the rules Gert proposes.

The question remains: why restrict our attention, in trying to determine what it would be rational for actual people to accept, to the attitudes of those who rely solely on the "rationally required beliefs" and a commitment to impartiality (or its functional equivalent)? Why think the approval of such people establishes what it would be rational for us to accept, given that their approvals depend on ignoring things we know (and on failing to value things we value)?

There is an answer to be found in *Morality*, one that brings us back directly to the claim that morality is, essentially, an informal public system that applies to all rational beings. Assuming that morality is such a system, it has to be both (i) known by, and (ii) rationally acceptable to, everyone to whom it applies.[30] If morality applies to all rational beings, it has to be known by and acceptable to all rational beings. Thus any system that could be justified only by appealing to beliefs not all rational beings might have would be a system that risked having aspects to it that not all rational beings could know and would rest on a justification some could neither know nor appreciate in a way required in order for them rationally to accept it. "[S]ince morality applies to all rational persons," Gert argues, "all of the essential features of morality must be understood and acceptable to all rational persons, and hence no religious, metaphysical, or even scientific belief that is not shared by all rational persons can be used to determine the essential features of morality."[31]

I should emphasize that Gert neither argues nor thinks that religious, metaphysical, and scientific beliefs are irrationally held. Indeed, in certain contexts—albeit contexts that not every rational being finds herself in—many such beliefs might be rationally required (so that one would not be justified in failing to have them). It is worth saying too that apparently, once such beliefs are onboard, particular people may, on the basis of such beliefs, rationally reject beliefs that, absent the new beliefs, would have been rationally required.

Of course, this introduces a serious complication when it comes to appealing to morality's standing as a system of rules acceptable to all. Those who do possess the religious, metaphysical, or scientific beliefs may, as I have suggested, find themselves unable rationally to accept the rules they would favor, were they relying solely on rationally required beliefs. Apparently, then, those who are more informed may find that, for them, accepting the rules is actually irrational. If so, that would undermine once again the claim that the rules would be acceptable to all to whom they apply.

Perhaps, though, if such people realize that morality is essentially an informal public system and that people can rationally fail to have the beliefs they do, then they may have reason themselves to bracket those beliefs in thinking about what all rational agents might accept. In the name of identifying rules all could understand, they might put aside much of what they know. Perhaps. Nonetheless, rules that would be understood by and acceptable to those who know very little may turn out to be rules that it would be positively irrational for those who know more to accept—even if they know that what makes it irrational for them to accept the rules are considerations not available to those who are more ignorant than they are themselves. The ignorance of others gives them reason to wish the ignorance away, not to ignore what they know.

We seem to face the following situation. On Gert's view, morality is an informal public system that must be both (i) known by, and (ii) rationally acceptable to, all rational agents. Any argument for a system of rules that required an appeal to beliefs not all could understand would fail to establish the rules as the sort of informal public system it would have to be (on Gert's view) in order to constitute morality. Thus, it appears, the justification for a set of rules—if it is to establish them as the rules of morality—must appeal to what each and every rational agent could be expected to understand. Yet, since some rational agents know, and so understand, a great deal more, they may find themselves unable rationally to accept what they could were they more ignorant. Any argument for a system of rules that requires an appeal *solely* to beliefs that all could understand would be an argument that would fail to establish the rules as the sort of informal public system it would have to be (again, on Gert's view) in order to constitute morality, since those who are more knowledgeable would be unable rationally to accept it (even though they would understand it). Either way, the rules will not stand as rationally acceptable to all, and so will not constitute an informal public system that applies to all rational beings. The natural question to raise is: why would someone think morality really is such a system?

Before turning to this question, let me flag one detail worth further attention: it might well be that one could identify a system of rules (Gert's ten rules, or Kant's single "treat yourself and others as ends and never solely as means," or Mills' "promote the greatest happiness") that are quite understandable to virtually anyone, although a compelling justification for accepting it would require an elaborate appeal to relatively esoteric beliefs that not all rational beings would have access to or understand. This suggests that we should distinguish (i) asking what it takes for a set of rules to be understandable from (ii) asking what it takes for it to be rationally acceptable as a standard for their own behavior, from (iii) asking what it takes to understand what makes it rationally acceptable. The three may be linked in interesting ways, especially if rationally accepting something turns, in important respects, on what a person understands about her situation and options, even when she knows not every rational being would have the same understanding. I will not pursue this issue here.[32]

Why Think Morality Is an Informal Public System That Applies to All Rational Beings?

Gert's defense of the appeal solely to those beliefs that are rationally required turns crucially on his claim that morality is an informal public system that applies to all rational beings. Why think this is true? There seem to be two sorts of argument offered in *Morality* for this assumption. One highlights the assumption as so obviously true that it doesn't need defense. The other holds that morality plays a distinctive functional role in our social life that can only be played by an informal public system. I will take them in order.

Frequently, especially early on in *Morality*, Gert simply asserts this as "an essential feature" or claims that "Nowadays everyone recognizes" morality's standing as an informal public system, or maintains that "It is uncontroversial that" it is such a system. Needless to say, every argument needs to rest on some assumption or other that is taken for granted. So an appeal to the obviousness of some assumption must, in more than a few cases, be perfectly appropriate, not least of all if, indeed, the assumption is uncontroversial or at least widely recognized. Nonetheless, this appeal to obviousness is highly dubious in the present case. There are two grounds for doubt, over and above the fact that it ends up playing such a crucial role in defending what is otherwise such an initially unintuitive limitation on whose approval matters morally.

One ground for doubt can be found in the observation that a number of Gert's criticisms of competing moral theories have as one crucial element the fact that they fail to recognize morality as an informal public system—appealing as they do to considerations predictably beyond the ken of many rational beings. This is, in effect, one of Gert's major criticisms of consequentialism: if consequentialism is true then what morality might require of people may be unknown by and even rationally unacceptable to those to whom it applies—an implication, Gert points out, that flies in the face of thinking morality is an informal public system.[33] Certain understandings of Kantianism have the same upshot when they treat application of the categorical imperative as a difficult exercise in practical reasoning.[34] For again, what morality actually requires ends up being elusive, to say the least. And certainly familiar versions of Aristotelian ethics have the same implications concerning the extent to which people may, as it happens, fail to know what morality demands of them. All of these substantive moral theories turn out to fly in the face of a putatively essential feature of morality. I infer from this that they, at least implicitly, reject the assumption that morality is essentially an informal public system. That is not to say morality is not such a system. It may be. The point is only that in this context it seems wrong to claim that the assumption is obvious or uncontroversial.

The other ground of doubt can be found in the fact that there are several attractive views that overlap with, yet differ in significant respects from, a view according to which morality is an informal public system that applies to all rational beings. The attractiveness of these alternative views might explain—without vindicating—Gert's contention that morality is such a system.

For instance, one might hold that morality is a public system that applies only to rational agents that have a fair bit of knowledge (knowledge substantially beyond that had by someone possessing only rationally required beliefs), although it extends its protection to all rational beings. On this view it is inappropriate to apply moral standards to people who have grown up in certain environments or lack knowledge of a certain kind, while it is appropriate to recognize such people as rational agents toward whom one has moral obligations (including, perhaps, obligations to educate). Thus one might agree with Gert that morality is an informal public system, but reject his view that it applies to all rational beings. Or one might think that morality is an informal system of rules (though not a public one) that applies to all rational beings and is such that they all have reason to accept the system, even though that system is not known to them all. On this view, there are compelling reasons to accept morality's demand though coming genuinely to understand and appreciate morality requires a kind of effort, insight, or education that cannot be expected of everyone. Or one might think that morality is a public system that is known to everyone but is such that not everyone is rational in accepting its demands. On this view, certain people might find themselves in situations in which it would be irrational for them to accept morality's standards whether or not others might rationally work to enforce the standards.

These alternatives bring out that in thinking about whether it really is obvious that morality is an informal public system that applies to all rational beings, we need to note that one might back off of this crucial claim by rejecting the claim that morality applies to all rational beings, or by rejecting the claim that it is known by all to whom it applies, or by rejecting the claim that all are rational in accepting its demands. Backing off any one of these claims is backing off something that is necessary to the initial argument for embracing the lowest common denominator standard of rational acceptability. I think it is not obvious that these alternatives are all wrong.

All told, then, there seems to me more than a little reason to think that morality's status as an informal public system that applies to all rational beings requires a substantive argument and cannot plausibly be offered as an uncontroversial or obviously true claim. Before turning to the substantive—functionalist—argument Gert might have on offer, I want to take a tour briefly through one of the features of Gert's view that I think is morally important, though puzzling: the requirement that moral standards must be known by those to whom they apply.

This knowledge requirement clearly plays a central role in Gert's system by constituting a condition on something counting as a *public* system. Yet, at least initially, the requirement seems to carry a strange implication. Gert holds that knowing morality's standards is a matter of knowing everything that they require and recommend.[35] Anything less and one doesn't yet have the requisite knowledge. At the same time, Gert acknowledges that determining what morality demands of one requires knowing all sorts of facts above and beyond those that would be known by those limited to rationally required beliefs.[36] At first this looks like a pretty serious tension. A system doesn't count as an informal public system unless it is known by all to whom it applies, and knowing it is knowing what it requires, yet it requires things in light of facts not known by all. As things turn out, we can alleviate the tension by distinguishing the fundamental demands of morality and the system of standards that constitute morality from morality's derivative demands. The fundamental demands apply to all rational beings and must be known by all to whom they apply, while the derivative demands apply only in particular situations, in light of the more fundamental demands, and they apply on the condition that the facts relevant for the derivation of the demands are known by the relevant people (rather than by all rational people).[37]

There is, at this point, an interesting twist in the view, for it turns out that, according to Gert, the facts that are relevant to the derivation count as known by the relevant people not because the agent to whom the demands apply knows them, but because they are known "by all qualified people"[38]—where being a qualified person is sometimes an esoteric qualification. This twist is at least a little peculiar, since it means that people may, after all, be subject to moral demands *they* may not know about or be able to understand. As long as these agents are able to recognize who is appropriately qualified, one might argue that they are, in the relevant sense, able to learn about the demands that apply to them even if they are not able to understand the considerations that make it the case that such demands do come into play. But this seems quite a stretch to the extent that actual understanding of morality's demands is seen as important to the legitimacy of those demands.

In any case, however that works out, there is a disturbing upshot of this general view. Sometimes, presumably, who is qualified will be clear to all, and all who are qualified will agree concerning the relevant facts. Yet at other times things will not work out so neatly and either there will be disagreement concerning who is qualified or disagreement among those who are qualified as to the relevant facts. In fact, this sort of disagreement is familiar and more or less rampant. As Gert would have it, under these circumstances, there is no correct judgment concerning the matter at hand and so no derivative demand. "If there is unresolvable disagreement among qualified people, or if there is unresolvable disagreement about who counts as a qualified person, then there is no right answer to the problem."[39] Thus it follows from the knowledge requirement, as Gert develops it, that if there is irresolvable debate among qualified people about facts relevant to whether abortion is wrong, or whether euthanasia is wrong, or whether capital punishment is wrong, or . . . then it follows that one side of each of these issues is right—the side that holds the practice in question is not morally wrong.

According to Gert, a "morally wrong action is one that all impartial rational persons would favor not doing."[40] In the case of derivative demands, this will require both that all impartial rational persons agree in favoring not doing a certain kind of action and that there is agreement concerning who counts as qualified concerning the facts at issue that underwrite the derivation and that they all agree. Moreover, "what is morally wrong is *always* determined," Gert maintains, "by what all qualified persons would decide at the time of acting or deciding,"[41] which means that there will be no relevant right answer in all the cases in which given merely the current state of information qualified people do not agree.

This generates a general argument—assuming there is the appropriate sort of disagreement either among the qualified or about who is qualified—to the effect that, say, abortion is not wrong. And this general argument might in turn be used to dismiss those who hold that it is wrong, on the grounds that they evidently do not understand the moral system. There is something suspicious going on here.

One might respond to this problem by pointing out that disagreements concerning the relevant facts cannot occur unless there is already substantial agreement concerning the fundamental rules in light of which the facts are relevant. What disagreement there is, then, will concern not the rules themselves but only their scope (do fetuses count as people?), or about when exceptions are justified (are they justified when a mother's life is endangered?), or about the interpretation of the rules as they apply in particular circumstances (is her life endangered?), and none of these, someone might hold, call the rules themselves into question. Would insulating the rules from disagreement in this way help to avoid the peculiar result that in controversial cases the right answer is always that there is nothing wrong? I don't myself see how, since the line of argument that generates this result turns not on whether the disagreement is ultimately a disagreement about the rules themselves but only on the result of what disagreement there is being that those who count as qualified do not agree or people do not agree as to who is qualified.

In any case, it is not at all clear that there is a sharp difference between disagreeing about the rules, on the one hand, and disagreeing about their scope, or about justified exceptions, or about their interpretation, on the other. If there is no sharp distinction to be drawn, then presumably it cannot be relied upon to avoid the peculiar consequences of holding that the fundamental principles establish derivative duties only in contexts where there is no reasonable disagreement concerning the relevant facts.

There are, then, two worries I have about the knowledge requirement, as Gert ends up developing it. First, it seems seriously problematic if the knowledge requirement has it turn out that when there is either disagreement concerning who is qualified when it comes to determining the relevant facts, or disagreement among those who are qualified about those facts, there is no relevant right answer and so no derivative moral demand that turns on the answer. In such cases, I think we ought to see the debates at stake as ones about which each side is committed to thinking there is an answer (perhaps even committed to thinking there might be some procedure by which the disagreement could, at least in principle, be resolved) but not committed to thinking that in cases of such disagreement those who think something wrong was being done are simply mistaken. To acknowledge our ignorance concerning relevant facts should not of itself resolve the moral debate in favor of those who claim there is nothing wrong. Second, it doesn't seem that one can successfully defend the theory by appealing to the distinction between disagreements concerning the rules and disagreements about, say, their scope, or legitimate exceptions, or their interpretations. Even if one grants the distinction, it doesn't seem to get around the untoward consequences. The distinction would allow us to treat some disagreements as disagreements not about the rules but about their scope (or whatever), but pretty clearly some serious disagreements would concern the rules themselves and others would concern the facts that the rules would render relevant, and in these cases the knowledge requirement (as Gert develops it) would still entail the implausible claim that the very fact of disagreement itself establishes that those who are arguing that some action is morally wrong are mistaken.

Let me get back to the question: why think that morality is an informal public system that applies to all rational beings? As I have suggested, this claim is not plausibly advanced as so obvious and uncontroversial as to need no defense. Gert does however suggest an attractive line of thought that might seem to recommend the claim. It starts by noting that morality, whatever else it might be, is a system of rules or principles that works to reduce harms and (perhaps) facilitate peace.[42] Thus morality performs a crucial function in our public life—most especially, it lets us substitute argument for arms in contexts where otherwise conflict would likely emerge. This role looks to be one that a system of rules could play, but only if the rules were widely known by those to whom they applied. Moreover, it could play the role only if, in addition to being known, it was rationally acceptable to those same people. So, one might think, the very function of morality could be fulfilled only by a system that was a public system—a system known to and rationally accepted by those governed by it.

Now my own sense is that this argument depends on false empirical claims. I see no reason to think that the system could be one of the best solutions to the problem of reducing harms and facilitating peace only if everyone to whom it applies could rationally accept it. The legal system provides a relevant example. It sure seems as if there are people subject to its rules who have, themselves, no reason to accept it. Nonetheless, it is a system that is better than many alternatives when it comes to regulating interactions among people in a way that reduces harms and facilitates peace.[43] At the same time, it seems that a system of rules might fulfill the crucial function even if it was not known by all to whom it applies—say because its requirements were available only on careful reflection of a sort that people do not often engage in (even as, perhaps, it encourages attempts to get people to reflect appropriately so that they could see for themselves the reasons they have to act as they are required to). So, even if one holds that morality should be seen as a system of rules that plays a crucial role in our social life, it is not at all clear that the only systems that might play that role well are public systems.

Moreover, it seems that which system of rules could effectively play the role might well vary dramatically, depending on facts about the people to be governed by the system. So, one worry is that if the moral system is designed especially to be acceptable to people who do not know things, people who do know a lot are going to find themselves in the awkward business—because of their commitment to morality (or impartiality)—of emphasizing rules even as, having more information, they themselves favor some other rules. They don't favor these other rules as a moral system because they would constitute a moral system only if they could be a public system. But they favor people acting in another way—a way that does not accord with the moral rules they are constrained—by the ignorance of others—to offer. This is a framework that risks being designed so that rationally informed people all the time have reason to violate (unless they happen to be committed to morality, or to regulating their behavior by rules that are impartial in Gert's sense). The upshot is that if one emphasizes the functional role of a system of rules, it may end up that the systems of rules that work well will differ dramatically from community to community as the nature and extent of the knowledge of the people change. And just as the Bauhaus theory of design holds that what makes a chair, for instance, a good chair, depends on the structure of the bodies that will use it, so too a good moral theory, on this view, should be structured to fit the body public (even if the theory is not public) in ways that accommodate it.

As I have said, I am puzzled by the knowledge requirement. Yet I am pretty convinced that something like a knowability requirement has got to be right. If an account of morality makes morality in principle unknowable, then it makes it in principle uninteresting. And if it is in principle knowable, then there is an issue about to whom it needs to be knowable and how. Moreover, it certainly seems (as Gert emphasizes) that it had better be knowable to all who are held responsible for acting according to its demands. After all, if one relies on the standards of morality as grounds for condemning people or punishing them, and those people couldn't have known about the standards (and so known they were violating them), then there is something seriously wrong—morally wrong—with condemning and punishing them. As a result, any account of morality that allowed as permissible such a practice would be, it seems clear, misguided. My sense, though, is that it would be useful here to distinguish two distinct roles knowability might play: it might serve as a constraint on what counts as morality (as Gert proposes) or it might serve as a substantive moral constraint. In the first role, the fact that some standard is unknowable to some rational people would establish that it does not constitute a moral standard. In the second role, in contrast, the fact that it is unknowable to some rational people would leave the standard's status as a moral standard unchallenged, even as it meant that such people could not legitimately be held responsible for violating it.

Any plausible moral theory, it seems, will need to include a prohibition (at least under normal conditions) on blaming, punishing, and holding people responsible for violating norms they justifiably didn't know about. Still, such a prohibition does not constitute a constraint on what might count as a moral system. Instead, it serves as a constraint, within the moral system, on various ways of reacting to violations of the system's requirements. Indeed, in recognizing it as a constraint on praise and blame, etc. *in the face of violations of morality's standards,* one is implicitly recognizing the standards as genuine despite their being unknown by at least some to whom they apply. Thus in accepting this substantive constraint one might, and may even have to, acknowledge that the standards in question—that were, by assumption, not known—are nonetheless standards of morality. In any case, I suspect that a lot of what might seem to recommend thinking of morality that it is a public system comes from the moral force of this substantive principle. A lot of people might embrace the substantive constraint without any commitment to the constraint on moral systems. And they may even find that the appeal of this substantive principle actually stands in the way of thinking that all the rules of morality must be known by those to whom they apply.

Notes

* Thanks are due to Walter Sinnott-Armstrong and Bernard Gert for suggestions on earlier drafts of this paper and for greatly appreciated help in working through the subtleties of Gert's moral theory.

1. Bernard Gert, *Morality: Its Nature and Justification* (New York: Oxford University Press, 1998), 316.

2. "It is . . . an essential feature of morality in all of its variations that everyone who is judged by it knows what morality prohibits, requires, encourages, and allows." As a result, "[s]howing that a proposed account of morality contains some part that is justifiably unknown to any people about whom moral judgments are made shows that the proposed account of morality is inadequate" (Gert, *Morality*, 6).

3. I should note in passing that Gert is not requiring that all rational people have positive reason to accept the system of rules he identifies. He only insists that the adequacy of the rules depends upon agents being able rationally to accept them. The difference is real, on his account, because rational acceptance is not a function of the weight of the reasons a person might have one way or the other. For the purposes of this paper, however, one could just as well hold that, to be adequate, an account of morality must offer rules or standards that all rational beings actually have reason, on balance, to accept, since, as it happens, accepting rules that in any way limit one's freedom, is (on Gert's view) rational only if one has adequate (positive) reason. In other contexts, though, Gert is concerned to emphasize that one may rationally do some things for which one has no reason and also that one can, in some contexts, be acting rationally despite acting contrary to what one has most reason to do. For instance, he thinks it is always rational to act in one's own interest no matter what reasons one might have for acting contrary to one's interest, even as he also thinks that when one has strong reasons to act contrary to one's interests one may rationally do so as well.

4. Gert, *Morality*, 6. See also 10. Later he claims that "Satisfying both of these requirements is necessary and sufficient for considering these rules as moral rules, that is, as part of a public system that applies to all rational persons" (*Morality*, 168).

5. It is useful to note the differences between Gert's proposal—that a system of rules is a candidate moral system only if the rules could be rationally accepted—and Thomas Scanlon's suggestion that the system must be such that "no one could reasonably reject" it. [See Scanlon's "Contractualism and Utilitarianism," in *Utilitarianism and Beyond*, ed. Amartya Sen and Bernard Williams (New York: Cambridge University Press, 1981), 103-28].

6. Significantly, on Gert's version of this approach, not all fully rational beings need favor the same things. Thus the proposal is not that a person is rational in doing (or accepting, or choosing) something if and only if *all* fully rational people, appropriately situated, would favor it, but only if and only if *a* fully rational person would. For some accounts this difference disappears thanks to the specific characterizations offered of what it is to be fully rational and to be appropriately situated. However, on Gert's view, even once these are specified, there is room for fully rational beings so situated to differ in what they favor. One is behaving rationally, Gert's thought is, as long as one has at least one fully rational being, appropriately

situated, favoring one's behaving in that way. That others might not favor it reflects a difference among rational agents, but it doesn't impugn one's rationality.

7. It is worth distinguishing the question of whether it would be rational for one to accept a set of rules as a limitation on, and guide for, others' behavior from the question of whether it would be rational for one to accept the set as a limitation on, and guide for, one's own behavior. Potentially, a set of rules that would be rationally acceptable for one role would not be so for the other. See chapter 7 of *Morality*, where this difference in role is especially important.

8. See, for example, Adam Smith's *A Theory of the Moral Sentiments* (New York: Cambridge University Press, 2001), and Roderick Firth's "Ethical Absolutism and the Ideal Observer," *Philosophy and Phenomenological Research* 12 (1952): 317-45.

9. See, for example, Richard Brandt's *A Theory of the Good and the Right* (Oxford, Eng.: Clarendon, 1984), and Michael Smith's *The Moral Problem* (Oxford, Eng.: Blackwell, 1994).

10. See John C. Harsanyi's *Essays on Ethics, Social Behavior, and Scientific Explanation* (Dordrecht, Neth.: Reidel, 1976) and John Rawls' *A Theory of Justice* (Cambridge, Mass.: Harvard University Press, 1971).

11. *Morality*, 36. He does acknowledge, though, that under some circumstances even the rationally required might without irrationality be rejected, but not under normal circumstances. This leads me to think that perhaps the "rationally required beliefs" Gert is after are best characterized as beliefs every rational agent holds, absent contrary evidence.

12. Such beliefs are, according to Gert, completely uncontroversial precisely because "they are the only beliefs that no rational person doubts" (*Morality*, 37).

13. *Morality*, 37. See also 158 and 167. Interestingly, Gert counts among the rationally required beliefs things like "some moral agents care about some sentient beings" (fn., p. 54). It is a little unclear to me whether Gert is assuming that all rational beings must have the concept of morality. The example makes it look as if he is, since without it they could not have the above belief. Nor is it clear whether, absent a fairly thick characterization of what it takes to count as a moral agent, the belief would be uncontroversial. After all, more than a few have claimed that no one genuinely cares about others. (Whether they would say that means there are no moral agents, or only that the moral agents there are do not, after all, care about others, will turn on what is built into the concept of a moral agent.) I agree that the view is implausible, but it doesn't appear to be one that a person would have to be irrational to accept it, except when in the possession of special evidence. On the face of it, absent evidence one way or the other the belief that no one cares about others seems roughly on a footing with the belief that some do care about others (although, of course, the latter is a bit weaker thanks to the "some").

14. *Morality*, 36.

15. *Morality*, 170

16. *Morality*, 44-45. According to Gert, a desire is rational if a person would be irrational were she to lack it and a desire is irrational if it would be irrational to act on it absent adequate reason. I should emphasize that in calling a desire irrational, Gert is not maintaining that it is always, or even usually, irrational to act on it—only that in order for it to be rational to act on it, one must have adequate reason. Other desires, Gert holds, are such that one needs no reason in order for one's acting on the desire to be rational. He is not, I think, holding that these not irrational desires actually themselves provide reason, only that, absent countervailing reason, acting on them is not irrational. In acting on them one may not be acting with a reason at all, even though, in so acting, one is not being irrational.

17. *Morality*, 161.
18. *Morality*, 167.
19. *Morality*, 167.
20. *Morality*, 168-69.
21. *Morality*, 170.
22. A system is shown to be weakly justified, in contrast, if it would be favored by *some* rational beings appropriately situated. See *Morality*, 18. According to Gert, that some would favor a system shows that it is not irrational to accept it; that all would favor it shows that it would be irrational not to accept it.
23. *Morality*, 167. And even the beliefs that are rationally required (absent contrary evidence) might well be rationally rejected by—and so have no influence on—those who have adequate contrary evidence.
24. In speaking of what they would rationally favor, I am imagining that they are relying solely on those beliefs of theirs that are rationally permitted (many of which will be rationally required of them, given their circumstances, even though those same beliefs would not be required of others, and so do not count as beliefs all rational agents are required to have).
25. *Morality*, 202. Gert "is not advocating an end to all civil disobedience." But he does hold that civil disobedience "is only justified when one has some reason to believe that disobeying the law will do something toward lessening that evil [which the law is causing]."
26. *Morality*, 202.
27. *Morality*, 167.
28. It is worth noting, however, that scientific beliefs—say that humans evolved from other mammals, or resemble nonhuman animals in many ways, or that people suffer psychological disabilities of various kinds—might significantly alter the sort of rules rational beings would accept or favor as well. Especially when we are asking what might cause a rational being to favor one thing or another we seem to be asking a question that, absent some quite substantive assumptions by the psychological impact of various sorts of beliefs cannot be answered in the abstract.
29. The rules Gert proposes all, as I have mentioned, admit of exceptions. So it is important here to mark the difference between embracing rules along the lines of those proposed by Gert and, in effect, abandoning the rules as independent standards of behavior—holding them merely as derivative rules of thumb, or summary rules, that are useful to promulgate. Someone who accepts utilitarianism may well find the rules Gert proposes roughly acceptable, but only as they have a utilitarian backing.
30. This follows directly from Gert's definition of informal public systems.
31. *Morality*, 144.
32. But it is worth noting that it raises an interesting issue about the sort of rational acceptance that might be required for a system to count as an informal public system. If a person counts as rationally accepting some set of rules as long as someone differently situated would favor accepting the rules, then a person's current commitments and what she happens to believe might only tenuously be connected to what it is rational for her to accept. Just how tenuously will depend upon the extent to which the favor of those who set the standard is sensitive to a person's actual situation, commitments, and beliefs.
33. G. E. Moore speaks to this view directly, if not all that persuasively, when he writes, "It might be urged, with more plausibility, that we mean by a man's duty only the best of those actions of which he might have thought. And it is true that we do not blame any man very severely for omitting an action of which, as we say, 'he could not be expected to think.' But even here it is plain that we recognise a distinc-

tion between what he might have done and what he *might* have thought of doing: we regard it as a pity that he did not do otherwise. And 'duty' is certainly used in such a sense, that it would be a contradiction in terms to say it was a pity that a man did his duty." *Principia Ethica* (Cambridge, Eng.: Cambridge University Press, 1903), 150-51.

34. Kant himself seems, with Gert, to think the epistemic accessibility of morality's demands—even if not the justification of those demands—is crucial to their legitimacy. Thus, in the *Critique of Practical Reason*, he argues that "The moral law commands the most unhesitating obedience from everyone; consequently, the decision as to what is to be done in accordance with it must not be so difficult that even the commonest and most unpracticed understanding without any worldly prudence should go wrong in making it." Kant, *Critique of Practical Reason*, trans. Lewis White Beck (Indianapolis: Liberal Arts Press, Bobbs-Merrill, 1956), 36.

35. See, *Morality*, 4, 7, 10, 26, and 150.

36. See *Morality*, 227 ff. and 236-37.

37. Alternatively, instead of distinguishing in this way between fundamental and derivative demands, treating only the former as part of the informal public system, one might hold that the supposedly derivative duties are actually conditional duties that, no less than the fundamental duties, must be known by all rational beings, even if they might not know whether the conditions are satisfied. One worry about this suggestion is that the conditional duties will require, for their articulation, the deployment of concepts that not all rational beings need possess. So there will remain a set of duties that are not knowable by all rational beings. See *Morality*, 151.

38. *Morality*, 324.

39. *Morality*, 324. When the problems are practical, as opposed to theoretical, the conditions on there being a right answer are often even more stringent: all qualified people must agree given only what is known at the time of decision or action. See 325-26.

40. *Morality*, 325.

41. *Morality*, 326.

42. This is a feature that Gert himself highlights in characterizing the distinctive nature of morality. See *Morality*, 13.

43. Of course I am not suggesting that the legal system is a kind of morality, only that it is a system of rules that has some claim to fulfilling the role the argument in question maintains can only be fulfilled by a public system, which the legal system is not.

Part II: Rationality and Reasons

4

Reasons and Rationality in the Moral Philosophy of Bernard Gert

Robert Audi

Few contemporary moral philosophers have proposed an ethical theory that is both comprehensive and detailed. Fewer still have systematically connected such a moral theory with an account of rationality. And Bernard Gert is the only one to provide both of these, to employ the latter as a basis for the former, and to center both on an intuitive list of basic standards for action, with irrationality and evil construed as more basic than rationality and goodness. *Morality* is an original and provocative book. It is rich, forceful, intensely analytical, and vividly concrete. It is also wise.

For several reasons, *Morality* constitutes a landmark in contemporary ethical literature. It offers an original account of rationality based on a list of substantive criteria and thereby provides a pluralistic view that contrasts both with the widely popular instrumentalist theories of rationality inspired by Hume and with the monistic accounts inspired by Bentham and Mill on one side and by Kant on the other. Its ethical principles are irreducibly plural, and it thereby contrasts both with single-principle views like utilitarianism and Kantianism as commonly understood and, as a rule theory, with virtue ethics. It portrays morality as public and universal, yet does not construe it as a rigid system that leaves no room for rational disagreement; and it defends the ethical priority of avoiding evil over promoting good without undermining the important role of moral ideals. It also explains how certain standards of rationality and morality can be universally and invariably applicable yet allow for exceptions. In doing all this, the book is concrete and readily applicable to ordinary life; its philosophical framework is balanced by an affirmation of commonsense moral rules and clarified by everyday examples.

Given enough time, I would like to discuss the entire project: not only the theory of rationality, but also the closely connected account of morality. That is impossible here, but I can consider the former with the latter in mind. Even that task is large; the rationality chapters are much too rich to explore fully in a single paper. I hope, however, to clarify and perhaps extend the theory of rationality and reasons for action. That is my special interest on this occasion. I begin, however, not with Gert's text but with some important background issues concerning the scope and purpose of a theory of practical reason. With these issues laid out, we can better appreciate both the magnitude of his achievement and some proposed directions of critical reflection and possible modification of his position.

The Theory of Practical Reason and the Foundations of Ethics

In very broad terms, one can think of the theory of practical reason as concerning standards for appraising action, just as the theory of theoretical reason may be seen as concerning standards for appraising belief. If one did not, with Gert, conceive rational action as simply action that is not irrational, one might be comfortable speaking of the theory of practical reason as concerned with standards for rational action and of theoretical reason as concerned with standards for rational belief. If we take his view of rational action, however, we are likely to characterize the theory of practical reason quite differently, for reasons that unfold below. In either case, it is plausible to view moral theory as a branch of the theory of practical reason. Since not all standards for evaluating actions are moral, it is only a branch; but it is a central one. (Some philosophers take it to be the highest branch, with a kind of commanding position over the others, but I see no need to address this controversial issue here and will not presuppose the supremacy of moral reasons.)

Systematic philosophers have commonly tried to show that, given a good theory of practical reason, we can derive a moral theory. Some of them have held that being a rational person implies being a moral one; and certainly many philosophers, including Gert, are committed to the more specific, behavioral view that moral action is always rational (hence never, on grounds of rationality, inappropriate for a rational person). Explicitly stated, the behavioral view I have in mind is that if an action-type, *A*, say making amends for injuring someone, is morally required of an agent, *S*, then it is rational for *S* to *A*, in a sense implying a strong positive reason for *A*-ing that goes beyond entailing merely that it is not irrational.

This formulation allows for a phenomenon important in understanding Gert. Call it a *type-token disparity*: even at a time when it is rational *for S* to *A*—hence, the action-type, *A*-ing, is rational for *S*—*S* might nevertheless *A* for a bad reason and thereby produce a nonrational action-token. *S* might, for instance, act on the basis of (a) an ill-considered desire which *S* would renounce on reflection and (b) an unjustified belief that the action would satisfy the desire. Such cases of disparity are important, but not usual. One might think that a bad reason, at least of this sort, is no reason at all; but presumably a reason may be normatively bad without ceasing to constitute any reason at all (beyond providing a reason *why* the action occurred—an explanatory reason, which might be as far from justifying the action as, e.g., mere fatigue, and is not the kind we are considering).[1] In a weak moment, a gambler might purchase a lottery ticket on the basis of such a desire to buy a flashy pickup truck and a belief that the ticket will very likely win the money. This act-token, being performed (wholly, I assume) for a bad reason, is not rational; but the act-type, buying a lottery ticket (in the same lottery) might be rational for the agent (a rational *kind* of thing for the person to do), given its low cost in comparison with the pleasure the agent tends to derive from such gambles. An analogy can be constructed for the domain of theoretical reason by distinguishing between a proposition's being, at a given time, a rational thing for *S* to believe (whether *S* believes it or not), as opposed to being rationally believed by *S* at that time. One could have excellent evidence for a proposition, yet believe it not on this rational ground but on the basis of a reading of tea leaves.

Whether or not one takes moral reasons for action (such as a promissory obligation) to be invariably good positive reasons from the point of view of rationality, the theory of practical reason is concerned with guiding action of any sort and with providing criteria for making optimal choices in day-to-day life. Thus, supposing there are times when morality leaves us free to do as we choose,[2] it is commonly thought by philosophers that there will be not only irrational choices we might make when we fail to use our freedom well, but choices that, though not irrational, are suboptimal from the point of view of what constitute good reasons for action. Some philosophers (in contrast with Gert) go further and maintain that even without being *ir*rational, suboptimal actions can fail to be rational or can be less rational than alternatives.[3] For these philosophers "irrational" is a strong term reserved for certain serious violations of the relevant standards.

If Gert wanted only to show that it is never irrational to do what is morally required, we could largely bypass the question of the implications of his view for the standards of choice appropriate to guide us where we are morally free, i.e. (roughly), there is nothing in particular we are obligated to do at the time and we may do as we like (within the omnipresent constraints of such negative requirements as abstention from harming others). But since he offers a general account of rationality and, in some detail, of reasons for action, it is natural to explore these implications. Even if his position turns out to be that, say, prudence is the source of nonmoral standards of choice among rationally permissible actions, it will be important to see how he conceives it in relation to rationality and why he is committed to holding that there cannot be degrees or gradations of rationality, for instance, where someone makes an imprudent choice that is not irrational but is nonetheless, from the point of view of rationality, inferior to an alternative.

Rationality and Reasons

To understand Gert's conception of rationality, it is useful to begin with some plausible constraints he expresses. He says that "to regard an action as irrational is always to want that it not be done by anyone for whom one is concerned."[4] More explicitly, irrational actions are such that "no fully informed rational person would advocate doing them to any person for whom he is concerned," where (a) it is types of action (kinds, not concrete tokens) that are in question here, (b) rational persons are "persons insofar as they have neither irrational beliefs, desires, nor motives, and are not acting irrationally" (30), and (c) presumably the kind of concern is intrinsic, since a merely instrumental concern with a person will plainly not do here.[5] Let us explore Gert's explication of some of the central normative notions he relies on, particularly the concepts of irrational action and irrational belief. These two notions are crucial for understanding the basic idea of irrationality and thereby for understanding rationality.

The definition of "irrational belief" comes earlier in the book than that of "rational action", even though Gert notes that "Rationality and irrationality are primarily concerned with actions" (3) and that "the concept of irrational action is necessary for explaining why some beliefs, desires, and motives are called irrational" (32). His short definition is this: "a belief is irrational if and only if it is held in the face of overwhelming evidence or logical truths that are, or should be, known to the person holding it" (34).[6]

As to irrational action, we are given an explicit definition of the term only "in the basic sense":

> An action is irrational in the basic sense if and only if it is an intentional action of a person with sufficient knowledge and intelligence to be fully informed about that action and who, if fully informed (1) would believe that the action involves significantly increased risk of his suffering death, nontrivial pain, loss of ability, loss of freedom, or loss of pleasure and (2) would not have an adequate reason for the action. A reason for action is a conscious rational belief that one's action will increase the probability of someone's avoiding any of the harms listed above or gaining greater consciousness, ability, freedom, or pleasure. A reason is adequate if any significant group of moral agents regard the harm avoided or benefit gained as compensating for the harm suffered. (83-84, all italics)

Gert seems to take it as clear enough how a nonbasic sense would be constructed. In looking for a plausible candidate for a *non*basic sense, my main suggestion would be to extend the formulation to nonintentional action. Suppose, for instance, *S* knowingly but not intentionally offends *x*, a powerful and resentful person, in the course of intentionally proposing *y* as a committee chair. Offending *x* could satisfy all the other conditions. It could indeed do so even if unintentional, provided *S* "should" know *S* will do it by proposing *y*. In any event, I shall simply assume that Gert supposes that any irrational action is such by virtue of bearing a certain intimate relation to one that is irrational in the basic sense, such as being (a) identical with that action under another description and, (b) under the relevant description, say "offending *x*", such that it would satisfy the definition of "irrationality" if intentional under that description.[7]

One might think that it is more natural to characterize certain kinds of desires as irrational and then define irrational action in relation to those. But this is not Gert's procedure. He tells us that "*A desire is irrational if it is always irrational to act on it without any adequate reason*" (45), where "*An adequate reason for acting is a conscious rational belief that* makes *the otherwise irrational action for which it is a reason, rational*" (57). What are the basic irrational desires, those Gert calls "fundamental" (51)? They are of course desires for items on the list of evils; specifically—and here I add a technical term that seems appropriate to Gert's concerns—I take them to be *intrinsic* desires for one or more of the following: death, pain, disability, loss of freedom, and loss of pleasure, where an intrinsic desire for something is a desire for it for its own sake. Even a rational intrinsic desire, however, is not strictly a reason for action; such reasons are (in Gert's terminology) always beliefs.

An important element in Gert's overall position is his insistence on the hybrid character of rationality. Although irrationality is egocentric, "reasons need not be egocentric in any way" (59). More specifically, "reasons for acting in a certain way are not limited to beliefs that acting in this way will benefit oneself, but also include beliefs that acting in this way will benefit someone else" (61). Moreover, "basic reasons" are all beliefs to the effect that someone will benefit, "either oneself or someone else" (61).

As one might expect, Gert notes that some reasons are stronger than others. One has a "better or stronger reason" to avoid imprisonment for four years as opposed to two (77); and more generally,

> reasons can be ranked by determining which irrational acts the reason can make rational. If everyone agrees that reason A would be an adequate reason

> for every otherwise irrational act that reason B would be an adequate reason for, and for some otherwise irrational acts as well, then reason A is stronger or better than reason B. (77-78)

Gert adds that although "What makes an action irrational is the harm that the agent will suffer" (78), "rational persons rank harms and benefits differently . . . [and] When rational persons disagree, I do not count either reason as stronger" (77).

In rough terms, the overall view is this: irrationality is the basic normative notion in the theory of practical reason. It is determined by the five-fold list of evils just noted. Rationality characterizes a kind of thing, such as action or belief, to which irrationality can apply, provided this action or belief, person, or other kind of entity is not irrational. And basic reasons for action are beliefs concerning harms or benefits. Action that one should believe produces one or more evils for oneself is irrational unless one has an adequate reason drawn from the basic kind; any other action is rational.

Some Problems of Interpretation

Despite the great clarity of an enormous amount of *Morality*, there are some significant problems of interpretation. I want to pursue some of the ones that seem both important and quite interesting.

Loss of Pleasure: Diminutions vs. Forgoings

First, how does "loss of pleasure" figure in Gert's theory of rationality? Ordinarily, one cannot lose what one does not (in some sense) have, and, in line with this idea, there are places where Gert apparently thinks of losing ability and freedom as changes in one's *present* condition, though to be sure they are losses of a dispositional property. One might then think that the irrationality in question—the kind basic in the theory of irrationality—consists in intrinsically wanting, or in acting solely in order to seek, loss of pleasure that one actually has, as where one wants to eliminate or reduce the pleasure one is taking in a concert. But this does not seem to be Gert's main conception of loss of pleasure. His first major point about it in the most pertinent subsection is this: "it is irrational to desire not to experience pleasure" (50). This is not to say that it is irrational *not to desire* pleasure; but it looks as if he is committed to saying that one must desire it *if* one believes one can achieve it. Note, for instance, that he says (plausibly) that "Someone who could not experience any pleasure, anhedonia, would certainly be suffering from a malady, even if she suffered none of the other evils" (106).[8] Here inability to have a pleasure is conceived as an evil, and "an evil is what it is irrational not to avoid without an adequate reason" (97), which strongly suggests that one should want to achieve pleasure, as opposed to simply wanting to be *able* to. (I say "suggests" rather than "entails" because what strictly follows is that one should seek to avoid inability to have pleasure. But why would this be so unless pleasure were itself to be sought, and indeed sought noninstrumentally given that there is non-instrumental reason to avoid inability to have it?[9])

There are, then, two conceptions of loss of pleasure that figure in the text. Some losses are deprivations, eliminations, or reductions of existing pleasures; call these *diminutions*, since that term covers unfavorable changes in quality as well as reduced quantity, even to zero. Other losses are constituted by forgoing available, or at least possible, future pleasures, including preventions of would-be diminutions in such pleasures; call these *forgoings*. The diminution reading fits much, but by no means all, of what Gert says about his theory better than the wider reading that also includes forgoing pleasure as a case of "loss" of it; for instance, forgoing pleasure even without an adequate reason is not clearly a case of suffering a harm.

More important, if it is irrational not to seek pleasure, then, contrary to the way Gert describes his theory, irrationality is determined in part by a positive good and not just by wanting or seeking evils without adequate reason. But even if Gert's theory would look quite different given the wider interpretation of loss of pleasure, his list of grounds of irrationality would be substantively much the same, as could his results for morality. (A similar argument can be developed for loss of ability and loss of freedom, though the difficulty there may be less serious in that forgoing and even diminution of pleasure are not clearly harms in the way loss of (at least basic) ability or of (basic) freedom is, nor is the possession of either of the latter as plausibly taken to be an intrinsic good, as is pleasure.)

The Diversity of the Grounds of Rationality

Suppose I am correct in suggesting that there may be, and Gert may even be committed to countenancing, rationally required desires not grounded in evils or in an avoidance thereof, above all desires to experience at least some kind of pleasure. Might there also be rationally prohibited desires that are not grounded in evils? Consider an intrinsic desire (not a mere wish) for something I should see cannot be achieved, say to fly to the moon on gossamer wings, a desire produced in me by posthypnotic suggestion or wishful thinking. One might argue that this desire is not rational for me owing to harm I might do myself in trying to satisfy it; it might then be irrational in a wholly derivative sense that Gert can countenance: I should know that I might suffer an evil in trying to satisfy the desire; hence I may not rationally harbor it without an adequate reason. But even if that is sometimes so, I might have beliefs about how such flight is to be achieved, say under the protection of a vigilant spaceship, that remove any appearance of danger. Granted, harboring such a desire could waste time or energy, say because it leads to my daydreaming about the prospect and asking questions of sympathetic scientists. But that need not amount to an evil. Thus, such a desire seems rationally permissible in terms of Gert's list as he apparently uses it. But is it rational?

For Gert, it is rational if it is not irrational; but ordinarily, there seem to be cases in which one might want to withhold "rational" yet not apply the strongly negative term "irrational". Gert would resist the suggested distinction between the merely nonrational and the irrational, but he might still agree that if I had many desires like the one imagined, even if none conflicted with any other, I would be an irrational *person*. He could note, for instance, that the whole is more than the sum of the parts. Still, granting that the parts need not be irrational to imply irrationality in the whole, there is some mystery about how having a large number of *rational* desires could yield irrationality in the person, even when they do not conflict nor are mutually unsatisfiable. An apparently more natural view is that such ill-grounded desires are for that reason at least *not* rational.

Whatever we think about this case, there remains some question about how the theory is to account for what is commonly considered a kind of *instrumental* irrationality: one wants to *A* solely in order to achieve *B*, say to take vitamin E in order to obtain immortality, but it is irrational for one to believe *A*-ing will achieve B.[10] People differ about whether this kind of desire—and actions wholly based on it—would be irrational; but we certainly try to eliminate desires of this sort in ourselves or those we care about, and we would do so even if we thought the action in question would do no harm. These desires and actions in question seem as it were to be infected by the irrationality of the underlying instrumental belief.[11]

A contrasting view would be that calling such desires and actions irrational displaces the appraisal from the underlying belief, whose irrationality Gert could explain: the clearest cases of irrational beliefs are indeed held in the face of overwhelming evidence. But I cannot see that this displacement hypothesis is as plausible as an infection hypothesis: the irrationality of the underlying belief may be what above all explains the irrationality—or at least the lack of rationality—of the desire or action, as opposed to the apparent irrationality of the desire or action being explained by our transferring that notion from its proper object—the instrumental belief. Thus, we are probably not mistaken in taking the former two to lack rationality as well: they seem in some way vitiated by the irrationality of their ground or, less metaphorically, are *ill-grounded* and so not rational.

There *may* be two strains in Gert's conception of rational belief. The dominant strain is apparently the view that irrationality in a belief is due to its being held in the face of opposing evidence or logical prohibition. But in some passages there are signs of another strain. Some of what he says suggests[12] that irrationality in the case of belief must *derive* from the irrationality of action. This is an intriguing idea that I cannot discuss in detail here. I doubt, however, that it is true. For one thing, I do not see how we could take anyone to know or justifiedly believe that certain kinds of beliefs will or may lead to *acting* in the harmful ways Gert considers basic for irrationality unless we *presupposed* standards of theoretical rationality, including criteria for rational and irrational belief. In any case, the second strain in Gert's conception of rational belief is not essential to his overall project. He does not need to reduce theoretical to practical rationality (and does not claim to). It is quite enough to provide an account of practical reason, and that account is the basis for his substantive ethics.

Reasons, Preferability, and Maximization

Another question of interpretation emerges if we recall the concern of the theory of practical reason with guiding action in the apparently vast domain of conduct that is neither required nor forbidden by considerations of rationality. Despite Gert's statement that rational actions have nothing positive in common, might his theory provide guidance here? One's first thought might be that we should maximize distance from harming ourselves. This is particularly plausible if we take forgoing possible pleasures as an evil. If we must avoid harm, and losing pleasure is a harm in the wide sense, there is prima facie reason to think we should seek to maximize (our own) pleasure unless we have adequate reason not to. For that would seem to contribute best to avoiding at least the evil of losing pleasure. In this sense, his theory provides *negative guidance* in the *discretionary domain*—the domain in which we are rationally free to do as we choose.

I believe, however, that there is no reason not to take Gert's theory to provide *positive guidance* as well, with reference to the kind or amount of some good, most notably our own pleasure, we may bring about. Indeed, it is not clear that a theory of practical reason can fully succeed if it counsels only the avoidance of evils. Still, two qualifications are critical. First, Gert is probably free to insist that the kind of preferability I describe does not imply a difference in rationality. It may, for instance, be just a difference in prudence. Second—and here I indicate a point applicable to much other theorizing as well—although he may be committed to taking quantity of good or evil seriously, he is not committed to a maximization standard for either negative or positive guidance. It is, for instance, one thing to say that *given* an actual choice to be made between *A* and *B*, we may not rationally chose *A* if we believe that *B* will produce more pleasure (or is superior by whatever relevant standard we use); it is quite another to say that we must have an overall commitment to seek to maximize our pleasure. A *preferential standard* applicable to choices different in the degree to which they yield some value does not entail a maximization standard relative to that value. We can be rationally required, in situations of actual choice, not to take less rather than more of a good thing, or to suffer more rather than less of an evil, *without* being rationally required, as a matter of general policy, to seek to maximize the good or minimize the bad.

At this point it becomes important to clarify just how forgoing pleasure stands in the scheme. Since the scheme is pluralistic, it is open to Gert to maintain that the quest for pleasure is qualified not only by the avoidance of evils other than its loss, but by the pursuit of other goods—a pursuit that can provide reasons for action strong enough to warrant even bearing pain or suffering death. (I return to this balancing issue next.)

Rationality as Applicable to Act-Types vs. Act-Tokens

My final question of interpretation concerns the type-token distinction for actions. Gert makes little or no explicit use of this, but I see no bar to his doing so. In one place, moreover, I prefer to read him as simply using a special term, "parasitic irrational action", to do the relevant work. Recall the case of José, whose desire to kill himself rests on anger and depression. Still, he sees that the life insurance money will immensely benefit his wife and children, who are sick. This gives him a reason (which we may assume is adequate) to kill himself, but it does not motivate his doing so; his motive is a desire to make them feel guilty. Commenting on such cases, Gert says, "if a person does kill himself, but has an adequate reason for doing so, his action is not irrational in the basic sense, regardless of whether that reason is a motive for his killing himself" (85). The action is irrational only in the parasitic sense that its motive is irrational, since his motivating desire to kill himself as a result of depression and (this) anger is a desire for an evil he does not see as compensated.

This diagnosis is what Gert's definition of irrational action—which is acausal—requires. But, to recognize the type-token disparity, he could instead say something like this. That definition is intended to apply to act-types, and where *S* has an adequate reason to *A*, the type, *A*-ing (e.g., lending one's car), is rational for *S*; but a token, say, a particular lending of the car, is rational only if it is (purposively) explainable by an adequate reason—hence motivated by that reason. We could now say not that José's action is irrational only in a parasitic sense, but instead that although the action-type, killing himself, is (in the circumstances) rational for him given his adequate reason, his actual suicide, the token of that type, is irrational, being a foreseeable harming of himself performed *for* no adequate reason. His adequate reason plays no role in his deed; in Kantian terms, he acts merely in conformity with it, not *from* it. Types could be said to be rational for one in virtue of reasons one *has*, tokens in virtue of reasons one both has *and* acts on. The substantive grounds of rationality and irrationality are unaffected by this.[13]

Indeed, one might think of José's motive as irrational because it is *for* death and not, say, *for death as a way to help his family*.[14] It has the wrong kind of ground, in a partly causal sense; its ground is something like an attraction to death for its own sake (or to some other evil). If his belief that dying will help his family does not save his motive from irrationality because it is not a ground of the motive, why would it save his action (token) from irrationality without being a ground of that?[15] I cannot find a good theoretical reason for treating the appraisal of the action differently on this score from that of the motive.

Rationality, Value, and Relativity

In the light of the main interpretive discussion so far, I want to make some critical comments that suggest possible modifications in Gert's theory of rationality.

Is Rationality Egocentric?

On the one hand, Gert holds that irrationality is egocentric; on the other, he allows that even basic reasons for action can include considerations of the welfare of others. Indeed, he goes so far as to say that "Any irrational act that would be made rational by a reason of self-interest would also be made rational by a reason of the same strength involving the interests of others. A mere change of person affected does not affect the strength of a reason" (78). These are plausible and important points, and the second is arguably crucial for any sound moral theory. But if an other-regarding reason can prevent an action's being irrational, and if that point is indeed essential to the very nature of irrationality, how can the notion of irrationality be essentially egocentric? If, for instance, you cannot tell whether my doing something obviously painful to me is rational until you know whether I have an adequate reason for doing it, and that reason may be other-regarding, it would seem that the criteria for irrational action include other-regarding considerations.

A natural suggestion to make here is that it is only the concept of a *prima facie irrational action* that is egocentric; that of a rational action simpliciter is not. Granted, a token of an irrational action may be irrational on *wholly* egocentric grounds; and perhaps they are the only *basic* irrationality-making considerations, and are necessarily so, not merely contingently so. But the *concept* of an irrational action is still not unqualifiedly egocentric.

A related move in the theory of rational desire would be to make use of the notion of intrinsic desire, whose relevance to the notion of rationality we have seen already. We might say that although the concept of an irrational desire is not egocentric, that of an irrational *intrinsic* desire is. Thus, if one's wanting something for its own sake is irrational, this must be because that object is on the prohibited list; anything else may be rationally wanted (intrinsically). In this spirit, one could say that the notion of an intrinsically motivated irrational action is egocentric. Still, so much of our action is performed for a further end, rather than for its own sake, that Gert is surely right to seek a conception of irrational action in general.

Is the Theory Valuationally Hybrid?

So far in this section, I have suggested that Gert's concept of rational action simpliciter is not unqualifiedly egoistic, though his concept of prima facie irrational action is. Similarly, I have suggested that his concept of an irrational desire is not unqualifiedly egoistic, though he might plausibly take the notion of an irrational intrinsic desire to be such. I now want to indicate another way in which the concept of irrationality (possibly including his own working concept) is more complex than one might think from some of his descriptions of it.

Even the concept of prima facie irrational action will be hybrid in one way if one's own pleasure is a positive good that one must want to achieve, on pain of irrationality. It will be *valuationally hybrid,* i.e., grounded not just in evils, but also in at least one good. I see no deep reason why Gert must disallow that, particularly since it keeps prima facie irrationality in the egoistic domain. To be sure, he does have reason to disallow it insofar as he has grounds to hold (as he does hold) that rationality permits declining to do beneficent deeds so long as doing that does not satisfy his (egocentric) criteria of irrationality. But must he maintain this? One may certainly wonder how the good of others can have enough normative weight to block irrationality, yet not enough *ever* to make it irrational not to do something for someone else. This deserves reflection.

Suppose I have nothing to lose, even prospective pleasure, from relieving someone's suffering and I believe this would be morally and intrinsically a good thing to do (something I may quite rationally believe, on Gert's view as on many others). I would be surprised at myself if I just stood there and looked on; but might I not also be to some degree irrational, or at least lacking in rationality, given my beliefs? Is there not some measure of irrationality, or at least some deficiency in rationality, in such a blatant disparity between belief and action? If so, as seems plausible, we should raise the question whether beliefs might play enough of a practical role so that acting inconsistently with them—at least when they are rational—can make an action deficient in rationality, or indeed irrational, even if one does not and should not see any evil or loss for *oneself* in the failure to act so. The deficiency or irrationality need not be deep or of a "high order," but there seems to be some kind and degree of deficiency in rationality. This is a view that may underlie some of the reasons to think that weak-willed action is irrational.[16] The global issue here (which I cannot pursue) is whether, far from being less basic than practical reason—at least where practical reason is conceived as egocentrically grounded—theoretical reason has some degree of apparently independent authority over it.

Are There Degrees of Rationality?

Let us move from the question of what constitutes irrationality to that of whether rational action is merely action that is not irrational. I have already indicated that once the role of positive goods in relation to irrationality is clear—and I think Gert is correct in his main points about that—it is strange not to attribute irrationality to certain failures to pursue a good for oneself. The point applies even more clearly, I have suggested, to taking less when given options differing in value. I now want to go further. Why may we not properly say that some pairs of actions that are not irrational can be differentially rational depending on how well they stack up as pursuits of one or more goods? Gert already seems committed to allowing that there can be better (certainly stronger) reason for one such action than for another, as well as more reasons of any given level of strength. Suppose I do something that is not irrational, but I do or should see that I have far better reason to do something else. Would I (or could I) not be acting less rationally than I might?

One might say there is no difference in the action's degree of rationality but only in the degree of its grounding in reasons. I find this an odd claim, but suppose it is true. It would still seem that the overall rationality of a person is in part determined by the proportion of the person's actions that are well-grounded in reasons, relative to those that are irrational or at least not well-grounded. Moreover, we can certainly compare persons in degree of rationality, which shows that the notion itself admits of comparatives. We can say we have never known anyone as rational as *x*, that *y* is more rational now that a good therapist has been helping, and that we sometimes wish we ourselves were more—or less—rational. If these points do not lead to differentiation in degrees of rationality for actions, there is a disparity between our criteria for rationality in persons and for rationality in action. A disparity like this is not an inconsistency, but a theory of rationality should avoid it except for compelling reason.

Whatever one says about the matter of degrees of rationality in action (or, more modestly, the possibility of comparison in respect to more and less), reasons surely figure in differentiating the advisability of different permissible acts. This is something Gert would grant, if only because there are degrees of likelihood of avoiding evils. I see no reason why he could not countenance such differences owing to different contributions which actions may be expected to make to promotion of goods that the agent recognizes.

Adequacy of Reasons, Consensus, and Relativity

The final problem I want to raise concerns Gert's notion of the adequacy of a reason. As it happens, he offers more than one formulation. On an early one, an adequate reason for action "makes *the otherwise irrational action for which it is a reason rational*" (57). An apparent implication of this is that whenever there is an adequate reason for which an action is performed, without that reason the agent would have performed a token of the same type irrationally. This would rule out the possibility that an agent (1) has two adequate reasons for an action, such as undergoing a painful exercise, (2) acts for only one of them, but (3) would have acted for the other if the former were not the operative reason.[17]

Gert's final formulation does not have this undesirable consequence: a reason is adequate, it says, "*if any significant group of moral agents regard the harm avoided or benefit gained as compensating for the harm suffered* (84). (The intention in the context is presumably to refer to the harm or benefit *the agent* believes will occur.) I have four, mainly clarificatory, points. First, I assume—controversially—that, without vitiating circularity, Gert can specify what constitutes a moral agent and a "significant" group of such agents.[18] Second, I take it that the intention is to refer to what any significant such group does *or would* regard as compensating, since clearly the formulation is meant to apply to actions not actually considered by anyone except possibly the agent. Third, I suppose Gert is here supplying only a sufficient condition for adequacy of a reason (which may be all his overall purposes require given the primacy of his interest in rational permissibility). To see that the condition (viewed in itself) is not plausibly taken to be necessary, consider an agent having no belief about any trade-off between an anticipated harm and a compensating good: an agent may (rationally) believe that an action will lead to pleasure and (quite rationally) not see any resulting harm at all. Why should we not consider such a belief an adequate reason? Gert's overall position does not preclude our so viewing it. I might add that in addition to not giving a necessary condition here, he is apparently considering only actions whose agents believe to have some harmful consequences for themselves (and if we do restrict his adequacy characterization in the context to such actions, a good case can be made to show that it does provide a necessary condition).

The first question I want to raise here is whether, if this condition on an adequate reason—call it the *significant consensus condition*—is the operative one, it imports more relativity than one would expect given most of what Gert says. Note that significant groups of moral agents can and do disagree on such matters. Thus, there can be adequate reasons both for an action and for a contrary option. This is not, however, necessarily objectionable, unless one thinks that an adequate reason for something is one that justifies *preferring* it over alternatives. But we should distinguish between a *preferential* and a *permissional* notion of adequacy. It seems consistent with Gert's overall view to invoke a parallel distinction applying specifically to reasons for action, a distinction between their *minimal (or permissional) adequacy* and their *preferential (or comparative) adequacy*: a reason having the former renders an action rationally permissible and may be matched by opposing permissional reasons, those licensing an action incompatible with the first; a reason having the latter renders the action rationally preferable to one or more alternatives and overrides any minimally adequate reasons for an alternative action.

This distinction allows that different agents, even in the same circumstances, can each have permissionally adequate reasons for incurring quite different degrees of harm. Gert recognizes no fixed hierarchy among harms and leaves individuals free to construct their own rankings. He does *not* say that any such consensus condition holds for preferential adequacy. If he should affirm one, consistency would seem to require him to say that one action is rationally preferable to another only relative to some variable, such as the valuation of some significant group appropriately considering it. The notion in question might still be objective, however, at least in the sense that what the relevant group would hold is a factual matter that can be determined by scientific or other objective procedures. What appears to be a far-reaching relativity, then, may be in fact only a kind of latitudinarianism, an endorsement of rational freedom that some readers of Gert might not be expecting him to make given the concreteness and apparent specificity of many of his normative claims. In rough but perhaps not inapt terms: an action is convicted of irrationality only if no significant subset of the jury would vote for innocence.

Another problem concerning the significant consensus condition—and not as likely to be eliminable by terminological adjustment—is that it forces us to say that a reason is adequate even if a significant group of moral agents has the appropriate belief only because its members are deceived by clever but sophistical reasoning into thinking there is such a compensation. Consider the analogous case of a deceived jury—assuming an acceptable procedure for selecting a competent jury in the first place. Intuitively, the members should *rationally* think the reason in question is adequate (or the accused innocent) if their belief is to be sufficient for adequacy of a reason (or to warrant acquittal). But if this were the requirement, we would need a notion of rational belief. I see no reason why Gert could not here invoke his notion of belief held in the face of overwhelming evidence. We need a theory of such evidence in any case. He sometimes speaks as if he thought we could get this kind of theory from his account of rationality, but I see no need for him to hold this. He is not (as suggested earlier) committed to deriving standards of theoretical rationality from those of practical rationality. Indeed, so far as I can see, he shows that the former standards are essential to fully working out the latter.

Possible Modifications in the View

If I have indicated some difficulties for Gert's account of rationality, I have also suggested how he can retain what seem its most important features with modifications that appear to be in the spirit of his overall project, that of providing an account of irrationality that leads to a theory of morality as mainly aimed at avoiding evil and as never requiring irrational action. Let me summarize the modifications I see as plausible if the problems I have noted are as weighty as they seem.

Both the priority of the avoidance of evil over the pursuit of good and the subordination of moral rules to the avoidance of evil can be retained even if one grants that practical reason has goods as well as evils at its base. The list of basic evils can be retained with loss of pleasure construed as diminution, a negative change in one's actual experience, such as an elimination of pleasure; but it appears that, at least in spirit, the theory takes failure to desire to experience future pleasure as irrational. If this is embraced, then the list of basic elements of irrationality gains in diversity to include a good, but it can remain egocentric.

A plausible feature of Gert's overall approach to rationality—one that I think reflects practical wisdom—is its antihierarchical character. One can retain this, allowing for different rational rankings of outcomes in terms of trade-offs among evils, among goods, and between evils and goods, but still allow comparisons in rationality within the domain of rationally permissible actions. If there are not differences in the degree to which rational actions are rational, surely some reasons are better than others and, as motivators of action, count more toward the rationality of agents.

A type-token distinction for actions—and indeed for desires and beliefs—can be brought in at several points without sacrificing anything major in the overall position. This would make it easy to affirm a causal requirement on the rationality of the tokens, though it would not require doing so. An action-token, for instance, is rational only if not based, in the relevant sense, on a vitiating consideration, such as an irrational desire or irrational belief; an action-type, by contrast, can be rational for a person merely in the light of what the agent believes—or perhaps rationally believes—about its overall consequences for good and evil. This may be so whether the agent does the deed or not and regardless of what actually motivates it if the agent does do it.

If these modifications are made, morally required conduct, understood as comprising those act-types required by moral rules, may still be plausibly argued to be always rationally permissible even if not, as such, rationally required. Moreover, if one countenances differences in degrees or gradations of rationality, one would now have more room to argue that there can be reasons to behave morally in the light of which a rational person under certain conditions will, or will tend to, do the things morality requires. Obviously, such conduct may be instrumentally required by rationality for some agents in virtue of conducing to their pleasure. But there may be noninstrumental cases as well, such as the one I sketched in which I believe I have nothing to lose by being moral and also believe that I ought to be. This, however, allows belief more rational authority than Gert's theory provides for in any explicit way. The question I am posing is how much of a departure from the main thrust of the view, if any, it would be to countenance such cases.

It will be obvious that I find a great deal that is both sound and insightful in Gert's account of rationality, particularly practical rationality. His account of the latter is among the leading candidates for serious discussion in the entire contemporary literature. Where I have found room for more than one interpretation, I have in many cases offered a reading that fits the overall text and yields a plausible thesis. Where I have found apparently untoward implications, I have suggested modifications that seem in the spirit of the text and can block those implications. There is no way to put forward such a multitude of ideas without being open to objections. But I believe that with modifications of the kinds I have suggested Gert is well positioned to revise his theory. He can do so in a way that preserves its most important elements, and he can thereby meet some major objections to his account of rationality and argue even more cogently for the main elements in his list-based, rule-centered, antihierarchical, and, by and large, straightforward and commonsensical moral theory.[19]

Notes

1. I cannot define the notion of such disparity here but will illustrate it. The notion of a reason for action, and the related concept of a bad one, are treated in some detail in my "Acting for Reasons," *Philosophical Review* 95, no. 4 (1986): 511-46.

2. This is by no means a trivial assumption; a maximizing consequentialism, e.g., might be held to require that we are never free to do anything that fails (at least relative to our beliefs) to maximize the value in question.

3. R. B. Brandt is probably a case in point. See, e.g., *A Theory of the Good and the Right* (Oxford, Eng.: Oxford University Press, 1979).

4. Bernard Gert, *Morality: Its Nature and Justification* (New York: Oxford University Press, 1998). References to this book will hereinafter be parenthetically included in the text.

5. One might still rationally and with full information advise someone one cares about (intrinsically) to perform an act one (truly) believes to be irrational act, provided doing so had good enough results for oneself or for others one similarly cares about, though that would seem *immoral* (I thank Walter Sinnott-Armstrong for calling my attention to this kind of case). If it is immoral, we should probably take Gert's intention to be to refer not only to intrinsic concern but to cases—which are not uncommon—in which there is also no competing motivation of a certain sort, say, no competing intrinsic concern. There is an interesting nest of questions here, but I leave them aside, in part because the advisability formulation is not Gert's main characterization of irrational action.

6. This does not seem to me equivalent to the longer characterization given just previously, and I think it may be preferable. I leave aside how "should know" is to be explicated and whether this is possible independently of an account of rationality.

7. In case a careful reader of Gert should think I simply overlook his description of two "parasitic kinds of irrational action" (84-85), I might note that there he is perhaps best read as not providing a nonbasic *sense* of "irrational" but a rationale for calling irrational actions that do not strictly deserve the name (in the way my imagined action does provided we simply widen the description in a simple way requiring no significant theoretical change). He mentions a case where *S* acts on an irrational belief but would (if "fully informed") not so act; here *S* satisfies the characterization of irrational action relative to this deed, so I take it this is not the parasitic case. That seems to be the next mentioned, in which the irrational belief

happens to be *true* but "if the situation were to change, the person would not react to it in a rational way" (84). Here the characterization would not be satisfied, since a fully informed person *would* (or might well) believe the same crucial (true) proposition (on a rational basis presumably), yet we may want to call the action "irrational" because it is only owing to the accidental set of circumstances that the agent gets in under the wire. Gert's second case deserves more discussion and is treated at length below.

8. He also treats as a malady a sexual dysfunction that prevents one from experiencing sexual pleasure and speaks here of "loss of pleasure" (106) even though there might be no such pleasure had and hence lost in the way in which ability can be lost by one's being disabled.

9. Later, in a subsection titled "Do Not Deprive of Pleasure," he says, "To trample on flowers in order to prevent someone from enjoying them is to deprive of pleasure" (165).

10. Gert implicitly addresses this question on 84-85, under the heading of "parasitic kinds of irrational action," but as pointed out in an earlier note I am not sure he deals with this altogether adequately. Further discussion of his strategy in those pages is provided later in this section.

11. Some, such as Brandt, would mention here cases in which we also call ourselves stupid because we should see that we can do better for ourselves by *A*-ing than by *B*-ing, but we *A* anyway, as where one buys something inferior to what one could have gotten at the same price had one paid better attention. Perhaps people who quite often do this may be considered irrational, but I am not sure these cases show any more than that one failed to act on one's best available reason.

12. He says, e.g., that "What I call irrational beliefs are appropriately called irrational because of their connection with irrational actions" (38); and that it is "primarily and basically actions that are judged rational and irrational" (38). Why might one say this? On 35 he says that "genuinely *holding* the beliefs that are put forward by the skeptic, *i.e.,* basing one's actions on these beliefs, would be irrational" (italics added). I do not think that even full-bloodedly holding a belief entails basing any action on it, but if one thinks anything close to this it may seem natural to take the rationality of beliefs to be less basic than that of actions—perhaps something like judging the health of a tree by the quality of its fruit (a venerable practice, within limits).

13. I have explicated the application of the type-token distinction to rational action and rational belief (a topic on which the distinction is also relevant to Gert's project) in "Rationalization and Rationality," in my *The Structure of Justification* (Cambridge, Eng.: Cambridge University Press, 1993), 405-30. For different views, see the papers by Carl Ginet ("Reasons Explanation of Action: An Incompatibilist Account") and Jaegwon Kim ("Mechanism, Purpose, and Explanatory Exclusion") in *Philosophy of Action*, ed. Alfred Mele (Oxford, Eng.: Oxford University Press, 1997), 106-30 and 256-82; and Hugh J. McCann, *The Works of Agency* (Ithaca, N.Y.: Cornell University Press, 1998).

14. Gert's description of the case begins with a suggestion that the agent wants to kill himself as a result of depression, which is compatible with his wanting it for its own sake—the kind of desire for death that is irrational. Later, Gert describes the motive as instrumental: José "believes that his wife and children will feel guilty" (85). The first description serves both Gert's and my purposes better here.

15. I defend this kind of approach in detail in "Rationalization and Rationality." In "Acting from Virtue," in my *Moral Knowledge and Ethical Character* (Oxford, Eng.: Oxford University Press, 1997), 174-92, I indicate passages where a similar commitment is made by writers as diverse as Aristotle, Hume, and Kant. Note that

the distinction between a ground and a mere cause is important here, as Gert would surely grant.

16. For a detailed treatment of the way in which weakness of will counts against the rationality of actions exhibiting it, see my "Weakness of Will and Rational Action," in my *Action, Intention, and Reason* (Ithaca, N.Y.: Cornell University Press, 1993), 319-33.

17. One might think that we may construe an adequate reason for action as one that *can* make an otherwise irrational action rational. But this will not do. Suppose I have almost good enough reason for an action that causes me some pain to make it rational. Then the addition of a minor reason might tip the balance so as to yield rational action, though that reason alone is not an adequate one for performing an action of that type. The notion Gert's formulation comes closest to capturing is perhaps that of an agent's *having minimally adequate reason* for an action; for without this, one might plausibly say the action is not rational, and for Gert this is equivalent to its irrationality. But this notion is not what is needed here, since the question is what constitutes *an* adequate reason, not *overall* reason (which may result from a mix of individually *in*adequate reasons) that is only *minimally* adequate.

18. One troublesome passage on this score is the one in which he counts "a reason as adequate if any significant group of otherwise rational people regard that reason as adequate . . . [in relation to] the harm avoided or benefit gained" (57) and quickly adds that "People count as otherwise rational if they do not normally act on irrational desires without an adequate reason" (57).

19. For helpful comments on this paper, I thank Andrew Boldt, Daniel J. Bush, and—especially—Bernard Gert and Walter Sinnott-Armstrong.

5

Gert on Reasons, Rationality, Harms, and Lists

David Copp

Over the past thirty years, and most recently in his new book, Bernard Gert has developed a distinctive account of reasons and rationality.[1] The account is central to Gert's overall project in moral theory, for he needs to use it in order to pinpoint the location of moral considerations in the space of reasons. My goal in this paper is to explore some of the central features of Gert's account. I believe that Gert is intuitively on strong ground, but I believe as well that there are problems with his story that make it difficult to accept. These problems fall naturally into four groups. His theory is a "list theory," and the first issue is whether list theories are theoretically fruitful or helpful. Second is a group of issues about the relation between reasons and rationality, including the issue whether desires give rise to reasons or make actions rationally defensible. The third issue concerns the relation between avoiding harms and seeking goods. And the fourth issue concerns the role of our values and life plans in constituting certain things as rational for us to pursue. I discuss the problems in roughly this order. Before doing so, however, I describe what seem to me to be the most interesting respects in which Gert's theory of reasons and rationality differs from more orthodox theories. I then turn to a kind of example that brings out intuitions that appear to motivate Gert's account. In the heart of the paper, I explore in detail the four groups of problems. I conclude by suggesting how Gert's account might be repaired to avoid some of the problems while doing justice to at least some of the intuitions that underlie it.

The Distinctiveness of Gert's Account

There is a widely shared idea that rationality is a matter of acting in one's *self-interest*. Derek Parfit suggested that all so-called "self-interest theories of rationality" can be viewed as giving each person the aim of realizing "the outcomes that would be best for himself."[2] But because there is disagreement about what would constitute an outcome as best for a person, Parfit distinguished three types of self-interest theory. According to hedonistic theories, the best outcome for a person is the one that would most contribute to his happiness. According to desire-fulfillment theories, the best outcome is defined in terms of the fulfillment of some or all of the person's desires, either his actual desires or the desires he would have in an ideal hypothetical situation. According to objective-list theories, there are certain things that would be good or bad for a person regardless of their impact on her happiness and regardless of her desires.[3] For my purposes, the important thing is the idea of a list theory. In Parfit's scheme, "list theories" agree with theories of the other types that the subject matter of rationality is self-interest, or achieving "the best" for oneself, but, unlike theories of the other types, they do not offer a unified substantive account of what this consists in.

Gert's account shares two characteristics with Parfit's list theories. First, certain lists are at the heart of his account. In Gert's case, these are lists of the kinds of actions that we have reason to perform and of the kinds of actions that it is irrational to perform. Second, Gert holds that there is no account that can be given of the subject matter of reason and rationality that is deeper or more authoritative than the lists themselves (51, 57).[4] Nevertheless, Gert's theory is different at a fundamental level from the theories in Parfit's scheme because Gert does not think that rationality requires aiming to achieve what would be *best* for oneself, or even something that would be *good* for oneself. Rather, a rational person must avoid certain harms or bads unless she has adequate reason to do otherwise. Gert's view therefore does not qualify as a self-interest theory, at least not according to Parfit's characterization of self-interest theories.

Gert does agree that we can *say* that it is always rationally permitted to act in one's "self-interest", and that all irrational desires are contrary to one's "self-interest" (71). But he would interpret "self-interest" in these contexts in terms of the lists that he gives of goods and bads (72). He holds that it is irrational to desire any of the listed bads either for oneself or for those one cares about, without adequate reason (57). In particular, it is irrational to desire to die or to permanently lose consciousness; it is irrational to desire pain or any other unpleasant feeling; it is irrational to desire to be disabled or to lose an ability; it is irrational to desire a loss of freedom to act or not to be acted on; and it is irrational to desire a loss of pleasure (45-50). These are the basic irrational desires (57). Gert holds that it is irrational to act on any such desire without adequate reason (45), but he would not *explain* this by saying that it is contrary to one's self-interest to act on any desire on this list. On the contrary, according to Gert, there is no account that can be given or that need be given to unify the list. Gert's theory is therefore distinctive, first, in being a list theory, and second, in not being a self-interest theory. That is, it does not take the idea of self-interest to be basic to, or explanatory of, the subject matter of rationality.

A third distinctive feature of Gert's theory is its "hybrid" character. There are two key notions in his theory, the notion of a reason for action and the notion of an irrational action. Irrationality is essentially egocentric, says Gert, whereas reasons are not necessarily egocentric at all (x). Both notions are defined by lists. The basic idea is that irrationality is a matter of acting in a way that one knows or should know increases the risk of harm to oneself, or to those one cares about, without adequate reason (59).[5] Reasons are beliefs about avoiding or reducing the risk of harm, as well as bringing about corresponding benefits, to anyone at all, even to those one does not care about (57). Here the notions of "harm" and "benefit" are defined in the end, as we will see, by relevant lists.[6] The upshot is that whereas irrationality is egocentric, in that it concerns harms or risks of harms to oneself or those one cares about, reasons are not egocentric in this sense. And whereas irrationality is a matter of courting harm, reasons can be concerned with attaining benefits as well as avoiding harm. Gert's theory therefore marries an account of irrationality with a related account of reasons. The relation between the accounts is not simply in the content of the lists. Gert explains that a reason is a rational belief that can make an otherwise irrational action rational (56), and irrationality is courting harm without adequate reason (39).

The fourth distinctive feature of Gert's view, and perhaps the most striking fact about it, is that it does not find any irrationality in failing to do what one sees oneself to have most reason to do. Gert disagrees with what is surely the standard view in these matters. He holds that it is not necessarily irrational to fail to do what one takes there to be the most reason to do, not even if one's judgment is correct, for so to act is not necessarily to countenance harm to oneself or to anyone one cares about. It is not even irrational to do something "for no reason," or simply "because one feels like acting in that way," despite recognizing very good reasons to do otherwise. For example, I might see very good reason to give to a charity yet decide not to do so simply because I don't feel like giving. Gert holds that there need be nothing irrational in this (60). Hence, Gert holds that a fully *rational* person might fail to be motivated to *any* degree to do what he recognizes that he has best reason to do (67). Although any reason *could* serve as a motive for a rational person, it is not the case that reasons always do serve as motives for rational persons (*x*). The explanation of these points traces to the fact that, for Gert, reasons are defeaters of irrationalilty.[7] He says, "*Reasons for acting are conscious rational beliefs that can make some otherwise irrational actions, rational*" (56, emphasis in original). Indeed, some reasons, such as reasons concerned with our ability to benefit other people, lack the power to give rise to rational requirements. These reasons can make an action rationally permitted that would otherwise be irrational, but they cannot create a requirement that would motivate any fully rational person. The basic idea in Gert's account is the idea of the *irrational*.

There are therefore at least four interesting ways in which Gert's account of reasons and rationality is distinctive. First, it is a list theory. Second, on Gert's theory, rationality does not require aiming to achieve what would be *best for oneself*. It merely requires avoiding certain harms, either for oneself or for those one cares about, unless one has adequate reason not to do so. Third, Gert's theory is a hybrid. Irrationality is egocentric and concerned with avoiding harms, but reasons are not necessarily egocentric and can concern benefits as well as harms. Fourth, reasons are essentially defeaters of irrationality. And because some reasons cannot give rise to requirements, it is not the case that fully rational persons must act in accord with the best reasons of which they are aware.

Some Useful Examples

Suppose that a man is driving along a road that follows a deep and fast flowing river. He loses control on a curve and the car flies off the road and into the river, where it quickly sinks until it can barely be seen below the surface of the water. The man escapes from the car, but his groceries are on the back seat. Fortunately, another driver has seen what happened and she rushes to the man on the riverbank. The man cries out that his broccoli and potatoes are in the car. Confident that she is a strong swimmer, the second driver quickly dives into the water to rescue the vegetables. It is difficult getting through the car window, and she cannot reach the groceries. She is forced to come up for air, but as she attempts this, her clothing catches on the car. She manages to free herself, and she surfaces coughing and gasping. She tries again, and this time manages to get the broccoli and potatoes out of the car. She and the man are extremely distressed and frightened, but they feel fortunate to have rescued the groceries.

In this example, which I will call the "Groceries Rescue Case," we naturally want to know what could explain the strange behavior of the woman in being willing to risk her life for some groceries. If the man had had a baby in the car, and if she were risking her life to save the baby, then we could see her as acting rationally. We could call this the "Baby Rescue Case." But in the Groceries Rescue Case, unless the woman had a very good reason for risking her life for some groceries, we are naturally inclined to view her actions as irrational. Perhaps there is a food shortage in the area, and perhaps the man had been driving for hours through dangerous terrain to bring the groceries to a group of starving people. If so, and if the woman knew this and believed that she might be able to rescue the groceries, then the woman's actions were rationally defensible. But otherwise, if she had no good reason for attempting the rescue—if she could say no more than that she "felt like" helping the man—we would say she was irrational or crazy to risk her life.

Our intuitions in the rescue examples tend to support Gert's idea that it is irrational to risk your life without good reason. Slight variations of the example also tend to support the related idea that it is irrational to harm yourself or to risk harming yourself without good reason. For instance, unless the woman had a special reason to rescue the groceries, we might agree that it would be irrational for her to jump into the river even if the only risk to her was the risk of the unpleasant sensation of being immersed in cold water.

It is important to see that there is something intuitively out of the ordinary about actions that risk harm to oneself. Suppose the man in my example had merely parked the car by the side of the road, instead of crashing it into the river. It would not be irrational, we think, for the woman to get the groceries out of the car in this case, not even if she had no reason for doing so beyond wanting to do it. These examples appear, then, to support Gert's idea that, as he says, irrationality consists in "not avoiding harms for oneself without adequate reason" (39). One might be led to agree with him by reflecting on the idea that irrationality is an especially egregious failure to respond to reasons. The reasons to avoid harms seem especially strong, and this might be thought to explain the irrationality of failing to avoid harms to oneself. But Gert appears to hold that nothing is irrational *except* failing to avoid harms to oneself, or to those one cares about, without adequate reason.

Suppose that the woman in the Groceries Rescue Case had *refused* to help the man to save his groceries. Given the risk of drowning that she faced, her reluctance to jump into the river surely will not seem to have been irrational. We might think she had adequate reason to help, if she could have saved some much needed food, but even if so, we would not think that she was irrational *not* to help. Gert embraces this intuition. In his view, the fact that the woman had reason to help means only that it would not have been irrational for her to help. It does not mean that she was rationally required to help. Rationality left her free to choose. Gert would add that it does not matter whether the woman had any reason *not* to help. In his view, she needed a reason to make it rationally defensible for her to help the man, given the risk of drowning, but she needed no reason to make it rationally defensible for her not to help him, since, by assumption, her not helping did not create any risk of harm either to herself or to someone she cared about.

Gert's intuitions might seem less plausible in the Baby Rescue Case. For even in this case, Gert would say that rationality leaves the woman free to choose between attempting to rescue the baby and not attempting to rescue it. He would say that the woman needed no reason to make it rationally defensible for her not to attempt the rescue, assuming that she did not care about the child. Even more striking are the views Gert is committed to in yet another version of the rescue case, which I will call the "Baby Rescue with Scuba Gear Case." Assume that the woman is wearing scuba diving equipment and a wet suit and that she is already in the river, exploring the bottom, when the accident occurs. In this case, there is no risk to her if she attempts to rescue the child caught in the car, not even a risk of getting a chill from the cold water. Gert would agree that she has good reason to attempt the rescue, but he would deny even in *this* case that she would be irrational to refuse to attempt the rescue, not even if she has no reason at all to refuse. If she does not feel like rescuing the child, she is not irrational to refuse to do so. She is rationally permitted either to attempt the rescue or not, just as she was rationally permitted to do either thing in the scenario in which her life would be put at risk if she attempted the rescue. This is curious. It means that the belief that a person's life can be saved is a sufficiently good reason for the woman to risk her life that it can make it not irrational for her to do something that would otherwise be irrational. Yet this belief is not a sufficiently good reason for the woman to attempt to save the person's life to make her irrational *not* to do so even if she has no good reason not to do so (60). This asymmetry can seem puzzling.

Matters would be different—there would not be this asymmetry—if we imagine that the woman *cares* about the baby trapped in the car. Gert thinks that it is irrational to fail to avoid harm to those one cares about, although he does not think it irrational to fail to avoid harm to those one does *not* care about. There is always *reason* to avoid bringing harm to a person, but if one does not *care* about the person, then it is not *irrational* to bring harm to her, Gert thinks, even if one has no reason to do so. In the Baby Rescue with Scuba Gear Case, if the woman *cares* about the baby trapped in the car, then she is irrational to let it drown. If she does *not* care about the baby, however, she is not irrational to let it drown even if she has no reason not to rescue it, but merely doesn't feel like rescuing it (30). So the asymmetry we noticed before does not exist in cases where people we care about are at risk of suffering harm. The woman's belief that a person she cares about can be saved can make it irrational for her not to try to do so. Yet the belief that a person she does not care about can be saved cannot make it irrational for her not to try to do so even if she has no good reason not to do so.

Given the fact that we care about people in different ways and to different degrees, it does not seem intuitively plausible to me that there should be this sharp a line, and a line of exactly this kind, between actions that harm those one cares about and actions that harm those one does not care about. And the asymmetry I mentioned is worrisome. I will return to these matters. But the point I want to make here is that Gert's view does respond to intuitions that can be evoked in certain of the rescue cases. In other rescue cases, however, especially in the scuba gear example, Gert's view seems to me to be counterintuitive. I turn now to discuss some of the theoretical problems that stem from the four distinctive features of Gert's view that I outlined.

A List Theory?

Gert holds that his list of irrational types of action is fundamental. He holds that no account can be given of the subject matter of rationality that is more authoritative than this list (51, 57). It might appear, however, that the list is unified by the fact that all the items on it are *harmful* kinds of action. Gert holds that this fact does not unify the list in an interesting way, any more than does the fact that all the items on the list are irrational kinds of action. He does suggest that a harm "is best defined as that which all rational persons avoid unless they have an adequate reason not to" (90-91). He therefore would define the concept of harm in terms of the concept of rationality. But he defines the concept of rationality in terms of the concept of irrationality (30), and he defines the concept of irrationality in terms of a list of types of action (82-84). Hence, Gert holds, the list is fundamental (51, 82).

Unfortunately, Gert gives us no argument to show that the items on his list *exhaust* the significant kinds of harm. In fact, Gert concedes that no such argument can be given (51). He appears to concede as well that if something on his list were not a harmful kind of action, then acts of that kind would not be irrational. For he appears to concede that if, as some religions hold, death did not bring about a permanent loss of consciousness, then it would not be irrational to kill oneself (46). Gert takes this to show that the reason it is irrational to seek death without adequate reason is that death involves the permanent loss of consciousness. What is fundamentally irrational is to seek the permanent loss of consciousness without adequate reason. But one might as well take the example to show that the fundamental point is that items belong on the list only insofar as they are harmful kinds of action.

Why then should we not take the concept of harm as basic or primitive in the theory, and take irrationality to be defined in terms of the concept of harm? Gert's list could then be viewed as a list of examples of kinds of harmful actions, and nothing would ride on whether it is exhaustive. Gert does not take this line himself because he thinks that if a concept is "fundamental," then it has to be "defined in terms of a list, for," he says, "all fundamental definitions must be ostensive rather than verbal" (82). Since the concept of irrationality is fundamental, we can do no better than a list. Unfortunately, this argument depends on a confused understanding of what is involved in ostension and in definition as well as a confused understanding of the role played by lists in Gert's own theory. After all, Gert uses his list in presenting a disjunctive "verbal" definition of irrational action (83-4). So his own view involves giving a verbal definition of the concept of irrational action, despite the fact that he takes it to be a "fundamental" concept. The issue I am raising is whether it would be preferable instead to regard Gert's list, whether or not it is exhaustive of the kinds of harmful action, merely as a list of central examples of harmful kinds of action. So understood, the list could be used to convey or to teach the meaning of "harmful action," but it would not be taken to be theoretically prior to the concept of harmful action.

The revision I am proposing would not alter the basic idea behind Gert's theory. Just as geometry can be axiomatized in different ways, with different propositions taken as axioms in the different axiomatic presentations, the fundamental idea behind Gert's theory can be presented in different ways, with different propositions taken as theoretically basic or primitive. Gert prefers to take it to be primitive that the items on his list are irrational actions because, he seems to think, we learn what counts as irrational or harmful action by being given examples of the items on his list. But one can agree with this without taking the list to be theoretically primitive. One can instead take the concept of harm to be basic in the theory, define irrationality in terms of harm, and take the list to be a (perhaps exhaustive) list of kinds of harmful action.

Given this, the question we need to ask is whether it would be philosophically or theoretically preferable to present Gert's fundamental idea the way I am proposing, in a theory grounded in the idea that it is irrational to increase the risk of harm to oneself without adequate reason, rather than the way Gert does, in a list theory. The analogy with the choice between different axiomatizations in mathematics suggests that there might be no deep theoretical issue at stake. Yet the approach I am proposing has at least an aesthetic advantage, and also, I think, explanatory and epistemic advantages. List accounts invite the question whether anything *unifies* the list in a way that *explains* why the items on the list belong there. And the explanatory weakness of the list theory makes also for an epistemic weakness. For the fact that a list theory provides no account of what unifies the list undermines the reasonableness of confidence that the list is exhaustive. Gert's approach is hostage to the undefended proposition that the items on his list exhaust the things that belong on the list. In my proposed alternative, nothing depends on whether the list is exhaustive since the fundamental point is that the items on the list deserve to be there because they are all harmful kinds of actions. Of course, my alternative leaves the concept of harm undefined in the theory, but it might be possible to define it, and, in any event, any philosophical theory must begin somewhere and take some notions as primitive. Hence, even if Gert is correct that his list is exhaustive of the items that deserve to be on it, and even though his list is unified by the concept of harm, there are explanatory, epistemic, and aesthetic advantages to taking it to be primitive that it is irrational to increase the risk of harm to oneself without adequate reason rather than, as Gert prefers, taking it to be primitive that the kinds of action on his list are irrational to perform without adequate reason.

The Hybrid Nature of the Theory: Those We Care About

In Gert's theory, irrationality is "egocentric." It is a matter of failing to avoid harms to oneself or those one cares about without adequate reason. But reasons are not essentially egocentric. They can concern benefits as well as harms, and benefits and harms even to those we do not care about. Harms to people we care about have a special relevance to the rationality of our actions that is lacked by harms to people we do *not* care about. Moreover, harms to people we care about have a special relevance to the rationality of our actions that is lacked by harms to *projects* we care about. These contrasts create tensions at the heart of Gert's theory.

To see this, return to the rescue examples. Assume that the woman's own son is trapped underwater in the car, and that the woman cares deeply about her son. Call this the "Woman's Own Son Rescue Case." In this case, as in the original Baby Rescue Case, the realization that the child's life can be saved is a sufficiently good reason for the woman to attempt the rescue that it can make it not irrational for her to risk her life. Yet if the woman realizes that the trapped child is her own son, and if she cares about him, she would be irrational *not* to save the child's life—that is, she would be rationally required *to* save the child's life—in a situation where she had no good reason not to do so. This is simply because she cares about her son. So in the "Baby Rescue with Scuba Gear Case," if the child were the woman's own son, then she would be irrational not to rescue him given that she cares about him. She would not be irrational to let the boy drown if he were a stranger to her, but, given that she cares about him, she would be irrational to let him drown.

The fact that we care about a person is constituted at least in part by facts about our desires. In the Woman's Own Son Case, the fact that the woman has certain relevant desires regarding her child makes the reason she has to rescue the child capable of rendering her irrational not to rescue him, provided there is no risk to herself. The fact that she has such desires can make it irrational for her to fail to rescue the child. But, Gert holds, it can do this without altering the *force* of the reason she already has to rescue the child. It does not make it a *better* reason, says Gert (77-79). Moreover, Gert is committed to denying that these desires give her a reason she would not otherwise have had. Gert wants to deny that desires are a source of reasons. Desires convert reasons into motives, but they do not give us reasons (62, ff.). Hence, although Gert is committed to acknowledging that certain desires have a special significance for the rationality of our actions, he would deny that these desires either give us reasons or alter the rational force of the reasons we already have. It is difficult to make sense of this combination of ideas. It seems incoherent to hold that a desire can make an action irrational that would not otherwise be irrational without either giving the agent a new reason not to do it or altering the force or quality of a reason she already had not to do it.

It is obvious that a person can care about her projects, her country, various artifacts, natural monuments, and the like, as well as about other people, such as her children. Gert does not give the kind of status to avoiding harms to *projects* that we care about that he gives to avoiding harms to *people* that we care about. At least, he does not overtly do so. So in the original Baby Rescue Case, in which the baby is a stranger to the woman, she has a reason to rescue the child, but even if she cares about *rescuing* the child, the fact that she does is irrelevant to the rationality of her rescuing or failing to rescue the child. In the Woman's Own Son Rescue Case, however, the fact that the woman cares about *the child* is relevant to the rationality of her rescuing or failing to rescue the child. This difference between the rational significance of caring about *rescuing* and the rational significance of caring about *the child* strikes me as poorly motivated in Gert's theory. For it is the fact that the woman *cares* about the child that gives him special significance in the theory, not any other fact about the child.

Let us therefore look more closely at the role of caring in Gert's theory. The question I want to ask here is whether, in Gert's view, it is *fundamentally* irrational to bring about harm to those we care about without adequate reason, or whether this is irrational only because and to the extent that bringing harm to those we care about has other consequences that no rational person would countenance without adequate reason. There is textual evidence to support both readings, but I will argue that the latter interpretation, on which it is only *derivatively* irrational to harm those we care about without good reason, is preferable.

The view that it is fundamentally irrational to harm those we care about without good reason presupposes the existence of a relevant threshold in caring, for it must accommodate the fact that we care about people in different ways and to different degrees. The threshold would have to be a way and degree of caring, let us say, way W to degree D, such that those we care about in way W at least to degree D are those we are irrational to harm without reason but that those we care about in other ways, or to a lesser degree, can be harmed without irrationality even for no reason. In a footnote to a passage in which Gert claims that no one wants a person for whom he is concerned to do anything he views as irrational, Gert says that those for whom a person is concerned in a *relevant* way are those he is concerned with as much as with anyone else, including himself, or those who have no conflict of interest with anyone for whom the person is more concerned, including himself (30, fn 1). This proposal gives us a threshold of the kind we need, but it is unclear why the irrationality of harming a person should depend on whether there is someone else for whom I am more concerned. It is unclear why harms to those we care about only somewhat less than ourselves count for no more than harms to complete strangers. On Gert's proposal, if I care about one of my children somewhat less than I care about another one of my children, then I am not irrational to cause harm to the former although I would be irrational to cause harm to the latter. Moreover, even if I care about both children more than I care about myself, it is not irrational to harm the child I care somewhat less about without reason even though I care more about her than about myself and it is irrational to harm myself without reason. This seems arbitrary.

I suspect that any threshold would seem arbitrary. For it will imply that harms to those we care about in way *W* but only to somewhat less than degree *D* would count no differently than harms to complete strangers. If I care about one of my children somewhat less than I care about another one of my children, then I might not be irrational to cause harm to the former even if I would be irrational to cause harm to the latter. In this case I can rationally treat harms to the less favored child as I would treat harms to a stranger, but I must treat harms to the other child as just as important as harms to myself, from the point of view of rationality. This seems arbitrary since there is no deep difference in my relationship to my children in the example, but only a slight difference in degree of caring. Moreover, the idea that the rationality of harming someone other than myself without reason depends on how I feel about her is difficult to reconcile with Gert's idea that harming myself without reason should count as irrational regardless of how I feel about myself. On Gert's view, even if I care very little about myself, I am irrational to harm myself without reason, even though, if I cared so little about another person I would not be irrational to harm her, even if I had no reason to do so. This also seems arbitrary: a difference in the degree to which I care for people is treated as significant to the rationality of my actions when it is a difference between how I care for people other than myself, but such a difference is treated as of no importance at all to the rationality of my actions when it is a difference between how I care about myself and how I care about someone else. I conclude, then, that the idea that it is fundamentally irrational to bring about harm to those we care about without adequate reason does not sit well with Gert's views about the irrationality of harming *oneself* and about the rational permissibility of harming those we do *not* care about.

There is textual evidence, however, that Gert's official view might be that the irrationality of bringing about harm to those we care about is derivative, not fundamental.[8] For in one passage he says it is irrational to bring about harm to those we care about *because* this will result in suffering for oneself (59, 78). Given Gert's view that it is irrational to cause oneself to suffer without adequate reason, it follows that it is irrational to bring about harm to those we care about without adequate reason. But bringing about harm to those we do not care about can also result in suffering for oneself, so at a fundamental level Gert's remarks in this passage suggest that those we care about have no special status in determining our rationality. Hence, Gert suggests, the only irrationality is failing to avoid a harm to oneself or failing to reduce the risk of one's suffering a harm without adequate reason (39, 59). This reading allows us to give a more plausible treatment of differences in ways and degrees of caring because it does not require a cutoff line between those it is irrational to harm and those it is not irrational to harm without reason. The irrationality of harming someone we care about is due to the harm that will be caused to oneself, and this harm might well vary with the way we care and the degree to which we care. This reading also enables Gert to explain away the apparent incoherence I mentioned before, and to do this without supposing that caring can give us reasons. Caring about someone can make an action irrational that would not otherwise be irrational because it can mean that an action would be self-harming that would not otherwise be self-harming. Caring in such cases does not defeat any prior irrationality, so, for Gert, it is not a reason.

The difficulty with this reading is that it has implications that conflict with Gert's apparent understanding of his own view. Gert formulates his position as if he thinks that harms to *people* we care about have a special relevance to the rationality of our actions while harms to *projects* we care about do not. But on the reading I propose, harms to people we care about have no different status than harm to pets we care about and harm to projects or ideals we care about. And if there were pills we could take that would make us immune to feeling bad at harms caused to those we care about, the link between irrationality and harm to those we care about would be broken. It is a superficial link. Gert appears to think it is a much more significant link than this for his formulations often mention harms to self and harms to others we care about in the same breath, as equally significant for the rationality of our actions. Yet his official definition of irrational action mentions only harms to self (83-84), so I shall adopt the reading on which harms to those we care about are only derivatively irrational.

If we adopt this reading, as I recommend, then, in Gert's usage, we can treat the term "irrational" as roughly equivalent in meaning and extension to the phrase "self-harming without adequate reason." As Gert puts it, irrationality consists in "not avoiding harms for oneself without adequate reason" (39).

This reading helps to explain why it is that although a reason can make rationally *permissible* an act that otherwise would be irrational, a reason cannot make rationally *required* an act that would otherwise merely be rationally permissible—unless the reason is a belief about how to avoid harms to *oneself*. In the Baby Rescue Case, for instance, the woman's belief that she can rescue the baby can make it rationally permissible for her to attempt the rescue, but it could not make it rationally required for her to attempt the rescue. That is, it could not make it irrational for her *not* to attempt the rescue. Not to attempt the rescue would not be self-harmful at all, so it could not be self-harmful-without-good-reason. Even in the Baby Rescue with Scuba Gear Case, where we imagined there would be no risk to the woman, the woman's belief gives her a good reason to attempt the rescue, but it cannot make it irrational for her not to attempt the rescue. This is because merely to carry on with her exploration of the river bottom could not be self-harmful-without-good-reason because it would not be self-harmful at all. Since the woman's reason to rescue the child cannot make it irrational for her *not* to attempt the rescue, it cannot make it rationally required that she attempt the rescue.

Harms and Goods

As we have seen, Gert's theory treats a list of harms as fundamental to the concepts of rational action and of a reason for action. It is irrational to bring about or to create a risk of causing a harm to oneself, unless one has adequate reason. There is reason to avoid bringing about or creating a risk of such a harm to any other person. There is also reason to bring about corresponding goods to any person. But might it not be irrational to fail to seek a good, whether for oneself or for someone else?

Gert appears to be ambivalent about this. There are certain goods, Gert says, that no rational person would give up or avoid without reason, including consciousness, ability, freedom, and pleasure (94), but this does not mean that these goods are such that any rational person would seek them. He says, "When an action involves no risk of harm to oneself, then it is rationally allowed to act for no reason at all, but simply on a whim or because one feels like doing so" (60). The remark suggests Gert thinks that it is not irrational to fail to seek a significant amount of additional ability, freedom, or pleasure, for no reason at all. But in another passage he says, "if one is not *deprived*, it is not irrational not to make any effort to gain a significant amount of additional ability, freedom, or pleasure" (92, my emphasis). Here, Gert appears to be allowing that one might be rationally required to seek additional ability, freedom, or pleasure, if one is deprived. Perhaps he thinks that to fail to attempt to get out of a state of deprivation is to countenance harm and that this is why it would be irrational not to try to get more of a good in order to get out of a state of deprivation.[9] If so, we can take his official position to be that it is irrational not to try to avoid harms, and it is not irrational to fail to seek additional goods unless doing so amounts to failing to avoid a harm. On this view, however, as Gert says, still with apparent ambivalence, "there *seems to be* an asymmetry in rationality between seeking additional goods and losing the goods one already has" (92, my emphasis). The idea that there is this asymmetry is problematic.

To assess the idea, we need to consider a case where deprivation is not an issue. If I stare at the sun, I will lose my vision. If I stare with my right eye, I will lose the vision in that eye, but I will not necessarily count as deprived as a result. For I will still be able to see with my left eye, and there might be corrective lenses that compensate for any loss of visual acuity that would otherwise be caused by the loss of vision in one eye. Let us assume that I have been given lenses of this kind so that the example can serve us as an example of a case in which I have suffered a loss but I am not deprived. Gert's position implies, quite plausibly, that I was irrational to cause myself to lose the vision in my right eye without good reason. But the situation I am now in, we are supposing, is that I already have no vision in my right eye. Suppose that my vision in the right eye can be restored painlessly by a quick and virtually risk-free operation. Gert's position implies that I would not be irrational to refuse the operation for no reason at all, simply on a whim. I find this quite implausible. It implies the possibility of one action's being irrational because it would involve the agent's knowingly choosing to be in condition *A* rather than condition *B*, while another action is not irrational even though it would involve the agent's knowingly choosing to be in condition *A* rather than condition *B*, where the only relevant difference between the actions is that in the case of the first, the agent began by being in condition *B*, while in the case of the second, the agent began by being in condition *A*. Imagine that the actions are cost-free, except for the fact that they leave the agent in condition *A*, and imagine that they bring no other benefits or harms to anyone at all. In my example, the choice is between being blind in my right eye and having sight in my right eye. In the "blinding scenario," imagine that staring at the sun is painless. In the "operation scenario," imagine that the operation is painless and risk-free. It seems quite implausible to hold that it would be irrational to stare at the sun in the knowledge that that will result in my being blind in the right eye but to deny that it would be irrational to refuse the operation in the knowledge that that will result in my continuing to be blind in the right eye when there is no relevant difference between the acts other than the fact that the status quo in the one case is that I am sighted in both eyes while the status quo in the other case is that I am blind in my right eye. It is difficult to see this differencc in the status quo to be relevant to the rationality of the actions.[10]

Gert suggests that we test the adequacy of a theory of rationality by asking what kinds of action are such that "every fully informed rational person would advocate that all persons for whom they are concerned, including themselves," never perform an act of that kind. For he thinks an action is irrational just in case (approximately) "every fully informed rational person would advocate that all persons for whom they are concerned, including themselves, never do that act" (31). We would not want our friends to stare at the sun, and thereby lose the vision in one of their eyes, without good reason. But if a friend had done this, we would not want her to refuse the operation. To paraphrase Gert, "would anyone favor people for whom one is concerned not [having an operation] that, with no side effects, will result in their no longer [being blind in one eye]?" (44) If Gert agrees that the answer to this question is negative, then he ought to draw the conclusion that not having the operation would be irrational.

The argument I have been giving suggests it is a mistake for Gert to identify irrationality with "not avoiding harms to oneself without adequate reason" (39). We were given no argument for identifying irrationality with failing to avoid harm except for appeals to examples and appeals to the above test. But if I am correct, the test suggests that failure to seek certain goods can also be irrational even when it does not amount to countenancing harm. Now I want to argue that when we value certain things, such as intellectual stimulation, or a certain life project, attaining these things can be good for us, and we can be irrational not to pursue or to seek these things.

Suppose that I have built my life around doing philosophy, and suppose I realize that burning my manuscript will destroy the product of all these years of writing. I have no reason to burn it. Burning it will not prevent or reduce the probability of anyone's being harmed nor will it benefit anyone. It seems clear in this case that I have good reason *not* to burn my manuscript and that I would be *irrational* to burn it, given its importance to my life project. Yet Gert's position implies that I would *not* be irrational to burn the manuscript, unless I know or should know, for example, that burning it will cause me some form of harm, such as unhappiness or regret. Indeed, his position implies that I have *no reason* not to burn the manuscript unless I believe that not burning it will either prevent or reduce the probability of someone's being harmed or bring someone a benefit. And only benefits and harms of the kinds that are on Gert's list can be brought into play. Intellectual stimulation and the pursuit of a life project are not on the list. It is true that if I value success in my life project, and if I have built my life around writing the manuscript, I am likely to regret burning it. But this does not seem to me to be sufficient to explain the irrationality of burning it. For suppose that I have a pill that will eliminate any regret I might otherwise feel if I were to burn the manuscript as well as give me a surge of compensating pleasure. I realize that if I take the pill as I light the manuscript on fire, I will not feel any significant regret or otherwise suffer from the loss of the manuscript. On this assumption, Gert's view implies that I have *no* reason not to burn it since, as we are assuming, I believe that burning it will not bring anyone a listed harm or deprive anyone of a listed benefit. His view also implies that I would not be irrational to burn it since I realize that burning it will not bring me any listed harm. In short, Gert is committed to saying that my life project and the fact that I value intellectual stimulation have no significance for the rationality of my actions unless, for instance, I know or should know that the pursuit of intellectual stimulation through my project brings me pleasure that could not be replaced by any other pleasure or helps me to avoid boredom or regret I could not otherwise avoid. These implications of Gert's view seem implausible, and they are implausible by the lights of Gert's own test for the adequacy of a theory of rationality. For we would not want anyone we care about to destroy the fruits of his life project in a situation in which doing so would neither prevent a harm to anyone nor bring about a benefit to anyone.

I am arguing in part that Gert's list of benefits and harms is incomplete, and I am also arguing that it can be irrational to fail to seek certain goods, as in the example of the operation to restore my eyesight. Most important, I am arguing that there are goods whose status as goods with the power to rationalize our actions depends on what we value. We have reason to pursue intellectual stimulation in part because we value intellectual activities and the stimulation they can give us. The reason it would be irrational for me to destroy my manuscript, given that nothing would be gained for anyone by my destroying it, is that the manuscript is the product of my life project, the project that is central to all that I value.

Reasons, Values, and Desire

Perhaps, however, Gert has an argument against my suggestion that our values give us reasons. He argues that "a belief that an action will satisfy one's desire is never a reason for doing that action" (62). Given this, if to value something is to have a kind of desire, Gert's argument would presumably show that a belief that an action would help to promote something one values is not a reason for doing the action. Of course, it might not be correct that to value something is to have a kind of desire for it, but the issue is beyond the scope of this paper. Let me simply assume here that to value something is to have a kind of desire.

Gert argues that since there can be irrational desires, which are "desires it is irrational to act on without a reason," it follows that "the belief that one's action will satisfy one's desire is not a reason for acting" (62). Given this, then if we assume both that values are a kind of desire and that there can be irrational values, it follows, by parity of reasoning, that the belief that an action will satisfy a value that one has is not a reason for acting. But I think that this does not follow. What would follow is something weaker than this. For suppose that one quite reasonably believes that there is nothing irrational about a value that one has. In this case, for all that Gert's argument shows, it could be the case that the belief that an action will satisfy that value is a reason for doing the action. There is nothing irrational about intellectual stimulation, for instance. Intellectual stimulation is a rationally permitted value. So for all that Gert's argument has shown, it might well be the case that if I believe that reading a particular book would give me intellectual stimulation, which I know I value, and if I realize there is nothing irrational about valuing intellectual stimulation, then I have reason to read the book.

Gert admits that "there is a sense of 'a reason' in which a desire does provide a reason." But he says, "this sense of 'a reason' has nothing to do with rationality; it simply explains one's actions. A reason must be able to make some otherwise irrational action rational" (63). Gert would say that I need no reason to read a book that will give me intellectual stimulation. So, he would say, citing this fact cannot show that my valuing intellectual stimulation gives me a reason to read the book. "[C]iting an action for which one needs no reason cannot show that [a value gives one] a reason" (63). The fact that I value intellectual stimulation might explain my reading the book, but it could not make reading the book rational in a case in which it would otherwise be irrational. But why couldn't it?

Suppose I have difficulty reading. Reading causes me eyestrain, which is mildly painful. On Gert's view, it would therefore be irrational to read a book without an adequate reason. But if I value intellectual stimulation, then, knowing that this value is rationally permitted, would I not be rational to read the book? Gert would agree that if reading the book will give me pleasure, then I can be rational to read it even though doing so will give me eyestrain (63). But perhaps I believe that reading the book will not give me pleasure. Suppose I think reading this book will be difficult work, but stimulating. I do not anticipate experiencing pleasure from reading it. In this case, Gert would have to say that I might have no reason to read the book. But it seems to me that I have the reason that reading the book will give me something I value, namely, intellectual stimulation. This seems enough to rationalize my action. If I value intellectual stimulation and believe I can get it from reading the book, then it seems to me that I would be rationally permitted to read the book given that intellectual stimulation is a rationally permitted value. It appears, therefore, that the fact that I value intellectual stimulation could make it rational to read a book in a case in which it would otherwise be irrational.

Gert's argument here turns on the thesis that "A reason must be able to make some otherwise irrational action rational" (63). It is not clear why he believes this. The fact that I value intellectual stimulation could justify reading a more stimulating book rather than a less stimulating book. Why is this not sufficient to show that the fact that I value intellectual stimulation can give me a reason?

This leaves the issue of irrational values. In Gert's scheme, such values would be self-destructive values or self-harmful ones. Of course, virtually any value might in some circumstances recommend an action that risks harm to oneself. In the Baby Rescue Case, for example, if the woman values helping people, she has reason to risk her life to save the baby. But this is not an example of a self-harmful value. When I speak of self-harmful values, I have in mind instances in which a person values one of the things or values risking one of the things on Gert's list of harms, such as death, disability, pain, loss of pleasure, or loss of freedom. Perhaps it would be irrational to act on such a value. But there is no conflict between this claim and the claim that I have been defending, which is that a rationally permitted value can rationalize action.

A Proposal: Values and Self-Government

The examples we have discussed suggest that although Gert has a hold on the elephant, he has not seen its true shape and size, nor the underlying skeleton that holds it up. Earlier in the paper, I complained that Gert's list theory left certain important questions unanswered, including especially the question why the various items on his list of irrational kinds of action belong on the list. The basic idea in Gert's view seems to be that it is irrational to risk harm to oneself without adequate reason. For this reason, I proposed taking it to be primitive that it is irrational to risk harm to oneself without adequate reason rather than taking as primitive the irrationality of doing the kinds of things on Gert's list without adequate reason. But even with this amendment, Gert's theory would leave unexplained why it is irrational to risk harm to oneself without adequate reason. In this section, I want to propose an explanation for this.

We can bring a variety of standards to bear on the evaluation of a person's actions. We can ask whether her actions are lawful, whether they are polite, whether they are prudent, whether they are morally permissible. Our question is about the standard relevant to assessing the *rationality* of our actions. What is the content of this standard? What makes it relevantly authoritative? There are a variety of views about the content of the standard. According to one view, rationality is a matter of appropriate responsiveness to all the reasons there are, whether they be moral reasons or reasons of any other kind. Call this the "comprehensive view" since it holds that evaluation of actions for their rationality takes into account the results of all other evaluations of our actions and offers an all-things-considered evaluation. Other views are more limited in that they take rational evaluation to be one kind of evaluation alongside others, and they do not take rational evaluation to be all-things-considered evaluation. The view that rationality is a matter of acting in one's self-interest is a limited view,[11] and so is Gert's view that rationality is a matter of avoiding self-harmful actions without adequate reason. What we are looking for, then, is a standard that provides for a limited kind of evaluation of actions. Failure to comply with the standard should seem a significant kind of failure, a failure of a kind that virtually everyone would want to avoid, such that it would be appropriate to call it "irrational." The account should accommodate and ground Gert's intuition that rationality requires avoiding risking harm to oneself without adequate reason. It should also accommodate the bulk of our intuitions in the cases I have been discussing.

We can evaluate a person on the basis of how well she is doing at *self-government*, where governing oneself consists in acquiring a coherent view of what is important in life and then living in accord with this view. It would be too much to expect that people have "life plans" in the sense that philosophers sometimes have in mind,[12] but, in my view, our having values consists at least in part in our having policies or general intentions about how to live our lives. We could then view our values as constituting partial plans for our lives. It seems to me that in normal circumstances where a person fails to have a coherent set of policies or values, or fails to act in accord with such policies, it makes sense to describe her as acting irrationally. This is a significant kind of failure that most people would want to avoid. For it is a failure to act in accord with what the person herself values in the situation, and this means it is a failure to act in accord with standards that the person herself cares to comply with.

The idea that rationality is a matter of self-government can go some distance toward accommodating Gert's intuition that one would be irrational to risk various listed harms without adequate reason. For many of the harms on Gert's list would tend to undermine a person's ability to govern her life in accord with her values. But Gert also thinks that we can never be rationally required to risk such harms. To see a possible basis for this idea, we need to understand that it is not always a failure of self-government to fail to act in accord with what our values would dictate. We can rationally decide to change our values at the point of action, for example, or to modify or to suspend them or to make an exception, at least in certain kinds of circumstances. But what interests me here is the idea that there can be "emergency" circumstances in which it is rational to suspend acting in accord with our values in order to preserve our ability to act in accord with our values. The woman in the Baby Rescue Case is in an emergency situation of this kind, if we assume that attempting to rescue the child is the act most recommended by her values, for she is in a situation in which acting on her values would put her life at risk. It would be a clear failure of self-government if a person ignored her values on a whim or momentary impulse. But a person who does not act on her values in an emergency situation in order to preserve her ability to be self-governing is not necessarily acting on a whim. A whim is something like a momentary desire that involves a change of mind that makes no sense. But if a person is in an emergency situation where her ability to serve her values is at risk, and if she chooses not to serve her values in order to preserve her ability to govern her life, her decision makes sense. It does involve a change of mind, and she might later feel regret. For example, she might have done something wrong by her own lights. Yet sometimes we feel regret even when we do what is *best* by the light of our values, for sometimes when we do what is best we fail to do well by something else that we value. So the fact that the person in an emergency situation who acts to preserve her ability to be self-governing might experience regret, and the fact that she does not act in accord with her values, are not enough to show that her action makes no sense. It seems to me that we cannot sensibly view her choice as showing a failure of self-government since she acts to preserve her ability to be self-governing.

In emergency situations, self-government pulls in two directions. On the one hand, it is no failure of self-government to act in accord with one's values. On the other hand, since doing so would put at risk one's ability to be self-governing, it is no failure of self-government not to act on one's values but to act instead to preserve this ability. Hence, it seems, failing to act in accord with one's values in such circumstances can exhibit good self-government, but so can acting in accord with one's values. In emergency situations, a person rationally may to do either thing.

Here, then, is a proposed standard of rationality that accounts, I think, for at least certain of Gert's central intuitions about the irrationality of self-harmful actions:

> a person is to have a coherent set of values and to govern her behavior so as to best serve these values, as assessed in light of her own epistemic situation, except that, in "emergency situations," she may instead act to secure her ability so to govern her behavior.

Call this the "autonomy standard."[13] In a nutshell, it calls on us to manifest or to secure our ability to be self-governing.

I will not be able to answer all questions that this formulation of the autonomy standard is likely to prompt, but I do want to attempt briefly to explain the basis for the standard as I see it. According to the conception of rationality that is expressed in this standard, the point of acting rationally is to manifest or secure self-government. *Irrationality* is a kind of failure to serve our *autonomy*. But if this is so, then in a situation in which acting in accord with our values would undermine our autonomy, or put it at risk, rationality must not require us to act on our values. For in such a situation, we would manifest or exemplify our self-government by governing ourselves in accord with our values, but we would also serve it and manifest it by acting to sustain our ability to be self-governing, which would mean declining to act in accord with our values. Given my proposal about the point of acting rationally, then, in emergency situations of the kind in question, rationality must permit us not to act in accord with our values in order to secure our autonomy. This is why the autonomy standard includes the exception for emergency situations.

We want more for our children and for people we care about than that they merely be rational. We also want them to be wise, to be morally upright, and to have a sense of fulfillment from their lives. We can be critical of their values.[14] But, on the conception of rationality that I am proposing, insofar as we want them to be rational, we want them in ordinary situations to govern their lives on the basis of their values. Wanting this for them does not always mean wanting them to do the thing that is most recommended by their values since in some extraordinary situations doing this thing would risk undermining their ability to carry on and govern their own lives. Insofar as we want those we care about to govern their own lives, we would be ambivalent in cases in which their values recommend doing something that would risk undermining their ability to govern their own lives. This ambivalence is reflected in the autonomy standard, which gives an agent the option of doing what is recommended by her values or of doing what will protect her ability to govern her life.

Consider then the rescue cases. My view implies that it is irrational for the woman to risk her life in these cases unless there is something she values that is at stake. This is because, in risking her life, she is risking her ability to govern her life on the basis of her values, or on the basis of anything else, for that matter. In the example of the eye operation, my position, unlike Gert's, implies that I have the same basic reason to regain my eyesight if it has been lost as I have to preserve my eyesight if it has not been lost. The reason is that the lack of eyesight, even if only in one eye, might interfere with my ability to achieve or to pursue what I value. In the manuscript example, since the manuscript is the product of my life project, which is central to all that I value, I will govern my life around the pursuit of this project, and if I am rational I will not intentionally destroy the manuscript except in extraordinary circumstances where something else that I value is at stake or where my ability to govern myself at all is at stake.

The picture I am proposing accounts for Gert's hypothesis that certain concerns have a special status in the life of a rational person. It accounts for the special status of concern to avoid death or the permanent loss of consciousness, concern to avoid being disabled, and concern to avoid the loss of freedom. For to suffer one of these harms is to suffer harm to one's ability to govern one's life, to achieve what one values. But my picture does not account for the status that Gert gives to a concern to avoid pain and other unpleasant feelings and a concern to avoid loss of pleasure. I think that Gert is mistaken to suppose that pain and pleasure have the status he gives them. Their status is derivative, I think, from the fact that we normally value pleasure and disvalue pain, and from the fact that, of course, pain can make it difficult for us to achieve what we value in life. It can be debilitating. But if I value doing philosophy, the pain and frustration of working on a manuscript is no reason to stop working on it, especially if I set no value in avoiding this pain. If doing philosophy in a serious way prevents me from having the time for certain pleasures that I do not especially value, this also is no reason to do less philosophy, not even if I get no pleasure from doing philosophy because of my dour nature. Presumably all of us do value a variety of pleasures and all of us disvalue pain and see that pain can be distracting and debilitating. So in most cases where an action risks pain or the loss of pleasure, my account and Gert's account will give us similar results. But the underlying point, I think, is that rationality consists in manifesting or securing our ability to be self-governing. It is because this is so that Gert's theory has the plausibility it does, given the values we have, and given that the harms on Gert's list interfere with our ability to govern ourselves by our values.

Gert is correct, I believe, to reject the common idea that rationality is a matter of acting in one's self-interest, as this idea is commonly understood. On reflection, the idea seems implausible since we value much that is not especially in our *self*-interest. Desire-satisfaction theories implicitly concede that rationality is not simply a matter of acting in one's self-interest, since the things we desire include many things that are not especially in our self-interest. But a rational person is able to decide on the basis of her values not to permit certain of her desires to establish goals for her to pursue.[15] A rational person governs herself on the basis of her values in this way, not simply on the basis of her desires. Nevertheless, a rational person would not necessarily permit herself to be led by her values to sacrifice her ability to govern her life. Insofar as Gert's list of irrational actions is well grounded, it is a list of kinds of actions that would undermine our ability to be self-governing. I agree with him that we are irrational to perform such actions unless we have adequate reason and that even when we have good reason so to act, we are not rationally required to do so. Gert's groundbreaking account of rationality points the way to this conclusion.[16]

Notes

1. Bernard Gert, *Morality: Its Nature and Justification* (New York: Oxford University Press, 1998). References to the book will be found in parentheses in the text. In the Preface (ix), Gert describes this book as "the last major revision of the moral theory that was first published in 1970." See Bernard Gert, *The Moral Rules: A New Rational Foundation for Morality* (New York: Harper and Row, 1970).

2. Derek Parfit, *Reasons and Persons* (Oxford, Eng.: Oxford University Press, 1984), 3.

3. Parfit, *Reasons and Persons*, 4. I have slightly modified Parfit's characterization of these positions. Parfit's classification does not comfortably accommodate Aristotelian perfectionist theories, so I do not believe it is exhaustive. Aristotelian theories propose a notion of excellence, or of human flourishing, and claim that what is best for a person is what would most contribute to or manifest his excellence. They therefore could be classified as self-interest theories, but they do not fit neatly into Parfit's categories. They do not qualify as hedonistic or desire-fulfillment theories since they do not explain the notion of the best for a person simply in terms of happiness or desire fulfillment. Nor do they qualify as objective list theories since they offer a unified characterization of the subject matter of rationality.

4. As we will see, Gert does propose a test for the adequacy of a theory of rationality (31), but it is a test for theories, not a definition of rationality. The test could perhaps be described as epistemically prior to Gert's theory, since we use it to test the adequacy of the theory, but the lists are basic in the theory so tested.

5. Gert's "final definition" of irrational action is more complex than this informal statement. Moreover, it does not include the provision that it is irrational to do something that will increase the risk of harm to some other person provided one cares about that person (83-84). I will discuss the provision for those we care about later in the paper.

6. As we will see, the notion of harm is defined in terms of rationality, rationality is defined in terms of irrationality, and irrationality is defined in terms of a list. I will not challenge Gert's view that reasons are beliefs, but it does need to be challenged. So does Gert's specific view that reasons are beliefs to the effect that an ac-

tion would be of kind *H*, where *H* is a kind of action that is on his list. First, suppose that someone believes doing *A* would be of a relevant kind *H* but believes that this is no reason to do *A*. In this case, it is hard to see how the person's belief that *A* would be of kind *H* could make sense of her doing *A*. Suppose that doing *A* would risk her life and she believes she has no reason to do *A* although doing *A* would be of kind *H*. It is tempting to think that it would be irrational for her to do *A*. The example tends to put in question Gert's view that reasons are beliefs to the effect that an action would be of some listed kind. Second, consider a belief that one has a reason to do something. Apparently Gert would hold that such a belief is *not* a reason; such a belief cannot make an action rational that would otherwise be irrational. On Gert's view, the belief that one has a reason to do *A* is true only if one has another belief, a belief to the effect that A would be of kind *H*, where *H* is listed. Beliefs about reasons are beliefs about beliefs with a relevant content. This is an odd position. Moreover, if the belief that one has a reason to do *A* is not a reason to do *A*, then, in Gert's view, such a belief cannot make doing *A* rational if doing *A* would otherwise be irrational. One might propose instead that it is rational to do what one rationally believes one has adequate reason to do. Scanlon holds that rationality consists in acting on one's beliefs about the reasons one has. T. M. Scanlon, *What We Owe to Each Other* (Cambridge, Mass.: Harvard University Press, 1998), 25.

7. Also relevant is the fact, which I discussed in the preceding note, that, for Gert, the belief that one has a reason to do something is no reason to do it. Such a belief cannot make an action rational that would otherwise be irrational.

8. In personal correspondence, Gert confirmed that this is his view.

9. In personal correspondence, Gert suggested that this is his view.

10. John Deigh and Douglas MacLean pointed out to me the relevance of "prospect theory" to these issues. I do not have the space to address prospect theory in this paper. See Daniel Kahneman and Amos Tversky, "Prospect Theory: An Analysis of Decisions under Risk," *Econometrica* 47 (1979): 313-27.

11. That is, it is a limited view provided it is accompanied by the recognition of other kinds of reasons, such as moral reasons. It is not necessarily a limited view.

12. In *A Theory of Justice* (Cambridge, Mass.: Harvard University Press, 1971), John Rawls proposed that we understand a person's good to be defined by a coherent life plan. We could view rationality as a matter of governing one's life in accord with such a plan.

13. I proposed a similar account in David Copp, *Morality, Normativity, and Society* (New York: Oxford University Press, 1995). See also "Rationality, Autonomy, and Basic Needs," in *Being Human*, ed. Neil Roughley (Berlin: de Gruyter, 2001); and "Grounding a Modest Conception of Rationality," forthcoming.

14. A person can value the things "or value risking the things" on Gert's list of harms, such as her own death, disability, pain, loss of pleasure, or loss of freedom. A person can also value or intend to promote the absence in herself of certain conditions of self-government, such as the ability to revise her own values. Leaving aside pain and loss of pleasure, let us call these values "irrational" on the ground that their content is such that promoting them would tend to undermine a person's ability to be self-governing. As I have formulated it, the standard of autonomy does not require that one have no values that are irrational in this sense. One might think that it should require this, but I want to leave the matter open.

15. This point has been made before by several writers. See, for example, Michael Bratman, "Identification, Decision, and Treating as a Reason," *Philosophical Topics* 24 (1996): 1-18. Bratman cites Rachel Cohon, "Internalism about Reasons for Action," *Pacific Philosophical Quarterly* 74 (1993): 265-88.

16. I am grateful to those who discussed an earlier draft of this paper with me at the 1999 Dartmouth College conference on Gert's Moral Theory. I am especially grateful to Daniel Bush, Bernard Gert, Stephen Nathanson, Geoffrey Sayre-McCord, Walter Sinnott-Armstrong, and Michael Smith.

6

Bernard Gert's Complex Hybrid Conception of Rationality*

Michael Smith

In the early chapters of his comprehensive, original, and startlingly systematic *Morality: Its Nature and Justification*, Bernard Gert argues that our concept of rationality—or, more accurately, our concept of practical rationality—has a hitherto unrecognized "complex hybrid" character.

> It is the failure to recognize the hybrid character of rationality that is responsible for the inadequacy of all the previous accounts of that concept. . . . It is only by recognizing the hybrid character of rationality, acknowledging that it has both an egocentric part (irrational actions) and a nonegocentric component (reasons), that an adequate definition can be formulated. (83)[1]

Despite Gert's various ingenious arguments for this claim, and the many lessons about the concept of rationality that he teaches us while arguing for it, I remain skeptical. Not only does an alternative theory of rationality, a version of what he calls the "cool moment" desire theory (42-44), seem to me invulnerable to his main objection, a version of that theory also, in my view, provides us with a far more plausible conception of practical rationality than the complex hybrid conception Gert recommends. So, at any rate, I wish to argue here.

The Commonsense Conception

Like all philosophical theories, theories of practical rationality must ultimately answer to the court of commonsense. Let me therefore begin by briefly explaining what I take the commonsense conception to be.

As I understand it, the commonsense conception of practical rationality has the concept of a reason for action at its very core. There are various reasons for action, where reasons for action are thought of as facts about which agents can gain knowledge via reflection. Moreover, some of these reasons are egocentric in character, whereas others are nonegocentric. The reasons we each have to avoid harm to ourselves, to help our friends, and the like, are in the former category—a specification of their content requires an ineliminable reference to oneself—and the reasons we each have to prevent the suffering of sentient creatures quite generally are in the latter.

Reasons, in turn, whether egocentric or nonegocentric, have different weights. Sometimes egocentric reasons outweigh nonegocentric reasons (the reason to provide a benefit of a certain magnitude to oneself, or a member of one's immediate family, or a friend, is weightier than the reason to provide that same level of benefit to a complete stranger); sometimes nonegocentric reasons outweigh egocentric reasons (the reason to prevent misery to a million strangers is weightier than the reason to prevent that same level of misery to oneself, or a member of one's immediate family, or a friend); and sometimes egocentric and nonegocentric reasons are of much the same weight (perhaps the reason to provide a benefit of a certain magnitude to oneself, or a member of one's immediate family, or a friend, has much the same weight as the reason to provide that same level of benefit to two [or maybe it is three or four. . .] complete strangers).

These various reasons with their associated weights are, in turn, capable of explaining what agents do, at least in those favorable cases in which agents know about their existence and give them the weight that they in fact have. But knowledge of the reasons that there are is sometimes impossible to gain. In determining the rationality of an agent's actions, the commonsense conception of practical rationality therefore insists that we ask not whether agents act as they have reason to, but rather whether they act (or whether it is as if they act) as they believe that they have reason to, and whether these beliefs about the reasons that there are, in turn, elude various ordinary forms of rational criticism to which all beliefs are subject.

When these conditions are met—and when various other familiar conditions on intentional action are met as well—the commonsense conception tells us that the actions in question are rational, and when they aren't, it tells us that we have a case of irrational action. Agents may therefore act rationally without acting as they have reason to, and they may act as they have reason to without acting rationally. What is important to determining the rationality of agents' actions is rather whether they act as they believe that they have reason to, and whether these beliefs are in turn well-grounded.[2]

My claim in what follows is to be that a version of the cool moment desire theory is preferable to Gert's complex hybrid conception of rationality inter alia because that theory better squares with this commonsense conception. Of course, if I am wrong that the conception of practical rationality just described is commonsensical, then my objections to Gert's complex hybrid conception will simply fail. But here is not the place to argue about that. Rather, assuming that the conception just described is commonsensical, I want to focus instead on which theory better squares with it.

Outline of Gert's Complex Hybrid Conception of Rationality

Here is Gert's full-dress definition of rational action.

> An act is irrational if and only if it is an intentional action of a person with sufficient knowledge and intelligence to be fully informed about that action and who, if fully informed, (1) would believe that the action involved significantly increased risk of his suffering death, nontrivial pain, loss of ability, loss of freedom, or loss of pleasure and (2) would not have an adequate reason for the action. A reason for acting is a conscious rational belief that one's action will increase the probability of someone's avoiding

> any of the harms listed above or gaining greater consciousness, ability, freedom, or pleasure. A reason is adequate if any significant group of moral agents regard the harm or benefit gained as compensating for the harm suffered. Any intentional action that is not irrational is rational. (83-84)

Let me bring out some of the crucial features and implications of this definition.

To begin, the definition assumes, rightly I think, that the only people who can act irrationally are those who have the capacity to be fully informed about their actions.[3] Those who are incapable of forming beliefs about the chances that their actions will have the features that they have—including that they cause harms such as death, pain, loss of ability, loss of freedom, and loss of pleasure, or that they cause compensating benefits in terms of someone or other's avoiding these harms or gaining increases in consciousness, ability, freedom, or pleasure—cannot act irrationally. But those who are capable of forming such beliefs may well act irrationally even when they act in ignorance of relevant considerations. Specifically, they act irrationally when they could and should have known better. I take it that this is why Gert couches his definition in counterfactual terms: "if fully informed, would. . . ."

Second, Gert's definition entails that it is always irrational for an agent to act so as to knowingly harm himself—that is, knowingly to cause himself pain or death or loss of ability or freedom or pleasure—without adequate reason. Thus, according to Gert's definition, people are one and all rationally required not to harm themselves without adequate reason. The concept of rational action is therefore substantive and egocentric: it gives special significance to the effects of an agent's own actions on himself. Here, in Gert's view, we see the grain of truth that lies in egoism.

Third, the definition entails that it may nonetheless be rational to act so as to knowingly harm oneself. For someone who knowingly harms himself in the presence of a conscious rational belief that his action will bring compensating benefits for himself or someone else thereby acts with adequate reason, and so does not act irrationally. Moreover, the strength of the reasons thus provided does not depend on whether the benefits are for the agent himself or for someone else. It is here, according to Gert, that we find the grain of truth that lies in Kantianism. Some reasons for action are nonegocentric, and even in those cases in which there are egocentric reasons, the strength of the egocentric reason is the same as the strength of the corresponding nonegocentric reason. It is thus rationally allowed for people to harm themselves in order to provide benefits either for themselves or for other people. Egoism goes wrong in so far as it denies this. To this extent Gert's definition is both substantive and nonegocentric.

Fourth, and finally, the definition entails that it may, however, nonetheless be rational for someone to act so as to knowingly harm someone else, despite the fact that he has adequate or even stronger reason not to do so. For so long as the action does not harm the agent himself, the definition tells us that the agent does not act irrationally, notwithstanding that he has reasons for acting otherwise. In Gert's view Kantianism goes wrong in so far as it denies this. This is the sense in which Gert's theory is hybrid in character. Contrary to Kantian theories, Gert thus thinks that it is always rationally allowed for people to harm others when doing so will not harm themselves. Here again we see the egocentric character of the concept of rational action. Egoism is once again on the right track.

Critical Discussion of Gert's Conception of Practical Rationality

Gert on Egocentric and Nonegocentric Reasons

According to Gert's theory, practical rationality is a hybrid concept, having "both an egocentric part (irrational actions) and a nonegocentric component (reasons)" (83). Moreover, as I emphasized in drawing out the second and third implications of his theory, he claims that the strength of an egocentric reason is identical to the strength of the corresponding nonegocentric reason. Here, accordingly, we find the first difference between Gert's conception of reasons and the commonsense conception.

As I said at the outset, while the commonsense conception agrees with Gert that there are both egocentric and nonegocentric reasons, it differs from Gert's conception in holding that these reasons may differ in their relative strengths. It holds that though egocentric reasons sometimes outweigh nonegocentric reasons, nonegocentric reasons may sometimes outweigh egocentric reasons, and these reasons may even sometimes be of the same strength. According to Gert, however, this commonsense view rests on a confusion.

> The question whether reasons of self-interest are stronger than reasons involving the interests of others arises only if one confuses reasons with motives. If the amount of harm to be avoided and the benefit to be gained is the same, the reasons involving self-interest cannot make rational any acts that reasons involving the interests of others cannot make rational. Any irrational act that would be made rational by a reason of self-interest would also be made rational by a reason of the same strength involving the interests of others. A mere change of person affected does not affect the strength of a reason. (78)

In other words, those who claim that egocentric and nonegocentric reasons may differ in their relative strengths are misled by the fact that people are sometimes *moved* by the fact that they will suffer a certain amount of harm themselves and left *unmoved* by the fact that others suffer that same amount of harm. But, Gert insists, while this is true it doesn't show that the strength of the reason isn't the same in both cases. It is the same, according to Gert, because a "mere change of person affected does not affect the strength of a reason."

The main problem with this diagnosis, however, is not just that it is at odds with commonsense, but that it is also at odds with Gert's own stated criterion for the way in which the weight of the reasons that there are gets fixed. "A reason is adequate," Gert tells us, "if any significant group of moral agents regard the harm or benefit gained as compensating for the harm suffered" (84). But in that case if, as seems likely given the commonsense view, some significant group of moral agents would each give more weight to their making it less likely that they will suffer greater harm themselves than they would give to their making it less likely that just someone will suffer greater harm, then it surely follows that, even by Gert's own criterion, the reasons have different weights. Gert's claim that a "mere change of person affected does not affect the strength of a reason" thus looks to be false even by his own lights.

The upshot is thus that we can reduce at least some of the distance between Gert's conception of practical rationality and the commonsense conception. On Gert's conception, we should suppose that reasons for action can be both egocentric and nonegocentric and that the weight of these reasons can differ. However we cannot reduce all the distance between Gert's conception of practical rationality and the commonsense conception, for according to the commonsense conception, reasons are facts, whereas according to Gert's conception, reasons are conscious rational beliefs. Let's therefore turn our attention to that aspect of his theory.

Gert on Reasons as Beliefs rather than Facts

Gert gives the following argument in favor of the view that reasons are conscious rational beliefs.

> If facts were reasons, it would weaken the conceptual connection between reasons, the rationality of actions, and the rationality of persons. Many facts are such that not only is the agent unaware of them, no one could be expected to be aware of them. These facts do not affect the rationality of an action when the rationality of an action counts in determining a person's rationality. (65)

He then gives an example that, in his view, illustrates the difficulty.

Imagine someone who acts in a way that she believes will cause her death—she takes an overdose of pills, say—but without believing that her doing so will be compensated for by the harms she prevents or the benefits she produces. However, suppose further that the pills she takes are the antidote to a poison that she unknowingly ingested at some earlier time, so that her act of trying to kill herself, far from causing her death, in fact saves her life. Gert points out that on the view of reasons as facts, this woman might well have acted as she had reason to. But, he insists, it would be extremely misleading to conclude, on this account, that she acted rationally. On the view of reasons as conscious rational beliefs, by contrast, he tells us that there is no reason to suppose that she acted rationally. Indeed, on his own account of irrational action, since the woman had no conscious rational belief that serves as an adequate reason for committing suicide, he claims that it follows that she acted irrationally. This, he tells us, is the right result.

Let me enter a parenthetical remark here. Though Gert claims that his theory would classify this woman's act as irrational rather than rational, it is not at all plain to me that it would do so. For remember, according to Gert's definition, the irrationality of an act does not depend on whether the person who acts *in fact* believes that she is acting in a way that will harm herself, and, if she does, whether she does not *in fact* have a conscious rational belief that provides her with an adequate reason for so acting. Rather it depends on whether she *would* have this constellation of belief and absence of belief if she were fully informed.[4] This was the point I emphasized when I spelled out the first implication of Gert's theory.

Suppose, then, that we add the following details to Gert's story. Though the woman he describes is in fact ignorant, both the fact that she has ingested poison and the fact that the pills that she is about to take are an antidote to that poison are suitably available to her. That is, let's suppose that she would, if fully informed, have both of these beliefs. Then, notwithstanding her actual ignorance, and notwithstanding that she actually acts in the belief that she is committing suicide by taking the pills she takes and that her doing so is not in any way compensated for by harms that she thus avoids or benefits that she thus produces, since, if she were fully informed, she would believe that her action of taking the pills benefits her rather than harms her, it follows that she does not act irrationally. And since acts that are not irrational are rational, so, according to Gert's definition, it would seem to follow that the woman acts rationally, not irrationally. Yet if, as it seems to me, the woman in this more detailed version of Gert's example plainly acts irrationally, then the fact she acts rationally according to Gert's own definition must surely count as an objection to it. Here ends the parenthetical remark.

I cannot see why Gert thinks that his objection to the claim that reasons are facts is so telling. Suppose we agree with him that the only facts that can affect the rationality or irrationality of an action are those of which an agent could have been aware, and suppose that we further agree with him that, since this is so, it follows that reasons cannot be grounded in facts of which agents cannot be aware. I am not positively endorsing the suggestion that we agree with him about this, I am merely suggesting that we imagine ourselves agreeing with him, for the sake of argument. Even with all this agreed it simply doesn't follow that reasons are conscious rational beliefs. All that follows is that, if reasons are facts, then they are facts of which agents could have been aware. But facts of which agents could have been aware are still facts. They are not conscious rational beliefs.

Worse still, it seems to me that Gert saddles those who think that reasons are facts with a view about the rationality of an agent's acts that they simply needn't hold. As I said at the outset, precisely because the commonsense conception holds that reasons are facts of which agents may be *unaware*, it holds that the rationality of an agent's acts is to be determined not by whether she acts in a way that she has reason to act, but rather by whether she acts in the belief that she has an adequate reason for so acting, where that belief eludes rational criticism. Thus, in Gert's example, those who favor the view that reasons are facts can insist that even though the woman did act as she had reason to, since she didn't act in the *belief* that she had that reason she did not, on that account, act rationally. Moreover, they can insist that if the belief about reasons on which she did act was rationally criticizable, then she acted irrationally. As far as I can see, this means that in both of the versions of Gert's example that we have been discussing here, those who hold that reasons are facts will say that the woman acts irrationally. This is the right result.

At one point, Gert seems to suggest that this view about the relationship between reasons and rationality is simply a terminological variation on his own theory of rational action.

> Of course we might distinguish between external and internal reasons. External reasons are facts and are the kind of reason normally referred to when one says "There is a reason." Internal reasons are beliefs and are normally referred to by saying, "One has a reason." If there are external reasons to do something, then if one knows of these facts, one has internal reasons to do it. If one has internal reasons to do something, then one believes that there are external reasons to do it. External reasons determine the external rationality, sometimes misleadingly called the "objective rationality" of an action. Internal reasons determine the internal rationality, sometimes misleadingly called the "subjective rationality" of an action. In the ideal case, which I hope is the normal case, external and internal reasons coincide, so that the external and internal rationality of an action are the same. However, sometimes the external and internal reasons do not coincide. For the ra-

> tionality of actions to have the appropriate relationship to the rationality of persons, internal rationality must be taken as the basic sense of rationality. Accepting internal rationality as the basic sense of rationality is regarding basic reasons as beliefs rather than facts. (65-66)

However it seems to me that this involves a serious misunderstanding.

The commonsense view, at least as I have described it—and, indeed, the view that Gert discusses in the passage just quoted—is one according to which reasons are themselves the objects of those of an agent's beliefs that determine his rationality. In other words, the propositional content of the beliefs that determine the rationality of agents is: that there is a reason for them to act in this way rather than that. The beliefs are thus about reasons, in a primary sense of the word "reason". They are not themselves reasons, in this primary sense. Of course, we can, if we wish, go on to define a secondary sense of the word "reason" to refer to beliefs that are about reasons in the primary sense. This is in effect what Gert imagines us doing in the passage just quoted. But, importantly, reasons in this secondary sense, even if we do choose to define such a sense, are beliefs that are about reasons in the primary sense.

This contrasts strikingly with Gert's own official view about reasons. Gert's official view is that reasons are beliefs which, when possessed by agents whose acts would otherwise be irrational, serve to make those actions rational. An example of such a belief, according to Gert, would be an agent's belief that cutting off his arm will save his life. For if we imagine this belief possessed by an agent who cuts off his poisoned arm to stop the poison spreading to the rest of his body, then, in Gert's view, the fact that the agent has this belief serves to make his cutting off his arm, an act which would otherwise be manifestly irrational, rational.

But we can now see the crucial difference between Gert's official view and the view of reasons described in the passage quoted above. The beliefs that Gert thinks reasons are are not the same as the beliefs that count as reasons in the secondary sense, for the beliefs that Gert thinks reasons are not beliefs about reasons, in a primary sense of the word "reason". Rather they are beliefs about the effects that acts have on the weal and woe of agents. Moreover, for this very reason, we can now see that Gert's theory is seriously problematic. For the acts of agents who act in the belief that their acts will have certain effects on the weal and woe of people, but who do not act in the belief that this sort of consideration is reason-giving, are surely no more rational merely for having been performed in the presence of the belief. Imagine, just to make the point vivid, that the agent believed that the consideration provided a reason *against* so acting. Would it be made rational then? I do not think so.

To have any effect at all upon the rationality of an agent's acts, an agent's belief that his act will have certain effects on the weal and woe of people must therefore be accompanied by the belief that that consideration is reason-giving. In other words, the agent must have a reason in the secondary sense described above, a belief about a reason in a primary sense of the word "reason". The idea that the beliefs that Gert thinks reasons are are capable of making otherwise irrational acts rational all by themselves thus seems to me to be in serious tension with our ordinary ways of thinking and talking about reasons. Despite his suggestion to the contrary, it therefore seems to me that there is no way that Gert can turn the commonsense view I have described into a version of his own theory by a feat of redefinition.

As further proof that this is so—in other words, as further proof that the view I have labeled "commonsense" really is commonsensical—imagine the parallel situation with reasons for belief, a parallel that Gert endorses (66-67). Suppose that someone says to me, "I know that you believe that *q*, but tell me what reasons there are for so believing." If I find myself unable to give an answer to this question then it seems to me that my natural inclination would be to reflect, and perhaps to investigate the world in which we live, in an attempt to discover what reasons there might be for believing that *q*, where this inclination, in turn, would be premised on the idea that reasons are facts, as opposed to beliefs, facts which I can find out about by engaging in acts of reflection and investigation. For it is only if reasons are such facts that I can so much as make sense of the idea that there might be reasons for believing *q* of which I am currently unaware. Moreover and importantly, given that we are comparing our ordinary ways of thinking and talking about reasons with Gert's, the inclination also seems to be premised on the idea that these facts are suitably independent of the acts of reflection and investigation via which I can come to have beliefs about them. There wouldn't, after all, be much point in my reflecting or investigating in order to discover what reasons there are for believing that *q* if the acts of reflection and investigation themselves could *change* the facts about the reasons that there are for believing that *q*.

On Gert's conception of reasons as conscious rational beliefs, however, none of this is true. For, on that conception, since I have no conscious rational belief that makes the belief that *q* rational, the proper answer to the question as to the reasons that there are for believing that *q* is that there aren't any such reasons. Reflection and investigation are thus pointless. Worse still, on that conception it seems that reflection and investigation would simply change the facts about the reasons that there are for believing that *q*. For, on that conception, though there will be reasons to believe that *q* after I reflect and investigate—let's assume that, as a result of reflection and investigation, I would come to believe both that *p* and that *p* entails *q*—the reasons that there will be for believing that *q* will be reasons that the acts of reflection and investigation themselves brought into existence. Engaging in reflection and investigation thus doesn't enable me to detect the preexisting reasons that there are for believing that *q*, it simply enables me to create some reasons for believing that *q*. It is thus, in a more or less quite literal sense, up to me whether or not there are any reasons for believing that *q*.

None of this seems to me to square with our ordinary ways of thinking and talking about reasons. Our ordinary thought and talk about reasons is simply shot through with the assumption that reasons are facts, facts which preexist our acts of reflection and investigation but about which we can form beliefs about by engaging in acts of reflection and investigation. The only conclusion to draw would therefore seem to me to be that we must reject Gert's conception of reasons as conscious rational beliefs and suppose, instead, that reasons are facts.

Gert's Objection to "Cool Moment" Desire Theories

If reasons are facts, then we desperately need to say what sorts of facts they are. My own view is that reasons are facts whose status as reasons is conferred upon them by their relations to idealized psychological facts.[5] Since this is similar to an idea that Gert considers and rejects—the idea that we can define rational action as that which satisfies the desires we would have in a cool moment—I want to consider briefly whether my own view is vulnerable to Gert's objection to cool moment desire theories.

Gert's objection to cool moment desire theories of rationality is, in essence, that they deliver the wrong results. Consider, for example, people who have an untreated mental illness (43). They might well desire, in a cool moment, that they kill themselves, or cause themselves pain, or to lose abilities, or to lose freedom, or to lose pleasure, in circumstances in which their so doing will not be compensated for by the avoidance of greater harms or the production of benefits.[6] But since, according to Gert, it could never be rational to do such a thing, it follows that cool moment desire theories classify as rational acts that are plainly irrational.[7] People are rationally required not to kill themselves when doing so will not be compensated for by the avoidance of greater harms or the production of benefits, no matter whether they happen to desire to do so in a cool moment or not.

An initial response to Gert's objection might be that it shows just that cool moment desire theories require augmentation. Those who accept such theories should say not that it is rational for an agent to do what he would desire himself to do, if he formed his desires in a cool moment, but rather that it is rational for him to do what he would desire himself to do, if he formed his desires in a cool moment, providing that when he forms those desires he is not mentally ill. According to Gert, however, this sort of amendment to a cool moment desire theory is tantamount to giving up the theory altogether. For what defines someone as having a mental illness is, at least in some cases, simply their possession of certain desires, desires which are irrational in a much more fundamental sense, a sense that eludes any illumination at all. Gert makes this point—that the irrationality of certain desires is basic, or fundamental—most forcefully in the following passage.

> I regard this list of five basic irrational desires (the desires for death, pain, disability, loss of freedom, and loss of pleasure) as complete. I cannot prove that it is complete, indeed I cannot prove that any of the desires that I have included in this list are basic irrational desires. I have not derived this list of irrational desires from any more basic account of irrationality. . . . I cannot and would not try to provide arguments for any item on the list. (51)

In Gert's view, then, no further account can therefore be given of the irrationality of desiring death, or pain, or disability, or loss of freedom, or loss of pleasure, in circumstances in which there is no compensation to be gained from the avoidance of greater harms or the production of benefits. The irrationality of these desires is the starting point from which all further conversation and argument about rationality begins. Their irrationality is a given.

Let me now spell out my own view about the nature of reasons in order to see whether it is vulnerable to a similar line of objection. My own view, to repeat, is that reasons are facts whose status as reasons is conferred upon them by their relations to idealized psychological facts. To be a little more precise, in my view the fact that an agent *A* can perform an action of a certain kind *K* in certain circumstances *C* by performing an act of kind *K** in those circumstances constitutes a reason for him to perform an act of kind *K** in *C* if and only if everyone, *A* included, would want that they themselves perform an act of kind *K* in *C* by performing an act of kind *K** in those circumstances if they were fully rational. If we call the possible world in which *A* has the inclinations and beliefs that he has in circumstances *C* the "evaluated" world, and the possible world in which he is fully rational the "evaluating" world, then, the idea is, the facts that constitute *A*'s reasons for acting in the evaluated world have their status as reasons conferred upon them not by what *A*, in the *evaluated* world, wants himself to do in the evaluated world, but rather by what he, in the *evaluating* world, wants himself to do in the evaluated world.

Thus, to illustrate, as I see things the fact that, in certain circumstances *C*, an agent's cutting off his arm will save his life constitutes a reason for him to cut off his arm in those circumstances if and only if everyone, *A* included, in possible worlds in which they are fully rational, want that, in possible worlds in which they themselves are in circumstances *C*, they save their own lives by cutting off their own arms. The fact that constitutes the agent's reason to cut off his arm—the fact that he can save his life by so doing—thus has its status as a reason is conferred upon it by its relation to idealized psychological facts, facts about the desires of fully rational creatures.

Note that this account of reasons provides us with an intuitive and compelling account of the nature of reasons for and against acting in a certain way. This is because, with regard to a particular set of circumstances, a fully rational agent could have several conflicting desires about what is to be done. Thus, for example, an agent might have a reason to cut off his arm in certain circumstances *C* because, if he were fully rational, he would want himself to do what is required to save his life, and cutting off his arm is what is required. And he might also have a reason not to cut off his arm in those same circumstances because he will cause himself pain by doing so, and, if he were fully rational, he would want himself to do what is required to prevent himself from feeling pain. The agent thus has a reason for and against cutting off his arm, and what he has reason to do all things considered is therefore fixed by the relative strengths of such desires: that is, by facts about what his fully rational self would overall want, or most want, himself to do in the relevant circumstances.[8]

The attraction of this sort of view, much as with the attraction of cool moment desire theories quite generally, should be plain. It is, after all, extremely plausible to suppose that what an agent has a reason to do is whatever someone perfectly placed to give the agent advice would advise him to do. But the person who is best placed to give an agent advice is simply himself, minus all of his imperfections and idiosyncrasies. It is the agent himself, in the possible world in which he is fully rational. In effect, the account of reasons just described simply makes this idea more precise. For the advice a fully rational agent would give is simply an expression of his overall preference among the various options that are available in the circumstances of action in the context of which he is giving advice.

At this point, Gert's objection might seem to loom large. For, he might say, the plausibility of the account of reasons just given is entirely dependent on the answer to a so far unanswered question. What makes an agent *fully rational*? It appears that we face a dilemma. On the first horn, we give an account of what it is to be fully rational that does not simply reduce to saying what Gert says. In other words, we give an account that does not amount to saying that to be fully rational is, inter alia, to lack desires for death, pain, disability, loss of freedom, and loss of pleasure in circumstances in which no compensation is to be gained from the avoidance of harms or the production of benefits. On this horn, Gert might say, the account of reasons is vulnerable to the same objection he made to cool moment desire theories. For such a theory is consistent with something that is manifestly false, namely, that agents can have reason to kill themselves in circumstances in which no compensation is to be gained from the avoidance of harms or the production of benefits. On the other horn of the dilemma, we say exactly what Gert says. In other words, we say that to be fully rational an agent must, inter alia, lack desires for death, pain, disability, loss of freedom, and loss of pleasure in circumstances in which no compensation is to be gained from the avoidance of harms or the production of benefits. But once we say this we abandon the project of giving an account of reasons of the sort just described in favor of adopting a view like Gert's. The fundamental idea lying behind the concept of a reason is conveyed by Gert's list of five basic irrational desires.

My own view is that we should grasp the first horn of this dilemma. However, in order to see why the first horn isn't as problematic as Gert supposes, we must first think a little more carefully about Gert's own positive view, his view that irrational desires are defined by a *list* of the five desires already mentioned. What really drives Gert in the direction of this positive view? The answer, it seems to me, is that Gert is driven to the view that irrational desires are defined by a list because of the high degree of confidence he supposes us all to have that the desires for death, pain, disability, loss of freedom, and loss of pleasure are indeed irrational. Indeed, as the argument given on the first horn makes plain, it is as though Gert thinks that if we posit a feature that unifies desires under the labels "rational" and "irrational," then that very fact will somehow call into question, or have the potential to undermine, the confidence we have that the five desires on his list really are irrational. But, of course, that is just a mistake. The unifying feature we posit might underwrite our confidence, rather than undermine it.

Moreover, and more importantly, no matter how high our confidence that the desires for death, pain, disability, loss of freedom, and loss of pleasure are irrational, provided that our confidence isn't 100 percent, the bottom line is that we *do* thereby grant that it is at least possible, even if only barely, that that confidence could be undermined by further reflection. But in that case, the very considerations which strike us as potentially relevant in undermining our confidence look like they will themselves contain the seeds of an explanation of what unifies desires under the labels "rational" and "irrational." In other words, they will provide us with a conception of what it is to be fully rational that *isn't* just equivalent to having no desires on Gert's list of five irrational desires.

So, let's ask the crucial question. What would undermine our confidence that the desires for death, pain, disability, loss of freedom, and loss of pleasure are irrational? Our confidence would be undermined, it seems to me, if we thought that, starting from uncontroversial premises, we could provide a compelling argument that the desires for death, pain, disability, loss of freedom, or loss of pleasure were part of a systematically justified set of desires. If the premises and the steps in the argument, taken together, are something about which we could be more confident than we are that the desires for death, pain, disability, loss of freedom, and loss of pleasure are irrational, then it is our confidence that these desires are irrational that would be undermined, not the former, and rightly so.

What are the characteristics of a desire set that is systematically justified? The answer, it seems to me, is that a desire set that is systematically justified comprises elements that are immune to revision on grounds of ignorance or error about matters of fact; the elements of the desire set cohere well with each other; the desire set, as a whole, exhibits a kind of unity; and so on and so forth. The idea, in other words, is that a desire set is systematically justified to the extent that it exhibits analogues of the standard *epistemic* virtues. One standard epistemic virtue, of course, is empirical adequacy. A desire set that is systematically justified must therefore have an analogue of that as well.

This is where Gert's confidence that the desires for death, pain, disability, loss of freedom, and loss of pleasure are irrational gets assigned its proper role. After all, we do not begin the task of constructing a systematically justified desire set utterly devoid of substantive views about which desires will, and which desires will not, be elements of a desire set that is systematically justified. Thus, for example, to the extent that we think that it would make no sense whatsoever for someone to desire death, pain, disability, loss of freedom, or loss of pleasure in circumstances in which there is no compensation to be gained from the avoidance of harms or the production of benefits, we start out with the assumption that no desire set containing these desires *could* be systematically justified. But the important point is that this is a *defeasible assumption*. It can be defeated by further reflection.

Suppose that, starting out from desires which we provisionally admit are systematically justified, we could provide a compelling argument for the conclusion that the set of desires that we would have if we were to add and subtract desires in the light of the information and considerations of coherence and unity *does* contain one or another of the desires for death, pain, disability, loss of freedom, or loss of pleasure, in circumstances in which there is no compensation to be gained from the avoidance of harms or the production of benefits. If such an argument could be constructed, then it seems to me that we might well happily concede that these desires *can* be elements of a systematically justified set after all. Even though we started out thinking that no fully rational agent could have such desires, we would have convinced ourselves that we were wrong, that they could.[9]

Here, then, we have a way of negotiating the first horn of the dilemma. Notwithstanding the fact we characterize a fully rational agent *without* reference to Gert's list—in other words, notwithstanding the fact that we characterize a fully rational agent as someone whose desire set is systematically justified, where a desire set is systematically justified if and only it comprises all and only those desires that survive after desires which we provisionally assume to be justified are formed into a maximally informed and coherent and unified whole—we still allow our *confidence* that certain desires are irrational to play a significant role in fixing what reasons there are. The role they play, however, is essentially that of providing us with a *defeasible constraint* on what reasons there are.

Gert on the Category of Rationally Allowed Acts

One of the reasons Gert gives in favor of his own theory of rational action is that it has the advantage over alternative theories of making room for acts that are rationally allowed, though not rationally required. So long as agents don't act so as to harm themselves, Gert claims, whatever they do is rationally allowed, notwithstanding the reasons that they might have for acting in one way rather than another. This was the point I emphasized when I spelled out the third and fourth implications of Gert's definition of rational action.

For example, suppose an agent faces a choice between buying himself a holiday and giving his money to a charity that alleviates the suffering of others, and suppose further that parting with his money does cause him some harm, at least insofar as it reduces his freedom by cutting down the number of options that he will have in any future choice situation. In such a case, Gert claims that the man is rationally allowed to give the money to charity, because the harms to others that are thus avoided more than adequately compensate for the harm that he thus causes himself. (It was in this sort of case, you will remember, that Gert claimed to find the grain of the truth that lies in Kantian theories.) But, Gert insists, the man described is not rationally required to give the money to the charity. For he is also rationally allowed to buy himself a holiday, as the benefits he gains by doing that would also more than adequately compensate for the harm he causes himself. (It was in this sort of case, you will remember, that Gert claimed to find the residual grain of truth that lies in egoism.) So long as an agent's action does not harm himself overall, he is therefore rationally allowed to do whatever he likes.

I think that Gert is right to emphasize that there is a category of rationally allowed acts alongside those that are rationally required, and I think that he is also right to insist that some of the so-called conflicts between morality and self-interest are best thought of in this sort of way. Agents have a free choice to decide in which way they will act, at least within certain limits. They are not rationally required to act in the one way or in the other. Moreover, I think he is right that a theory of rational action that suggested otherwise would be flawed in a quite decisive way. But I think he is wrong that his hybrid conception of rationality is unique in making room for the category of acts that are rationally allowed, as opposed to rationally required. The view of rational action I described above makes room for the class of rationally allowed acts as well. It does so by allowing that certain reasons are disjunctive in form.

Thus, in the case just described, we can imagine that if the man had the set of desires that would result if we take those of his desires that we provisionally agree to be justified, and then add and subtract desires in order to find a set that is maximally informed and coherent and unified, then he would desire himself, in the circumstances of action he faces, either to buy himself a holiday or to give his money to charity. Since his desire has this disjunctive content it follows, on the theory of reasons for action that I described, that the reason for action he has is disjunctive in form as well: he has a reason either to buy himself a holiday or to give his money to charity. If no other reasons are in play, apart from this disjunctive reason, and if the man believes that this is so, and if his belief eludes rational criticism, then, according to the view of rational action described above, it follows that the man will be rationally allowed either to buy himself a holiday or to give his money to charity. Whatever he does will be rational notwithstanding the fact that he had adequate reasons for acting in the alternative way.

The upshot is thus that Gert is wrong to claim that his theory is alone in making room for the category of acts that are rationally allowed, as opposed to being rationally required. Indeed, it seems that any theory can make room for that possibility simply by acknowledging the existence of disjunctive reasons.

Conclusion

Despite Gert's various ingenious arguments for his complex hybrid conception of rationality, it seems to me that, in the end, we should reject it. This is not to say that there isn't much Gert says with which we can and should agree, there most certainly is: the idea that a theory of rational action must combine egocentric and nonegocentric elements; the idea that certain desires wear their irrational nature more or less on their sleeve; the idea that rational actions come in two forms, acts that are rationally required on the one hand and acts that are rationally allowed on the other; and so on. My point is simply that we do not need to move beyond a theory which is, for all intents and purposes, much like the cool moment desire theory insofar as we agree with Gert on these crucial issues.

Notes

* An earlier version of this paper was read at *A Conference on Gert's Moral Theory* held at Dartmouth College, May 1999. I would like to thank Robert Audi, Ruth Chang, David Copp, David Cummiskey, Bernard Gert, Joshua Gert, Shelly Kagan, Geoffrey Sayre-McCord, Stephen Nathanson, Walter Sinnott-Armstrong, and Susan Wolf for their many helpful criticisms and suggestions.

1. All otherwise unexplained references are to Bernard Gert, *Morality: Its Nature and Justification* (New York: Oxford University Press, 1998).

2. Walter Sinnott-Armstrong has suggested that we can usefully make a distinction between the claim that *there is a reason for an agent to act* in a certain way and the claim that *the agent has a reason to act* in that way. In his view, claims of the latter sort (claims about *the reasons that agents have*) are best analyzed as claims about the beliefs that agents have about claims of the former sort (in other words, they are claims about *the reasons that agents believe that there are*). In these terms, the commonsense conception of practical rationality insists that we ask not what reasons there are for agents to act in certain ways, but rather what reasons they have for acting in those ways. As we will see, Gert himself says that he embraces something like this distinction (65-66). Despite the good company I would keep, I am reluctant to accept this distinction, as ordinary usage seems to me not to support it. "Though John has a reason to act in a certain way, he doesn't believe that he has a reason to do so" doesn't seem to be equivalent to the claim that though John believes that there is a reason to act in a certain way, he doesn't believe that he believes there is a reason to act in that way. It seems, instead, to be equivalent to the claim "Though there is a reason for John to act in a certain way, he doesn't believe that there is a reason for him to act in that way." Claims about the reasons there are for agents to act in certain ways thus seem to me to be equivalent to claims about the reasons they have for acting in those ways. When an agent asks whether there is a reason for him to act in a certain way, that is just a way of asking whether he has any reason to act in that way.

3. Note that when Gert says that someone is "fully informed," he means not that she is omniscient, but rather that she is has all the information that is suitably available to her (184, note 11).

4. Though remember what Gert means by "fully informed" (see note 3 above).

5. Michael Smith, *The Moral Problem* (Oxford, Eng.: Blackwell, 1994).

6. Remember that, for Gert, the greater harms referred to here are death, pain, loss of ability, loss of freedom, and loss of pleasure, and the benefits referred to are greater consciousness, ability, freedom, or pleasure. This will be important subsequently (see note 9 below).

7. Why could it never be rational? According to Gert, it is a constraint on any adequate theory of rational action that it not classify as rational acts that "every fully informed rational person would advocate that all persons for whom they are concerned, including themselves, never [perform]" (31), and an agent's knowingly harming himself when his doing so will not be compensated for by the production of benefits or the avoidance of harms is such an act.

8. Michael Smith, "The Incoherence Argument: Reply to Schafer-Landau," forthcoming in *Analysis*.

9. How likely is it that a fully rational agent would have one or another of the desires for death, pain, disability, loss of freedom, or loss of pleasure, in circumstances in which there is no compensation to be gained from the avoidance of harms or the production of benefits? Well, remember that the harms referred to here are death, pain, loss of ability, loss of freedom, and loss of pleasure, and that the benefits he refers to are greater consciousness, ability, freedom, or pleasure (see note 6). The question is therefore: how likely is it that a fully rational agent would desire death, pain, disability, loss of freedom, or loss of pleasure in circumstances in which something other than these harms and benefits provides the compensation? For example, how likely is it that a fully rational agent would desire death, pain, disability, loss of freedom, or loss of pleasure in circumstances in which the loss enables the preservation of a work of art or area of rain forest? Certainly it doesn't seem impossible.

Part III: Consequences and Rules

7

Gert on Aid to Others

Shelly Kagan

"It is worse than pointless to claim that
morality requires helping the deprived."
Bernard Gert

Introduction

Let me start by telling you two things I believe. The first is this: morality often requires us to aid others (for example, helping the deprived). The second is this: reason often requires the same thing. That is, we are often *rationally* required to aid others.

Now I happen to believe particularly strong versions of both of these claims. I believe that morality actually requires us to do as much good as we possibly can do—and I believe that reason requires the same thing. And since doing all the good we can do typically involves aiding others, I believe that we are very frequently required to aid others—both morally required and rationally required.

But of course one might accept more modest versions of either of these claims. For example, one might accept the existence of what are sometimes called "deontological constraints" which would rule out certain methods of aiding others. Thus one might think that it is immoral to deliberately harm an innocent person, even if this is the only way to aid others by an even greater amount overall. And one might hold, as well, that we are rationally required to conform to such constraints. Accordingly, one might reject my bold versions of the two claims, and accept instead the more modest claims that we are required—both morally and rationally—to do all the good we can within the limits set by those constraints. Even so, since we can often aid others without violating any constraints, we are often morally and rationally required to aid others.

Or one might accept even more modest versions of these two claims. For example, one might accept the existence of "options" which make it permissible to forgo promoting the good when the cost to you of doing so involves too great a sacrifice in terms of the various other things you care about. And one might hold, as well, that it is rationally permissible to act on these options—forgoing the chance to promote the good—when the cost to you of promoting the good is too great. Accordingly, one might insist merely that we are required—both morally and rationally—to do all the good that we can (within the limits set by constraints) provided that the cost of doing so is not too great. Even so, since the cost of aiding others is often quite reasonable, we will often be morally and rationally required to aid others.

Or we might be more modest still. One might hold that there is no moral or rational requirement to concern ourselves with the provision of mere *goods* (for example, mere bodily pleasures, or the enjoyment of beauty). Perhaps we are only required to prevent evils (for example, pain, disease, or death). Then one might say that we are morally and rationally required to prevent harm to others (within the limits set by constraints) when the cost of doing so is reasonable. Even so, since we often can prevent harm (and other evils) to others at reasonable cost (and within the limits set by constraints), we will often be morally and rationally required to aid others.

As I've already noted, I do not personally accept any of these possible modifications. Rather, I accept the pair of claims in quite bold form. But that is not my concern in this paper. It suffices to note that one can accept one or both of the claims in quite modest forms as well. And, indeed, I rather suspect that many people do accept one or both of these claims in some (perhaps modest) form.

For example, if you have the opportunity to save a drowning child, at little or no cost to yourself—suppose you are the only one near enough to throw a life preserver—then I suspect that many people would agree that you have a *moral obligation* to do this. And at least some people, I suppose, might even agree that it would be *irrational* of you not to help in this situation.

If I understand him correctly, however, then, with one important kind of exception, Bernard Gert rejects both of these claims. He does not believe, first of all, that we are *rationally* required to aid others—not even when this prevents serious harm, not even when this costs us little or nothing, and not even when we can help without violating any constraints. And, more strikingly still, Gert does not even believe that we have a *moral* requirement to aid others (not even if we can prevent harm, at little cost, without violating constraints).

The important exception is this. Gert recognizes that in what he calls "civilized societies" there is often a conventional, socially imposed duty to rescue (210).[1] So if you happen to live in such a society and you come across the drowning child, Gert too will admit that you are morally required to provide the requisite aid. Similarly, your society might impose upon you various other relevant duties to aid others, deriving, perhaps, from your job or other social roles (for example, you might be a lifeguard).

Presumably, however, this means that if you are not a member of a "civilized society"—and have no other similar socially imposed duties—you face no similar moral obligation.

Suppose, then, that you live in the wild and there come across the drowning child—far from any society whatsoever. And suppose, as well, that it is not your job to aid drowning children in the wild, that you've not made any promise to save such children, and so forth. I take it, then, that Gert's position is that in a case like this, there is no requirement at all—neither a rational requirement, nor a moral requirement—to save the drowning child.

Still, it seems to me that a good many people would insist that even in this situation there is indeed a *moral* requirement to provide aid: to fail to throw a life preserver to a drowning child (even if you are in the wild, and it's not your job) is simply *immoral*. And at least some people will agree as well that there is in fact a *rational* requirement to provide aid in such cases. So when Gert denies both of these, it seems to me that he is making some rather striking claims.

Accordingly, what I want to do in this paper is to investigate Gert's various arguments for these striking claims. My goal, then, is a modest one. I won't attempt to defend the alternative view—that there *are* rational and moral requirements to aid. I will restrict myself, instead, to trying to see whether Gert has given us any good reason to *deny* the existence of these requirements. As we shall see, I believe his arguments are unsuccessful.

Before proceeding, however, two preliminary remarks about exposition are in order. First, as I have already explained, it is possible—and, indeed, common—to accept a requirement to aid with various qualifications and restrictions in place. But it is clumsy, and tiresome, to be forever talking of "a requirement to aid others—so as to prevent harms or other evils, when this can be done at reasonable cost within the limits set by constraints." Thus, I will typically talk simply of "a requirement to aid others." But those who accept the various qualifications should certainly keep them in mind.

Second, Gert's presentation of his views is lengthy and complex. He often revisits issues he has discussed before, sometimes modifying or refining earlier theses, arguments, and objections. It is quite possible, then, that I have overlooked some relevant passages, or misconstrued the precise intent of those that I have identified. But it would of course be tiresome in a different way to have the discussion that follows constantly flagged with reminders to this effect. And so, for the most part, I will let this single, initial reminder suffice.

Rationality

I trust it isn't particularly controversial for me to claim that Gert rejects the existence of a rational requirement to aid others. Consider his official account of irrational action (83-84). For our purposes the key part of the account is this. Gert claims that an action is irrational only if the (suitably informed) agent would believe that the act significantly increases his risk of suffering some significant evil (for example, pain or death).

Now to be sure, Gert insists repeatedly (and it is an important part of the official account) that it can be rationally permissible for the agent to act in a way that he believes will increase the risk of his suffering some significant evil—provided that the agent has an "adequate reason" for doing so. And Gert insists as well that the fact that the act will aid others (providing a benefit, or preventing a harm) can count as an adequate reason. Thus it can be rationally permissible for an agent to act in a way that will cause harm to himself, so as to aid others. Still, the fact remains that on Gert's account the *only* way that an act can be irrational is if it runs the risk that the *agent* will suffer some evil.

According to Gert, then, an act is irrational if and only if it risks harm to the agent in the absence of an adequate reason. Thus, if the agent does *not* have an adequate reason for "disregarding" this evil to himself, his act is irrational. But note that there is nothing irrational—according to Gert—about similarly "disregarding" evils to *others*. If no harm to oneself is involved, it is perfectly rationally permissible to act in a way that harms others, or fails to prevent or eliminate harms to others—even in the complete absence of some further "adequate reason."

That's why, on Gert's view, there is no rational requirement to aid others, not even to prevent harm to them. One does not need some special adequate reason to disregard the welfare of others. One can rationally disregard it for no reason at all. As Gert puts it at one point: "it is only failure to act on reasons concerned with one's own self-interest that is ever irrational; failure to act on reasons concerned with the interests of others is never irrational" (73).

The question we need to put to Gert, then, is this: why should we accept this claim? Why not believe, instead, that one can be irrational for failure to act on reasons even when those reasons are concerned only with the interests of *others*? Obviously enough, Gert's official account of irrationality rejects this more encompassing approach in favor of a more restricted view. But what exactly is Gert's argument for accepting this more restricted view about rationality?

Before answering this question, however, we have to deal with a complication. In developing his theory of rationality, Gert attempts to make use of what we might call a No Controversy Strategy. The idea is roughly this: Gert only wants to label something as irrational if it is reasonably uncontroversial that this kind of act is indeed irrational. (Presumably, this is because Gert frequently goes on to rely on arguments which make use of premises asserting that some type of act is irrational; Gert wants those premises to be as uncontroversial as possible.) Unfortunately, however, Gert's use of the No Controversy Strategy makes it difficult to pin down his views on the issues we are discussing.

Here are two typical statements of this strategy:

> Whenever there is any significant disagreement as to whether an action is rational or irrational, I shall regard it as rational. Thus if any significant group of rational persons, as characterized previously, regard an action as rational, I shall regard it as rational. (32)

> However, I do not want to classify as irrational any action that anyone can plausibly want to classify as rational. When I show an action to be irrational, I expect complete agreement that it should not be done. (86)

Now on the face of it, all that these remarks seem to tell us is something about when Gert is prepared to *label* an act as irrational. But if that's right, this leads to a rather surprising way of understanding Gert's various claims about rationality and irrationality, including his official account of irrational action. Gert is willing to *call* an action "irrational" only if everyone agrees that it is irrational. But this means that it is possible, and perhaps even likely, that there may be other kinds of action that are irrational as well, but where, as it happens, there is not yet any kind of agreement about this fact. Since there is no agreement, these other irrational acts won't be *called* "irrational" by Gert; but of course, this in no way shows that they are *not* in fact irrational.

Thus when the official account of irrational action asserts that the only irrational actions are those that harm the agent without an adequate reason, what this actually *means* is that this is the only kind of action that Gert is prepared to *call* irrational, because it is the only kind of action concerning which there is general agreement that it is irrational. So construed, the official account doesn't actually say that the only irrational acts are those that harm the agent without an adequate reason (appearances to the contrary notwithstanding). What it actually says—or should be understood as saying—is that this is the only *uncontroversially* irrational action.

Similarly, then, when the official account implies that it cannot be irrational to fail to prevent harm to others (even in the absence of an adequate reason), all this actually *means* is that if this kind of action *is* irrational, this fact is controversial. Thus, on this reading, it is perfectly compatible with Gert's official account of irrational action to hold that there is a rational requirement to aid others. Presumably, if there is such a rational requirement, there is no general agreement about this, so Gert won't be prepared to *call* failure to act on such a requirement irrational. But, of course, it will be irrational for all that.

Thus, on at least one possible reading suggested by Gert's appeal to the No Controversy Strategy, we may not actually have any evidence at all that Gert truly does reject a rational requirement to aid others. He appears to say things that explicitly reject such a requirement (or entail its rejection); but the appearances are deceptive. Gert is actually talking in a kind of code. And for all we know Gert may actually agree with me that there is such a requirement. It's just that Gert can't say it out loud.

And yet, I can't help but feel that Gert does disagree with me about this. And surely the reader of the official account of irrational action will be excused for thinking this as well. So I think we had better look for a second way to understand the relevant passages.

Luckily, an alternative understanding is not hard to find. This second interpretation begins by laying stress upon the fact that Gert is interested in the agreement of *rational* people. In discussing his account of rationality, Gert frequently reminds us that he is only attempting to state the beliefs and actions of people "insofar as" they are rational. Here are two more typical passages:

> When I talk of "rational persons" in this context, I mean "persons insofar as they have neither irrational beliefs, desires, nor motives, and are not acting irrationally." Thus, in talking about rational persons, I am not making any empirical claims about actual rational persons, but am simply making explicit what is involved in being rational. (30)

> No rational person insofar as she is rational (this phrase is always to be understood when I talk of rational persons). . . . (90)

Now recall that in stating what I have dubbed the No Controversy Strategy, Gert tells us that he only wants to call an action irrational if (virtually) all rational persons regard the action as irrational. Combine this with the realization that Gert is only interested in the opinions of rational persons insofar as they are rational. This suggests that the proper way to understand Gert is as follows: he only wants to call an act irrational if all rational people *insofar* as they are rational would agree it is irrational. Which is to say, I take it, that Gert is interested in knowing what *perfectly* rational individuals would agree to be irrational. (By a "perfectly" rational individual I simply mean someone who is "completely" rational—lacking all irrational beliefs, and so forth. Focusing on perfectly rational individuals in this sense guarantees that we attend only to the views of rational people *insofar* as they are rational.)

But this doesn't yet solve the problem. After all, it is still true that what Gert actually tells us is that he is not going to "classify" an act as irrational in the absence of the agreement of rational persons. Thus, Gert's appeal to the No Controversy Strategy still allows for a reading according to which some type of act might still be irrational, even though not all perfectly rational people agree about this. All that Gert would be saying, then, is that he won't *call* such an action irrational, even though it is. Thus we would remain in the unpleasant exegetical situation of having no clear evidence that Gert rejects a rational requirement to aid others, even though he certainly appears to do so.

Perhaps, however, I have been misconstruing the No Controversy Strategy. I've been interpreting it as a statement of Gert's unwillingness to *label* something irrational in the face of disagreement. This does seem to me the most natural way to interpret Gert's remarks. But perhaps we should understand it, instead, as a statement of Gert's *belief* that an act cannot be irrational if people disagree about this. That is, perhaps what Gert actually thinks is something like the following: an action *is* irrational only if all perfectly rational people would agree that it is.

Admittedly, Gert doesn't quite say this. But it is not unreasonably far from the various things that Gert does say. Furthermore, it seems like a reasonably plausible view to hold.

Note that it would not be an especially reasonable view to hold if it were a claim about ordinary, imperfectly rational people. That is, it wouldn't be especially plausible to claim that an act is irrational only if ordinary, imperfectly rational people would agree that it is. After all, it is difficult to see why imperfectly rational people shouldn't sometimes (or often) make mistakes about what kinds of acts are irrational. But the view does seem far more plausible once we insist—with Gert—that what we are interested in are the beliefs of perfectly rational people (that is, the beliefs of rational people "insofar as" they are rational). For it does not seem implausible to suggest that a (well-informed) perfectly rational person can't be mistaken about what kinds of actions are irrational. So unless there is agreement among perfectly rational people, the act can't be irrational.[2]

Note, furthermore, that if we do ascribe this view to Gert—that an act is irrational only if perfectly rational people agree it is—then we can take him at his word in his various other pronouncements about rational and irrational actions. In particular, when Gert *says* that the only irrational acts are those that harm the agent without adequate reason, we can now straightforwardly assume that he *means* it. No other sorts of acts are irrational, Gert would be telling us, for there are no other sorts of acts that all perfectly rational people agree to be irrational.

I tentatively conclude, accordingly—albeit with considerable hesitation—that Gert does hold the view that we've just been discussing. An act is irrational, according to Gert, only if perfectly rational people agree that it is irrational.

But now, of course, our question to Gert is this: is it, or is it not, the case that all perfectly rational people will agree that there is a requirement to aid others?

Presumably, Gert thinks that they will *not* agree that there is such a requirement. This is reflected in his official account of irrational action. But again, what we need to know is, what is Gert's argument to this effect? Why is Gert so confident that at least some perfectly rational individuals won't accept a requirement to aid others? (Note that Gert need not claim that *all* perfectly rational individuals would reject such a requirement; it suffices if *some* would.)

Many of Gert's pronouncements concerning matters of rationality are made *ex cathedra*. He simply informs us that something is, or is not, irrational. Given our current understanding of his position, however, we can interpret these remarks as implicit claims about the beliefs of perfectly rational people. And indeed, often enough Gert explicitly appeals to claims about what everyone does, or does not, accept (e.g., 51, 71, 88, or 90). But it is difficult to be sure how exactly such claims are to be understood, given the confidence with which Gert makes them.

Suppose we had concluded that what mattered were the actual opinions of reasonably educated, and reasonably rational (albeit imperfectly rational) individuals—the readers of Gert's book, say (see 32). Then we might well have taken Gert's pronouncements to be empirical claims about the beliefs of those individuals. But of course, given Gert's repeated insistence that what matters is not the actual empirical beliefs of imperfectly rational beings, but rather the agreements of perfectly rational beings, it is difficult to know what to make of his repeated pronouncements about what everyone believes. For what Gert needs to be talking about are the views of *perfectly* rational people—and I find it hard to see what makes Gert so confident that he knows what *perfectly* rational people believe.

I don't mean to be unduly insulting about this, but I take it that *none* of us is perfectly rational. So even if Gert is right in his claims about what "we" all believe (or what some of us believe), it isn't especially relevant, unless Gert can give us reason to believe that the views he cites are views we have "insofar as" we are rational. And as far as I can see, this is something that Gert simply doesn't do.

For all I know, then, perfectly rational people *would* all agree that there is a rational requirement to provide aid. Obviously enough, the existence of such a requirement is denied by many ordinary, imperfectly rational people. But for all that Gert has shown us, this denial may not be one made by them insofar as they are rational. Perhaps, were they perfectly rational, they would see that there is such a requirement after all.

Mind you, I haven't given you any reason at all to *believe* that all perfectly rational people would agree that there is a rational requirement to aid others. I am simply trying to make it clear that Gert hasn't given you any reason to believe the contrary either. His confident pronouncements notwithstanding, Gert hasn't actually given you any reason to believe that at least some *perfectly* rational people would *reject* such a requirement.

Now I don't mean to be embracing skepticism concerning our ability to identify the beliefs of perfectly rational people. We are, after all, ourselves rational, even if only imperfectly so. I presume this means that we have a real, if flawed, ability to evaluate a variety of possible arguments about what perfectly rational people would accept. And in fact, in those rare cases where ordinary, imperfectly rational people are indeed in agreement about what is rational, this may well provide evidence (although, no doubt, only defeasible evidence) that perfectly rational people would hold the same views. But when ordinary people disagree about whether something is irrational—and this, I take it, is the case with regard to a requirement to aid others—we'll need to turn to more complicated arguments.[3] Mere confident assertions about the beliefs of perfectly rational people won't be especially compelling.

Let me close this section by noting one possible argument of this more complicated sort—really it's just a sketch of an argument—that builds on material that Gert himself provides. In discussing the idea of an adequate reason, Gert notes that it makes no difference to the strength of a reason *whose* interests are at stake (whether the agent's or someone else's).

> If the amount of harm to be avoided and the benefit to be gained is the same, then reasons involving self-interest cannot make rational any acts that reasons involving the interests of others cannot make rational. Any irrational act that would be made rational by a reason of self-interest would also be made rational by a reason of the same strength involving the interests of others. A mere change of person affected does not affect the strength of a reason. (78)

Gert offers no argument for this claim, and I don't actually think it is self-evident. But suppose we accept it. One might then think that it must generalize. If mere change of person affected cannot affect the force of a reason, then perhaps mere change of person affected cannot affect other aspects of what is rational as well. If so, then once we agree that it would be irrational to disregard harm to myself (in the absence of an adequate reason), we will have to hold as well that it is also irrational to disregard harm to others (in the absence of an adequate reason). But this would mean, of course, that Gert's official account of rationality would be mistaken, for it would be stated too narrowly, giving special place to harm to the agent. Instead, we would need to adopt the more encompassing, "impersonal" view, according to which disregarding *anyone's* harm (in the absence of an adequate reason) can be irrational. And this would mean, of course, that there will indeed be a rational requirement to aid others.

Obviously, Gert himself will have none of this. As we know, Gert insists that "failure to act on reasons concerned with the interests of others is never irrational" (73). Gert rejects a rational requirement to aid others. Thus, he clearly thinks that the point about the irrelevance of mere change of person does not generalize. But if he has a reason for holding this more restricted view, I do not see what it is.

Morality

Let's turn now to our second question, whether there is a *moral* requirement to aid others. As I noted in the first section, many people think that there is such a requirement. Indeed, even among those who deny the existence of a rational requirement to aid others, many nonetheless accept the existence of a moral requirement.

What's more, or so it seems to me, we might well have expected the existence of such a requirement to follow from Gert's own basic ideas concerning the nature of morality as an informal public system for guiding conduct that applies to all rational persons.

As Gert is at pains to point out, in determining what morality permits or requires, our concern is not with what any given rational person would or would not favor—not even a perfectly rational person—but rather with what an *impartial* rational person would favor. The concept of impartiality is central to a proper understanding of morality. In particular, according to Gert, a morally wrong action "is one that *all* impartial rational persons would favor not doing" (325).

But on the face of it, at least, I would have thought it rather plausible to suggest that all impartial rational people would often oppose failing to aid others. Presumably, after all, rational individuals would often want aid for themselves or their loved ones (in cases involving significant evils, if nothing else; see 52-53). But an *impartial* person, one with "an impartial concern for all persons" (168), would lack an "egocentric attitude" (171). Thus it seems that an impartial rational person would want aid for anyone at all (at least, in cases involving significant evils).

So, in at least many cases, all impartial rational people would oppose failing to aid others. Which is to say, such failure to aid would be morally wrong. But this, in turn, is equivalent to saying that aiding others is often morally required.

What's more, I would have thought it rather plausible to suggest that impartial rational people would favor some sort of moral *rule* requiring aid to others. After all, as Gert explains, "talking about moral rules is a convenient way of talking about those general kinds of actions that are morally required and prohibited" (109). If, as seems plausible, aid to others would often be morally required, then it does seem as though it would be convenient to note this fact with some sort of moral rule, such as, perhaps, "aid the needy."

Of course, as we know, Gert denies all of this. He claims that there is no such moral rule. That's obvious enough from a quick glance at what Gert takes to be the complete list of moral rules (216): there are ten rules altogether, but none of them requires aiding others (special circumstances aside).[4] But in any event, Gert makes the point explicitly: "Moral rules do not require promoting good for oneself or for others. They do not even require preventing harm to others" (116).

And lest one think that Gert's point is merely that there is no moral *rule* requiring aid—that he believes that aid is indeed morally required, even though there is no *rule* requiring this—it may be helpful to quote Gert yet again: "it is worse than pointless to claim that morality requires helping the deprived" (365).

Admittedly, Gert does think it morally admirable to aid the needy. He recognizes the existence of "moral ideals" (see, e.g., 126). But he is at pains to insist that these ideals cannot themselves ordinarily generate moral requirements: "There is no similar requirement to act in accordance with those general precepts encouraging people to prevent or relieve the suffering of evil or harm, the moral ideals" (122). Since our question is why Gert rejects the existence of a moral *requirement* to aid others, we can, I think, safely put aside further consideration of these "mere" ideals.

One might think, for similar reasons, that we could also put aside Gert's defense of his claim that there is no moral *rule* requiring aid to others. After all—or so one might think—what we want to know is whether or not there is a moral requirement to aid others. And even if Gert is correct that there is no moral *rule* requiring aid, this is, strictly, irrelevant to our concern. For even if there is no such moral *rule*, it might still be the case that agents are often morally *required* to provide aid. Or so one might think.

But if this is right, then we will be rather hard pressed to come up with any understanding of why Gert rejects a moral requirement to aid. For he actually has very little to say directly on this subject. He repeatedly asserts that there *is* no such requirement, but he offers little by way of direct argument for this view. What he actually argues against, rather, is the existence of a moral *rule* requiring aid. Yet if the nonexistence of such a moral rule has no implications for the existence of a moral requirement, then Gert's arguments to this effect—even if successful—won't show that there is no moral *requirement*.

However, to dismiss Gert's discussion of a moral rule requiring aid as irrelevant in this way would be too quick. For there is clearly *some* kind of connection between the existence of a moral rule and the existence of the corresponding requirements. Again, recall Gert's remark that "talking about moral rules is a convenient way of talking about those general kinds of actions that are morally required and prohibited" (109). Unfortunately, the exact nature of the connection is not altogether clear. Presumably, on at least some possible views about the connection, Gert would indeed be entitled to move from the claim that there is no moral rule requiring aid to the conclusion that there is no moral requirement either. But, obviously, a great deal will depend on the details of the correct account of the connection.

Unfortunately, Gert has surprisingly little to say about this topic. This is indeed *surprising*, given the central emphasis upon moral rules in Gert's theory. One might have expected a rather careful discussion of the precise connection between moral rules, on the one hand, and the moral status of a given act, on the other (that is, whether the act is required, forbidden, or optional). But Gert doesn't offer such a discussion, and so we will have to consider some alternatives on his behalf.

Suppose, for example, that Gert accepted a simple view like the following: an act is morally required if and only if failure to perform it would violate (one or more of) the moral rules. The desired inference would certainly go through on this view (that is, the absence of a rule would entail the absence of a requirement). For if we assume, for the moment, that Gert is right, and there is no moral rule requiring aid, then failure to provide aid won't violate any moral rule, and so providing aid won't be morally required.

As I say, a simple view like this would certainly do the trick for Gert. But it is quite clear that this is not, in fact, Gert's view. For the simple view entails that it is always morally forbidden to violate the moral rules.[5] Yet Gert insists upon the existence of *justified* violations of the moral rules. Gert argues repeatedly, and at length (see, especially, 221-46), that in various situations it is permissible to violate the moral rules—roughly, in those cases where impartial rational people would publicly advocate allowing the rule to be violated.[6] Since Gert holds that violating a moral rule is sometimes morally permissible, he obviously cannot accept a view according to which it is *never* permissible to violate the moral rules. So he cannot accept the simple view.

Perhaps, then, Gert's view if this: an act is morally required if and only if failure to perform it would be an *unjustified* violation of the moral rules. This is a more complicated position than that of the simple view, but the desired inference still goes through, since it still implies that the only way that one can be required to perform an act is if some rule requires performing the act. (Not all violations of the moral rules are forbidden, but *only* violations of the moral rules are forbidden.) Assuming, as before, that Gert is right, and there is no moral rule requiring aid, it will still follow that there is no moral *requirement* to aid.

But I think that this can't quite be Gert's view either. To see this, we need to consider more carefully the status of justified violations of the rules. Take a case where violating the rules is indeed justified. Obviously enough, then, performing the act in question (that is, the act that will justifiably violate the rules) is not morally forbidden. So, at the very least, performing that act will be morally permissible. But mightn't it also be the case—in at least some instances of justified violation—that violating the rules is not only morally permissible, but in fact morally *required*?

I think that Gert wants to allow for this second, bolder possibility. He remarks, at one point, that

> the moral attitude does not encourage blind obedience to the moral rules. On the contrary, it allows that quite often they need not be obeyed. Less often, all impartial rational persons may even favor their not being obeyed. Not only are there justified violations of the moral rules, there is even unjustified keeping of them. (171-72)

But if obeying the rules is unjustified, I take it, violating the rules is morally required. So in at least some cases, one is not only permitted to violate the rules, but actually morally required to do so.[7]

Now it would be possible, I suppose, for someone to claim that the *only* time one can be morally required to violate a moral rule is when doing this is necessary to satisfy some *other* moral rule. Thus, it would only be when moral rules conflict that one is required to violate one of them. If so, the desired inference would *still* go through, since there could still be no requirement to provide aid in the absence of a rule requiring aid.

It is, however, far from clear what would support a claim like this. And in any event, it doesn't seem to be Gert's view either. Indeed, at one point Gert seems to explicitly recognize the possibility of being required to violate a rule even though this is not done so as to satisfy some other *rule*: "an action that is in accordance with a moral rule when all impartial rational persons would publicly allow violating the rule in order to follow a moral ideal also counts as a morally wrong action" (328).

Apparently, then, Gert recognizes that one can be required to violate a moral rule, even though there is no other moral rule that requires the required act.[8] Thus, an act can be morally required, even though it is not required by any moral rule. As I say, this does in fact seem to be Gert's own view, and in any event it seems plausible in its own right.

Note, however, that at this point the desired inference no longer goes through. For we have now recognized the possibility that an act can be required even though it is not required by any moral rule. So even if Gert is able to convince us that there *is* no moral rule requiring aid, he himself will have to admit that it still might be the case—for all that—that providing aid to others is morally required.

Presumably, the situation boils down to this.[9] An act is required if and only if all impartial rational persons would oppose failure to perform the act. (Recall Gert's account of a wrong act as one that "*all* impartial rational persons would favor not doing" (325).) Sometimes, perhaps typically, required acts will be required by one or another moral rule. But not always. So even if Gert is right, and there is no moral rule requiring aid to others—it simply won't follow that there is no moral requirement to provide aid. Indeed, for all that Gert would have shown, it might be that a moral requirement to aid others is extremely common.

Of course, if a requirement to aid others is all that common—as I believe it is—it would still be puzzling why there would be no moral *rule* to that effect. So even if the point I have just been making is correct—and we can't infer the lack of a moral requirement from the mere lack of a moral rule—it remains of interest to us to consider Gert's various arguments against the *existence* of such a rule. So let us ask, at long last: why does Gert believe there will be no moral rule requiring aid to others?

One answer is straightforward: Gert believes that all moral rules are negative; they can be stated as prohibitions. Since a rule requiring aid would be positive, it can't be a genuine moral rule. Gert tells us that "Moral rules do not require promoting good for oneself or for others. They do not even require preventing harm to others. Rather they require avoiding causing evils or harms. It is not an accident that all moral rules can be stated as prohibitions" (116).

But why should we follow Gert in this regard? Why believe that all genuine moral rules are negative?

As far as I can see, Gert's initial argument for this conclusion simply comes to this: all of the rules on his initial list of sample moral rules are negative (116, cf. 111). Now he is certainly right about this generalization, but it is hard to take this argument seriously. Anyone who believes in a moral rule requiring aid will simply insist that the initial sample is too narrow in this regard. Positive rules can be moral rules as well.

A more significant argument—indeed what I take to be Gert's central argument here—turns on the claim that all moral rules must be *general* in a particular way. According to Gert, genuine moral rules must be obeyed "all of the time" (122) and "with regard to everyone" (123). Of course this isn't strictly true, since there are cases of justified violations (122). But *except* for cases of justified violation, one must obey a moral rule all of the time, and one must obey it with regard to everyone. When a moral rule is general in this way, Gert says that it is possible to obey it "impartially" (that is, at all times, toward everyone).

But Gert argues that this simply can't be done for rules requiring aid (like "aid the needy"). Given human limitations on how much good any one of us can do, and given widespread human need, it simply isn't possible to provide aid to everyone who needs it. "Moral rules require acting in accordance with them all of the time with regard to everyone equally. Since positive actions cannot be done all of the time with regard to everyone equally, the moral rules cannot require positive actions like preventing evils or promoting goods" (127).

Gert's argument, then, is this. A rule requiring aid to others cannot be obeyed impartially, hence it cannot possibly be a genuine moral rule (cf. 126, 136).

It is not clear to me, however, that Gert's argument is successful. I can, in fact, imagine two possible replies.

First, suppose we grant that it is indeed literally impossible (given human limitations) to obey a rule like "aid the needy" at all times, and with regard to all people, given that one cannot possibly aid all of those who actually need aid. Imagine, for example, that some agent has exhausted all of his resources, and can literally provide no further aid to others. It might plausibly be suggested—against Gert—that if the agent literally cannot aid anyone else, this will simply be recognized as a valid justification for his failure to aid anyone further.

That is, presumably, all impartial rational persons will publicly allow failure to aid the needy in those cases where the agent literally cannot provide any further aid. Thus our agent's ensuing failures will all be cases of justified violations of the rule in question. But as Gert himself notes, the generality of moral rules does not require obeying the rules when violating the rules is justified (122). Thus from the mere fact that it is humanly impossible to aid all of the needy, it simply won't follow that a rule requiring aid would lack the requisite generality.

This first reply grants Gert's assumption that a rule requiring aid would necessarily be violated. It simply insists that any violation that is truly unavoidable will be a justified violation, and so the necessity of violating the rule does not show that the rule cannot be properly general.

A second possible reply, however, might take issue with Gert's assumption that the rule must—as a matter of necessity—be violated. After all, the unavoidability of violation only follows if we interpret the rule "aid the needy" as requiring one to provide aid to each individual person who needs it (something that, clearly, no human can do). Typically, however, rules like this are interpreted in a more limited fashion. They are understood to involve one or another implied restriction—so that they require less of us than literally aiding everyone who needs aid.

For example, one might understand the rule "aid the needy" as simply requiring that one provide as much aid to the needy as one *can*—but no more. If this is how the rule is to be understood, obviously enough, then it is no longer impossible to fully obey it. After all, if one can do no more, then one has done all that one can; and so failure to aid anyone else won't constitute a violation of the rule.

And, of course, the relevant restriction might be even more significant. Recall that many who accept a moral requirement to aid others accept only a modest form of the requirement. In particular, most people believe that you only need to aid others when the cost of doing so is not too great. On this view, then, the rule "aid the needy" should be understood as having an implied "cost" restriction: one must aid the needy, but *only* if the cost of doing so is reasonable. Once again, it seems, there will be nothing impossible about fully obeying the rule, provided that it is understood in this restricted fashion; and so, again, the rule will have the requisite generality after all.[10]

I am not at all sure how Gert would respond to these two replies. Perhaps he would admit that, if either reply is correct, when I inevitably fail to aid some needy individual, this need not be an unjustified violation of the rule (either because it isn't a violation at all, or because the violation is justified). But he might insist, nonetheless, that it is still impossible to obey the rule "impartially." After all, it is still true that some needy individual will go unaided by me, and so perhaps I still have not obeyed the rule "with regard to everyone." That is, Gert might argue that I simply *can't* obey the rule impartially, since I *must* pick and choose who to aid, from among all those who need aid.

I am not at all confident that Gert *would* say this, but if he did, he would clearly be right about at least one thing: given human limitations, and widespread need, I literally cannot give aid to all who need it. So it is certainly true that in *this* sense of the term I cannot obey the rule "impartially." But is this a problem? Does it show that the rule "aid the needy" is not a genuine moral rule?

Of course, one might have thought that if a rule cannot be obeyed impartially, unjustified violations of the rule are inevitable. (Indeed, it seems to me that Gert's discussion sometimes suggests that these two notions come to the same thing. See, e.g., 124.) If so, then it would indeed be plausible to hold that if a rule can't be obeyed impartially, it can't be a genuine moral rule.

But I have just argued, in effect, that even if a rule cannot be obeyed impartially (in this special sense of the term), it does not follow that unjustified violations are inevitable. In particular, I have argued that even though the rule "aid the needy" cannot be obeyed "impartially," unjustified violations are not inevitable. And once we see this, it is not at all clear why we should *care* whether or not a rule can be obeyed "impartially."

Nor should it be thought that the kind of impartiality at stake here follows trivially from the fact that genuine moral rules are those that would be favored by all *impartial* rational persons. For it certainly seems possible, at least in the absence of further argument, that impartial rational persons might nonetheless favor rules that allow agents to treat other individuals in differing ways—for example, aiding only the *needy* (as opposed to aiding everyone), or aiding only those who need the aid the *most*, or aiding only those among the needy who can be helped at a reasonable *cost*, and so forth. Even if such rules cannot be obeyed "impartially"—in the strong sense of the term—it still seems possible that impartial rational people might favor such rules.

In short, even if the rule "aid the needy" cannot be obeyed "impartially," it is not at all clear why we should care about this fact.

In fairness to Gert, however, it should also be noted that I am not at all confident that he *does* care about whether a rule can be obeyed impartially in this extremely strict sense of the term. For at one point he considers restricted versions of some positive precepts and he says that these precepts *can* be obeyed impartially (181).[11] Presumably, Gert's thought here is that by virtue of the restriction, one can (in the relevant sense) obey the precept with regard to everyone—in that whenever the rule applies (which is less often than it would, absent the restriction) one can obey it. But this suggests that the idea of impartiality that Gert is actually concerned with is not the extreme one after all. And this would mean, of course, that the rule "aid the needy" (perhaps suitably restricted) may be one that *can* be obeyed impartially, in the only sense of the term with which we should be concerned.

I simply do not know whether or not this is Gert's considered view. That is, I am not sure whether Gert would agree that it is irrelevant whether a rule can be obeyed "impartially" in the extremely strict sense of the term. But regardless of whether this is Gert's view, it seems to me correct nonetheless. The validity of the rule "aid the needy" is not threatened by the fact that it is literally impossible to aid everyone who needs aid. What is important, rather, is the fact that unjustified violations of the rule are not inevitable. And so, as far as I can see, we don't yet have any good reason to reject a moral rule requiring aid to others.

Gert's other main argument can be discussed more briefly. It turns on the idea that genuine moral rules are those that impartial rational people would be prepared to enforce, by punishing those who unjustifiably violate the rules (177-82). But Gert believes that rules requiring aid to others are such that it simply isn't true that all impartial rational people are prepared to punish unjustified violations. Thus, there can be no genuine moral rule requiring aid.

But why should we believe Gert's claim that impartial rational people need not favor punishing unjustified violations of rules requiring aid to others? We've already noted that impartial rational people would presumably *want* everyone to aid others. Why, then, wouldn't they be prepared to enforce a rule requiring such aid?

Gert's answer here seems to presuppose the inevitability of unjustified violations of such rules (181). Clearly, if unjustified violations are truly inevitable, then everyone would be "liable to punishment all the time." And it does not seem implausible for Gert to suggest that a rational impartial person may not be prepared to "increase everyone's chance of suffering evil" in this way.

I've already argued, however, that a rule like "aid the needy" is *not* one that must inevitably be unjustifiably violated. (If violations are truly inevitable, they will be justified; and if the rule is properly restricted, violations won't even be inevitable.) Yet if unjustified violations are not inevitable, it is not inevitable that everyone would be liable to punishment all the time. And so it is no longer clear why impartial rational persons would not be prepared to enforce the rule.

Perhaps, however, Gert's position is actually this: even if unjustified violations are not literally inevitable, the fact remains that they are overwhelmingly *likely*. Given familiar facts about limited human sympathy for others, it would be very plausible to suggest that unjustified violations of a rule requiring aid, even a modest rule, would be extremely widespread (even if not literally unavoidable). Thus it remains true that everyone, or almost everyone, would remain liable to punishment. And so Gert might still insist that at least some impartial rational persons won't be willing to enforce the rule, on the grounds that the imposed suffering won't outweigh the potential benefits (181).

But even this reply seems to me inadequate, for it fails to keep in mind Gert's own insistence that liability for punishment does not entail that one *must* be punished. As Gert explains:

> I have said that all impartial rational persons adopt as part of their moral attitude that unjustified violations *may* be punished. I said that unjustified violations may be punished, rather than that they are to be punished because the latter would have needed to be qualified. Situations may arise in which punishing unjustified violations would cause significantly more evil than would result from failure to punish. . . . (181-82)

> [An impartial rational person's] primary goal is to minimize the amount of evil suffered, which is generally best served by punishing unjustified violations. But if it is not, an impartial rational person advocates only that those who unjustifiably violate the rules *may* be punished rather than that they are to be punished. (182)

Gert's idea, then, seems to be this: punishing unjustified violations is a means to an end—the end of reducing suffering and other evils. But it is always an empirical question whether or not punishment will actually serve this end well. In many cases it will; in others it won't. In those cases where punishment would be counterproductive, impartial rational persons won't approve of it—even in the face of unjustified violations of the moral rules.

But if this is right (and it certainly strikes me as plausible), then I am no longer able to see what Gert's objection against a rule requiring aid comes to. Even if we grant that unjustified violations of such a rule will be common, this does not entail that punishment must actually be imposed for all these violations. If, as Gert fears, ubiquitous punishment would do more harm than good, this simply shows that a policy of punishing all such violations would be counterproductive. And so, of course, impartial rational persons need not favor imposing punishment in this fashion. Presumably, they would favor, instead, a more restricted policy here—punishing, perhaps, only especially egregious failures to aid the needy.

The details, of course, would depend on empirical questions concerning the ultimate effects of alternative policies with regard to enforcing a rule requiring aid. But for our purposes the important point is this: none of this in any way shows that a rule requiring aid cannot be a genuine moral rule. For as Gert himself insists, being a genuine moral rule only requires that unjustified violations leave one *liable* to punishment; it does not entail that punishment must actually be imposed, when doing so would be counterproductive. Thus even if Gert is right, and it would be counterproductive to routinely impose punishment (given widespread unjustified violations), this does nothing to show that there can be no rule requiring aid.

I conclude, therefore, that the appeal to punishment does not succeed. Gert still has not given us adequate reason to hold that there can be no genuine moral rule requiring aid to others.

But the arguments that I have reviewed are, as far as I can see, the only arguments Gert offers. Since none of them are successful, I conclude that Gert hasn't actually provided us with a good reason to accept his claim that there can be no moral rule requiring aid.

Of course, the mere fact that such a rule would in principle be *possible* would be of little interest to us, if we were nonetheless of the opinion that there can in fact be no moral *requirements* to provide aid. But I have already argued that from the point of view of Gert's own basic account of morality we should in fact expect there to be moral requirements to aid others, and that Gert, in any event, has given us no good reason to think otherwise. If Gert has an adequate defense of his striking claims about morality—that there is no moral requirement to provide aid, and no moral rule requiring one to provide such aid—I simply don't see what it is.

Are we, then, ever required to aid others? As I indicated at the start of this paper, I believe that the answer is yes. I believe that we are often morally required to aid others, and I believe that we are often rationally required to aid others. Of course, I have not offered any positive defense of these claims here. I have contented, myself, instead with an examination of Gert's arguments for the opposite view—that aiding others is neither rationally nor morally required. Had Gert succeeded in establishing either of these, it would indeed have been a striking and significant accomplishment.

But it would also have been a tremendously disappointing accomplishment. For it would have been disappointing indeed to learn that neither morality nor reason was concerned enough about the suffering of others to require us to come to their aid. Speaking personally, I expect rather more from both morality and reason. Perhaps, then—and here I close—those of us who have rather higher ambitions for both morality and rationality can take some small comfort from Gert's failure.

Notes

1. All parenthetical page references are to Bernard Gert, *Morality: Its Nature and Justification* (New York: Oxford University Press, 1998).

2. This is not to say, however, that the view is without its difficulties. For it is not clear what work is done by appealing to *agreement* among perfectly rational people, as opposed to merely looking for the beliefs of any given perfectly rational person. If perfectly rational people can't disagree, then of course no harm is done in saying that an act is irrational only if all perfectly rational people agree it is; but it would be simpler to assert that an act is irrational only if a perfectly rational person would say so. Explicitly bringing in the concept of agreement only makes sense if people can still disagree, despite being perfectly rational (and well-informed).

Now it seems to me that Gert does think that even perfectly rational people can disagree about what kinds of acts are irrational; but this claim is itself problematic. For example, it seems to mean that when two (well-informed) perfectly rational people disagree, at least one of them will be *mistaken* about the rationality of the act in question. Yet one might have thought that perfectly rational people can't be mistaken about fundamental matters concerning what is and what is not rational. Similarly, one might have thought that if it is *true* that an act is irrational only if perfectly rational people agree it is, then perfectly rational people will recognize this truth, so once one of them holds an act is rational, all others will see that it must be rational after all, and so any disagreement will dissolve. But I will have to leave these complicated questions aside.

3. At one point, Gert suggests that basic claims about irrationality can't be backed with arguments—for then they won't be basic (51). So perhaps Gert wouldn't allow the possibility of arguments of this "more complicated" sort after all. But it seems to me that Gert's remark confuses being fundamental with being self-evident.

4. Again, recall that one might have a socially imposed duty, or one might have made a promise to provide aid, and so forth. But for simplicity, we can assume that we are concerned with cases where these special circumstances do not arise; and in such cases, according to Gert, one will not be required to aid.

5. According to the simple view, you are required to perform an act if failure to perform that act violates the rules. But obviously enough, whenever you fail to avoid violating the rules you violate the rules, and so—according to the simple view—you are *required* to avoid violating the rules. Thus, according to the simple view, all violations are forbidden.

6. Gert distinguishes between "strongly justified" violations (where all impartial rational persons would publicly allow the violation) and "weakly justified" violations (where impartial rational persons can disagree) (151, 222-23). For our purposes, however, the distinction is unimportant.

7. Other remarks of Gert's (e.g., 328) seem compatible with this interpretation as well, though several (e.g., 109, 137) are somewhat more ambiguous, since they merely talk of "encouraging" the violation of the rule—which leaves it open that the violation might not actually be required.

8. This assumes, of course, that if an act is morally wrong one is morally required not to perform it. (In effect, it assumes that "wrong" is equivalent to "forbidden" or "prohibited.") But Gert may reject this entailment. (In particular, Gert may think that an act is required only if—in addition to being wrong—one may be punished for failing to perform it. I can't actually find a passage in which Gert asserts this; but it seems compatible with what he does say.) And if Gert does reject the entailment, then perhaps he does hold the view, after all, that one can be required to perform an act only if there is some moral rule requiring that act. Our question, then, will be whether Gert has good reason to reject the existence of a rule requiring aid. I turn to this below.

9. So far, we've only recognized the possibility of an act being required—even though no moral rule requires it—when the required act violates some moral rule. Presumably, however, it would be implausible to claim that the *only* time one can be required to perform an act not required by a moral rule is when doing so *violates* a moral rule. After all, if an act can be required, merely for the sake of following some moral ideal, even when this violates a moral rule, it should also be possible for an act to be required, in the service of a moral ideal, even when this involves violating *no* moral rules whatsoever.

So it looks as though we must move to a view something like this: an action is required if and only if failure to perform the act would be (1) an unjustified violation of the moral rules or (2) opposed by all impartial rational persons. But since unjustified violations *are* opposed by all impartial rational persons, the first clause collapses into the second, as a mere special case.

10. Might Gert object to this understanding of the rule, on the ground that it is open to dispute what counts as a "reasonable" cost? I don't think that he can, given that his own account of the requirement to rescue makes use of a similar restriction (210). As Gert notes, in a different context, "Justifying the moral rules does not eliminate all moral disagreement" (217). Or perhaps Gert would object that this rule does not have "the simplicity required of general moral rules" (181)? That's hard to say, though to my mind, at least, the rule seems simple enough, even with the implied restriction.

11. I should note, however, that even here all that Gert explicitly says is that the restricted precept can be "impartially obeyed all the time" (181). So perhaps he still thinks (though he doesn't say) that it *cannot* be impartially obeyed "with regard to everyone," and that this is still objectionable.

8

Gert contra Consequentialism

Walter Sinnott-Armstrong

Bernard Gert is ambivalent about consequentialism. It might not seem so, since he criticizes consequentialism and utilitarianism repeatedly and viciously. Here are some of my favorite excesses: "All forms of consequentialism, including negative consequentialism, are so vague as to be almost totally useless as moral guides" (253).[1] "I think utilitarianism not only an incorrect position but an extremely dangerous one" (373). Gert is less restrained in casual conversation, as I can testify.

In response, I will argue that, when consequentialism is properly understood, it is not useless or dangerous, as Gert claims, because its project is different than his.

Is Gert a Closet Consequentialist?

He doth protest too much, methinks. Despite his vehemence, Gert's own moral theory and system have important consequentialist elements that allow it to be interpreted as an indirect form of consequentialism. Or so I will argue.

At the very foundation of Gert's moral theory lies his theory of rationality and reasons. One section heading reads, "No beliefs unrelated to avoiding harms or gaining benefits are basic reasons" (74; cf. 61). Since the consequences of an act include both the harms it avoids and the benefits it gains, Gert holds that all basic reasons for an act must be beliefs about the consequences of that act or about some feature of the act that is related to consequences.

This last disjunct is needed so that a belief that an act violates one of Gert's second five moral rules will always count as a reason not to do that act. Such beliefs are reasons only because "moral rules are good rules" (75), since moral rules pick out act kinds whose instances usually increase the risk of some bad consequence. A belief that a particular act is of such a kind is a reason to believe that the particular act will increase the risk of some bad consequence. This reason can be undermined; but, if all we know about an act is that it breaks a promise, for example, then this is a reason to believe that it risks some harm to somebody. That does not mean that each individual violation actually increases the objective probability of some bad consequence (pace 127); but it does mean that, in the absence of any underminer, we will always have some epistemic reason to believe that such an act will increase the risk of some bad consequence. That seems to be why such beliefs count as basic reasons for Gert.

In contrast, if a rule or custom is not good in this way, then the belief that an action is or would be in accordance with that rule or custom is not a basic reason for doing it (75). Gert also insists that beliefs about past wrongdoing are not basic reasons to punish (74; compare 103) and beliefs about past favors are not basic reasons for showing gratitude (74). In all of these cases, Gert goes against common views (as he recognizes on 61, 74, and 103) and instead sides with consequentialists about reasons.

I am not criticizing these positions. I hold them myself.[2] My point is only that they are consequentialist. What makes Gert's theory consequentialist is not that he holds that *some* reasons have to do with consequences. Any plausible theory holds that. What makes Gert's theory of reasons consequentialist is its claim that *every* basic reason is a reason because of its relation to consequences.

When such a fundamental part of his moral theory is consequentialist in this way, it should not be surprising that other parts of his moral system also turn out to be consequentialist. The most important example is Gert's morally decisive question, which asks "What effects would this kind of violation being publicly allowed have?" (236) This question asks about effects and effects only. Another theory might have asked whether acts of this kind should be publicly allowed or whether any rational impartial person would favor publicly allowing acts of that kind.[3] Such formulations would allow answers to be based not only on consequences but also or instead on moral intuition or some social contract device or God's will or whatever. In contrast, Gert's version of the decisive question requires us to consider only "the consequences of everyone knowing that this kind of violation is allowed" (237). Gert again exclusively focuses on consequences, so this crucial step in his moral system is also consequentialist.

Admittedly, Gert does not refer to actual effects of particular actions. His decisive question asks about hypothetical and even counterfactual effects in a different possible world than the actual one in which the act is done. But that does not remove Gert from the consequentialist camp. Even act consequentialists consider counterfactuals insofar as they compare consequences of alternative acts that are not done. Moreover, rule consequentialism is often formulated in counterfactual terms by its proponents, including John Austin, who wrote that, when asking about the tendency of an act, which determines its moral rightness or wrongness,

> The probable specific consequences of doing that single act, of forbearing from that single act, or of omitting that single act, are not the objects of the inquiry. The question to be solved is this:—If acts of the *class* were *generally* done, or *generally* forborne or omitted, what would be the probable effect on the general happiness or good?[4]

The test of moral wrongness for Austin, thus, compares the consequences in two possible worlds, one or both of which are not actual. Austin presents his view as a "general" version of utilitarianism, and his contemporaries saw it that way. Thus, the fact that Gert's theory, like Austin's, does not focus on consequences in the actual world does not show that it is not consequentialist (pace 215).

Nor does the fact that his rules and procedure for justifying violations refer to factors other than consequences. Rule consequentialists, such as Austin, usually endorse rules that seem nonconsequentialist, but only because those rules have a consequentialist foundation.

Gert's rule consequentialism is, however, more sophisticated than most versions of rule consequentialism. Instead of asking, "What would happen if everyone *did* that?" Gert asks, "What would happen if everyone knew that they were *allowed* to do that?" This is an important improvement. As Gert points out (121), it would be disastrous if everyone stood on their heads all day, but nothing disastrous would happen if everyone knew that they were allowed to stand on their heads all day, since very few would choose or be able to do it. That explains why it is not morally wrong for one person to stand on her head all day.

Another advance is that Gert tells us what *that* is, i.e., which kind of act is done or known to be allowed. Austin blithely refers to "the class" of acts with no limits on which classes might be relevant. That lack of limits leads to well-known problems when one tries to formulate rules precisely (cf. 214). If "the class" is acts that maximize utility, "acts of the class [a]re generally done" when everyone does acts that maximize utility, and then "the probable effect on the general happiness" would be very good. Thus, every single act that maximizes utility passes Austin's test, so Austin's formulation reduces to act consequentialism.[5] Gert avoids that reduction by specifying a canonical description of the act type in terms of morally relevant features (225 ff.).

Admittedly, Gert restricts morally relevant features to concepts that all rational people share, so that justified violations, like moral rules, will be known or knowable by all agents who are bound by the moral system (150-151, 226). Some consequentialists might question why this much knowledge and publicity is necessary for a theory of moral wrongness as opposed to moral responsibility. Nonetheless, each rule consequentialist needs to decide which kind of rule and which procedure for justifying violations determine the moral wrongness of acts.[6] The rationale for making moral wrongness depend on one kind of rule or procedure rather than another need not itself be consequentialist in order for the theory to be consequentialist. Gert does not give a consequentialist rationale for focusing on universal public rules and procedures.[7] Nonetheless, once Gert decides to seek universal public rules and procedures to determine moral wrongness, and once the canonical description of an act is specified, then Gert judges competing candidates for the role of being publicly allowed solely by their consequences. Here again Gert displays the exclusive focus on consequences that makes him a consequentialist.

Of course, Gert's theory is not hedonistic or quantitative or additive. Gert never tells us exactly how to determine whether the consequences of universally publicly allowing all acts of a kind are better than the consequences of not so allowing. He says that he would put more weight on preventing harms than on gaining benefits. He probably also would consider other factors in addition to the total harms and benefits of the options, including distribution. But that is still compatible with consequentialism, as Gert recognizes (213). Consequentialism about moral oughtness or wrongness claims only that whether an act morally ought to be done or is morally wrong is determined solely by the consequences of something, such as the particular act or universally publicly allowing all acts of the same kind. This broad claim is compatible with almost any way of comparing values. Thus, even if Gert does not quantify or add harms or benefits, and even if he considers distribution as well as objective goods, none of that keeps him from being a consequentialist in a broad sense that is common in moral theory.[8]

I conclude that Gert's own moral system can be interpreted as a sophisticated form of negative objective universal public rule consequentialism.

Sophisticated Act Consequentialism

Even so, Gert's system still contrasts sharply with act consequentialism. That is the view that Gert criticizes so strongly.

It is easy to poke fun at simplistic versions of act utilitarianism, but refuting the crudest versions of a class of views will not refute the whole class. To assess act consequentialism in general, we need to compare Gert's sophisticated rule consequentialism with the best sophisticated version of act consequentialism.

I will sketch one such version. I will not endorse, much less argue for, this system here. I cannot even spell out all of its details. All I hope to do is to make it clear enough and plausible enough to set up a fair fight with Gert.

Act consequentialism is an instance of direct consequentialism. Direct consequentialists determine which acts a person ought to do by the consequences of that person doing those acts. They can also determine which public rules our society ought to have by the consequences of our society having those public rules. They can also determine which motives (and states of character) a person ought to have by the consequences of that person having those motives (and states of character).[9] What ought to be at each level is determined by the consequences of the very thing being assessed. That is what makes this view direct.

In contrast, rule consequentialism about acts is indirect in that whether an act ought to be done is determined not by the consequences of the act itself but instead by the consequences of some group obeying or accepting a general rule that the act violates or conforms to. Such indirect consequentialism strikes many people as implausible to the extent that it is hard to see why one thing should be evaluated by the consequences of something else. Direct consequentialism also enables us to explain our ambivalence in complex conflicts by allowing different evaluations at different levels, such as when an act morally ought to be done although it violates a good moral rule. The plausibility and power of direct consequentialism then extend to its part, act consequentialism, which is the claim that an agent ought to do an act if and only if that act has better consequences than any alternative act.

This claim itself says nothing about which consequences are best, so it needs to be supplemented by separate claims about value. Classical utilitarians held hedonistic or subjective theories of value, but most today reject hedonism, so our consequentialist theory will probably seem more plausible if it includes some values that are objective in the sense that they are independent of any conscious mental state. For example, one can have life and freedom even while one is sleeping so deeply that one has no conscious mental states at all. To make the contrast with Gert stark, I will assume Gert's own theory that the only basic goods are pleasure, freedom, ability, and life (or consciousness), and the only basic evils are pain and losses of goods. Personally I would add other items, such as false beliefs (217n1), and take away some items, such as life (which has no value independent of pleasure and some ability to control consciousness, pace 93); but these minor changes do not affect my points here, so I will ignore them.

This list of goods and evils does not itself tell us how to determine which is better among the total sets of consequences that result or would result from different actions. It does not even tell us which consequences count, or for whom. Act consequentialism can be held about all reasons or just about morality. There are consequentialist systems of prudence, which consider only consequences to the agent, and even aesthetics, which does not consider economic effects.

Our concern here is a moral system. Consequently, I will assume that the system is universalistic in the sense that harms and benefits to everyone count and that it is egalitarian in the sense that the harms and benefits to each count equally (in some sense). The theory can still depart from classical utilitarianism by allowing comparisons of total consequences to be affected by the distribution and mix of values within the total consequence (213). There might be some algorithm, but I do not know of any; so I will discuss a version of act consequentialism on which one total consequence is objectively better than another in a morally relevant way if the first would be preferred by all rational impartial persons. We can again follow Gert in allowing disagreements among rational impartial persons. If some rational impartial people prefer one total consequence, and others prefer another, the total consequences are incomparable in the sense that neither is better and they are also not equal. (Compare 77-78.) This shows how some moral disagreements and conflicts can be unresolvable.[10]

This version of act consequentialism, thus, shares many of the advantages of Gert's own system. Insofar as Gert's theory gains plausibility by allowing reasonable moral disagreements, as he claims, that plausibility will be inherited by this version of act consequentialism. Insofar as Gert's theory of harms and benefits is plausible, that plausibility will be inherited by this version of act consequentialism. Insofar as Gert's emphasis on universal public rules is plausible, act consequentialists can talk about which universal public rules morally ought to be used, taught, and enforced. This will be just one special application of their basic system. Sophisticated act consequentialism can thereby incorporate much of Gert's own moral system. Moreover, it has the additional virtues of directness and flexibility. So I hope it seems plausible, at least initially. Anyway, this is the version of act consequentialism that I will discuss henceforth.

Gert's Criticisms

The crucial question is whether any such act consequentialism can adequately respond to Gert's main objections. I will argue that it can.

Too Much Impartiality

Gert's first main criticism is that act consequentialism requires or demands too much. Gert makes this charge specifically with regard to impartiality:

> it is humanly impossible for anyone to act impartially with respect to preventing or relieving the pain or suffering of all moral agents, much less to promoting their pleasure or happiness. It is absurd to claim that morality *requires* one to act impartially toward all moral agents with respect to the consequences of one's action on their happiness when it is humanly impossible to do so. (136, my emphasis; cf. 123, 152)

This might seem confused. It is not literally impossible to be impartial toward all moral agents. In each case, one can use an arbitrary and hence impartial method (say, flip a coin) to choose whom to help (cf. 133). This is not far from what people do when they help those needy people whom they happen to meet or hear about.

Gert might respond that we cannot be impartial all the time. However, one could donate a dollar per year to a charity that reduces suffering as much as possible with no regard to who is suffering. Then, for each portion of the year, one donates a portion of a dollar and hence does something impartial.

Gert can still respond that not all of our acts can be impartial in this way, because human nature gives us all such a strong tendency to favor ourselves and our families and friends in at least some acts. This makes universal impartiality *humanly* impossible.

Some act consequentialists, such as Godwin, might respond that all this shows is that human nature leads us to do what is morally wrong. After all, human nature also leads people to seek revenge even when doing so is irrational, and so on. But Gert could respond that it is humanly possible to lead a whole life without ever seeking revenge, whereas it is humanly impossible to live a whole life without ever being partial to oneself or anyone else.

The argument then seems to depend on the principle that "ought" implies "can," or at least that one must be able to avoid doing what is morally wrong. This principle could be challenged.[11] Moreover, even if one cannot avoid ever acting partially, one can avoid each particular act of partiality. That seems to be enough to save act consequentialism from Gert's argument.

Nonetheless, I will focus on another response that is available to act consequentialists. Act consequentialists can simply distinguish what is morally *required* from what morally *ought* to be done. The principle of act consequentialism, as I and most others formulate it, determines what agents morally ought to do. Still, some acts that morally ought to be done are not morally required. An act is morally required only when failure to do that act is morally wrong. Moral wrongness in this view implies some kind of punishability. As Mill wrote,

> We do not call anything [morally] wrong unless we mean to imply that a person ought to be punished in some way or other for doing it—if not by law, by the opinion of his fellow creatures; if not by opinion, by the reproaches of his own conscience. . . . There are other things, on the contrary, which we wish that people should do, which we like or admire them for doing, but yet admit that they are not bound to do; it is not a case of moral obligation; we do not blame them, that is, we do not think they are the proper objects of punishment.[12]

Mill's distinction between what is morally wrong to omit and what morally ought to be done, of course, parallels Gert's distinction between moral rules and ideals. My point is that a similar distinction can be drawn within act consequentialism.

The resulting theory of moral wrongness will be indirect insofar as the moral wrongness of an act depends on the consequences of a different act (of punishment), but that much indirectness is plausible if claims of moral wrongness are used primarily for judging other people or for imagining how other people should judge us, since then the main issue is how one person should react to acts by another person. Moreover, the basic principle of what morally ought to be done can remain direct act consequentialism.

One might object that the notion of punishments and punishability are vague. Granted. But they are no clearer in Gert's theory. Gert does say that punishment must inflict evil, and he does chide Mill for including "reproaches of his own conscience" (16), but beyond this Gert never specifies what counts as punishment for him. Imprisonment and flogging are clearly punishment, but what about fines and civil damages? What if you privately or publicly rebuke your neighbor? What if a misdeed makes you refuse to hire or promote someone? What if you just refuse to invite them to a party? Are these punishments?

Gert can draw a line, of course. The problem is to justify drawing the line in one place rather than another. In discussion, Gert said that punishment must be inflicted "by authorized persons in accordance with some established procedure." But what is needed for authorization? Gert sees parents as authorized to punish their children, but who authorizes them? Gert's main model seems to be law. However, what is morally wrong should not depend on what is legally punishable, because one role of morality is to determine what legal systems may and may not punish. Moreover, many moral wrongs should not be punished legally or by parents. Even if no parent or legal authority should get involved, it still might be morally wrong for me to lie to a friend. Is that friend authorized to punish me somehow? Is a mutual friend so authorized? Since it is not clear who counts as "authorized" or when a procedure is "established," it is still not clear what counts as punishment in Gert's system.

My own view is that we should distinguish different degrees of obligation and moral obligation according to different kinds of negative reactions that are warranted by violations, so there is no need to draw a hard and fast line between punishment and nonpunishment. Mill could agree, but Gert needs a stable line between punishment and nonpunishment in order to draw his distinction between moral rules and moral ideals. It is not clear where or how he will draw or justify that line. Anyway, however Gert eventually defines punishment, act consequentialists can adopt or adapt the same definition. Thus, if Gert can contrast moral rules with moral ideals in terms of punishability versus encouragement, then act consequentialists should be able to use the same tools to distinguish what one is morally required to do from what one morally ought to do.

Armed with this distinction, act consequentialists can agree with Gert that impartiality with regard to consequences is not always morally *required* (136, 152). Specifically, such impartiality is not morally required when partiality is not morally wrong or morally ought not to be punished. It morally ought not to be punished when punishment would not have the best consequences. When is that? Sidgwick argues plausibly that we should grade on a curve: "we think that moral progress will on the whole best be promoted by our praising acts that are above the level of ordinary practice, and confining our censure—at least if precise and particular—to acts that fall clearly below this standard."[13] Sidgwick admits that this line "must be inevitably vague," but the basic idea is clear. When so many people are so partial, there are too many cases to censure them all, so it is best to pick out the worst offenders for censure. If we censure those who show only moderate partiality in cases where almost everyone else would also, this will do little good and will probably discourage the worst offenders from raising themselves up to the norm, since even then they will not escape censure. For such reasons, we should reserve censure and punishment for cases where people show too much partiality or show it in situations where impartiality is especially important, such as in courtrooms or classrooms or in other situations where Gert counts a kind of act as an unjustified violation of a moral rule. It is only in those cases, then, that partiality is morally wrong and impartiality is morally required.

Act consequentialists can still explain why very rich people might be morally required to contribute a great deal to charity, much more in absolute terms and in percentages than the middle class. There is more to be gained by inducing a single very rich person to contribute. Moreover, that person has less to lose, since a multibillionaire would still be very rich if he gave away a billion dollars. Consequently, if private or public censure would increase the billionaire's charitable contributions and would not have too many bad side effects, then censure morally ought to be applied. The government could pass steeply graduated taxes enforced by legal punishments, but moral censure still might be useful in addition to taxes. The billionaire could not complain that he is censured without moral wrongdoing, if he did fail to contribute enough, since whether that failure is morally wrong is the issue at stake. At least a billionaire who gives little to charity morally ought to censure himself by feeling guilty for not giving more. Those emotions of guilt would be justified by their consequences in such circumstances. Insofar as such censure and guilt feelings count as punishment, their being justified implies some degree of moral requirement for the very rich that did not exist for the middle class. Act consequentialism thereby retains much of its radical and reformative character, even while it limits what is morally required for most people.

Many details remain to be worked out, but enough has been said to show how act consequentialists can avoid the charge that they *require* too much (or too little) impartiality. Act consequentialists still hold that everyone morally *ought* to be impartial in a way that would greatly affect most people's lives, but that weaker claim does not seem so implausible, at least to act consequentialists.

Too Much Information

A separate but related criticism is that act consequentialism requires too much information. Gert writes,

> If the relevant consequences are taken to be actual consequences, then act utilitarianism leads naturally to skepticism. No one can possibly know all the future consequences of his proposed action, let alone all of the actual future consequences of all of the possible alternative actions, so there is no way that anyone can ever know that any given act is morally good or right. (129n9)

If one rejects such moral skepticism, act consequentialism will seem inadequate, at least "if the relevant consequences are taken to be actual consequences."

One popular response is for act consequentialists to turn to foreseeable consequences. Gert recommends this move, and it is available within the general framework of act consequentialism.

But there are reasons to resist this temptation. The turn to foreseeable consequences raises a question, "Foreseeable by whom?" Gert talks about what is foreseeable by the agent whose acts are judged, but that produces problems. If you do not know and have no way of knowing that your act of keeping a trivial promise will cause many deaths, but an observer does know this and also knows that this act will have no benefits for anyone, then that observer should *not* say (to you or to another) that you morally ought to do this act. If possible, the observer should tell you that you morally ought *not* to do it. This "ought" is moral because it is based on harm to others, rather than harm to self, economic benefit, law, religion, or anything else apart from morality; and you are able to respond to advice from the observer. Of course, if you do kill those people because of a reasonable mistake, then you have an excuse, you are not responsible, and you should not be blamed or judged to be a morally bad person, because you had no way of knowing that you were killing. Such moral judgments about responsibility and persons, then, might depend on whether consequences are foreseeable.[14] Also, of course, agents have to decide on the basis of consequences that they can foresee. But judgments about the moral rightness or wrongness of acts, when made by observers, do not seem restricted to what was foreseeable by the agent.

Moreover, Gert's decisive question asks about the consequences of publicly allowing all acts of a kind. The relevant kind of act is determined by what is foreseeable to the agent of that act, so different agents can do the same kind of act only if they are able to foresee the same consequences of their particular acts. But different agents still might foresee and be able to foresee very different consequences of publicly allowing all acts of that kind. Thus, whether it is morally wrong for an agent to do an act of that kind cannot be determined by whether that agent can foresee that publicly allowing all such acts would have worse consequences than not publicly allowing all such acts. If it did so depend, then acts of the very same kind would be morally wrong for one agent but right for another. Active euthanasia, for example, would be morally wrong for some doctors but not for others, even when the doctors are able to foresee the same consequences of their acts. That is a result that Gert wants to avoid. So his decisive question, at least, cannot refer to effects that are foreseeable by the agent.

Gert might respond that what matters is what is foreseeable by the observer making the moral judgment. But that leads to other problems. There could be several observers. Suppose a first observer knows that your act will cause many deaths, but a second observer cannot foresee these or any bad consequences of your act. Accordingly, the first observer says that your act is morally wrong, and the second observer says that your act is not morally wrong. Both of these moral judgments would be correct if what is morally wrong depended on the consequences that are foreseeable by the person making the moral judgment. But these judgments cannot both be correct (even though both might be justified, given different epistemic situations of the two observers). Consequently, act consequentialists should not make what is morally wrong depend on what is foreseeable by the person making the moral judgment. This leaves no satisfying answer to the question "Foreseeable by whom?"

Other problems arise when we ask when a consequence is foreseeable. Does it have to be foreseeable given what the person actually believes or what the person should believe or should we subtract false beliefs or just beliefs the person should know are false? Different theories give different answers, and no answer fits all of our intuitions.

It is hard to see any way to avoid such problems except by making what is morally wrong depend on actual consequences (or some equivalent, such as an ideal observer). This conclusion might, however, seem problematic when applied to retrospective moral judgments. Suppose again that you have no way of knowing that your act will cause many deaths, and nobody warns you, so you do it, and it does cause many deaths. According to act consequentialists who count actual consequences, your act was morally wrong. Gert claims that no normal speaker would say this. I am not so sure whether this is so or why.

Gert argues that such retrospective judgments would be like judgments of nonhuman animals, but we do not make moral judgments about nonhuman animals (21-22). However, act consequentialists can accept that we do not classify a judgment as moral unless it is about humans. That fact about common usage might merely reflect the inability of nonhuman animals to follow advice given in moral judgments. After all, we also do not advise animals to brush their teeth. In contrast, even when a normal adult human has no way of knowing that an act will cause many deaths, such a human is still capable of responding to advice if an observer says that the act will cause deaths and that the human morally ought not to do it. Even after the act is done, a human is still the kind of agent who is normally responsible and subject to moral judgment, and who was capable of responding to advice if any had been given in advance. So, even if you could not have foreseen the deaths, you are not like an animal in any way that need preclude retrospective moral judgments of your acts.

Moreover, after you cause the deaths that you could not have foreseen, you and your victims wish that someone had warned you, since your act turned out to be the wrong thing to do. Its wrongness was not prudential or economic or aesthetic or religious or anything other than moral. What makes it wrong is harm to others without adequately compensating benefits, as in standard cases of moral wrongness. Such considerations might lead some to call your act morally wrong. Of course, they should immediately add that you were not responsible, blameworthy, punishable, or bad as a person; but the moral wrongness of your act is a separate matter.

The reason why speakers are so reluctant to call such acts morally wrong might be just that we usually make such retrospective judgments in order to blame agents, so an audience might be misled into thinking that the agent is blameworthy or a bad person. This explanation can be supported by the oddness of saying that your act was morally right when you killed so many people. For different reasons, then, we usually avoid expressing either moral judgment out loud. But it still might be correct that your act was morally wrong, even if nobody likes to say it.

The other problem is that actual consequences go on forever, so they seem unknowable, and this version of act consequentialism seems to lead quickly to skepticism about moral knowledge. (Recall 129n9.) This implication would hold if knowledge required certainty. One cannot ever be certain about the long-term consequences of any particular act, so, if moral wrongness depends on those consequences, one cannot ever be certain that any particular act is morally wrong. But that implication does not seem absurd, if one does not forget that one still can know that the agent is punishable on the basis of what was intended or foreseeable.

Moreover, agents and observers can still have very good reasons to believe that the overall consequences of an act will be good or bad. It is extremely unlikely that the overall consequences would be good if I killed my neighbors right now. It is possible that these deaths will lead to world peace, but that is unlikely. There is at least as much reason to think that they would lead to world war. Thus, although I cannot be certain, I can be justified in believing that my killing my neighbors now would be morally wrong, according to act consequentialists who count actual consequences. In other cases, where it is harder to justify beliefs about overall consequences, it is harder to be justified in believing that an act is morally right or wrong. But that just shows that life is tough. No news there. And no problem for actualistic act consequentialism, since any plausible moral theory should admit that we often cannot tell what is morally right or wrong.

Even if it still seems implausible to count actual consequences, it does not matter for my purposes whether act consequentialists count actual consequences or some kind of foreseeable consequences. So here I will not take either position. Since Gert counts foreseeable consequences and usually assumes that act consequentialists do the same, I will write as if act consequentialists count foreseeable consequences. Any remaining differences with Gert must then be due to other factors. Readers who favor actual consequentialism still may reformulate my points in terms of actual consequences. Whichever version of act consequentialism seems best, the question here is whether that best version is as plausible as Gert's moral system.

To compare these systems, we need to determine whether Gert's moral system avoids the epistemic limits of consequentialism. He claims that "everyone who is judged by it knows what morality prohibits, requires, encourages, and allows" (4; cf. 7, 10, etc.). This is too strong as it stands. One problem is that Gert's second morally relevant feature requires us to determine the consequences of each particular act in order to determine what kind of act it is (228). The fifth, sixth, and eighth morally relevant features also refer implicitly or explicitly to consequences (231-33). Gert tells us that he refers to foreseeable consequences of acts and their alternatives and public allowings. However, an agent might not *actually* foresee or know consequences that she is *able* to foresee or know. Then the agent will not actually know what kind an act is or whether that act is morally permissible.

Gert might respond that at least the moral status of the act is *knowable* because its consequences are foreseeable. However, even if he can solve the above problems about foreseeability, this weaker claim does not fit with his limitation to rationally required beliefs and concepts in his moral theory. Many beliefs and concepts that are not actually shared by all rational people, nonetheless, *could* be held by all rational people. This includes much science, if what could be known is broad enough. It is not clear why those additional beliefs and concepts should not be used in moral theory if agents are judged not by what they do foresee but by what they could foresee.

Even if this tension can be resolved, Gert faces worse epistemic problems regarding his morally decisive question, which asks about the effects of a kind of violation being publicly allowed (236). This speculative counterfactual question about the consequences of a practice that we do not follow in a world that we do not inhabit will be harder to answer than the act consequentialist's question (especially if the act consequentialist counts only foreseeable consequences of particular acts). Gert seems to assume that it is easy to extrapolate from what would happen in our society to what would happen if we all started to think differently about what we are allowed to do. This is not at all easy, because so many other social circumstances might change along with this change in our public allowings. For example, if we all viewed ourselves as allowed to break laws when doing so causes and risks no harm, then this might undermine "the order and stability that is essential for any society to function well", as Gert claims (208). Or it might lead to very few and minor illegal acts. There need be no increase in murder, rape, theft, or any harmful or dangerous acts, since those acts are still ruled out. Some people would drive through stop signs on clearly deserted streets, but other drivers would know to watch more carefully. This new attitude to law might even lead to reforms of the legal system, including better enforcement to increase risks of punishment and better laws in areas where breaking the law harms nobody. All of this is speculation, but it can be countered only by more speculation or ideology (238). So justified beliefs about moral rightness and wrongness are at least as hard to obtain on Gert's version of rule consequentialism as on act consequentialism.

Gert will probably respond that his moral system has the advantage of concrete rules, whereas act consequentialism cannot be applied without detailed examination of each situation. This might seem to make act consequentialism useless as a guide to conduct in those cases where we cannot form justified beliefs about consequences. Moreover,

> Consequentialism provides no procedure for weighing foreseeable beneficial consequences against foreseeable harmful ones or even for weighing one kind of evil against another. It says nothing about how probabilities are to be considered, nor does it answer any questions about distribution or even about the scope of morality. (253)

Gert is, unfortunately, right about most of this. Consequentialists do need to do much more to solve these problems. Still, nothing within the general framework of consequentialism precludes making progress by specifying and justifying a particular way of weighing harms against benefits and other harms.[15] Regarding probability, decision and game theorists have developed many ways to deal with risk and uncertainty. Dominance, maximin, disaster avoidance, and other principles constrain what is rational in situations where we cannot know even the probabilities of various consequences.[16] These principles can be adapted to morality by act consequentialists so as to provide some moral guidance when agents cannot form justified beliefs about the probabilities of consequences of acts. The resulting theory will still be a version of act consequentialism because such principles apply directly to the particular circumstances of particular acts, just as does the basic principle of act consequentialism itself.

Moreover, Gert does no better. Gert himself "provides no procedure for weighing foreseeable beneficial consequences against foreseeable harmful ones or even for weighing one kind of evil against another" and "says nothing about how probabilities are to be considered" and does not "answer any questions about distribution or even about the scope of morality" (253). Gert does refer to what impartial rational people would favor, but act consequentialists could do the same, and that will not tell us how to determine what they would favor.

Most important, even when act consequentialism does fail to provide any direct practical guidance, that failure is beside the point, if the goal of the theory lies elsewhere. Some moral systems try to provide a direct practical *guide,* that is, a step-by-step method that agents can self-consciously go through in order to reach decisions about acts and attitudes when they face moral problems. Some even want their guide to be *public*, that is, taught and accepted by all. Other moral systems seek a very different goal, namely, *conditions* of moral oughtness, rightness, and wrongness, that is, a formulation of the necessary and sufficient conditions for an act to be morally right or wrong or to be an act that morally ought or ought not to be done.[17] If agents cannot readily determine whether these necessary and sufficient conditions are met, then these conditions cannot be used as a guide in everyday life; but that does not show that those conditions are not necessary and sufficient for an act to have the relevant moral status. That is all they are claimed to be.

This divergence between guides and conditions is common outside morality. The condition of rightness for investments is actual net income and capital gain, but financial advisers often say to diversify, focus on blue chip stocks, and so on. These practical guides tell investors not to aim directly at the conditions of rightness, because that would be too risky. Gert admits this divergence in theoretical cases and some practical areas, including the stock market, but then he claims that practical guides do not diverge from conditions of rightness in moral contexts (325-26). He gives (and I see) no good reason to deny that the same divergence occurs within morality, where the term "right" is used with the same meaning.

Although act consequentialists seek primarily to specify conditions of moral rightness, they can construct practical guides as well. Indeed, their conditions of moral rightness can be used to determine the right practical guide. Act consequentialists will prefer one practical guide over another when following that guide will make it more likely that agents will bring about the best consequences in the circumstances.[18]

Act consequentialists can agree with Gert that people do not, cannot, and should not appeal directly and self-consciously to consequences alone when they decide what to do in most everyday situations.[19] Act consequentialist conditions of moral rightness might be useless and even dangerous if misused as a direct practical guide. But that is not their intended use, and these dangers of misuse do not show that such conditions of moral rightness are useless (pace 253). They can still be useful in determining which practical guide is best.

In choosing a guide for everyday use, act consequentialists will have to consider the fallibility of humans. Gert criticizes act consequentialism for "fail[ing] to recognize that the fallibility of persons is an essential presupposition of morality" (205-6; cf. 245). But the most that they do is refuse to build fallibility directly into their conditions of moral rightness.[20] Their practical guide still can and should be tailored to reflect common mistakes and also to help people work with the information that is available to them in various situations. By providing such a practical guide that is separate from its conditions of moral rightness, act consequentialism thereby avoids requiring too much information.

Act consequentialists can even incorporate publicity and universality, since they ask which rules should be publicly announced and taught as rules for all people to use self-consciously, that is, as public guides. The results might be very close to the content Gert's moral system.

But there will still be differences. Suppose two people get married. Each wants both to feel free to have sexual relations with others, so their marriage vows include no promise of sexual exclusivity. Later each does have sex with others and tells the spouse. This does not bother either of them, because they know that they really love each other, regardless of how each gets physical pleasure on the side. They do not have children who could be harmed by their activity; and they keep it secret from their neighbors, because they know that their neighbors and most of their society disapprove of adultery, and they do not want to upset anybody unnecessarily. They do not care whether other marriages are like theirs, but they like theirs the way it is. Nonetheless, Gert would say that their acts of adultery violate his moral rule against cheating if the institution of marriage in their society requires sexual exclusivity, as in modern Western societies, according to Gert (196-97). His point cannot be that this couple violates any explicit or implicit promise, nor that they deceive others by representing themselves as having promised sexual exclusivity, since he insists that his rule against cheating is independent of his rules governing promises and deception (192, 208-9). Gert's claim is that this couple's acts of adultery are morally wrong just because publicly allowing adultery like theirs would undermine the existing institution of marriage, that institution is generally beneficial, and their only reason to violate it is to get sexual pleasure.

Old hippies and libertarians might respond that here Gert takes publicity too far. To these critics, it seems unfair to let the dominant public institution determine the moral status of their private sexual lives. Act consequentialists can agree with these critics insofar as, even if a public prohibition on adultery has better consequences generally, this unusual couple's private sexual acts are not morally wrong, when those acts have the best consequences among their alternatives. Whether or not you agree, the point here is just that act consequentialism remains at least plausible and distinct from Gert's system.

What enables act consequentialists to adopt such a position is that they can separate conditions of moral rightness from their universal public guide. Gert conflates these stages into one when he claims that the universal public guide determines what is morally right and wrong. This conflation prevents Gert from drawing distinctions that others can. In this respect, act consequentialists can provide everything Gert does, and more.

Indeed, act consequentialists can provide many practical guides. One question asks which practical guide has the best consequences when everyone knows that everyone knows that everyone follows it. Less universal but no less public practical guides might, however, be best for certain societies or certain groups within society, such as doctors. A slightly different practical guide might have the best consequences if followed by a given individual. Opponents might scorn this proliferation of practical guides or any nonpublic or nonuniversal morality (215), but act consequentialists can respond that their theory thereby recognizes more of the levels and complexities of our moral lives (pace 6).

Even if this flexibility is not seen as an advantage, at least the two approaches seem to be at a standoff. Gert seeks direct practical guidance or rules for all to follow publicly and self-consciously. Act consequentialists instead seek to specify conditions of moral rightness. Gert cannot fairly complain that they do not give him what he wants, if they are not trying to do that. Gert's project is not the only worthwhile project in moral theory. If act consequentialists are up to something else, that cannot be used against them.

Too Little Common Sense

Some of you are probably feeling impatient. Haven't I left out the most obvious and strongest criticism of act consequentialism? Yes, but no longer.

The most common criticism of act consequentialism is that it has absurd implications in particular cases. It is supposed to license harming one person to benefit others, which is supposed to violate the victim's rights. Many examples have been given, including proverbial sheriffs hanging innocent people to stop riots, doctors cutting up one healthy person to get organs to save five dying patients, and so on.

Gert agrees that such acts are morally wrong, but he argues that sometimes it is permissible to kill an innocent person in order to prevent more harm to more people (124-25). So Gert's main counterexample to utilitarianism is different: "It is a universally accepted criticism of some forms of utilitarianism that it would allow the infliction of pain on one person in order to promote a great amount of pleasure for many others if a sufficiently large number will receive the pleasure" (124; cf. 15, 231, 373). One common example is Romans forcing slaves to fight lions as entertainment for citizens in the coliseum stands.

It is not clear that act consequentialists must allow any such act. Even hedonistic act utilitarians can argue plausibly that there will always be some better form of entertainment with less cost in the long run. Sophisticated act consequentialists can also count the freedom and life lost by the slave; and they can assign relative values so that those losses always override any entertainment value. Act consequentialists can also count distribution in a way that magnifies losses to those previously deprived, and they can discount pleasures at pain to others.[21] Such moves enable sophisticated act consequentialists to minimize divergence between their view and common morality.

Gert will insist that act consequentialism still diverges from common morality in some examples. One of his favorites involves cheating on a medical school final exam (cf. 203). To ensure that cheating has the best consequences and the student can foresee this, Gert needs to add details: the student must be able to know that more harm will result if he does not cheat (because there is no other way to avoid failing, and failing will hurt his career and his parents, who are doting and dying). He must also be able to know that no or less harm will come if he does cheat (because he won't be caught or feel too guilty, he won't become an incompetent doctor or a bad person, and other students won't be harmed in later competition or because these grades are curved). The student must also be able to know that more good will come if he does cheat (since he will pass and be happy, his parents will be very proud of him, and he will get his degree, start his career, help many patients, and live happily). If enough details are spelled out properly, cheating will have the best consequences, and the student will be able to know this, so act consequentialism will imply that the student morally ought to cheat.

Gert claims that this implication of act consequentialism conflicts with common morality and also with his and most moral intuitions. He backs up this moral intuition with an argument from publicity: rational impartial people would never advocate publicly allowing cheating in circumstances like these, because publicly allowing this kind of act would make impossible all restricted tests or would lead to too many abuses, as students make mistakes about the consequences of cheating and its alternatives.

Act consequentialists could respond by adjusting their theory of value so that cheating does not have the best consequences in this case, or they could argue that it is not really counterintuitive to hold that cheating is morally permissible in such extreme circumstances. However, I would like to explore a third possible response, namely, that, even though act consequentialism is counterintuitive in such examples, that does not refute it.

The crucial question for this response asks why it is so bad for a theory to be counterintuitive. At first, Gert answers this way: "it would not count as *justifying morality* unless the code of conduct being justified was virtually identical to the moral system that is now implicitly used in deciding how to act morally and in making moral judgments" (7). This test has to be hedged by the term "virtually", because no moral progress is possible without some change, and also because Gert's own theory is not completely identical with the moral system in current use. Once that hedge is inserted, however, it is not clear why act consequentialism fails this test. As Sidgwick argued in some detail, act consequentialism agrees with common morality in a wide range of cases.[22] There is even more convergence with sophisticated versions of act consequentialism. Partly because secrets are hard to keep, better consequences will almost always be produced by following common morality or Gert's rules, except when violations are justified by Gert's procedure. So these systems are "virtually" identical, unlike Nietzsche's system (17-18).

These systems still differ somewhat, so we need to ask whether a theory is refuted if it diverges at all from common morality. Gert himself goes on to say, "Any divergence counts against the adequacy of the generated system and ultimately against the moral theory that generated it. This is precisely what happened to utilitarianism" (7). Here Gert claims that every divergence counts, but how much? Act consequentialism has virtues that might override some minor divergence from common morality, so its critics also need to show that its counterintuitive implications are numerous and important enough to refute it.

Gert and other critics do claim this, but why? Maybe because the systems diverge in so many cases. One book lists over a hundred counterexamples to utilitarianism (although many do not apply to sophisticated act consequentialism, and many that do apply are questionable). In principle, act consequentialism diverges from common morality and from Gert's system in an infinite number of possible cases. But the raw number is not decisive. Act consequentialists can respond that divergence occurs only in cases that are recognizably abnormal both statistically and in the sense that they are emergencies, a feature that Gert admits to be morally relevant (235).

More importantly, the rare cases are unrealistic. Cheating seems to have the best foreseeable consequences in Gert's case only because the student knows more than any real student could ever really know or justifiably believe. As the number of convictions shows, students do not know as much as they think they know about whether they will be caught. As Raskolnikov found out in Dostoevsky's *Crime and Punishment*, it is also hard to tell how guilty one will feel, or how such an act will affect one's character and future actions. Similarly, when critics talk blithely about cutting up one person to save five, they forget that real transplants require many staff members, any one of whom could leak information that would ruin the doctor and the hospital. Such counterexamples depend on secrecy, but secrecy is fragile in real life. These critics also forget that doctors never know whether transplants will work, that often another treatment might work without costing lives, that such acts affect the agents' characters and future actions, that it would be a massively unlikely coincidence if five patients all happened to be compatible with a complete stranger who happens to walk into the hospital, and so on. Such details are essential and justify calling such counterexamples unrealistic.

These examples are still logically possible. If act consequentialism is supposed to hold necessarily, such cases refute it if the acts in such examples are morally wrong. So why does it matter that these examples are unrealistic?

This lack of realism matters because the arguments against act consequentialism rest on moral intuitions that these acts are morally wrong. Our moral intuitions evolved to help us deal with normal and realistic cases. They were then shaped by social indoctrination and teaching that was also aimed at the most common kinds of cases. Only philosophers worry about unrealistic situations. Given their origin, it is not at all clear why moral intuitions should be trusted in rare and unrealistic cases. If moral intuitions should not be trusted in such cases, then they cannot refute act consequentialism.[23]

These cases still might leave a dirty taste in one's mouth. No teacher likes to say that it is morally permissible to cheat. No doctor likes to say that it is morally permissible to cut up one person to save five, even in unrealistic circumstances. However, act consequentialists can easily explain why we are and should be reluctant to publicly announce and even think that such acts would be morally permissible. If we announce these permissions to others, or if we think them to ourselves, then we or our audience will be more likely to make mistakes and cheat or cut up when such acts are not morally permissible, which is all or almost all of the cases that we will really encounter. Our speech acts and thoughts affect our actions, so those speech acts and thoughts can be evaluated by their consequences. But those consequences of speech and thought still need not reveal the truth of those claims and thoughts or the moral status of the acts that those claims and thoughts are about. So this explanation is compatible with act consequentialism.

This response would not be available if act consequentialists proposed their system as a public guide. But we already saw that what act consequentialists propose is conditions of moral rightness. Act consequentialists can agree that no acceptable public guide would ever allow students to cheat or doctors to cut up healthy patients. Nonetheless, even if no act consequentialist moral system should be publicly announced or taught in medical schools, acts that are forbidden by the best public guide still might be morally right in abnormal emergencies where those acts have the best consequences. That is all that act consequentialists need to claim in order to defend their conditions of moral rightness.

Conclusion

I have not argued and I do not claim that act consequentialism is correct. All I have tried to show is how sophisticated act consequentialists could best respond to Gert's criticisms. I doubt that Gert or his followers will be persuaded by these responses, but that does not settle the question of whether Gert's arguments succeed in refuting act consequentialism.

My answer to that question is that the force of Gert's criticisms depends on the purpose of one's moral theory. As Sidgwick pointed out,

> There are two distinct ways of treating ethical questions. . . . We may begin by establishing fundamental principles of abstract or ideal morality, and then proceed to work out deductively the particular rules of duty or practical conceptions of human good or well-being, through the adoption of which these principles may be as far as possible realized, under the actual conditions of human life. Or, we may contemplate . . . the body of opinions as to right and wrong, good and evil, which we find actually prevalent in the society of which we are members; and endeavor, by reflective analysis, removing vagueness and ambiguity, solving apparent contradictions, correcting lapses and supplying omissions to reduce this current body of opinions, so far as possible, to a rational and coherent system.[24]

The former project is that of act consequentialists. The latter is that of Gert, as he makes clear when he says that his moral system is analogous to a grammar (4-5) and aims to provide "an explicit description of common morality" (379).

If you share Gert's goal of systematizing common morality, then the counterexamples to act consequentialism will seem to have great force. If you want universal public rules as practical guides, then act consequentialism will seem to demand too much impartiality and information. For such projects, Gert's system might seem to have advantages over the most sophisticated act consequentialism.

On the other hand, if you have doubts about common morality, so that you countenance the possibility of radical moral progress and seek a deeper justification, then Gert's appeals to common morality and moral intuition will strike you as inadequate. And if you want to specify conditions of what morally ought to be done in particular situations that could ground a distinct practical public guide, then Gert's arguments against act consequentialism will seem to miss their target. For projects like that, there is much to be said in defense of and for sophisticated act consequentialism.[25]

Notes

1. All parenthetical page references are to Bernard Gert, *Morality: Its Nature and Justification* (New York: Oxford University Press, 1998). Gert is almost as critical of other traditional theories (6).

2. Walter Sinnott-Armstrong, "An Argument for Consequentialism," *Philosophical Perspectives* 6 (1992): 399-421.

3. This formulation dominates earlier editions without the morally decisive question, such as Bernard Gert, *The Moral Rules* (New York: Harper and Row, 1966), 92.

4. John Austin, *The Province of Jurisprudence Determined and the Uses of the Study of Jurisprudence* (New York: Noonday Press, 1954), 38-40. First published 1832, so this kind and sense of rule utilitarianism is not a recent invention.

5. Austin might respond that some acts that maximize utility also belong to other classes whose general instantiation would reduce utility. But that is true of any act that causes any harm, since, if "causing harm" were "generally done," "the probable effect on the general happiness" would be bad. So this cannot show that an act is morally wrong. For more on reduction, see David Lyons, *Forms and Limits of Utilitarianism* (Oxford, Eng.: Clarendon Press, 1965).

6. Gert's emphasis on public permissive rules is shared by John C. Harsanyi, "Morality and the Theory of Rational Behavior," reprinted in *Utilitarianism and Beyond*, ed. Amartya Sen and Bernard Williams (New York: Cambridge University Press, 1981), 39-62. On page 59, Harsanyi says that rule utilitarians will always have to ask the question, "What would be the social implications of adopting a moral rule permitting that promises should be broken under conditions A, B, C, etc.—assuming that all members of the society would know that promise breaking would be permitted under these conditions?" Thanks to Josh Gert for this reference.

7. In personal communication, Gert does cite consequences as reasons to include some features but not others on his list of morally relevant features.

8. A different sense is used by some recent moral philosophers, including Frances Howard-Snyder in "A New Argument for Consequentialism? A Reply to Sinnott-Armstrong," *Analysis* 56, no. 2 (April 1996): 111-15. Howard-Snyder's definition of consequentialism makes her criticisms miss their target, me, as cited in note 2. See my "What Is Consequentialism?," *Utilitas* 13, no. 3 (November 2001): 342-9.

9. For a direct consequentialist account of virtue, see Julia Driver, *Uneasy Virtue* (Cambridge, Eng.: Cambridge University Press, 2001).

10. See my *Moral Dilemmas* (Oxford, Eng.: Basil Blackwell, 1988), 58-71.

11. See my "'Ought' Conversationally Implies 'Can,'" *Philosophical Review* 93 (1984): 249-61.

12. Quoted by Gert on his pages 15-16 from John Stuart Mill, *Utilitarianism*, ed. Roger Crisp (Oxford, Eng.: Oxford University Press, 1998), chapter V, paragraph 14. Mill also calls punishability "the real turning point of the distinction between morality and simple expediency." Nonetheless, I will assume that some acts *morally* ought to be done even though they are not morally required and omitting them is not morally wrong. Also, if Mill claims that an act is morally wrong whenever it ought to be punished, then sometimes one morally ought to do what is morally wrong. To avoid this odd implication, I will assume that Mill means to claim that an act is morally wrong if and only if it both morally ought not to be done and also morally ought to be punished (if the agent is responsible and punishment would not be impractical).

13. Henry Sidgwick, *The Methods of Ethics*, Seventh Edition (New York: Dover, 1966), 221. Originally published in 1907. For the description of such views as "grading on a curve," I am indebted to Nomy Arpaly.

14. These judgments about excuses, blame, condemnation, and responsibility show some ways in which act consequentialists can "recognize the fallibility of humans" despite what Gert says (205-6; cf. 245). We will see another way below.

15. See, for example, John Broome, *Weighing Goods* (Oxford, Eng.: Blackwell, 1991).

16. See, for example, Gregory Kavka, *Moral Paradoxes of Nuclear Deterrence* (New York: Cambridge University Press, 1987), 57-77.

17. This distinction is implicit in Mill and Sidgwick, but recent discussions seem to derive from R. E. Bales, "Act-utilitarianism: Account of Right-making Characteristics or Decision-making Procedure?" *American Philosophical Quarterly* 8 (1971): 257-65. I avoid the more common phrase "decision procedure," because this is often taken to imply completeness, and Gert denies that there can be any complete moral decision procedure (11). I also refer to conditions instead of criteria, because conditions of oughtness and rightness need not be as easily accessible as Wittgensteinian criteria. Finally, there can be conditions and guides for both moral oughtness and moral wrongness. I will focus on moral wrongness, because here I am answering objections that are usually formulated in terms of what is morally wrong.

18. See R. M. Hare, *Moral Thinking* (Oxford, Eng.: Clarendon Press, 1981), 46-48, 50, 137, 156, etc.

19. See Henry Sidgwick, *The Methods of Ethics*, 405-6 and elsewhere.

20. Act consequentialists do not even refuse to do this if they count only foreseeable consequences. They can also let fallibility affect standards of responsibility, as I mentioned in note 14.

21. Compare Ronald Dworkin, *Taking Rights Seriously* (Cambridge, Mass.: Harvard University Press, 1978), 234 ff., on external preferences. This also might explain Bentham's inclusion of purity in his hedonic calculus.

22. *The Methods of Ethics*, book 4, chapter 3, and *passim*.

23. See R. M. Hare, *Moral Thinking*, 132-35, and Timothy Sprigge, "A Utilitarian Reply to Dr. McCloskey," *Inquiry* 8 (1965): 272-84. For separate arguments that anticonsequentialist moral intuitions should not be trusted because they lead to mysteries or incoherence, see Shelly Kagan, *The Limits of Morality* (New York: Oxford University Press, 1989).

24. Henry Sidgwick, *Practical Ethics* (New York: Oxford University Press, 1998), 31. Originally published in 1898.

25. For helpful comments on drafts, I thank Robert Audi, Marcia Baron, Julia Driver, Shelly Kagan, David Phillips, Bill Throop, and, especially, Bernie Gert.

9

The Role of Rules*

Susan Wolf

In academic philosophy, the role of rules in morality has been steadily de-emphasized over the last quarter of a century. Though in earlier decades both Kantian and utilitarian moral theorists stressed the importance of rules in the moral life, contemporary writers tend either to reject these earlier accounts of morality or to ignore them while shifting attention to other moral philosophical topics. Thus, rule utilitarianism, once hailed as the most promising way to reconcile the attractions of a utilitarian account of the foundations of morality with deeply held convictions about what morality in practice requires one to do, seems to have virtually vanished from the academic scene. Advocates of deontological theories inspired by Kant have meanwhile turned away from the projects of earlier theorists who defended specifiable perfect and imperfect duties, bringing out instead a variety of attitudes, virtues, and habits of thought that embody Kantian respect for persons and the value of rational autonomy. Even Bernard Gert, whose conception of morality gives rules a central place, has increasingly retreated from a description of his theory that highlights the role of rules. Revised editions of the book that elaborates and defends Gert's theory trace this shift in emphasis in their very titles: the 1970 edition of *The Moral Rules* gave way to the 1988 edition of *Morality: A New Justification of the Moral Rules*. The newest presentation of Gert's theory finds rules nowhere mentioned in its title.

By "rules" I mean directives or commands that specify in relatively general and concrete terms a kind of action that is either generally forbidden or generally required. In other words, I mean the kind of thing exemplified by Gert's proposed set of moral rules, including such directives as "Do not kill," and "Keep your promises." By contrast, a principle like "Maximize utility" is too abstract to constitute a rule in my sense, and a judgment like "When in need of money for the sake of one's own welfare one should not borrow it if one cannot be sure that one will be able to honor one's promise to pay it back" is too specific.

A number of factors have contributed to the disfavor in which thinking about morality in terms of rules has fallen. Philosophers in recent years have rightly called attention to some of the intellectual dangers that an approach to morality that concentrates on rules invites, and to the inadequacy of a conception of morality that identifies it wholly with a set of rules. Perhaps the pendulum of academic ethical thought had swung too far in the direction of envisioning morality in terms of a set of rules. Contemporary work in moral philosophy may be interpreted as a corrective. At this point, however, one may wonder whether the pendulum is swinging too far in the other direction. More specifically, the very important role Gert assigns to rules, whether highlighted in his book titles or not, seems to me to get some things right about morality that other philosophers may not appreciate. This paper is primarily a defense of the idea that an adequate morality must give something like a set of rules a central place. But this statement is too general. As we shall soon see, not *any* central place, not any understanding of the importance of rules, will do. This paper, then, is more precisely a defense of the role rules play in Bernard Gert's moral theory. For Bernard Gert, as for some other moral theorists, rules do not constitute the bottom line in moral reasoning, nor are they absolutely binding. Nonetheless, they are *very* important. Indeed, they are ineliminable from moral thought, and, in a certain sense, form the core of morality.

Outside of the studies and seminar rooms of moral philosophers, it would seem that thinking of morality largely in terms of a set of rules is the default position. If one asks the proverbial man on the street what morality is, or what morality says, or what morality instructs him to do, he will most likely answer with a list of rules: "Don't kill"; "Don't steal"; "Keep your promises"; "Tell the truth."[1] In light of this, it would seem that the burden of proof rests with those whose theories of morality do not mention rules or assign them a central place. Rather than begin with an account of why morality needs rules, then, let me begin with why some philosophers have thought it wise to avoid them.

Problems with Rule-Centered Accounts of Morality

By far the biggest problem philosophers have with rules involves the thought that rules are objectionably rigid. If one subscribes to a rule forbidding lying or killing, this seems to commit one to the view that one should *never* lie or kill. It suggests that all lies, all killings are alike, and wrong. Moreover, many people who have internalized moral rules do take them as absolute guides to conduct and moral judgment. To such people, once an act is identified as a case of lying, cheating, or stealing, for example, the moral issues are settled: the act is wrong, and a person who performs it is guilty of a high crime or misdemeanor. Such absolute adherence, particularly to the simple sorts of rules we are taught as children, seems to give the wrong moral advice, however. Most of us believe that some lies or acts of theft may be justified if they can prevent a great harm (keep the psychotic murderer from finding the victim he seeks; save a poor man's children from starvation). To many people, even acts of violence and killing are justified under some circumstances. Nor are all unjustified violations of the moral rules that we are taught growing up on the same level. Some lies, some cheatings, some breakings of promise are worse than others.

Philosophers concerned with defending a strongly rule-oriented account of morality have often responded to this concern by suggesting corrections to the rules. As they would point out, the rules we are taught as young children must, for obvious reasons, be simple and easy to follow. But we may see them as simplifications of a more complicated but still rule-bound moral truth. As we mature, we learn to make exceptions and finer distinctions: for example, we may come to think that killing is wrong except in self-defense (or in the defense of others or in acquiescence of the rational competent patient's request). Correct moral rules, then, will tend to be more complex and refined than those that can be explained to a four-year-old, but they will avoid the crude oversimplifications that we wish to avoid.

The reminder that adherence to rules need not be adherence to simple or simplistic rules answers some of the worries connected to rigidity that a rule-centered approach to morality engenders. Ironically, however, it may reinforce or encourage others. For the idea that the correct set of rules or the correct description of them will contain within it specifiable exceptions implicitly retains the idea that once the rules are specified correctly, with all the exceptions listed and built in, they will function as absolute guides to conduct and to judgment. In one way rules with exceptions built in may be said to be less rigid that the simpler rules. But if the idea is that once the rules are stated correctly, they are to be taken as absolute, it may be thought that the rules remain rigid in another way.

Many philosophers, however, will be skeptical of the idea that any set of discriminations or exceptions will yield a set of rules that we can confidently regard as giving correct moral guidance. What reason is there to expect morality so perfectly to fit such a rule-bound model, they will ask. Moreover, they may think that whatever statement of a rule against lying or stealing or killing we come up with must be tentative—for how can we guarantee that a counterexample will not arise from some yet unimagined situation?

The failure of many rule-oriented ethicists to address these questions points up another reason philosophers in recent years have been wary of rule-centered approaches—namely, that such approaches tend to be intellectually shallow. People who think of morality in terms of rules often think of them as constituting "the bottom line" in moral thinking. Whether an act or policy is morally justified depends, for them, on whether it accords with the rules, but their accounts have no resources for explaining or defending the rules themselves. Once they have justified a moral judgment that some act is wrong, say, because it involves lying, they cannot go further to say *why* lying is wrong. "It just is wrong" is all they have to say.

Such an account is both intellectually unsatisfying and metaphysically puzzling. Intellectually, it seems legitimate to ask for reasons that lie behind the rules and support them—to ask, in other words, what makes it plausible, commendable, desirable that these rules be followed. A conception of morality that offers no answer to these questions but insists that nonetheless these rules tell us what to do is also metaphysically suspicious—where do these rules come from? what gives them their authority? what reason is there to believe in them at all?[2]

Because there is a conception of morality prevalent in our culture that not only largely identifies morality with obedience to a set of rules but takes these rules to constitute the bottom line in moral reasoning, philosophers may well associate a focus on rules with adherence to this familiar conception. Insofar as this conception of morality *is* objectionably rigid, shallow, and metaphysically puzzling, philosophers are right to be wary of thinking of morality in terms of rules. But one may believe that rules are important in morality without taking them to constitute the bottom line. One may take rules seriously and assign them a central place without either taking them to give absolute moral guidance or to be rationally foundational.

Looking at the use and the role of rules in other contexts may remind us of these other possibilities. To be sure, some rules do function as rigid, absolute, and rationally foundational: in bridge, the rule that one must follow suit on a trick if one can dictates absolutely, and the reason one must is simply that *that is the rule*—that is how the game is played. Etiquette requires that one answer a third-person invitation in the third person. Again, this is simply how things are done—there is no room for flexibility or further justification. But other rules in bridge and even in the domain of manners function rather differently. Bridge players are taught to open a hand with thirteen points, but the rule does not dictate absolutely. People brought up with good manners are taught to use the large spoon for the soup, but if the less-cultivated guest of honor begins the meal with the small one, it may be more polite to follow her lead.

It is possible to try to understand these examples as cases of rules too crudely stated. The real rules, or the more accurate statement of them, one may suggest, will build in the exceptions which allow a player to open with less than thirteen points, or a diner to use the dessert spoon for the soup. It is not obvious, however, that this is the best way to understand how these rules function. If, instead of looking for a description that will capture a specifiable set of exceptions, we consider why these simple rules are, for the most part, justified in the first place, we may at once have a deeper understanding of the game or domain in which these rules have a place and a basis—as opposed to a list—for seeing when these rules would be better ignored or overridden from the point of view of the values or goals embodied in the game or domain itself.

Similarly, philosophers who take rules to have an important place in morality are not committed to thinking that such rules constitute a bottom line. Gert's use of rules is a prime example of this: Gert's list of rules occupies a central place in his theory—it comprises, at the least, a first answer to the question of what morality requires one to do—but it does not govern conduct absolutely nor does it constitute the end of the moral justificatory line. We can explain the rules and in conjunction understand the circumstances under which they may or should be broken.

How Can Rules Play an Important Role in Morality If They Are Neither Foundational nor Absolute?

If rules are not to be understood as constituting a bottom line, however, it may not be clear what is meant by saying that they hold an important place. All but the most radical particularists are apt to give *some* role to rules in moral reasoning. At a practical level, rules are useful heuristics that help us move through the world efficiently. They supply rough and ready first answers to the question of what morality requires us to do. In other words, they function as rules of thumb. Philosophically, however, it may seem that such rules are not very interesting; moreover, it may seem that such rules must be in principle eliminable at a deeper level.

The role of rules in a utilitarian conception of morality can illustrate this concern. According to a standard account of utilitarianism, actions are morally right insofar as they bring about the greatest good for the greatest number. Since one typically brings about greater good if one refrains from killing, lying, and so on, the utilitarian will support actions that are in accord with such familiar rules as "Don't kill" and "Don't lie." Moreover, because calculating expected utilities is time-consuming and sometimes difficult, and because agents may be prone to certain kinds of distortions in their estimates of what benefits and harms their actions are apt to bring about, agents would do better on the whole in actually maximizing utility if they did not try to calculate on a case-by-case basis, but rather looked to the general rule in deciding what to do. So utilitarianism supports the use of rules in moral deliberation. Indeed, if one thinks, plausibly, that agents do *much* better by following familiar moral rules than they would if they tried to act on individual calculations, a utilitarian might say that he *strongly* supports such rules, that he gives them a central and important place.

Nonetheless, when one considers that the reason we ought to follow the rules is that by doing so we are most likely to maximize utility, and that morality permits us to violate the rules whenever we can (or whenever we have strong reason to believe we can) maximize utility by doing so, one might be inclined to regard the place of rules in this conception of morality to be philosophically superficial, however practically important. Rules are important on this view, it might be said, only because of human limitations on time, intelligence, and clear-headedness. If it were not for these weaknesses in human nature, there would be no need for rules in morality at all. Moreover, what really matters in morality—the good- and the right-making features of actions and states of affairs—do not involve rules at all. Rules, on this view, seem to be in principle eliminable from moral theory.

This train of thought suggests that if utilitarianism were correct, rules would have practical but no philosophical importance. They would play but a superficial and in principle eliminable role in moral thought. (Indeed, this train of thought does seem to be behind the disappearance of rule utilitarianism from the philosophical scene.) But now one might wonder whether the same sort of argument would not apply in the case of any moral theory that refrained from regarding moral rules as the bottom justificatory line. It may seem that any theory that explains why we ought to follow the rules with an appeal to a deeper principle or other sort of moral justification, and that offers a corresponding story for when one might neglect the rules or decide among them or make an exception will, in effect, be assigning rules a superficial and in principle eliminable place. Thus, one might say that, although a Kantian might subscribe to the rule that one ought not to commit suicide, or to make a false promise, what she really cares is about is not acting on a maxim that one cannot at the same time will as a universal law.[3] On this view, rules function for the Kantian, as they do for the utilitarian, only as short-cuts in moral deliberation.

To take a more contemporary example, Scanlon argues in *What We Owe to Each Other*[4] that actions are wrong insofar as they would not be allowed by principles that rational creatures could not reasonably reject insofar as they, too, are seeking principles of mutual governance which other rational creatures could not reasonably reject. Though Scanlon's reference to principles make his proposal appear to give rules a central place (at least if "principles" are just another name for "rules"), one might wonder whether this reference to the level of rules or principles is doing any work for him. Mightn't one just as well capture his view by saying an *action* is wrong if it could be reasonably rejected by rational creatures interested in mutual cooperation, or by saying more simply that an action is wrong if it, in all its specificity, could not be justified to others?

Finally, we may apply this general line of argument to Gert's theory of morality. To the question "Why ought we obey the moral rules?" Gert answers that they would be advocated by all rational people as part of a public system according to which the violation of such rules may be punished.[5] To the question, under what conditions should we make exceptions to these rules, Gert answers "when impartial rational persons would publicly allow such an exception."[6] Here, too, we might say, the essence of the view seems to be that morality is a matter of acting in ways that rational people would be willing publicly to allow. Though, in fact, this will exclude most cases of killing, lying, and so on, and because of this, rules like "Don't kill," "Don't lie" may serve as a general guide, reference to these categories or rules is in principle eliminable. Whether an act is right or wrong and what is right or wrong about it can be fully assessed and understood directly and without any reference to the moral rules.

Though I announced earlier that the purpose of this paper was to defend the idea that rules occupy an important and central place in the structure of morality, the line of thought pursued in this section raises a question about what that can mean. For it shows us that once we abandon the idea that rules constitute a bottom justificatory line in morality, we abandon as well the possibility of assigning rules a certain, especially deep sort of importance in morality. The theories that I want to compare (especially, utilitarianism, Kantianism, and Gert's moral theory) all acknowledge that if something is a moral rule—that is, a general directive that specifies in relatively general and concrete terms a kind of action that is either generally forbidden or required—there must be some explanation of why it is a moral rule that shows its relation to the point or the nature of morality as a whole. And this point might be expressed by saying that according to any of the theories under consideration, what is really wrong with an act is never that it is a killing or a lie, or, more generally, a violation of any articulated moral rule, but rather something deeper, which relates more directly and precisely to what morality fundamentally is.

Insofar as this statement suggests, however, that the reference to rules in morality is not essential, it is dangerous and misleading. In fact, I believe that none of these theories are ones in which rules are really even in principle eliminable. But some of these theories assign rules a more important and deeper role than others. Kantian conceptions of morality, I shall argue, assign rules a deeper and more important place in morality than purely consequentialist conceptions do. And Gert's (and some others, such as Hobbes's and Mill's) conceptions of morality assign rules a deeper and more important place than at least some Kantian conceptions do. As I have already mentioned, I believe that this more central role is the right one. But even if we cannot reach agreement about this, it will be worthwhile to understand more clearly what the differences among the competing views are and what is at stake in the disagreement.

The Role of Rules in Utilitarianism

Even an advocate of utilitarianism, the moral theory in which the superficiality of moral rules seems most evident, will not, on reflection, take rules to be mere corrections for limitations in time and accuracy in moral deliberation, in principle eliminable from moral thought. For utilitarians want to bring about the greatest good, that is, the greatest overall human or sentient well-being, and it is an undisputed fact of human life that we fare better, as a group or a community, if we can set up institutions and practices that involve organized schemes of cooperation in which we can rely on each other to do our assigned and expected parts. Public understanding and allegiance to rules are essential to the existence of these institutions and practices. Not even a community of perfectly accurate and instantaneous calculators of the consequences of actions could achieve the benefits of such institutions as promising, private property, a criminal justice system, or even rules of the road without the existence of conventional public rules. Thus it will be essential to morally right action, on a utilitarian conception, to refer to these rules and to the utility of generally promoting and maintaining them in moral deliberation.[7]

The acknowledgment of the ineliminability of rules due to the benefits of publicly coordinated activities, however, may still be thought to be morally superficial. For one thing, it might be suggested that the rules that a utilitarian must acknowledge as essential to moral deliberation are not themselves *moral* rules. The example of rules of the road is a striking case in point. "Drive on the right" is surely a rule to which utilitarians have reason to attend (in the United States). By following the rule rather than neglecting it they significantly contribute to the efficiency and safety of the system of transportation. Moreover, such a rule is not eliminable in practical deliberation, since it functions by convention to coordinate people's behavior rather than as a summary of how people are observed to behave independently of the existence of the rule. No one, however, would suggest that "Drive on the right" is a moral rule. Though there are moral reasons (among others) for obeying it, the rule is not itself a part of morality.

Similarly, it might be argued, rules that specify how one may behave with respect to the property of others, what taxes one should pay, what obligations one takes on by signing a contract, are, to a large extent, legal rather than moral rules. Though obedience to these rules may be described in terms that we familiarly identify as moral, invoking such moral terms as stealing, cheating, and fraud, if we speak strictly, we may distinguish the legal rules themselves from the moral reasons we may have to obey them. Indeed, Gert himself does this: the rules that constitute positive law are not themselves (at least, *qua* positive law) moral rules in his system. But his system contains one moral rule—"Obey the law"—that guides our action with respect to all of them.

Not all conventions that allow us to realize our goals more effectively by coordinating behavior are legal rules, and so not all rules that utilitarians will have reason to take seriously (ineliminably, and not as mere heuristic devices) will be legal rules. "Keep your promises," for example, is a rule utilitarians will have moral reason to obey, and it is hard to know what, if anything, is at stake in deciding to call this a moral rule or instead a nonmoral rule that, because of its utility, utilitarians have strong moral reason generally to obey. A second consideration, however, suggests that however we label the rules that set conventions general obedience to which increases utility, they function for a utilitarian (or more generally a consequentialist) in a relatively superficial way. Specifically, utilitarians will find reasons to obey these rules (that is, to conform to the practice of promising, and so on) only on those instances when such obedience can be expected to maximize utility. If, taking all consequences into account, utility would be slightly increased by breaking the rule, the utilitarian will approve the action that breaks the rule. That the act would be a case of following the rule (that it would be the keeping of a promise, or a following of the law, for example) does not itself carry any moral weight from a utilitarian perspective. Thus, though even for utilitarians, rules are not eliminable from moral deliberation, and not just for the contingent reasons that calculations are time-consuming and prone to error, they may be said to occupy a superficial role.

The Role of Rules in Kantian and Mixed Moral Theories

For Kantians, however, and indeed for proponents of any moral theory that takes respect for persons to generate nonconsequentialist reasons for constraining one's behavior in certain ways, the story will be different. The requirement to treat people as ends in themselves directly obliges us to behave and to refrain from behaving in certain ways in regard to them. We may not, for example, interfere with their ability to exercise their practical reason in deciding what to do. This means that obedience to at least some rules, such as the rule not to lie, function not merely as a means to the production of morally good effects. Rather obedience to such rules is partly constitutive of moral practice. Respecting people just *is* in part a matter of following certain rules toward them.

For a utilitarian, lying is wrong only insofar as it produces worse effects than not lying. That an act would be a case of lying is thus not itself (independently of its particular effects) a reason not to perform it. Arguably, however, lying is always a case of disrespect. Thus, for a Kantian, there is always a reason to obey this sort of rule. It is part of the very way of being moral.

Even rules whose justification stems from the beneficial consequences of general obedience to them will have a different and more secure status for moral theorists who incorporate a principle of respect for persons into the foundation of morality than they will for pure consequentialists. For such theorists, there will be reasons to take even these rules seriously over and above the reasons that consequentialists recognize. I have in mind the sorts of reasons associated with the thought that it is wrong (and not just counterproductive) to be a free rider. By obeying rules general obedience to which is necessary for the rules to have their function, one not only probably contributes to the goals for which the rules are designed (i.e., to overall utility), one definitely participates on an equal basis with others to whom the rules equally apply. In other words, one's abiding by the rules that one expects and relies on others to obey implicitly acknowledges that one is on an equal plane with them, that one lacks any authority that would allow one to make an exception of oneself, even for the sake of the greater overall good. Such behavior therefore directly expresses a respect for others, a recognition of others as equals. This sort of reason is often discussed in support of the claim that one has a moral obligation to obey the law (*qua* law). It does not imply that the reason is absolute—only that it is a reason in addition to whatever reason is given by the consequences of following the law in that instance, and which therefore has weight even when the value of the consequences of obeying the law are in question or even appear to be worse than the consequences of breaking it. Insofar as we believe that morality does include the value of respect for others as equals, and takes this to be best understood as generating reasons that are not teleological in form, we have reason to give rules a more central place than consequentialists would assign them.

Both consequentialists and Kantians, then, must afford rules a greater and more important place in morality than many recent discussions of their theories have tended to notice. The goals of morality, on either sort of theory, cannot be fulfilled without the existence of rules, and moral values, especially on a Kantian conception, urge us to take these rules seriously in practical deliberations. Nonetheless, the role of rules on either of these theories remains relatively limited. Insofar as rules are necessary to fulfill some important moral purpose (whether it be the increase in social welfare or the expression of respect to others), we should construct them; and insofar as rules have been constructed and adopted by the community (ies) of which we are a part, we should recognize moral reasons to obey them. For Kantian theories, obedience to some rules will follow directly from the requirement to treat people as ends in themselves. Still, on neither of these theories would obedience to a set of rules be plausibly construed as constituting the core of morality. Leading a moral life, for either a Kantian or a consequentialist, is not to be assessed by noting whether the agent in question is succeeding in following such rules. To the contrary, the criteria for leading a moral life, on either theory, might be said to reach under whatever rules morality endorses, and to permeate one's life in a more comprehensive way. (As I understand these theories, the relevant criteria are very different in the two cases: for at least one kind of consequentialist, the moral life is whatever life does the most good. The criterion is, in a sense, totally public, realized in the physical world. For the Kantian, on the other hand, the moral life is the life in which the good will conditions all of one's activities. It is a purely psychological criterion.)

The Role of Rules in Gert's Theory

By contrast, Bernard Gert's moral theory *does* place rules at the center of morality. To be moral is, in the first instance, to behave in accordance with the moral rules (or, if not, to meet the standards of making a justified exception). If one does so behave, then at least a certain core standard of moral acceptability has been met. To be sure, Gert (rightly, I think) insists that this is not all there is to morality. A morally good person, maybe even a morally decent person, does not just obey the moral rules (or make justified exceptions) and stop there. She will cultivate and exercise moral virtues and aspire to moral ideals. Still, obedience to the moral rules does in itself constitute an identifiable and important moral status: it means that one is fulfilling one's moral obligations, meeting moral requirements, acting morally permissibly.

Though other moral theorists are not as explicit as Gert in discussing moral rules—rarely, for example, do any so boldly propose an actual set of them—I believe that a number of them (for example, Thomas Hobbes, John Stuart Mill, P. F. Strawson, and Thomas Scanlon)[8] would or should support the assignment of a similarly central place to them. But the place I have described may seem to be exactly what recent generations of moral philosophers have found to be objectionable. This identification of rules with the core of morality, and the corresponding weight placed on the distinction between moral requirements and recommendations may be precisely what moral philosophy has been trying to get away from.

Different Conceptions of Morality, Different Conceptions of the Role of Rules

In discussing the difference between the Kantian's and the consequentialist's attitude toward rules in morality, we saw that the role of rules in morality depended on what, at a deeper level, one thought the goals and values of morality fundamentally are. Here, too, I believe, the even more dramatic difference between the role of rules in Gert's moral theory and their roles in Kantian and utilitarian theories, is explained by these theories' different assumptions about what morality is.

It is fashionable these days to say that moral philosophy asks, or should ask, "How should one live?" Such a question, it is said, is larger than the questions "What should one do?" or "What actions should one perform?" since living is not simply a matter of acting, but also of feeling, of caring, perhaps even of being. Moreover, such a question is larger than the question "How is one required (or obliged) to live?" since, at least arguably, there are many things one should do (and should feel and should care about) that one is nonetheless not obliged to do (or feel or care about). Finally, it will be noted, such a question cannot possibly be adequately answered by providing a list of rules or any other sort of mechanical procedure the following of which will guarantee *eudaimonia*.

This way of understanding the subject matter of ethics is often voiced in the context of a critique of traditional modern moral theories—of Kantianism and utilitarianism, for example,—and, it might seem, *a fortiori* of such theories as Gert's.[9] Because Kantians and utilitarians concentrate so much on action and on what is morally required, these critics say, they either fail to address or to appreciate much of what is valuable in life, or, even worse, their moral theories instruct us to behave in ways that are incompatible with some of these values. Kantians and utilitarians have generally answered that these criticisms misinterpret the theories to which they are directed. They point out the ways in which their theories do offer advice and judgment about character, emotion, friendship, and so on, and they argue that, when one understands the advice, one will find it at worst compatible with the values the theories are accused of neglecting and at best properly supportive of them.

It is worth noting that this response accepts the premise that moral philosophy should be about the question "How should one live?" and responds, roughly, with the reply "But we do address that question, and address it well." It is easy to see how, hand in hand with this response, would go a de-emphasis of the role of rules in these theories. Much recent moral philosophy is occupied with taking sides in the debate over whether this reply is successful. But my interest here is with the availability of another response to the initial concern, a response that one can see in the way Gert develops his moral theory.

This response, too, may accept the premise that moral *philosophy*—or, synonymously, ethics—should range over all the questions relevant to thinking about how one should live. But it insists that moral philosophy is one thing, morality another. More precisely, morality is one thing that is relevant to the question of how one should live, and so it is a subject within the larger field of ethics. As Gert points out, there may be a great many things that contribute to living well, things one might offer as advice about how one should live and that we might urge all people to do: "Greet everyone with a smile." "Learn to draw." The best-selling series of *Life's Little Instruction Books* are full of such advice. But to take this advice as moral advice, to take the reasons to follow them to be moral reasons, is both to fly in the face of ordinary linguistic usage and to forfeit a valuable linguistic tool for singling out one important set of concerns and questions from others.

On Gert's view, morality has a distinct and specific subject matter, much narrower than the question "How should one live?"[10] Morality has to do with social life—with how to live *with other people* and with how one wants other people to live with you (and those you love). A few salient points about this conception of morality are worth highlighting. First, because our sociality is both a fundamental aspect of our human nature and a pervasive feature of our physical existence, it will play an extraordinarily important role in shaping our answers to the broader question of how to live. Second, the importance and character of our interest that others live cooperatively and on an equal basis with us and those we care about gives us a unique and distinctive reason for wanting to *insist* that people behave in certain ways (and refrain from behaving in others). That is, we have a reason for wanting to put pressure on people to treat others in certain ways that is lacking in connection with our reasons for wanting people to smile and to learn to draw.[11] Finally, understanding morality to be about a specifiable aspect of our lives implicitly acknowledges the existence of other aspects that are potential sources of value and of reasons to live one way rather than another. Although living cooperatively on an equal basis with others and having others live in such a way with you are important contributors to the possibility of living well, they are far from sufficient, at least for most people. There is more to life than morality. Putting the last two points together, it seems that we have reasons for wanting to require of people that they behave in certain ways with respect to others and reasons also for wanting not to require too much. We want, in other words, a set of requirements that are limited in their demands, so as to allow people the freedom to live lives that they can find to be good and rewarding.

Within the domain of morality, on this view, the domain roughly concerned with how to live with others cooperatively and on an equal basis, there is reason to want to be able to specify a limited set of requirements on which we can insist (requirements, in other words, that it would be legitimate to punish people for failing to meet). But it would be unreasonable—and, arguably, undesirable—to require or insist on too much. What we morally require of others and what others may legitimately require of us should not constrain our concrete physical options so much as to severely reduce our ability to find and to shape a way of life that is personally rewarding nor should it constrain our psychological options so much as to interfere with our ability to love and to attend to those features of life that make it worth living. How can such requirements be specified? The most obvious and, I think, also the best way is by offering a set of rules.

The very idea that morality should contain a set of requirements on which we can insist implies the need for a structure that is at least somewhat rule-like in form. It must be possible publicly and generally to express what is expected (otherwise how can we insist that the expectations be met?) and to indicate the status of what is expected as required or obligatory. For these reasons, lists of virtues or portrayals of ideals, as well as particularist descriptions of the moral life will not serve this conception of morality adequately.

This fails, however, to explain why we need a set of rules—that is, a set of relatively concrete directives that specify kinds of actions that are either generally forbidden or required—rather than insist directly on conformity to one or more of a set of abstract principles that can be applied to any given situation. It fails to explain why we need something like the set of rules Gert proposes, on the order of "Don't kill," "Don't lie," and "Keep your promises," rather than, or in addition to, such principles as "Maximize utility," "Act always on maxims that you can at the same time will to be universal laws," or even "Act only in a way that fully informed, impartial rational persons would publicly allow." Whereas the reason we need rules in addition to virtues is that on this conception, we want morality to require *something*, the reason we need rules in addition to such abstract principles as are mentioned above is that we do not want morality to require *too much*. Rules, it seems to me, provide a structure especially well-suited to meeting this condition.

On this conception of morality, we want a set of requirements that do not threaten to take over our whole lives. Though it is hard to say precisely how limited the moral requirements must be, there should be limits not only on how these requirements constrain our concrete physical options but also on how they constrain and define our psychological lives. In other words, we want requirements that, if we have been properly socialized, we can for the most part meet without thinking, or with relatively little thinking. It is unclear whether abstract principles can satisfy this condition.

Neither standard interpretations of utilitarianism nor standard interpretations of Kantianism build this condition into their conceptions of morality. On these interpretations, if maximizing utility or following the categorical imperative swallows up one's whole life, so be it. For on these interpretations, morality is not restricted to the domain of living with other people. Nor is morality just one very important value among others—it is rather a supreme value, or a supreme source of reasons. Even if we consider modified versions of these theories, or theories like Gert's in which morality is explicitly conceived as occupying a specific and limited aspect of life, it is hard to see how abstract principles could keep from being too intrusive without summoning the aid of rules. For the need to consider these principles with every choice one makes would interfere significantly with our ability to act spontaneously, to act out of love, to get carried away by the excitement or grip of an engrossing challenge. If, on the other hand, we do not consider these principles as a matter of course, how will we know that we are behaving in accord with them? The structure of rules allows us to meet the challenge of establishing important requirements on which we can insist in a way that is minimally intrusive.

On this conception of morality, it is important to distinguish requirements on which we can insist from whatever further goals, values, ideals, and virtues we would like people to have that complement, reinforce, and enhance the possibility of living cooperatively with others on an equal basis. Fulfilling these requirements constitutes one sense or one level of what it is to be moral. As such, it may be considered the core of morality. Because, due to reasons just mentioned, the best way to specify such requirements will take the form of a set of rules, rules will have a very important, albeit not foundational, place in morality. For the requirements of morality on this view just *are* the requirements set by the rules. Fulfilling one's moral obligations just is a matter of obeying the rules (or making the exceptions that the more abstract principle specifically allows). Thus, on this view rules are more central to morality than they are on a utilitarian view, in which rules are only a means to some further moral goal, or even on the Kantian view, in which rules are a way of being faithful to some deeper and broader moral commitment.

Conclusion

I have argued that, depending on what one thinks morality is—what goals and values one believes are fundamental to it, or what, so to speak, morality is for—the importance of rules and the force they have in our moral practical deliberations will vary. Utilitarians have reason to take rules seriously. Kantians, I have argued, have even more. Another group of moral theorists—we might call them "social moralists"[12]—has, I believe, still more reason to give rules a central and ineliminable place in their theories.

The question will be raised, is one of these conceptions of morality the right one? Is there a fact of the matter about what morality fundamentally is? My own response to this question is "yes and no."

On the one hand, the different questions that the various moral theories differently identify as questions of morality (for example, How should one live? and What do we owe to each other?) all deserve answers. There is room to ask all of them both in philosophy and in life. The question, then, of which questions are to be identified as the subject matter of morality seems mainly to be a question of how to use certain words. Does faithfulness to ordinary language give us a determinate answer to this question? I doubt it. The word seems stretched and narrowed in different contexts, to emphasize different strands and there is little reason to expect that a single strand or a unified set of strands will emerge from linguistic analysis as sufficiently dominant to answer the question decisively.

Still, there are two things to be said on behalf of Gert's (and the other contractualists' and social moralists') conception:

One is that, as I said at the beginning of the paper, such rules as "Don't kill," "Don't lie," "Keep your promises," do for many people constitute the paradigm or the core of morality. It is the default position of what morality to the man on the street is. If our subject matter is to be rooted in ordinary conceptions of morality, it is plausible to root it in this. That is, it is plausible to take as the question that identifies the subject matter of moral theory "What is the best explanation—and ideally, the best justifying explanation—of allegiance to the set of rules understood by most people to comprise the core of morality?" This is indeed Gert's approach.

The other is that there is an important and distinct question to be asked—what ought we to *require* of each other in order to live peaceably and well in a common world? There is, in other words, reason to be interested in a distinct set of rules, to which punishment is legitimately attached, which people have reason to obey and to encourage others to obey in the interests of social peace and well-being. In other words, if these rules were not already out there in the consciousness and discourse of the men and women on the street, in the instructions of parents, teachers, rabbis, and priests, and in the conversations we have with each other, we would have to invent them. It would not be absolutely necessary to refer to this set of rules as "The Moral Rules," or to refer to the larger system of ideas and values that concern living cooperatively and on an equal basis with others as "morality." But it would not be a bad idea.

Notes

* I am grateful to the participants of the Gert Conference and to the members of Philamore for their very helpful comments on an earlier draft of this paper.

1. At least, this is one likely answer. Citing the Golden Rule is another.

2. Divine Command theories which take morality to be a set of rules commanded by God may be understood as answering the metaphysical questions. On such views, the metaphysical status of morality is derivative from God's existence. If one has no metaphysical problems with that, the metaphysical status of morality will be unproblematic. Such views, however, wear their intellectual shallowness on their metaphorical sleeves, since the answer to "Why should one not lie, kill, etc.?" is explicitly modeled on "Because I say so, that's why."

3. As I am understanding the term, "maxims" are not another name for rules—they are not nearly so general and their specification must include the motive for action.

4. Thomas Scanlon, *What We Owe to Each Other* (Cambridge, Mass.: Harvard University Press, 1998).

5. Gert, *Morality*, 223. Strictly speaking, this is Gert's answer to the question "What makes these rules *moral* rules?" or "What makes these rules right?" One may press on to ask why we should do what is right, or, in other words, why we should be moral. Gert addresses this question in chapter 13, 338-61.

6. Gert, *Morality*, 222-23. Note that Gert distinguishes between weakly justified and strongly justified exceptions.

7. Since any plausible form of consequentialism will at least include among the consequences to be maximized the benefits to human welfare afforded by such institutions and practices as I have mentioned, the ineliminable reference to rules will be a part not only of classical utilitarianism but of any plausible consequentialism.

8. See Thomas Hobbes, *Leviathan* (Oxford, Eng.: Oxford University Press, 1998); John Stuart Mill, *Utilitarianism*, ed. Roger Crisp (Oxford, Eng.: Oxford University Press, 1998), chapter 5; P. F. Strawson, "Social Morality and Individual Ideal," *Philosophy* 36 (1961): 1-17; Thomas Scanlon, *What We Owe to Each Other.*

9. See, e.g., Michael Stocker, "The Schizophrenia of Modern Moral Theories," *Journal of Philosophy* 73 (1976): 453-66; Bernard Williams, *Moral Luck* (Cambridge, Eng.: Cambridge University Press, 1981), especially essays 1 and 2; and Bernard Williams, *Ethics and the Limits of Philosophy* (Cambridge, Mass.: Harvard University Press, 1985).

10. Questions similar in scope but with different emphasis that link them more explicitly to Kantian and consequentialist moral theories include "How does one have reason to live?" ("What does one have reason to do?") and "What life would be best?"

11. It may be thought that what distinguishes moral rules from rules such as these is that moral rules pertain to important matters while these are relatively trivial. But moral rules may be obeyed or disobeyed in both important and trivial ways (consider, e.g., using a business envelope for a personal purpose) and nonmoral advice (such as "appreciate beauty") can be of great personal importance.

12. There is a strong connection between a conception of morality as something that would arise from a social contract and a conception of morality as occupied with maintaining a basis for living cooperatively with others on an equal basis. Thus, one would expect most, if not all, contractualists to be what I am calling "social moralists." Since the idea of a contract need not figure explicitly into the conception of morality I am concerned to highlight—indeed, it does not figure in explicitly to Gert's moral theory—the conception I am advocating is one that may be held by theorists who do not think of themselves as contractualists.

Part IV: Ideals and Goods

10

Moral Ideals

John Deigh

Philosophers now commonly write about morality where two centuries ago they wrote about morals. Consider these great works of eighteenth century ethics: Hume's *Enquiry Concerning the Principles of Morals*, Kant's *Groundwork of the Metaphysics of Morals*, Bentham's *Introduction to the Principles of Morals and Legislation*, and Price's *Review of the Chief Questions and Difficulties of Morals*. By comparison a list of significant works in ethics produced over the last thirty years includes Gewirth's *Reason and Morality*, Harman's *The Nature of Morality*, Geoffrey Warnock's *The Object of Morality*, Donagan's *The Theory of Morality*, Kagan's *The Limits of Morality*, and Bernard Gert's book, now titled *Morality: Its Nature and Justification.*[1] Whether this comparison shows some real change in the subject of moral philosophy over the course of two centuries or just a shift in terminological preferences is hard to say. While I am confident that David Gauthier's *Morals by Agreement* deals with the very same subject as Alan Gewirth's *Reason and Morality*, I am less confident about there being a similar identity of subject between either of these works and book III of Hume's *Treatise*. Hume meant the study he pursued in the third book of his *Treatise* to be continuous with the studies he pursued in the first two books, and this is to say that he understood the study of morals to be continuous with the studies of the understanding and the passions. Whether one could understand the study of morality to be similarly continuous with those of the understanding and the passions seems to me a real question, and consequently that the subject of ethics may have changed from Hume's time to ours a real possibility. Be this as it may, in our time morality is what moral philosophers chiefly study.

The prevailing philosophical view of morality goes something like this. First, morality consists of rules and principles. These rules, these principles, govern the behavior of human beings in their relations with each other as members of a community. They specify both the actions no one may do to another and the actions everyone must do for others. They define, in other words, a set of prohibitions and requirements on conduct towards others. Second, morality is universal. Its rules, its principles, apply to everyone who has the powers of reason and self-control necessary to understand and follow them. No one who has these powers is exempt from their governance. Consequently, either the rules of morality do not vary significantly from one human community to another, or human beings as such form a global community and morality governs their behavior in the relations they have with each other as members of this global community. Finally, the rules and principles of morality are distinct from the moral customs of any particular society. Indeed, they represent the standards moralists and social critics use to evaluate and criticize such customs. Moral customs, being among the settled habits and practices of the members of a society, are concrete phenomena properly studied by ethnologists and sociologists. Morality, by contrast, being an abstract system of rules that men and women can comprehend by reflecting on and reasoning about their relations with and conduct towards each other, is a paradigm object of philosophical study.

The chief aims of this study are to formulate, systematize, and justify morality's rules and principles. Many of the most important works in contemporary moral philosophy have been organized around these aims. Bernard Gert's book is exemplary. Gert's project in the book is to provide rational foundations for morality, and he mainly pursues it by formulating a list of ten rules, working out a systematic account of how they provide the basis for all moral prohibitions and requirements, and arguing for their justification as what reason endorses as the fundamental rules of morality. At the same time, Gert acknowledges that morality comprises more than the ten rules on his list and the procedures for determining when their violation is justified. Recognizing that some moral judgments about the goodness or badness of an action are different from moral judgments about an action's being required or prohibited, he has incorporated into his theory a set of moral ideals through recourse to which the theory accounts for these judgments.[2] Accordingly, he takes moral ideals as forming a part of morality that is distinct from the part the moral rules form. They are similar to the moral rules in being precepts, but they differ from them in that they do not set requirements or prohibitions on conduct. In sum, on Gert's theory, morality is a system of precepts that is divided into two parts. One part consists of the ten moral rules and is the basis for determining whether an action is morally required or prohibited. The other consists of moral ideals and accounts for morality's concern with an action's being good or bad apart from its being morally required or prohibited.

The dominant focus of Gert's book in its earliest editions was the ten moral rules. As a result, the book inspired criticism that it misrepresented a part of morality for the whole, that it shortchanged the subject by concentrating on the minimal demands of morality, its requirements and prohibitions, to the exclusion of morality's loftier concerns with conduct of merit and worth.[3] In later editions, to correct this misperception, Gert has paid increasingly greater attention to moral ideals. Though the major focus of his project continues to be the ten moral rules and their justification, a full understanding of his theory, he now makes clear, requires reflection on his account of moral ideals. This account is the subject of my paper. It represents an attractive view of how moral ideals are related to the requirements and prohibitions of morality. Nonetheless, I believe that it is seriously flawed. In the first and longest section of the paper, I critically examine Gert's account with the aim of bringing out the flaws in its view of how moral ideals are related to moral prohibitions and requirements. In the paper's second and much shorter section, I briefly offer a different account of moral ideals and a correspondingly different of view of this relation.

I

Gert's account of moral ideals proceeds from the distinctions he draws between them and moral rules. Both are moral precepts. But—and this is the first distinction Gert draws—only moral rules set requirements and prohibitions on conduct.[4] Moral ideals, by contrast, merely encourage certain conduct. Accordingly, they support judgments applauding such conduct as morally good or deploring its omission as morally deficient, whereas moral rules, together with the procedures for determining when their violation is justified, support judgments condoning or sanctioning certain conduct as at least morally permissible and condemning its opposite as morally wrong. This first distinction between ideals and rules turns, then, on a difference in their force. I will refer to it as Gert's functional distinction. The second distinction he draws, which I will refer to as his substantive distinction, turns on a difference in their content. Moral ideals, Gert holds, call for the prevention of harm or evil. Moral rules, by contrast, call for the avoidance of causing harm or evil.[5] What Gert has in mind in drawing this distinction is not clear on its face, however, especially since some acts of preventing harm are also acts of avoiding causing harm. A parent, for instance, who sterilizes a needle before using it to remove a splinter lodged in his child's finger is preventing the finger from being infected and also avoiding causing an infection. Similarly, the signs "Prevent Forest Fires" that the government posts along country roads and mountain highways are meant to be a call to avoid causing forest fires.[6] So one has to look further into Gert's text to figure out what he intends in drawing his substantive distinction. The search will take us to the heart of his account.

One indication of what Gert intends by this distinction comes from comparing examples of each kind of precept with examples of the other. Consider the following rules from Gert's list. "Do not kill," "Do not cause pain," "Do not disable," "Do not deprive of freedom," "Do not deceive," and "Do not cheat." Each speaks against doing a certain action that either causes harm directly to someone or leaves someone vulnerable to suffering harm, and conforming to any of these rules means not doing that action. These points then apply to the other rules on the list, though their application to three of them, "Keep your promises," "Obey the law," and "Do your duty," needs some explanation because the negative element is not evident in their formulation. The points do not apply, however, to moral ideals. Gert offers several examples of these as representative of the entire class.[7] His examples include "Preserve life," "Relieve pain," "Help the needy," and "Prevent immoral behavior." These ideals do not speak against doing a certain action. On the contrary, they direct one to engage in certain actions. This contrast suggests, then, that what Gert has in mind when he distinguishes moral rules from moral ideals according as their object is the avoidance of causing harm or the prevention of harm is a difference between a call for negative action and a call for positive action. The text, moreover, supports this suggestion. In one place Gert glosses this distinction by characterizing it as one between precepts conformity to which "[does] not generally require positive action but only the avoidance of certain kinds of action" and precepts conformity to which generally requires positive action.[8] And similar remarks occur elsewhere.[9]

At the same time, Gert never explains how he understands the distinction between positive and negative action or what it is about the distinction he thinks supports his account. This is unfortunate, for the distinction is a well-known snare.[10] Plainly, he cannot understand it simply as a distinction between acts described positively and acts described negatively. Too many acts can be described either way. Thus, one can either say that *S* ignored *G* or that *S* did not pay attention to *G*; or again one can either say that *S* forgot *G*'s birthday or that *S* did not remember *G*'s birthday; or that *S* revealed his sources or that *S* did not keep his sources confidential, and so forth. Gert himself makes such an observation about promise keeping when he points out that keeping a promise and not breaking a promise are equivalent descriptions.[11] So there is good reason to assume that he does not mean to be using the grammar of an act's description as the criterion of whether the act is positive or negative.

Perhaps the safest interpretation is that Gert intends the distinction commonly made in the law between acts that proceed from the initiation of bodily movement and acts to which no initiation of bodily movement is essential.[12] Accordingly, yelling counts as a positive act since one cannot yell without moving one's vocal chords, but keeping quiet counts as a negative act since one need not move any part of one's body to keep quiet. Yet Gert's substantive distinction between moral ideals and moral rules is just as untenable on this interpretation as on the last. For there are plenty of circumstances in which conformity to a moral rule requires moving one's body. For instance, if some buck private were to go several weeks without showering or bathing, he would cause a good deal of visceral distress to his mates in the barracks in which he bunks. Hence, in these circumstances, his conforming to the moral rule "Do not cause pain" requires his showering or bathing. Similarly, suppose the same circumstances and that the private has contracted some highly contagious disease. Because he would threaten the health of his mates if he remained in the barracks, conformity to the rule "Do not disable" requires that he get himself to the infirmary. Other examples of this sort are easily generated. Indeed, the literature on killing and letting die is now replete with examples of homicide by omission, which is to say, of circumstances in which conformity to the rule "Do not kill" requires positive action. Nor are these examples mere philosophical fictions. The *New York Times* recently reported on a tragic case of a young mother whom the Bronx District Attorney is prosecuting for manslaughter on the grounds that she starved her infant son.[13] Clearly, then, we cannot safely assume that Gert understands the distinction between positive and negative action in the way it is commonly made in the law.

One might hope to mine Gert's text for evidence of how he understands the distinction. But unfortunately this evidence is mixed. His several references to positive action are not consistent in their meaning. For example, in a passage reaffirming that moral rules, given their negative formulation, do not demand positive action, Gert illustrates this proposition by pointing out that "The rule prohibiting depriving of freedom can be obeyed by doing nothing."[14] This point suggests that he takes the initiation of bodily movement to be the criterion of positive action. But elsewhere it appears he does not. Thus, in the passage quoted earlier in which he opposes positive action to the avoidance of certain kinds of action, it would seem he has a different criterion in mind.[15] For it is obvious that sometimes one must initiate some movement of one's body to avoid doing certain actions, as when I must swerve to avoid hitting a pedestrian or change the subject to avoid causing embarrassment. And in a later passage one finds Gert using the grammar of an action's description as the criterion of positive action. Thus, in discussing whether the moral rules admit of positive formulations, he writes, "[The moral rules] do not require positive action, except in those cases where there is no difference between requiring action and prohibiting action. There is no difference, except in style, between saying 'Keep your promises' and 'Don't break your promises.'"[16] Here Gert must be using the grammatical criterion, for otherwise one could not make sense of his conceding that a moral rule can be said to require positive action when it admits of a positive formulation.

In all of these passages the uncertainty about what Gert intends by the distinction arises from difficulties in understanding his view that moral rules do not require positive action. It does not, however, arise only from these difficulties. Similar difficulties also attend his view that moral ideals require positive action. Take his first example of a moral ideal, "Preserve life." To preserve something is to keep it safe from deterioration and destruction. To preserve life then is to keep it safe from these effects. "Do not let life deteriorate or be destroyed" is therefore an equivalent formulation of this ideal. Or in other words, one cannot say that the ideal requires positive as opposed to negative action if the criterion of whether an action is positive or negative is the grammar of its description. Nor would switching to the criterion common in the law improve the prospects for Gert's view. Preserving something, after all, does not always require action that proceeds from initiating a bodily movement. As my wife and I have learned over the years, the best way to preserve our good china is not to use it. In sum, unless Gert has some other criterion in mind for distinguishing positive from negative action, we would seem forced to conclude that the distinction between these kinds of action is useless to understanding what he means by his substantive distinction between moral ideals and moral rules.

It is possible, though, that Gert does have some other criterion in mind. He sometimes observes in support of his substantive distinction that because conformity to a moral ideal requires positive action, one cannot follow that ideal all of the time.[17] He takes this observation to support his substantive distinction because, as he also observes, one can follow any moral rule all of the time since none requires positive action.[18] It is a cardinal point of Gert's account of moral ideals that, unlike moral rules, one can sensibly ask how much time one should devote to following them, and it is evident that he sees this point being reaffirmed in these observations.[19] So, evidently, he sees some connection between an action's being positive and its being such that one cannot always be following a precept conformity to which requires it. Of course, he may make this connection because he is applying the criterion for distinguishing positive from negative action common in the law. But his point, in that case, would be mistaken. The necessity of initiating movements of one's body to conform to a moral rule could, if one's circumstances were sufficiently strange, be as great as the necessity of initiating such movements to conform to a moral ideal. There is, however, a different explanation of why he makes the connection, and from this explanation one can extract a criterion for distinguishing positive from negative action that renders Gert's substantive distinction meaningful.

The explanation is this. The reason why it makes sense to ask how much time one should devote to following moral ideals is that the ideals prescribe ends, and people cannot be expected to live their lives exclusively and always in pursuit of these ends. By the same token, the reason why it shows confusion to ask how much time one should devote to following the moral rules, the rules on Gert's list, is that these rules do not prescribe ends. Rather they set constraints on the pursuit of whatever ends people adopt, and everyone can be expected always to live within these constraints. Thus Gert makes the connection between an action's being positive and its being such that one cannot always follow a precept conformity to which requires it, because he sees that no one can be expected always to act in pursuit of the same end. On this explanation, then, what Gert means by a positive action is an action with a certain end.[20] Accordingly, on Gert's account, moral ideals require positive action because each calls for the promotion of a certain end, whereas moral rules do not require such action because none of them calls for the promotion of some end. Gert, in other words, intends his substantive distinction to capture the difference between precepts that call for pursuing a certain end—the lessening of evil—and precepts that call for avoiding, in whatever pursuits one undertakes, certain consequences—the instantiations of harm and evil. Hence, on this latest criterion of positive action, his thesis that the object of moral ideals is the prevention of evil, the object of moral rules the avoidance of causing evil is explicable.

To be sure, Gert's equivocal use of the term "positive action" makes any interpretation of what he means by it less than certain. The passages cited above are evidence that sometimes he uses it with the grammatical criterion in mind and sometimes with the criterion common in the law in mind. Nonetheless, there is decisive reason to interpret him as having this latest criterion in mind when he draws his substantive distinction, for unlike the other two criteria, this criterion renders the distinction unmysterious. Accordingly, let us assume that Gert intends the distinction to be one between precepts that call for the promotion of certain ends and precepts that do not. The assumption then allows us to move forward. Gert's account of moral ideals results from his combining his functional distinction with his substantive distinction, and we can now examine whether this combination is sound.

The combination yields a thesis about the place of the promotion of ends in morality. The thesis is that morality merely encourages the promotion of some ends. This thesis is in fact a conjunction of two propositions, first that morality encourages the promotion of some ends, and second that there is no end the promotion of which morality requires or indifference to which morality prohibits. The first proposition, which follows from Gert's functional characterization of ideals as encouragements and his substantive characterization of them as precepts calling for the promotion of some end, is uncontroversial. The second, however, which follows from Gert's functional characterization of moral rules as setting requirements and prohibitions on conduct, his substantive characterization of them as precepts that do not call for the promotion of any end, and his assumption that each of his distinctions divides the universe of moral precepts into the same disjoint classes, is not uncontroversial. Many philosophers would reject it. For many philosophers believe that there is a general duty of benevolence towards humankind and that this duty amounts to a moral requirement that one take the good of human beings as an end and act accordingly. In other words, they reject Gert's assumption that no moral precepts setting requirements and prohibitions call for the promotion of some end. They reject his assumption that his functional distinction divides the universe of moral precepts into the same disjoint classes as does his substantive distinction, that the two distinctions are isomorphic to each other.

Gert, it is worth noting, rejects the possibility of a general duty of benevolence toward humankind when he rejects Kant's distinction between perfect and imperfect duties.[21] The general duty of benevolence, in Kant's ethics, is one of two main imperfect duties, and what distinguishes them from perfect duties is that they require the adoption of an end, whereas perfect duties require the conformity of conduct to an external standard. Gert regards his distinction between moral rules and moral ideals as an improvement over Kant's distinction, and the reason he does is now clear: he believes there are no moral requirements to adopt certain ends. Call this the Gert-contra-Kant belief, or the "GCK" for short. What needs to be examined then are Gert's arguments for it. These are the arguments on which he bases his assumption that his two distinctions, the functional and the substantive, are isomorphic to each other.

He gives three arguments for the GCK. Two are implicit in the arguments he makes for his substantive distinction. We will examine them shortly. A third appeals to the necessity of understanding moral rules as precepts enforced by punishment. We can deal with it immediately, for it cannot be sound if neither of the other two is sound. Examining them, in other words, is sufficient for our purposes. So we can set his third argument aside once we see how its fate is tied to that of the other two. As a convenience, I will continue to refer to it as Gert's third argument for the GCK and will refer to other two as Gert's first and second arguments for this belief.

The major premise of his third argument is that moral rules are those precepts and only those precepts "toward which all impartial rational persons adopt the appropriate moral attitude," where the appropriate moral attitude toward a precept includes favoring making unjustified violations of it punishable.[22] From this premise Gert argues that, since impartial rational persons would not favor making any violation of a precept that required the promotion of some end punishable, such a precept cannot be one toward which all impartial rational persons would adopt the appropriate moral attitude. Hence, it cannot be a moral rule. And the reason Gert gives to explain why impartial rational persons would not favor making violations of such a precept punishable is that any distinction they tried to draw between justified and unjustified violations of it would be arbitrary, owing both to the impossibility of complying with the precept all of the time and to the impossibility of complying with it impartially with respect to everyone.[23] These last two points, that neither constant nor universally impartial compliance with such a precept is possible, are also premises of Gert's first and second arguments for the GCK. Consequently, by virtue of these shared premises, the fate of his third argument for the GCK is tied to the fate of the other two. Let us then turn directly to examining them.

We are already acquainted with one of them. It occurs when Gert argues for his substantive distinction on the basis of the two observations, (a) that no precept calling for positive action can be followed all of the time and (b) that every moral rule can be followed all of the time. For, given our assumption that in this argument Gert takes "positive action" to mean action with a certain end, (a) means that no precept calling for the promotion of a certain end can be followed all of the time, and given Gert's functional distinction, (b) implies that one can always act such as to be in compliance with every moral requirement. Hence, the thrust of this argument, Gert's first argument for the GCK, is that no moral precept can set a requirement to promote some end. Or, put simply, there are no moral requirements to promote certain ends.

This is a puzzling argument. The conclusion appears to follow from the premises, yet there are evident counterinstances. After all, no one expects the parents of small children to be advancing their children's interests all of the time. Even the parents of small children are allowed some time to themselves and allowed on some occasions to put their interests ahead of their children's. Yet it doesn't follow that they are not morally required to promote their children's welfare. Similarly, if I promise to take care of your cat while you are away for a week, you certainly wouldn't expect me to spend every waking minute of that week attending to your cat's welfare. Yet it doesn't follow that I am not morally required to take care of your cat. Indeed, even on Gert's theory, parents are morally required to promote their children's welfare, given the usual custodial duties parents have toward their children and the moral rule "Do your duty," and likewise I would be morally required to take care of your cat, given the promise I made and the moral rule "Keep your promises." Why Gert should deny that morality ever directly requires the promotion of some end when at the same time he allows that it can indirectly require the promotion of ends in virtue of these moral rules and the possibility of duties and promises to promote certain ends is a puzzle in itself.[24] But the more pressing puzzle is why this first argument for the GCK appears cogent when applied to general precepts calling for the promotion of some end yet clearly fails in cases of specific duties and promises like the duties of parents to look after their children and the promises of friends to take care of their friends' pets.

To resolve this puzzle we need to look more closely at such duties and promises. A duty to promote someone's good or a promise to look after someone requires one to engage in action with a certain end, but it does not require that one constantly engage in that action. Rather what is required to fulfill the duty or promise is that one take as one's end the good of the person who is its beneficiary and act in furtherance of that person's good in all circumstances in which failure to do so would convict one of not having taken it as one's end. The point is that to take something as an end is an inner state or condition whose existence does not depend on constant outward expression or manifestation. To take someone's good as one's end is to be disposed to be guided by that person's good in one's deliberations and decisions, and though there will certainly be circumstances in which one could not omit exercising this disposition without having lost it, one need not be constantly exercising it to continue to have it. Consequently, even though there are times when one does not promote the person's good, one may still have his good as one's end, just as I may do things unintended to promote my health, such as driving to work or even indulging my taste for fried food, without having abandoned my health as an end. Hence, Gert's point that one can always act such as to be in compliance with every moral requirement, whatever its merits, does not imply that there are no moral requirements to promote some end. For one does not need to be engaged in an action promotive of some end to be in compliance with a requirement to promote it. On many and perhaps most occasions, one's having adopted the end and thereby become disposed to be guided by it suffices for meeting the requirement. Gert's first argument for the GCK therefore appears cogent only when one loses sight of this fact about such requirements.

Gert's second argument for the GCK is similar to the first. It too is implicit in an argument he makes for his substantive distinction. Moral ideals, Gert argues, are distinct from moral rules because, as precepts calling for positive action, one cannot follow them impartially. That is, because a moral ideal is a precept calling for positive action, one cannot, in following it, act equally toward everyone whose interests the ideal protects. By contrast, moral rules, being precepts that do not call for positive action, can be followed impartially. When one follows a moral rule, one always acts equally toward everyone whose interests the rule protects.[25] From these observations we can then obtain an argument for the GCK in the same way as we obtained Gert's first argument for it from parallel observations about the impossibility of following a moral ideal all of the time and the possibility of always following a moral rule. The actual construction of the argument I leave as an exercise for the reader.

This second argument, it should be clear, is no more cogent than the first. Its conclusion too has evident counterinstances. The executive director of UNICEF,[26] for instance, who no doubt has a duty to promote the welfare of the world's children, cannot possibly advance the interests of every child in the world equally. Yet it does not follow that she is not morally required to promote the welfare of the world's children. Similarly, if I promise to take care of your ten children for a day, I cannot possibly look after all of them equally. Some are bound to get more of my attention than others. But it hardly follows that I am not morally required to look after your children. The second argument thus goes wrong in the same way as the first. It too misrepresents what counts as meeting a requirement to promote some end. For what the duty the executive director of UNICEF has and the promise I make requires is the promotion of the good of all who belong to a specific group, and one meets such a requirement if one adopts their good as one's end and acts in furtherance of it in every circumstance in which failure to do so would convict one of not having taken it as one's end. Hence, one can meet the requirement even though one does not act equally toward every member of the group in advancing their good, since a disparity in the way one treats the members does not in itself convict one of not having adopted their good as one's end.

This point parallels the point on which the first argument founders. The latter, recall, is that one need not constantly be engaged in action that contributes to someone's good to have adopted the person's good as one's end. One can, in other words, omit contributing to someone's good on Tuesday, say, having contributed to it on Monday, without thereby showing indifference to the person's good. Such disparity over a period of time in one's conduct toward someone is consistent with constancy throughout the same period in one's attachment to his good. Similarly, then, one need not contribute to the good of each member of some group, or contribute as much to each member's good as to every other's, to have adopted the good of all as one's end and be equally well disposed toward each. One can, in other words, omit contributing to the good of some members, having contributed to the good of others, or contribute to the good of some less than one has contributed to the good of others, without thereby showing that one is indifferent to the good of some members or not as well disposed toward them as one is toward others. Such disparity across the group in one's conduct toward its members is consistent with one's being uniformly attached to the good of all. Thus Gert's claim that every moral requirement can be complied with impartially is no reason to exclude requirements to promote some end from the class of moral requirements. For one need not contribute equally to the good of all who benefit from a requirement to promote some end in order to have complied impartially with that requirement. It is sufficient to have adopted their good as one's end and to be equally well disposed towards each as a result.

The temptation to think otherwise comes from thinking that any disparity in one's treatment of the members of a group whose good one is required to promote must be due to some bias or prejudice favoring some members and disfavoring others. But this need not be so. One may simply have greater opportunities to contribute to the good of some than of others, and taking advantage of these opportunities is consistent with being attached to the good of all who belong to the group and equally well disposed toward each. A teacher who has several students all of whom are working on separate projects is required to help them advance their projects. At the same time, though, she may have more opportunities to help some than others just because some have remained nearby and some have moved away. Yet one shouldn't suppose that the greater time she therefore spends helping those who live nearby betrays a bias in their favor or a weaker commitment to the success of the projects of those who have moved away. As long as the teacher continues to take as an end her students' success in their projects and education and to be equally well disposed in this regard to each, she will have complied impartially with the requirement to advance her students' projects.

To be sure, the question of when one's actions convict one of not being attached to someone's good or the good of all who belong to some group is not always cut-and-dried. A good example of this uncertainty can be seen in the controversy, currently popular in moral philosophy, over whether those of us who can save starving children in faraway lands by making donations to international relief organizations are morally required to do so, given that we certainly would be morally required to save a drowning child in a shallow pool whom we could save by wading into the pool and lifting him out of danger. Some philosophers argue that we are morally required to donate to international relief organizations, since we would be morally required to save the drowning child and there is no morally relevant difference between the circumstances in the two cases.[27] Others, however, resist this conclusion, for they regard it as contrary to common sense about what morality requires. Like Gert, they hold that sending donations to international relief organizations is something morality encourages but does not require. While the issue in dispute here is complex and no doubt open to several interpretations, one of them is whether meeting the general duty of benevolence toward humankind is consistent with one's not sending money overseas to save starving children, given that it is inconsistent with one's doing nothing to save a drowning child in a shallow pool should one happen upon a child in such trouble. And on this interpretation one can see sufficient reason to resist the conclusion of the philosophers who hold that the moral necessity of saving the drowning child implies the moral necessity of sending money overseas to save starving children.

The reason lies in the difference in how certain we can be in each case that the omission of life-saving action is a sign of the actor's indifference to the good of human beings. In the case of the drowning child, declining to wade into the pool and lift the child out of danger is a sure sign of such indifference, whereas in the case of the starving children, declining to send money overseas for their relief need not be. Its significance in this regard is much more open to doubt. For one thing, a person who had already sent money overseas to save starving children, say within the last month, might then decline to send money for this purpose without thereby showing indifference to the good of human beings, whereas letting a child drown whom one could save would be a sign of such indifference whether or not one had saved a child in similar danger within the last month. For another, a person who donates to local efforts to help the poor or the sufferers of some dread disease like AIDS might decline to send money overseas without thereby showing indifference to the good of human beings, whereas one could not, without showing such indifference, ignore a drowning child because one was too busy building houses for the homeless. Generally, then, we cannot be as certain about someone's declining to send money overseas to save starving children, that it is a sign of deficient attachment to the good of human beings, as we can about someone's declining to lift a drowning child out of a pool, for whether the latter is such a sign depends much less than whether the former is on the context of the omission and on the actor's prior and ongoing efforts at promoting human welfare. It admits of determinate and firm answers, whereas the question of the former's significance, in all but extreme cases of selfishness, clannishness, and chauvinism, does not.

These last points reinforce our conclusion that Gert's first and second arguments for the GCK fail. What is more, they remove the worry lying behind these arguments that any general moral requirement to promote the good of human beings places impossible demands on the time and resources of moral agents and entails the impossible task of involving them impartially in the lives of billions of people. They make clear that meeting such a requirement, at least if it is of the sort that Kant and others identify as the duty of benevolence toward humankind, need not entail an unreasonable expense of time and resources or excessive involvement in the lives of strangers. Hence, while there may still be difficulties in taking as a general requirement of morality a requirement of this sort, while there may, in particular, be difficulties in Kant's understanding of it as an imperfect duty, neither of Gert's first two arguments for the GCK has uncovered any. A duty of benevolence like the one Kant affirms would therefore appear to be one plausible form of the moral requirement to promote the good of human beings that escapes these arguments. And in the absence of some new and cogent objection to taking it as a general requirement of morality, Gert would appear to have no solid grounds for his denying that morality includes any such requirement.

What of Gert's third argument for the GCK? Could it be the source of some new and cogent objection? To be sure, the argument is unsound just as his first and second arguments for the GCK are. It too includes among its premises Gert's faulty claims about the impossibility of constant and universally impartial compliance with precepts requiring the promotion of some end. But though the argument is unsound just as they are, the worry lying behind it is different from the worry that lies behind them. This worry, the one lying behind the third argument, is that such precepts cannot be fairly or usefully enforced by punishment, and unlike the other worry, it is completely separable from the faulty claims on which the argument it lies behind are based. Consequently, even though these claims make that argument unsound, the worry that lies behind it might still be a source of a cogent objection to taking a duty of benevolence like the one Kant affirms as a general requirement of morality. So we ought to consider whether Gert could give a different argument that substantiates that worry.

Specifically, since the argument Gert gives to substantiate it consists in his presenting reasons why impartial rational persons would not favor making unjustified violations of precepts that require the promotion of some end punishable, we ought to consider whether Gert could present different reasons explaining why impartial rational persons would not favor making unjustified violations of such precepts punishable. If he could, then these reasons would constitute a new and different argument for the GCK. He would then have produced a new objection to taking as a general moral requirement the duty of benevolence that Kant and others affirm.

This possibility may seem promising as a way of restoring cogency to Gert's view. Gert does, after all, treat the attitude impartial rational persons would take toward unjustified violations of moral requirements as independently important to understanding the nature of those requirements. And a new argument for the GCK that drew on that attitude without relying on the faulty premises of the third argument would represent this independent importance Gert assigns to his account of the attitude.[28] But though this possibility may seem promising, it cannot succeed. It certainly could not succeed if Gert held that the attitude impartial rational persons took toward unjustified violations of moral requirements was one of favoring punishment for every such violation. To favor punishment for every unjustified lie and broken promise and for every petty utterance of cruel words would be to favor a cure for these wrongs that was far worse than the disease. What Gert must and does hold is that the attitude is one of favoring punishment of unjustified violations where the cost of imposing the punishment is not greater than the benefit of its deterrent effect.[29] This by contrast is a sensible attitude to attribute to impartial rational persons, so sensible, in fact, that it is hard to fathom what reasons Gert could give to show that such persons would decline to take it toward unjustified violations of requirements to promote a morally significant end such as the good of human beings.

The chief difficulty, in any case, is that whatever new argument for the GCK Gert constructed from such reasons would be subject to the same counter-instances that proved fatal to Gert's first and second arguments. We undoubtedly think, for instance, that parents of small children, given the usual custodial duties such parents have, should be subject to some threats of punishment for neglecting their children's welfare, and likewise think that people who promise to look after their friends' children, given the obligations such promises create, should be subject to threats of punishment were they to neglect the welfare of these children once they were put in their care. We think, in other words, that such duties and promises entail requirements to promote their beneficiaries' welfare and that unjustified violations of them should not be immune to punishment. No reasons Gert could give purporting to show how impartial rational persons could think otherwise would even be credible. And the same holds for reasons purporting to show how such persons could favor making immune to punishment unjustified violations of a requirement to promote the good of human beings like the one Kant and others identify as the duty of benevolence. To be sure, we can assume that impartial rational persons would, as a result of balancing the costs of punishment against the benefits of its deterrent effect in each case, favor stricter enforcement of the former requirements than the latter. But whatever the results of these calculations, the point is that there is nothing in the latter to distinguish it from the former as a requirement whose enforcement by threats of punishment impartial rational persons would, as a matter of principle, not favor.

The duty of benevolence that Kant and others affirm represents, then, a general moral requirement calling for positive action that confounds Gert's arguments against the possibility of such requirements. His actual arguments fail as a result of his misconstruing what compliance with such requirements involves when they are requirements to promote some end. And even possible arguments suggested but not developed in the text that avoid this misconstruction fall short. The impact of this result on his account of moral ideals is immediate. The account follows directly from his combining his functional and substantive distinctions between moral rules and moral ideals, and his combination of the two distinctions depends on his assumption of an isomorphism between them. Since the possibility of a general moral requirement to promote some end is incompatible with the assumption, the failure of Gert's arguments against this possibility means that the assumption on which his account depends is unwarranted. And insofar as the criticisms showing that failure make a strong case for including among the general requirements of morality a requirement to promote the good of human beings like the one Kant and others identify as the duty of benevolence, there is little hope for supporting the assumption by some other argument.

The end result of these criticisms, therefore, is that Gert's account of moral ideals cannot be sustained. For without the assumption on which it depends, Gert must either abandon his substantive distinction or abandon his functional one. That is, he must either allow that some moral rules call for positive action or allow that some moral ideals require action and do not merely encourage it. And neither is an option Gert can embrace. Plainly, he cannot embrace the second option, for if he did, he could no longer oppose moral ideals to moral requirements and prohibitions. Specifically, he could no longer point to moral ideals as accounting for moral judgments of good and bad action that are distinct from moral judgments of required and prohibited action. But equally clearly he cannot embrace the first option, for if he did, he would be hard pressed to find a precept that counted as a moral ideal rather than a moral rule. After all, nothing in his theory, apart from the substantive distinction, explains why "Preserve life," "Relieve suffering," "Help the needy," and so on are moral ideals and not moral rules. Hence, once the theory abandoned this distinction and allowed that some moral rules call for positive action, it would need some basis for explaining why not all precepts calling for action that prevents evil are moral rules, that is, why some are moral ideals, and it is hard to see what that basis could be. Indeed, as Gert himself recognizes, once he admitted as a moral rule a precept that called for the promotion of the good of human beings, all of the precepts he counts as moral ideals would be consequences of this rule. Thus, short of discovering some wholly new and cogent objection to the possibility of moral requirements that call for positive action, there is no saving Gert's account of moral ideals and their relation to moral requirements and prohibitions.

II

Gert takes moral ideals to be precepts. On his account, they belong to the same category of standards as moral rules. They are standards one complies with or obeys. There is a different way to understand moral ideals, however. One can take them, instead, as models of conduct. Accordingly, they belong to a different category of standards from rules. Models of conduct are standards one lives up to or realizes. The difference between the two categories is evident both in their modes of expression and in their modes of guidance. Where precepts take the form of an imperative, models are presented in images, pictures, and portraits. Where precepts guide by explicit direction, models guide by inviting emulation or imitation. As children, for instance, we learn that standing during the playing of the national anthem at community events is the proper thing to do. Typically, we learn this both by being directed to stand by our parents or other authority figures when the national anthem is about to be played and by seeing our parents and these other figures stand during its playing and following their lead. In the one case we learn by prescription; in the other we learn by example. Having found serious flaws in the initially attractive account of moral ideals that Gert expounds, the account on which they are understood as precepts, let us briefly consider an alternative account on which they are understood as models of conduct.[30]

As my observation about learning suggests, we get our ideals from examples that people whom we look up to or admire set. These will not only be people, such as our parents and teachers, whom we know directly but also people whom we see from afar and learn about through the news or whom we meet in literature, history, theater, and film. The latter point is well illustrated in philosophy by the portrayal of Socrates in Plato's early dialogues. Countless readers of these dialogues have taken Socrates's conversations and activities, as portrayed by Plato, both as a model of how one conducts a philosophical inquiry and a model of intellectual and moral integrity. Admiring Socrates's refusal to profess knowledge he does not have and his unwavering commitments to truth and right action, these readers have found in the early dialogues an ideal of truth seeking and justice that has captured their imagination and favor. Plato's portrayal is perhaps a sufficient illustration of my point, but for the sake of variety let me offer two others. One is Thoreau's description of his two-year sojourn at

Walden pond. His experiment there to show that "a man is rich in proportion to the number of things he can afford to let alone"[31] is our foremost ideal of a life of solitude lived close to nature and without dependence on material wealth. The other is the figure of Mohandas Gandhi, whose leadership in the campaigns against the injustice of British colonial rule, first in South Africa and then in India, inspired many to adopt his methods of nonviolent struggle against tyranny and to model their conduct in such struggles on his. Gandhi, both through his actions and his writings, thus conveyed to many disciples and admirers powerful ideals of a life dedicated to advancing justice through radical social reform and without violence or malice toward one's opponents and of the courage, patience, and self-discipline necessary to persevering in such a program.

There are of course a great many other ideals that guide people in the conduct of their lives: ideals of athletic prowess, artistic achievement, romantic love, family life, triumph over the elements of nature, and so on. Plainly, it would be a mistake to construe all of them as moral ideals. So the question is how should one distinguish these from all the others. One possibility is to suppose that they are ideals that have a certain content. This way of distinguishing them will recommend itself to anyone who, like Gert, holds that morality has a definite point. Thus, if like Gert you believe that the point of morality is to lessen harm and suffering, then it would be reasonable for you to define moral ideals as the ideals whose realization tends to have this result. Another possibility, though, is to suppose that moral ideals are ideals that bear a certain formal or functional relation to moral requirements and prohibitions. This way of distinguishing them will recommend itself to anyone who either holds that morality has no definite point or does not have a view on the matter. At the same time, it would not preclude anyone from distinguishing moral ideals by their content since they would, by virtue of being formally or functionally related to moral requirements and prohibitions, inherit whatever content was distinctive of those requirements and prohibitions. Hence, this second way of distinguishing moral ideals has the distinct advantage of avoiding controversies over whether morality has a definite point and what that point is if it does. It is, for this reason, a better initial way of distinguishing them than the first.

The question therefore becomes one of finding a formal or functional relation that ideals can bear to moral requirements and prohibitions and that can serve to distinguish those that do as moral. Ideals, I suggest, give meaning or purpose to a life. Certainly, people who devote their lives to the pursuit of some ideal, as Mother Teresa, for instance, devoted her life to ministering to the poorest of the poor, give to their lives in this way a distinct and compelling purpose. But even for those of us who have not devoted our lives wholly to the pursuit of a single ideal, whose lives consist of some of this and some of that, the ideals that we do hold to and that do guide our lives help to give meaning and purpose to our various activities and conduct. Suppose, then, that moral ideals are ideals allegiance to which gives meaning or purpose to moral conduct, specifically, to one's compliance with moral prohibitions and requirements. They are, in other words, ideals that people can take themselves to be realizing through such compliance. On this proposal, moral ideals function in people's lives by enlarging their understanding of the significance and value of compliance with moral requirements and prohibitions and thus strengthening their disposition to comply. Accordingly, any ideal that so functions in a person's life is for that person a moral ideal.

Distinguishing moral ideals in this way is consistent, needless to say, with recognizing other ways in which people find meaning or purpose in their complying with moral requirements and prohibitions. Nothing in this proposal, in other words, implies that holding to some moral ideal is a necessary condition of finding such meaning or purpose. Indeed, for the most part people may simply see the purpose of their complying with moral requirements and prohibitions in the necessity for social life that general compliance with moral requirements and prohibitions has or in the advantages of an untarnished reputation that personal compliance with them brings. That is, for the most part people may see a purpose to moral conduct without recourse to any moral ideal. Still, there are times when one's circumstances invite acts of dishonesty or infidelity that would neither disrupt social life nor sully one's reputation. One finds a lost wallet, say, containing a wad of cash, or one becomes privy to insider information from which one can gain significantly though illicitly. At these times, allegiance to a moral ideal will give meaning or purpose to compliance with the applicable moral requirement or prohibition that would otherwise escape one. At these times, allegiance to a moral ideal keeps one from falling prey to the perspective of Hume's sensible knave.

From that perspective, the perspective of Hume's knave, moral requirements and prohibitions appear as externally imposed restraints on one's conduct. One sees a general purpose as well as personal advantage to observing those restraints and, like Hume's knave, is willing to observe them in circumstances in which their violation jeopardizes social harmony or risks damage to one's reputation. But from the knave's perspective one finds nothing self-affirming or self-realizing in observing them. By contrast, then, from the perspective of someone who holds a moral ideal, moral requirements and prohibitions are felt as self-imposed restraints. The ideal represents a way of acting or living to which one aspires, which is to say, with which one identifies, and in virtue of this identification, the restraints cease to appear external. I think something like this point is expressed by Harry Frankfurt when he writes, "Especially with respect to those we love and with respect to our ideals, we are liable to be bound by necessities which have less to do with our adherence to the principles of morality than with integrity and consistency of a more personal kind. These necessities constrain us from betraying the things we care about most and with which, accordingly, we are most closely identified. In a sense which a strictly ethical analysis cannot make clear, what they keep us from violating are not our duties or our obligations but ourselves."[32]

Moral ideals, therefore, on this understanding of them, do not belong to the system of rules and principles of which morality, on the prevailing philosophical view of it, consists. They are not, contrary to Gert's understanding of them, a type of precept whose function in morality complements the function of those moral precepts that set requirements and prohibitions on conduct. Rather, moral ideals exist within the large class of images, pictures, and portraits of ways of acting and living that appear worthy of realization and inspire pursuit. These are images, pictures, and portraits on which we draw to give meaning or purpose to the various activities and practices that make up our lives. Compliance with the demands of morality, its requirements and prohibitions, is commonly a source in people of uncertainty about whether it serves any of their own purposes, and thus moral ideals answer directly a common uncertainty about the meaningfulness of one type of conduct. They specifically work to alleviate this uncertainty, as the development and strengthening of allegiance to moral ideals transforms their possessor's sense of morality's demands from that of being externally imposed constraints into that of being self-imposed ones. Moral ideals, then, do not come into the study of morality as an integral part of the system of rules and principles that, in contemporary philosophy, is seen as the proper object of that study. Perhaps they don't come into the study at all.

Alternatively, though, if the study of morality were understood not so much, let alone exclusively, as an examination of a set of social norms regulating conduct and were understood, instead, as more of an examination of those habits and springs of action distinctive of a moral personality, then there might be a place for them in the study. In other words, if there is any merit to the thought at the outset of this paper that the subject of moral philosophy may have changed over the past two centuries, then one might find a place for them in a return to the older understanding of the subject. Accordingly, introducing moral ideals into the study might help to reverse this change. It might, that is, serve to bring the study of morality back to something closer to a study of morals.[33]

Notes

1. Bernard Gert, *Morality: Its Nature and Justification* (New York: Oxford University Press, 1998). All references will be to this work.

2. See 318-319, 322. Note that Gert does not take every judgment that an action is morally bad to be one made apart from the act's being morally prohibited, but he does hold that some are.

3. See preface, ix-x.

4. Gert, *Morality*, 247. See also 109.

5. Gert, *Morality*, 126.

6. Of course, one might think, in view of these and similar examples, that preventing harm is a kind of act one of whose species is avoiding causing harm. But Gert, however he understands the distinction between preventing harm and avoiding causing harm, does not think that the latter is a species of the former. For if it were, then violations of moral rules would frequently count as failures to act on a moral ideal, and it is clear that Gert sees violations of moral rules as importantly different from failures to act on moral ideals. Thus he writes (157), "Failing to act on a moral ideal never warrants punishment, whereas violating a moral rule often does."

7. Gert, *Morality*, 248.

8. Gert, *Morality*, 123 and 126.

9. See, e.g., Gert, *Morality*, 127, 189, and 249.

10. I follow N. Ann Davis's discussion in her very perceptive and instructive essay "The Priority of Avoiding Harm," in *Killing and Letting Die*, ed. Bonnie Steinbock (Englewood Cliffs, N.J.: Prentice Hall, 1980), 172-214.

11. Gert, *Morality*, 188-89.

12. See Bentham, *Introduction to the Principles of Morals and Legislation*, ed. H. L. A. Hart and J. H. Burns (Oxford, Eng.: Oxford University Press, 1979), 75-76 (ch. 7, pars. 8 & 9).

13. Nina Bernstein, "Placing the Blame in an Infant's Death: Mother Faces Trial After Baby Dies from Lack of Breast Milk," *New York Times*, 15 March 1999, 1(B).

14. Gert, *Morality*, 189.

15. Gert, *Morality*, 123.

16. Gert, *Morality*, 189.

17. See Gert, *Morality*, e.g., 126 and 249.

18. Gert, *Morality*, 122 and 126.

19. Gert, *Morality*, 122-23.

20. That this explanation yields a separate criterion of positive action from the other two should be clear. For example, on the criterion it yields, my growing a beard would be

a positive action; my letting my beard grow would not. The two actions would thus be classified differently on this criterion. By contrast, on both the grammatical criterion and the criterion common in the law, they would not be. On the former, both my growing a beard and my letting my beard grow would count as positive actions, whereas on the latter neither would count as a positive action.

21. Gert, *Morality*, 16.

22. Gert, *Morality*, 180. See also 126-27.

23. Gert, *Morality*, 181. Using "Promote pleasure" as an example of a rule toward which impartial rational persons could not take the appropriate moral attitude, Gert's argument, verbatim, is

> Unlike the . . . moral rules, this rule cannot possibly be obeyed all of the time. Nor is it likely that it can ever be impartially obeyed with regard to everyone. Thus an impartial rational person would either have to adopt the attitude that everyone be publicly allowed to violate the promote-pleasure rule whenever and with regard to whomever he feels like doing so, or else to hold that everyone is liable to punishment all of the time. To do the former would make it pointless to adopt the moral attitude toward the rule; to do the latter would be to increase everyone's chances of suffering evil. I conclude that no impartial rational person would adopt the moral attitude toward the rule 'Promote pleasure.'

I have taken the liberty of interpreting this argument as one in which Gert is appealing to the arbitrariness of distinguishing between justified and unjustified violations of the promote-pleasure rule to explain why its being impossible to obey the rule all of the time and impartially with respect to everyone are grounds on which impartial rational persons would not favor making violations of the rule punishable. Nothing in what follows, however, depends on the soundness of this way of interpreting Gert's argument. The important thing is that Gert takes the impossibility of constant and universally impartial compliance with a rule as the grounds on which impartial rational persons would not favor making violations of the rule punishable, and that he does so is plain from the passage quoted in this footnote.

24. Gert could undo this inconsistency by reversing himself on the question of whether keeping a promise and not breaking a promise, fulfilling a duty and not violating a duty, are equivalent descriptions and by reformulating the rules about promises and duties to read "Do not violate your duties" and "Do not break your promises." For he could then say, using "positive action" in the sense we are assuming he means, "One can follow these rules all of the time, even at those times when one is not engaged in the positive actions necessary to fulfilling some duty one has undertaken or keeping some promise one has made." But this inconsistency in his views is not the problem. It is just a symptom. The problem is that parents are morally required to look after their children, a promise to promote an end does create a moral requirement to promote the end, and Gert cannot affirm either of these propositions without abandoning one or the other premise of the argument we are considering.

25. Gert, *Morality*, 123-24.

26. Carol Bellamy.

27. Peter Singer, *Practical Ethics* (Cambridge, Eng.: Cambridge University Press, 1979), 168-71.

28. See Gert, *Morality*, 126-27. Cf. 180-81, where Gert does not as clearly treat his account of the attitude as being important to understanding the nature of moral requirements independently of his functional and substantive distinctions but does suggest its independent importance in citing the attitude to explain why such contrived precepts as "Offer to prevent pain for the first person you see each day" are not moral rules.

29. See Gert, *Morality*, 182.

30. On the notion of ideals as models of conduct presented in images and pictures, see P. F. Strawson "Social Morality and Individual Ideal," *Philosophy* 36 (1961): 1-17.

31. Henry David Thoreau, *Walden*, ch. 2, par. 1. *Walden, and Civil Disobedience* (New York: W. W. Norton, 1966).

32. Harry Frankfurt, *The Importance of What We Care About* (Cambridge, Eng.: Cambridge University Press, 1988), 91.

33. I am grateful to Marcia Baron, Paul McNamara, and Walter Sinnott-Armstrong for helpful comments they sent me on an earlier draft of this essay. I benefited too from the comments offered by the participants and audience at the conference on Gert's *Morality: Its Nature and Justification*, where I presented the first part of this essay.

11

Accentuate the Negative: Negative Values, Moral Theory, and Common Sense*

Douglas MacLean

Ethics is about respecting people, preventing evils, and not harming other sentient beings. The subject is also widely thought to include fashioning ideals for individual lives and societies and figuring out ways to remove the barriers to progress in approaching those ideals. Moral theorists, like the rest of us, worry about the evils in life, but they also look on the bright side. Bernard Gert defends a conception of morality that he claims to be based on common sense, and he argues that the focus of such a system should be predominantly on the negative. The history of the subject is not on Gert's side, and I believe common sense gives only partial and not full support to Gert's view. As I see it, the positive and the negative are both part of common morality, and both of these themes figure prominently in the history of moral philosophy.

Positive Goods, Moral Theories, and Common Sense: An Historical Glimpse

Consider some examples. Aristotle begins the *Nicomachean Ethics* by noting that all human actions aim at an end, which is some good.[1] The main purpose of ethics, as he understands the subject, is to discover and analyze the proper end of human activity, the end that is final, complete, and self-sufficient. The reasons for this study are practical as well as philosophical. For, as Aristotle remarks, "surely knowledge of this good is also of great importance for the conduct of our lives, and if, like archers, we have a target to aim at, we are more likely to hit the right mark."[2]

The idea of the highest good in Aristotle's ethics is based on common beliefs of his day. He says that most people agree about it, at least in name. "Both the many and the cultivated call it happiness, and suppose that living well and doing well are the same as being happy."[3] Philosophy is needed because the many and the wise disagree about what happiness is. Interestingly, happiness is thought by Aristotle in some degree to be the absence of harm or misery, which is why the same person changes his mind about it, "since in sickness he thinks it is health, in poverty wealth."[4] But Aristotle's understanding of happiness—as activity expressing virtue—is primarily a positive achievement of reason.

Where Aristotle differs most markedly from us is in believing that happiness can be understood as a single, objective thing. He believes this, of course, because of his views about the activities that most positively engage reason. The greatest happiness and highest virtue come from the activity of study or contemplation, and "it is agreed" that activity expressing wisdom is the most pleasant of activities. It is the most self-sufficient of activities, but more importantly, study alone allows us to transcend our human natures and express the divine element within us. But even if Aristotle had a less intellectual and more pluralistic conception of the highest human good, the positive and teleological character of his conception of ethics would not have been compromised. Of course it may be that our modern view of morality is more narrowly focused than Aristotle's conception of ethics, but he was clearly arguing from common sense, as he understood it, and focusing on positive as well as negative values.

John Stuart Mill also regarded morality as aiming primarily at achieving some positive end, and one of the basic aims of moral philosophy was to make this clear. "From the dawn of philosophy, the question concerning the *summum bonum*, or, what is the same thing, concerning the foundation of morality, has been accounted the main problem in speculative thought."[5] It is possible that the foundation or point of morality may be positive—in Mill's system the realization of the *summum bonum*—but the content of morality, its rules and prescriptions, could be exclusively negative. This could be the case if a moral code restricted to negative rules and prescriptions was likely to achieve more good than any other code. It is also true that Mill believed that most of the point of moral rules and duties was to relieve the sources of misery and other impediments standing in the way of happiness. Once these impediments are removed the natural human desire for happiness would lead people to seek and find it, just as removing debris from a stream allows the natural flow of water downhill.

But the utilitarian system of morality that Mill defends is not restricted to negative rules, and Mill arguably did not regard the negative aims of morality as in any way prior to the positive prescriptions aimed at promoting happiness. The theory Mill defends in *Utilitarianism* calls not only for defining rules to prevent people from impeding the flow of happiness, and punishing those who break them, but also for directly promoting happiness or pleasure where possible.

Moral theory for Mill, as for most utilitarians, is a theory about what makes actions right or wrong. Mill's own view, as I interpret him, regards right and wrong actions, as it were, asymmetrically. The "greatest happiness principle" holds famously that "actions are right in proportion as they tend to promote happiness."[6] Mill says that wrong actions are those that "tend to produce the reverse of happiness."[7] But later he says, "We do not call anything wrong unless we mean to imply that a person ought to be punished in some way or other for doing it."[8] Thus, right actions for Mill are those that promote happiness, and wrong actions are those that deserve punishment. Morality for Mill consists both of producing right actions and preventing wrong ones, and the former requires an understanding of the good that is to be promoted.

Mill's view of the relation of the utilitarian morality to common sense is more complicated. He sees utilitarianism as a revolutionary development in moral thinking, which can be applied to attack commonly believed moral prejudice as well as other sources of human misery. He thus understands why the doctrine provokes such controversy and criticism in his day. But a large part of his defense of utilitarianism consists in clearing away the misunderstandings of its critics, so that the intuitive or commonsense core of the doctrine can shine through. After addressing a series of these misunderstandings in chapter 2 of

Utilitarianism, Mill claims that "mankind must by this time have acquired positive beliefs as to the effects of some actions on their happiness; and the beliefs which have thus come down are the rules of morality for the multitude, and for the philosopher until he has succeeded in finding better."[9] Mill's attempt to prove the principle of utility in chapter 4, moreover, rests on the assumption that, "No reason can be given why the general happiness is desirable, except that each person, so far as he believes it to be attainable, desires his own happiness."[10] The argument relies on Mill's unsuccessful attempt to show that all the things we desire as ends are means to or constituents of our own happiness, but the proof can be seen as a further attempt to link the utilitarian doctrine to common beliefs.

Kant's view, as usual, is more complicated still, but he must also be read both as attempting to build on commonsense morality and as requiring us to promote positive goals as well as constraining our actions to eliminate evils. In the first section of the *Grounding of the Metaphysics of Morals*, Kant's strategy is to argue from ordinary knowledge of morality to a determination of its first principle. The title of the section, "Transition from the Ordinary Rational Knowledge of Morality to the Philosophical," makes this intention clear.[11] For Kant, the ideas that the good will is the only unconditional good, and that we can understand the good will by taking up the concept of duty, are merely to elaborate on common sense. He writes, "This concept [of a good will] already dwells in the natural sound understanding and needs not so much to be taught as merely to be elucidated."[12] The concept of duty, which includes a good will, is simply how the requirement to respect the rational law as the first principle of morality appears to human beings. We see the rational law as a duty because we have desires and inclinations, which Kant unreasonably assumes we would all rather be without. In the second section of the *Grounding*, Kant proceeds to argue from common sense, or Popular Moral Philosophy, to a Metaphysics of Morals. In this section, however, he repeats that "all moral concepts have their seat and origin completely a priori in reason, and indeed in the most ordinary human reason as much as in the most highly speculative."[13]

That Kant's moral theory also requires promoting positive goals can be seen in each of the formulations of the categorical imperative. The first formulation, which tells us to act only on that maxim that we can at the same time will to be a universal law, can be interpreted as a procedure through which we filter our natural motivations. The categorical imperative disallows acting on evil maxims that generate contradictions of a rational will, while allowing the others to pass through. This procedure cannot be interpreted exclusively in a negative way, however, which merely prohibits wrongful acts, for it also requires us to develop our own natural talents and to provide aid to others. Failure to act on these maxims, Kant argues, contradicts a rational will.[14]

The second formulation of the categorical imperative, which requires us to treat humanity always as an end and never merely as a means, is more complicated. This formulation has a clear negative aspect, which prohibits us from using other people in immoral ways, but it must also be interpreted as requiring positive actions that promote the rational nature of other human beings, which include duties to aid others in achieving their rational aims.[15] The third formulation, which gives the "complete determination of all maxims," requires us to see ourselves and all other rational beings as united in a "kingdom" by a common set of moral principles.[16] In this kingdom, all principles proceeding from my own will "ought to harmonize with a possible kingdom of ends as a kingdom of nature."[17] This formulation is clearer than the others in emphasizing the positive aspect of the categorical imperative. Kant explains that by saying that morals regards a possible kingdom of ends as a kingdom of nature, he means that this is "a practical idea for bringing about what does not exist but can be made actual by our conduct."[18]

One might argue that Kant is going beyond the scope of morality when he discusses duties to oneself. Some philosophers would insist that the subject of morality is restricted to conduct that affects other people. Kant would have thought such a restriction to be arbitrary. In selecting examples to illustrate the categorical imperative, Kant carefully chooses examples of perfect and imperfect duties, to oneself and to others, in order to test his conclusion on all the kinds of duties morality was understood to encompass. More importantly, however, Kant's own view of morality is not fundamentally tied either to self-regarding or to other-regarding conduct. Its aim is rather to respect rational nature and its laws wherever they occur, and in our world rationality happens to be embodied in human nature, both in ourselves and in every other normal human we encounter.

Negative Moralists

There are, of course, exceptions to theories that emphasize the positive in morality. One kind of exception can be seen in the underappreciated writings of the Stoics and Epicurus.[19] The stoics seemed to be nearly exclusively concerned with the causes of misery and ways to eliminate them. Epicurus appears to be more positive, for he regards pleasures of the mind as essential for living a good life. But these pleasures, as he understands them, turn out to be mainly negative. One pleasure of the mind is recognizing that death is merely the limit of experience and thus not a thing to be feared. A second pleasure comes from recognizing that the gratification of desires that go beyond what is necessary for sustaining life results in greater pain than pleasure. And a third pleasure comes from the study of natural philosophy, the point of which is to remove our natural fear of the gods.[20] The good state that results from cultivating these pleasures, which the Stoics called *ataraxia*, is better characterized as the elimination of suffering that brings peace of mind than as some more positive state of the sort that we usually associate with pleasure.

The main modern exception to moralists who see the subject as including positive aims is commonly believed to be Hobbes, who views morality as a way of escaping the evils present in the state of nature. One should notice, however, that in describing the state of nature as a state of war, in which people lack the benefits of cooperation, Hobbes emphasizes the goods missing in that state as well as the evils that exist there. He writes, "In such condition there is no place for industry, because the fruit thereof is uncertain, and consequently, no culture of the earth, no navigation, nor use of the commodities that may be imported by sea, no commodious building, no instruments of moving and removing such things as require great force, no knowledge of the face of the earth, no account of time, no arts, no letters, no society and which is worst of all, continual fear and danger of violent death."[21] The lack of such goods together with the fear and danger that exist in the state of nature are what make the life of man in that state "solitary, poor, nasty, brutish, and short."[22] Hobbesian man has a rational nature, however, which includes passions that incline him to peace. Hobbes describes these passions as a fear of death, a desire of such things as are necessary for commodious living, and a hope of obtaining them by industry.

Hobbes has been wrongly criticized for holding an excessively pessimistic view of human nature. He is not strictly a psychological egoist, as he is often interpreted to be, for Hobbesian man cares as passionately for his family and friends as he does for himself. The pessimism in Hobbes's view of society, in any case, comes from his sociology, not his psychology. It comes from seeing that the outcome of individuals successfully pursuing their own interests in a state of nature is not to be led by an invisible hand to some optimal result. Without the guidance of law or some other authority, men face what contemporary game theorists call assurance problems and prisoners' dilemmas, which they cannot solve acting in isolation. The collective outcome of the rational pursuit of individual interests in the state of nature is a disaster for each and every person. This disaster is what morality as a rational agreement aims to avoid.

We could be led to see the rationality of the social contract, however, either by focusing on the benefits that we could attain in civil society or the evils we could avoid there. Hobbes believed that we are moved by both concerns but that our desire to avoid evil is stronger. He writes, "Everyone is moved by an appetite for what is good for himself, and by an aversion for what is evil for himself, but most of all by the greatest of natural evils, which is death. This happens by a certain necessity of nature, no less than that by which a stone is carried downward."[23] It is perhaps for this reason that Hobbes believes that we do better by focusing on the negative in defending our moral theory.

This concludes the quick historical tour. My point is to show that at least some of the most important moral theorists were concerned to explain morality in a way that sees it both as preventing evils and as promoting good. Even the theorists I regard as focusing on the negative do so only in a manner of emphasis and degree, and not from any more restrictive view of the scope of the subject. Most of these theorists also claim to be starting from and elucidating common sense.

Bernard Gert's Negative View

Among contemporary moral theorists, probably none is more consistent or thoroughgoing in emphasizing the negative than Bernard Gert. He defines the goal of morality as "the lessening of evil or harm."[24] Promoting good, he says, is not normally a matter of morality at all. Acknowledging the Hobbesian influence on his own views, he writes, "The moral virtues are praised because of the calamities everyone avoids if people act morally."[25] The positive themes in Gert's view come grudgingly. He says, "[Morality] prohibits the kind of conduct that harms others and encourages the kind of conduct that helps them."[26] But the encouraging, positive aspects of morality turn out to be restricted to removing harms and barriers. They do not include promoting more positive ends. In defending this negative emphasis, moreover, he insists that his view is simply the elucidation of common morality. Gert's emphasis on the negative aims of morality sets him apart from most of the classic moral theorists we have considered. He shares with them, nevertheless, the attempt to claim that his view is an elucidation of and thus supported by common sense.

The main components of Gert's system are the moral rules and the moral ideals. The rules, he explains, "do not require promoting good for oneself or for others. They do not even require preventing harm to others. Rather they require avoiding causing evils or harms. It is not an accident that all moral rules can be stated as prohibitions."[27] The moral ideals "embody the nature of morality more than moral rules, for following moral ideals is acting so as to achieve the point of morality, the lessening of evil or harm being suffered."[28] The ideals can be derived from the rules, more or less, by replacing the "don't"s or prohibitions of the rules with positive injunctions to prevent, relieve, or help. But the content of the ideals remains negative. They concern "lessening the amount of harm or evil suffered."[29] Gert's view is thus negative in two ways. First, rules are at the heart of his system, and they express negative duties in the sense that they are stated as prohibitions. They tell us what we cannot do, not what we must do. Secondly, the content of the rules, which carries over to the ideals, consists of negative values. They are evils and harms that we aim to prohibit or reduce, not goods we might reasonably want to produce or increase.

Why does Gert insist that morality is primarily negative? The answer, I believe, is that his view rests on the assumptions that morality is limited in scope to behavior that affects others, and that rules are at the core of common morality. The question about whether morality is restricted in scope to behavior that affects others is to some degree, of course, a terminological issue. I will argue presently that common sense does not fully support Gert in this claim, but this does not get to the heart of the issue about negativity. For even if he conceded that our common morality includes self-regarding actions, as Aristotle and Kant certainly thought it did, Gert could simply argue that his system applies only to the part of morality that concerns our behavior that affects other people. To see why Gert insists that this subject, whether it is a part or the whole of morality, should be oriented toward the negative, we have to look at the assumption that rules are at the core.

At one point Gert considers and then quickly dismisses the view that morality is about producing the best state of affairs. The only way the best state of affairs could be relevant to morality, he says, is if it were connected to what one ought to do. But he argues that sometimes we are in no position to bring about the best state of affairs, and at other times we might be in a position where we can realize the best state of affairs only by using morally unacceptable means.

Now these are curious reasons for dismissing the relevance to morality of "the best state of affairs," for two reasons.[30] First, someone who thought this concept provided the appropriate target for our actions, in the sense explained by Aristotle, could reply that the target's remaining out of reach does not diminish its importance as a guide. Nor would a theorist who thinks the idea of the best state of affairs is crucial to determining the goal of morally right action need to deny that we are constrained in the acceptable means we can use to work toward the ideal. Secondly, the very same objections could be brought against any list of evils we are meant to minimize. Sometimes we are in no position to reduce evil, and sometimes we might be able to reduce evil only by using morally unacceptable means, as in the case of "dirty hands" problems. Gert's objection, impartially applied, would seem to count against his own interpretation of the moral ideals. What moves Gert to press this argument against the relevance to morality of "the best state of affairs," I suspect, is his conception of the place and structure of moral rules in a moral system.

Common morality, as Gert sees it, is essentially a rule-based system. In his analysis of the formal conditions of moral rules, Gert argues that they must be public, universal, impartial, and what I shall call humanly feasible. It is also part of his analysis of a moral rule that violations of rules deserve punishment. These formal conditions of rules lead to negativity in the first sense. Being universal, the moral rules apply to all persons. Because their violations deserve punishment, the rules are similar to perfect duties in the sense explained by Kant and his predecessors. That is to say, rules imply duties owed to others, the performance of which others can claim as their right. Moral rules imply duties that are owed to all other people, each of whom is thus entitled to make rational claims against us. Only negative duties can be perfect duties in this sense, however, if they are universally applied and obedience to them is humanly feasible. Positive general duties would have to be imperfect duties, or else either their demands would be impossible to fulfill or nobody would be able to claim their performance as a right. There cannot be a rule commanding a duty of charity, therefore, because those deserving charity are too numerous, and no individual could feasibly satisfy the claims they would all be entitled to make against us. Negative duties, like the duty not to harm others, can be expressed by the moral rules, because any person can obey such rules simply by refraining from doing certain things. Every person can demand from all others that they refrain from harming them in certain ways. Only prohibitions can be thus universally, impartially, and feasibly obeyed as part of a public system of rules.

Gert rejects the suggestion that "the best state of affairs" is relevant to morality, therefore, for the same reason that he rejects the idea that we could have a duty to promote pleasure. He writes, "[T]he precept 'Promote pleasure' is not and should not be followed impartially with regard to everyone protected by the moral rules. It is not only possible but relatively easy to obey all moral rules all of the time, but it is humanly impossible to follow the precept 'promote pleasure' all of the time."[31] The content of the moral rules is thus determined to be negative by the structure of the rules. Gert gives further support to this negative content with his argument about rationality, which emphasizes the irrationality of certain harms and the rational permissibility of whatever is not irrational.

Now, the negative values that constitute the content of the moral rules give morality its point in Gert's view, and it is appropriate therefore to express these values as moral ideals. If harms are bad, then moral ideals call on us to reduce or eliminate them where we can. The ideals are conceptually dependent on the rules in this system, in the sense that the ideals follow from a determination of the content of the rules. Gert emphasizes, however, that the moral rules are not necessarily *morally* prior to the ideals. He argues that it may be permissible to break a moral rule in order significantly to promote a moral ideal. The procedure for justifying exceptions to the moral rules determines when such violations are permissible.

Gert's Appeal to Common Morality

We must now ask why moral rules have this privileged position in Gert's system. The only reason I can find is that Gert sees his project as giving an account of "common or universal" morality, and he claims that this morality has rules at its core. He regards one of the tasks of moral theory to be to justify common morality, which he attempts to do by showing that all rational people would favor adopting the system he describes. But this argument does not prove that rules are essentially at the core of morality. Gert assumes that rules have this position. This assumption is part of his account of common morality. From this assumption, as I have argued, both senses of negativity follow.

If we interpret common morality to be timeless, as Gert does, then I don't think he is justified in claiming that morality is about avoiding and reducing harms, not about promoting good and achieving ideals. I have attempted to show that some moral theorists give accounts of morality that are not restricted to prohibiting and reducing harms, and they also claim to start from and remain consistent with common morality.

Perhaps we should not look to the past to determine the core of common morality. Even if moral truth is timeless, as Gert believes it to be, it may be that our ancestors were confused and had false views when they theorized about the subject. Some contemporary philosophers, such as Derek Parfit, suggest that moral philosophy as a rational discipline, one that attempts to free itself from religious views and other prejudices, is relatively new. Parfit claims that we should not be surprised if we are only now beginning to make real progress in morality, nor that our moral beliefs will in the future change quite drastically as a result of appeal to rational philosophical arguments.[32] The ancients, both the many and the wise, might have been as confused about morality as they were about science.

I believe this move does not help us, however, for two reasons. One is that the moral views of a philosopher like Aristotle seem to most readers today to contain more and deeper truths than his scientific writing, which would suggest that the ancients had a better grasp of human affairs than of science. The second reason is due to the lack of progress in moral philosophy as compared to science. If our ancestors did *not* have a good grasp of morality, then the relative lack of progress in moral philosophy so far should lead us to be skeptical that our own common morality is much closer to the truth.

Gert's claim that morality is about avoiding harms and not about promoting positive goods is justified only to the extent that he is justified in claiming that rules are basic to morality, but I don't see any way of justifying that claim without begging the question. The only reason Gert gives for not allowing morality to include promoting goods such as pleasure or ideals of life, is that these ideals cannot fit the requirement that they be subjects of moral rules. But we need some independent reason for believing that rules are basic to the structure of common morality, as Gert takes them to be.

One useful way to think about common morality, which can temper some of the extreme claims of philosophers as well as the sophistical claims of insincere students, is to ask what a reasonable person teaches her children as she tries to raise them to be morally responsible people. My guess is that throughout history and across cultures, people teach their children by means of rules, and the rules often take the form of prohibitions. "Don't lie." "Don't steal." "Don't hit people." We explain to children why they should obey these rules in ways similar to those Gert uses to justify the moral rules. There can be no question that such rules and their justification are basic elements of morality.

We also tell people, including our older children, that they should try to make something of themselves, develop their talents, and be generous and kind. Gert would not deny the value of these injunctions, but he does not consider them to be part of morality. We also encourage our children to develop a taste for art, an appreciation of natural beauty, and a love of sports, but these injunctions appeal to values and ideals that surely do go beyond what most of us take to be morality. Nevertheless, many of us would regard attempts to develop certain virtues of character in our children as part of their moral education. Some people will agree with Gert that we should resist thinking that we have any moral duty to make something of ourselves or to develop our talents. They will agree with Gert that our duties to be generous or kind cannot be moral duties because they cannot be owed to others who can claim them as entitlements. But I don't see how this issue can be settled without begging the question. In any case, the idea that morality could be directed in part at one's own perfection is certainly not an alien notion in the ethical writings of Aristotle, Kant, or many other philosophers.

Moreover, I think we have some strong intuitions that lead us to a more inclusive conception of the scope of common morality. Consider the most drastic way of failing to make something of oneself, which is for a young and talented person to commit suicide. Most moral theories condemn suicide in these circumstances. Some of them try to express this condemnation as a violation of a duty owed to another, for example, a duty owed to God or the state. But common morality has other resources available to it. Some things may be moral wrongs without being violations of duty. Some actions that do not violate rules or harm others may nevertheless be shameful, and shame has certainly been a part of most moral cultures. Shameful acts, failures to develop one's talents, and suicide may all be instances of failing to respect the best aspects of human nature. These aspects of humanity account in part for our understanding of human dignity and thus help to explain why each human being deserves to be included among the beings that deserve respect and can claim rights not to be harmed in certain ways. It does not stretch our common understanding too much to see these aspects of our natures as comprising the basis for other kinds of judgments about wrongful acts and what we owe each other.

Not all of these perfections can be regarded as individual in nature. Generosity and kindness are essentially social, I would argue, even though they do not give rise to perfect duties. If we focus on the positive reasons for cooperating within civil society and include the gains of commodious living of which Hobbes wrote, then we can easily appreciate the important role of virtues like generosity and kindness and the need for their widespread development. In Kant's system, the failure to will these virtues as universal law would count as a failure of rationality, and on most views, I believe, these virtues would be seen to be connected to the goals of morality. If we think about a young person in despair, who fights his desire to commit suicide in order to develop his socially valuable talents, I think we would all agree that he shows courage and deserves praise. Common morality would consider this kind of courage to be a moral virtue, and I don't see any good argument in Gert for denying that it is.

I have argued so far only that Gert's negativity is difficult to defend if it depends on arguing for a privileged position of rules in our common understanding of morality. Rules would have to be shown to comprise not just an important part of morality but the whole core of the subject. I don't see how to make this argument without begging the question against widely believed common assumptions.

A Direct Appeal to Moral Ideals: The Asymmetry Between Good and Evil

I want to consider now a different way of trying to defend Gert's emphasis on the negative, which moves away from his system and its commitment to rules, and argues instead directly for the priority of negative moral values. How important is it to the point or goal of morality to reduce negative values like pain and suffering? In this and the next section, I will consider two arguments for thinking that negative values capture most of what matters in morality. The first argument appeals to some assumptions that seem initially plausible, I believe, and are often accepted, but in the end must be rejected for empirical reasons. The second argument rests on empirical claims that I believe are correct but will concede are difficult to defend. In the final section, I will elaborate briefly on the Hobbesian reason for seeing morality as aimed at positive goods as well as avoiding negative harms, even when we restrict morality to social goals and our conduct toward others.

In many contexts there seems to be an asymmetry between good and evil. Gert notices one in his discussion of rationality. It seems easier to list some specific evils that it is irrational to want than it is to list goods that it is irrational not to want. Similarly, we feel confident in saying that pain is a bad thing, and if we find someone who appears to desire pain, we need him to provide us with a good reason for this desire in order to withhold a judgment of irrationality. The reason would take the form of a benefit to be gained that outweighs the pain. The situation seems different with desires for some good or some pleasure. It is hard, in fact, to think of any pleasure that would lead us to judge someone irrational simply because he lacked a desire for it. It is only when lacking a desire for some good leads to a harm that we consider the lack of desire to be irrational, as when a lack of desire for food leads to physical harm.

Perhaps this asymmetry is due in part to something we tend to believe, which philosophers like Aristotle and Kant did not. There are plural conceptions of the human good or ideals of human life that are incommensurable and incompatible with each other. If this is true, then it may be the case that there is no good that it would be irrational not to desire, because there are always other reasonable ideals to pursue that are incompatible with it. Some evils or pains, however, may prohibit a person from realizing any of the most important goods and would thus be irrational for anyone to desire.

This asymmetry also takes a different form, however, which becomes clear when we focus on simple pains and pleasures. Pain seems to be an unconditionally bad thing in a way that pleasure does not seem to be unconditionally good. If we see someone experiencing pain, and we are in a position to relieve that pain without great sacrifice, we seem to have a reason to act to relieve the pain. Of course we risk failing to understand that the pain is possibly being endured for some greater purpose. Our reason for acting to relieve pain in such a situation is only a prima facie reason, but it is a reason nevertheless. If we see someone failing to get some benefit or pleasure, however, and we are in a position to get that benefit or pleasure for her without great sacrifice, we do not seem to have the same kind of reason to get them that benefit. Perhaps if we can see that she wants the benefit and is trying to get it, then we have a reason to help her do so. But if we do not see that she wants the benefit, then our helping her to get it seems simply to be interfering in her life in an unacceptable way. We might have moral admiration for someone who devoted considerable time and energy looking around for occasions to relieve suffering and acting to relieve it wherever he could. But if someone spent time and energy instead looking for occasions to bring pleasure to people—not helping people get what they want, but helping them get more pleasure, whether or not they had a desire for such pleasure—we would not admire such a person at all. We would regard him as a busybody whose interest in the welfare of others was inappropriate.

Bad things also seem scalar in a way that good things are not. Pain, harms, and other evils seem worse if there is more of them, while pleasures or good things are not necessarily made better by increasing their quantity. A pain that lasts longer *seems* worse than a shorter one of equal intensity, but pleasure is not necessarily better if it lasts longer. As John Broome points out in an insightful discussion of these issues, a short, great symphony would not be improved at all by the addition of another movement that was pretty good but not great.[33] The world is a morally better place, *ceteris paribus*, if there is less suffering in it, but it is not necessarily a better place for containing an increase in pleasure or other good things. There is no reason to think, for example, that the world would be better if there were more people in it than are alive today, even if each additional person were living a happy life. The failure to notice this fundamental asymmetry between happiness and suffering seems to me to be a major defect in some classical utilitarian theories.

This asymmetry suggests that happiness or pleasure is good only on condition that people desire it, and that without this desire, additions of pleasure or happiness have no positive moral value at all. Similarly, we might say that pleasure itself has no intrinsic value, but that pleasure is good for the person who has it, and only on condition that the person desires it. Pain and suffering seem different. Pain seems to be a bad thing wherever it occurs. The badness of pain seems unconditional and does not depend on a personal desire not to experience it. This is why the existence of pain seems to support a reason to relieve it, but the possibility of pleasure does not seem to support a reason to produce it, especially in someone else. This asymmetry, it seems, gives us a good reason to focus especially on the negative and to regard relief of pain to be the point of morality. In focusing on pain and suffering, we are at least focusing on things that have intrinsic or unconditional moral value.

The problem with this argument is that it seems to be undermined by empirical research. In the first place, Daniel Kahneman and his colleagues have discovered that preferences for the relief of pain do not fit the model that more pain is worse than less.[34] They have shown this in experiments in which subjects undergo two painful episodes of different durations. For example, in one episode subjects hold their hand for a minute in water cold enough to be painful. In the second episode, subjects hold their hand for a minute in water exactly the same temperature, followed by a half minute during which the temperature of the water, still cold, is raised to a point where it is noticeably less painful. (While the episodes are occurring, the subjects are indicating how painful they find the experience.) After the two episodes, the subjects are asked which one was worse, or which episode they would prefer to repeat if they had to repeat one of them. Most subjects prefer the longer to the shorter episode. (The order in which the episodes are experienced does not affect this result.)

If pain were objectively bad and scalar in type, so that more of it was worse than less (either in intensity or in duration), then the longer of the two episodes would be worse than the shorter, because it contains all of the intensity of the pain of the shorter episode and more of its duration. The "experienced" utility of the episodes confirms that the longer one contains more pain than the shorter one. But the hypothesis that these experiments seem to confirm is that people cognitively process painful experiences in a different way. It appears that we do not remember or form preferences for painful episodes on the basis of some function of their intensity and duration. Rather, we process these episodes cognitively as a function only of the experience at its peak and at the end. We tend, in other words, to ignore the duration of the painful episode. Since the episodes have identical peaks but the longer one is less painful at the end, that is the one people judge to be less bad and would prefer to repeat if they had to repeat one of them. (Pleasant experiences are judged in the same way, as a function of the pleasure at the peak and at the end, with neglect of their duration.) Thus, people tend to prefer more painful episodes to less painful ones, when the peaks are identical but the longer one ends less badly.

I take these results have troubling implications for morality. Consider, for example, a physician who must inflict pain on her patient in the course of a treatment. As the treatment is ending, let us suppose that the physician can end the pain immediately or draw it out while lessening it gradually. If we believe that pain is objectively bad, then it would seem that we should decide what to do on the basis of experienced utility and end the painful episode as soon as possible. If, on the other hand, we believe that decision or preference utility is morally more important, then the physician should extend the pain while gradually lessening it.

Some people will insist that it would be wrong to extend pain beyond what is necessary. They regard pain as objectively bad, and they would probably agree that happiness and suffering are asymmetrical in the way I described above. But I am inclined to think that such a decision shows an unacceptable degree of paternalism, and that we should administer more pain when this is clearly what the patient would prefer. In endorsing this view, I am suggesting that there might not after all be a defensible asymmetry between happiness and suffering and that pain is bad only on condition that people prefer to avoid it, just as the goodness of pleasure is similarly conditional. If I am right, then this intuitively plausible appeal to an asymmetry between pain and pleasure as a reason for focusing on harm rather than benefits in morality cannot be justified.

An Epicurean Theme

A different reason for thinking that morality should focus on negative values comes from Epicurus. A theme of stoicism worth considering is that once our basic needs are met, which provide us the means to relieve the pain and suffering that it is within our control to relieve, we have achieved about as good a life as we can expect to have. This point has two aspects. The first is to appreciate how much we gain in relieving pain and suffering, and the second is to see how little is left to gain once pain and suffering are relieved.

When we realize how people tend to value their own lives, often clinging to life in the face of great adversity, it should be clear to us that for most people life itself is a very good thing. Human lives include many kinds of joy and suffering. It is of course possible that suffering and the prospect of future suffering can become so great that a person could rationally judge that it is no longer worth continuing to remain alive. Except where the prospect of continued life is very short, however, it is exceptionally rare for people to reach this state. I doubt that this is because many people who have clear reasons to believe that their prospects are bleak mistakenly expect that the future will bring them great happiness. Rather, it is a simple fact that life itself seems to most people to be a very good thing. If we subtract all the pleasure and pain that a human life contains, what remains is not a neutral shell but something of great value. For most people, it is good simply to be alive. This thought is reflected in the Epicurean view that happiness consists primarily in freedom from pain.

This view gains further support from a closer look at the nature of pain and suffering that it is the goal of morality to relieve. Specifically, we have a particularly narrow conception of suffering if we think of it exclusively as a negative physical sensation. One of the reasons it is good simply to be alive is that conscious life typically contains an unending parade of new and interesting experiences, which can capture and fascinate us even without bringing pleasure. Without the normal flow of experiences, life becomes boring, and real boredom (as opposed to moments of nonstimulation that lead teenagers to complain that they are bored) is a terrible thing. Sensory deprivation is a form of torture. Even if boredom is not a painful sensation, it is a form of suffering, so that a morality that focuses on the negative must also focus on relieving tedium and boredom.[35]

Gert writes, "Education and medicine are social goods: the former increases knowledge, which is an ability; the latter decreases disabilities as well as preventing and relieving pain." On Gert's view, therefore, it would seem that medicine but not education should be the concern of morality. I would argue, however, that basic education should be seen, like medicine, to decrease disabilities. In most modern cultures, for example, illiteracy is a serious disability. Not only does illiteracy severely limit one's opportunities for employment, enjoyment, and simply getting around in one's society, it is also typically a source of embarrassment and shame which illiterate people take pains to conceal.[36] Illiteracy is thus a form of suffering. Once we realize that boredom and illiteracy are forms of suffering and not simply a lack of positive goods, we can better appreciate how comprehensive a morality that focuses exclusively on the negative can be.

The second aspect to this Epicurean theme is that once suffering is eliminated from a person's life and his basic needs are met, his life is about as good as it can be. The further result that comes from satisfying mere desires, Epicurus thought, is often to produce more pain than pleasure.

This is a controversial empirical claim, but I think common sense and some evidence give it some support. Satisfaction of desires tends to breed further desires as much as it produces happiness. People whose basic needs are met often focus more on status or positional goods, the desire for which can be satisfied only when they have more or better goods than others. It follows logically that the greater the number of people who form such desires, the greater the number of people who will fail to be satisfied.[37] Most attempts to measure happiness across economic classes show that once poverty is eliminated, greater wealth brings little or no increase in happiness. Measures of happiness across time produce similar results. Although economic standards of living show great gains in industrial societies over the past five decades, surveys aimed at measuring happiness show no gain or a modest decrease in happiness.[38]

There is today also a revival of interest among some economists in the nature and causes of our "joyless" economy.[39] One of the causes that these studies cite is the tendency I just mentioned increasingly to desire positional goods after basic needs are met. Another cause, however, is the tendency to seek increasing comfort, which ironically hinders the ability to experience joy or pleasure. This is because pleasure appears to require change in one's psychic state of a sort that increasing comfort makes more difficult to achieve. This research and much common sense support the conclusion that if morality focuses exclusively on the negative values of relieving harm and suffering, not only will it have accomplished its most important goal, it will have done about all it can do to produce happiness.

A Hobbesian Reservation

I conclude that the case for moral philosophy accentuating the negative is a strong one, but in closing I will mention my primary reservation in embracing this conclusion, which comes not from Aristotle or Kant but from Hobbes. The Epicurean argument focused on individual goods, where I believe the case for accentuating the negative is strongest, but Gert insists that morality is limited to behavior that affects others. Even if we insist that Gert focuses on only part of morality, however, Hobbes gives us a reason not to think that the subject is essentially negative. As I have pointed out, the means for commodious living that Hobbes mentions, including arts, letters, knowledge of the face of the earth, and an account of time, are primarily social goods. For Hobbes it was the lack of these things, as well as danger and the fear of death, which make life brutish in the state of nature. We could add to this list the requirements of distributive justice for achieving social equality (which both Hobbes and Gert notably seem to ignore as part of morality), the preservation of natural beauty, and the public rituals, ceremonies, and monuments that foster social ties and a sense of community. These are all essentially social goods, which means that they are goods that can only be achieved by social cooperation. They would also seem to be an indispensable element in any adequate conception of a good life, to the extent that we see our pursuit of good lives to be the activities of beings that are also essentially social in nature. The good life, including its irreducibly social features, must surely be included within the scope of morality, even if we limit morality to behavior that affects others. It has to be part of the subject. If morality is a system of social cooperation, then the securing of these goods must be part of its point.

When harm and suffering are eliminated, we have most of what we could reasonably gain as individuals. But the good life demands some essentially social goods as well, and so I must conclude that although social morality may instruct us to "accentuate the negative," the subject also necessarily includes promoting positive values. Moral theory, as well as common sense, must deal with both evils and goods. Morality looks in both directions. Just don't mess with Mr. In-Between!

Notes

* This paper was originally written for a conference honoring the work of Bernard Gert, Dartmouth College, May 13-16, 1999. I have benefited from the discussion of the paper at the conference, and I am especially grateful for comments and suggestions from Robert Audi, Bernard Gert, Frances Kamm, Walter Sinnott-Armstrong, and Susan Wolf.

1. *NE* 1094a2. [All references to Aristotle are to the *Nicomachean Ethics*. Page numbers refer to the standard Bekker edition of the Greek text. The translation is by Terence Irwin, *Nicomachean Ethics* (Indianapolis: Hackett, 1985)].
2. *NE* 1094a24.
3. *NE* 1095a19.
4. *NE* 1095a24.
5. John Stuart Mill, *Utilitarianism* (Indianapolis: Hackett, 1979), 1.
6. *Utilitarianism*, 7.
7. *Utilitarianism*, 7.
8. *Utilitarianism*, 47.
9. *Utilitarianism*, 23.
10. *Utilitarianism*, 34.
11. *Grounding*, 7 (393). [All references to Kant are to: Immanuel Kant, *Grounding for the Metaphysics of Morals*, trans. J Ellington (Indianapolis: Hackett, 1981). Page references are to the Ellington translation. The numbers in parentheses refer to the standard Prussian Academy Edition of Kant's Works.]
12. *Grounding*, .9 (397).
13. *Grounding*, 22-23 (411).
14. *Grounding*, 31-32 (423-4).
15. "Now humanity might indeed subsist if nobody contributed anything to the happiness of others. . . . But this, after all, would harmonize only negatively and not positively with humanity as an end in itself, if everyone does not also strive, as much as he can, to further the ends of others." *Grounding*, 37 (430).

16. *Grounding,* 39-40 (433).

17. *Grounding,* 41-42 (436).

18. *Grounding,* 43 (438).

19. For example, Gert has no references to Epicurus in his book and only one to stoicism, which he claims to lack sufficient overlap with common morality to be a moral theory.

20. See Epicurus, *Letter to Menoeceus:* Diotenes Laertius 10.121-135. In *The Epicurus Reader: Selected Writings and Testimonia,* trans. B. Inwood and L. P. Gerson (Indianapolis: Hackett, 1994), 28-31.

21. Thomas Hobbes, *Leviathan* part I, chap. 13, sec. 9.

22. Hobbes, *Leviathan* part I, chap. 13, sec. 9.

23. Hobbes, *Leviathan.*

24. Bernard Gert, *Morality: Its Nature and Justification* (New York: Oxford University Press, 1998), 13.

25. Gert, *Morality,* 9.

26. Gert, *Morality,* 9.

27. Gert, *Morality,* 116.

28. Gert, *Morality,* 247.

29. Gert, *Morality,* 247.

30. There may be better reasons for rejecting the idea that "the best state of affairs" has a central place in morality, for example, that it has no clear meaning. See Philippa Foot, "Virtues and Vices," in *Virtues and Vices and Other Essays in Moral Philosophy* (Berkeley: University of California Press, 1978).

31. Gert, *Morality,* 124.

32. Derek Parfit, *Reasons and Persons* (Oxford, Eng.: Clarendon Press, 1988), 452-54.

33. John Broome, "More Pain or Less?" *Analysis* 56 (1996): 116-18.

34. D. Kahneman, B. Fredrickson, C. Schreiber, and D. Redelmeier, "When More Pain is Preferred to Less: Adding a Better End," *Psychological Science* 4, no. 6 (1993): 401-5.

35. For this point, I am indebted to conversations with Bernard Gert.

36. This theme is nicely illustrated in Bernhard Schlink's novel, *The Reader* (New York: Vintage Books, 1998).

37. See Robert Frank, *Luxury Fever: Why Money Fails to Satisfy in an Era of Excess* (New York: Free Press, 1999).

38. See Robert E. Lane, *The Loss of Happiness in Market Economies* (New Haven, Conn.: Yale University Press, 2000).

39. See Tibor Scitovsky, *The Joyless Economy: The Psychology of Human Satisfaction,* rev. ed. (New York: Oxford University Press, 1992).

12

A Note on Harms and Evils in Gert's Moral Theory

F. M. Kamm

Bernard Gert claims that "the goal of morality is the lessening of evil."[1] He thinks well of Hobbes's view that "The utility of moral and civil philosophy is to be estimated, not so much by the commodities we have by knowing these sciences, as by the calamities we receive by not knowing them."[2] In addition, he thinks this view represents common morality, as he aims to provide a justification of that common morality.[3]

In this note, I shall consider whether morality on Gert's understanding really is concerned with evils in a Hobbesian manner. First, I shall briefly describe Gert's views on evils and goods and conduct related to them. Then I shall provide my own characterization of the various ways in which the evil/good and harming/not aiding distinctions may interact in this view. Having done this, I shall consider how concerned with lessening evils Gert is.

Gert's Views

According to Gert, the point of morality is to relieve evils, not to promote goods. Evils are things it is irrational for an agent to seek or not avoid. This includes loss of goods. Gert also thinks it is an evil to be in a deprived state, that is, to have insufficient goods relative to a social standard of sufficiency. Among the primary rules of morality are the first five telling us *not to cause evil*; Do not cause death, pain, loss of ability, loss of freedom to act or be acted upon, or loss of pleasure (or opportunities for pleasure). To cause loss of goods such as freedom or pleasure (or the opportunity for the latter) is to cause evil. A moral ideal—not a moral rule—tells us to prevent evils. Sometimes we can break rules not to cause evil in order to prevent evils. It is only a utilitarian ideal, not a moral ideal, that tells us to promote goods.

The Negative and the Positive

I believe there are two senses of the contrast between negative and the positive in Gert's system. The first is that between evils and good. The second is that between harming and aiding. It will help us in thinking about the relation between Gert and Hobbes to consider these factors in relation to each other. The following chart presents some relationships among these four factors. (It does not necessarily represent in all cases Gert's thinking about these factors.)

	Evils (N)	Goods (P)
Harm (N)	(1) NN	(2) NP (3) NP
Aid-ing (P)	(4) PN (5) P(NN)	(6) PP (7) PP (8) P(NP) (9) P(NP)

Evils (N) is intended to represent *only* the evils which are *not* the loss of goods; for example, pain or disability with which one began life. Arguably, death is an evil only because and when it involves the loss of goods of life or because life itself is a good. I shall refer to evils that involve loss of goods as N*. Loss of ability, freedom, and pleasure are also evils which involve loss of goods.

(1) represents causing evil.

(2) represents interfering with goods someone has (and would have continued to have). Hence, it involves causing N*, the loss of goods.

(3) represents interfering with someone getting new goods. When Gert speaks of causing loss of opportunities for pleasure, I think he has this in mind. Hence, it involves causing N*.

(4) represents preventing (or relieving) evil that is not caused by human interference.

(5) represents preventing (or relieving) evil that is caused by human interference. The distinction attended to between (4) and (5) is not, I believe, given importance in Gert's system. Some, however, may think it important in deciding whether to aid or not, that they would be preventing an evil caused by human interference.

(6) represents preventing (or relieving) the loss due to natural causes of a good someone has (or had). As such, it prevents an evil N*.

(7) represents providing someone with a new good. It may involve preventing an evil N* if the person is deprived. Otherwise, it does not prevent an evil, but just provides a good.

(8) represents preventing (or relieving) the loss, by way of a person's interference of a good someone has (or had). Hence, it prevents an evil N*.

(9) represents preventing (or relieving) the loss by way of a person's interference of an opportunity for a good. Hence, it prevents an evil N*.

Gert claims that there can be a fine line between preventing the loss of a good like pleasure when someone is not deprived (part of the moral ideal of preventing evil) and simply providing the pleasure (a utilitarian ideal). Strictly, however, preventing losses takes precedence over providing good, even when the loss would leave someone no worse off than someone else will be if he does not receive a good, even when the loss would leave someone *better off* than someone else will be if not given a good, even when the loss would reduce someone's conditions slightly and our aid could produce a great benefit to someone else.

Gert, Hobbes, and Common Morality

I shall now raise three points in support of the claim that Gert and common morality are more concerned with the harm/aid distinction than with the evil/good distinction as Hobbes might be taken to have understood it.

(A) In Gert's system, suffering a loss (through natural or human intervention) is an evil. Often even a large loss (hence not trivial) will leave one still quite well off. Yet Gert thinks there is a moral rule not to cause such losses. Could these be the sort of evils that Hobbes thought we should flee the state of nature to avoid? As they leave us still well off, it seems unlikely. If all people ever did to each other was cause the loss of pleasure or cause occasional broken legs, it seems unlikely that life would be short, nasty, and brutish without morality. I am not denying that there are many losses that do result in very bad conditions, and so we might flee a state of nature to avoid them. I am only pointing out that Gert's system does not make a point of *only* ruling out such flee-state-of-nature losses.

Gert seems to be more concerned with the not harming/aiding distinction understood as the distinction between (a) not causing someone a set back of his condition (regardless of how badly off this leaves him) and (b) helping improve his condition. (This is different from the no loss/gain distinction which Gert also accepts, but to which he gives less weight. The latter distinction alone could give as much importance to helping prevent a loss as to not causing it.[4] Gert gives less weight to helping prevent a loss than to not causing it, though he thinks preventing a loss has more weight than providing a gain, even when persons would wind up in the same position through loss and no gain.) Concern for the not harming/aiding distinction (and even the no loss/gain distinction) contrasts with concern for the distinction between people not being in bad conditions and their being in good conditions. It is the latter distinction which is more likely suggested by the ordinary contrast between evils and goods. Insofar as Gert is concerned with the not harming/aiding distinction, even when losses do not lower someone to bad conditions, I believe he is really concerned with *a morality that gives great emphasis to the separateness of persons*. Such a morality says that we have a strong duty to avoid interfering with what others have independently of us and a weaker duty to aid because to have a duty to aid requires interference with what we have independently of someone else.[5] (This coheres with Gert's frequent assertions that we could abide by the first five moral rules with respect to everyone without doing anything, but would have to do something [and hence probably not do something for everyone] if we had to aid.)

(B) If Gert really believed that common morality were concerned with reducing evils, he should, for example, think it permits killing one person in order to save two from death (or from being killed) or maiming one to save another from death. This would also apply to evils of loss that would leave us not very badly off. Yet he does not endorse minimizing evils in general. Rather he thinks that the amount of evil we would prevent has to be very much larger than the amount of harm we would do in order for the rule against causing evil to be overridden by the moral ideal to prevent evil.[6] In other words, there are probably rules which would reduce evils more than Gert's rules do, yet they are not the rules of common morality.

(C) If the loss to you of obeying the moral rule to not harm someone is even greater than the loss you would cause her, common morality still insists that you may be required to suffer the loss. For example, if a villain (or natural disaster) threatens to break your leg and your arm unless you break someone else's arm, it does not seem permissible to break the arm. If common morality were concerned with reducing evils (understood either as bad conditions or losses), such action should be permissible.

I conclude that Gert and the common morality he seeks to describe and justify are more concerned with respect for the separateness of persons than with the avoidance of evils.[7]

Notes

1. Bernard Gert, *Morality: Its Nature and Justification* (New York: Oxford University Press, 1998), 253. All references are to this volume, hereafter referred to as *Morality*.

2. Noted on page 2 of Gert, *Morality*.

3. Gert, *Morality*, 13.

4. For more on the difference between the no loss/gain and not harming/aiding distinction, see my "Moral Intuitions, Cognitive Psychology, and the Harming/Not Aiding Distinction," *Ethics* 108, no. 3 (April 1998): 463-88.

5. This is only a shorthand description of an account of the not harming/aiding distinction I have given in *Morality, Mortality Vol. II* (New York: Oxford University Press, 1996).

6. Gert, *Morality*, 125.

7. This note began life as a comment on an paper by Douglas MacLean on Gert's emphasis on the negative. I am grateful for the stimulus to thought provided by MacLean's paper.

13

Is the Lessening of Evil the Only Goal of Morality? A Role for *Eudaimonia* in Gert's Moral System

E. J. Bond

For Gert the moral rules, which lie at the base of his system and are architectonic of the whole, consist entirely of prohibitions (or can be so construed): prohibition of killing, causing pain, disabling, depriving of freedom, depriving of pleasure, deceiving, breaking promises, cheating, breaking the law, neglecting one's duty, all of which are said to cause, or to increase the probability of, evils.[1] Doing any of these things *without justification* is morally wrong, i.e. one is morally obliged *not* to do any of these things unless there is a publicly acceptable justification. However breaking a promise is a failure to keep it and neglecting one's duty is a failure to do it.[2] Only in these two cases is it natural to speak of a positive obligation. Even obedience to the law consists for the most part in not doing certain things, and in all the other cases the obligation is straightforwardly negative. But all can be construed as prohibitions (limits to the permissible), and all have to do with the not causing (avoidance of causing) harm or evil.[3]

Gert has correctly seen that *deontic* morality (the ethics of moral requirement) has to do with the avoidance of wrongdoing (causing or contributing to evil) and not with the disinterested promotion of good. In an important respect it is like the law. Just as the law prohibits some actions and requires others, otherwise leaving us free to do as we please, deontic morality forbids some acts and requires others (keeping our promises, doing our duty), leaving all other acts *morally permissible*, i.e. things we may either do or not do *without moral transgression either way*. The idea that we are under a *perpetual obligation to promote good disinterestedly*, as most forms of consequentialism imply, is merely absurd.

Thus Gert is absolutely right in seeing moral *obligation* or requirement (what I have called *deontic* morality) as entirely concerned with the not causing of evils or harms. And he is also right in saying that the kinds of acts that are morally wrong (unless there is a publicly acceptable justification) are those from which, when performed by others, we ourselves could suffer evils or harms, or things we could not rationally wish upon ourselves or those we care about. And he is also right in saying that we advance from this egocentric position to the moral position when we consider not just what no rational person would have publicly allowed (because she herself or those she cares about might suffer), but what no *impartial* rational person would have publicly allowed (which requires a person to count her/himself in). He is right too in describing *deontic* morality (i.e., moral *requirement*) as belonging to a public system. But Gert takes the big leap from these truths to supposing that *anything at all* that can justifiably be called "moral" must be tied to the not causing, or preventing, or alleviating of evil. This is plain from the section in chapter 1 headed "The definition of morality" which concludes with the following (italicized) statement (13): "*Morality is an informal public system applying to all rational persons, governing behavior that affects others, and includes what are commonly known as the moral rules, ideals, and virtues* ***and has the lessening of evil or harm as its goal*** [my additional emphasis]." It is this final clause that I wish to challenge in this paper.

Gert is consistent in this broad claim almost throughout the book.[4] Thus when he comes to deal with ideals (chapter 10), a moral ideal is said to consist in going beyond moral requirement in pursuit of the goal of morality—the lessening of evil—by acting so as to prevent, remove, or alleviate evils. And when he discusses virtues and vices (chapter 11), his claim is that a moral virtue can only be so called if it is tied to one or more of the moral rules or ideals. The others (e.g., courage, temperance, prudence) are to be understood as primarily tied to one's own well-being and only secondarily to what affects others (via the role they may have to play in our following a moral rule or pursuing a moral ideal). These he calls "personal" virtues.

The moral ideals are all related to the moral rules—*preventing* the evils that the moral rules require us *not to cause* (250). Together these constitute the "moral system." The moral virtues and vices "involve free, intentional, voluntary actions related to the moral rules and ideals" (283). Thus, in the end, the *whole* of morality is related to the moral rules, which in turn are related to the five evils (not causing them directly or increasing their likelihood). Evil or harm is architectonically built into Gert's moral system at its very foundation, and benefit, as distinct from harm (except in the political arena) is thereby excluded. It is not surprising, then, that he sees morality as entirely concerned with the lessening of evils or harms. Now Gert may, indeed, erect this structure, and no one can object, but while he sees himself as doing no more than giving an account of the common understanding of morality, his account, in this particular regard, seems to be at variance with that understanding, as I shall attempt to show.

What I wish to claim is that an informal public system guiding behavior and applying to all rational persons, one that is justifiably called "morality," while it is first, in order of importance, concerned with the lessening of evils or harms, need not be seen as exclusively concerned with that limited goal. Indeed that goal may itself be seen as part of what I wish to claim is morality's ultimate purpose (and ground), namely, the social good, a necessary condition for the well-being of individual persons, and hence desirable for everyone. In connection with this I would like to make several points.

But first let me make it absolutely clear that I am not supposing that it is even a part of the business of morality to go about, like Santa Claus, disinterestedly promoting the good of others! With regard to this, let me note that there is something quite ridiculous about the current "random acts of kindness" movement where people go to shopping malls or wander the streets, handing out goodies (e.g., flowers, stuffed animals, candies) to people as they pass (or are passed). If these "favors" are random, they are certainly disinterested, but how might they be considered kind? Is this done from kindness of heart or simply to meet some abstract idea of moral goodness? How many people would actually like a flower pressed upon them on the main street or in the mall? And if they didn't happen to want the flower, would they be happy to find such wonderful goodness in the world and be touched by such kindness of heart? Not if they knew it was not spontaneous but part of a "movement"!

1. Gert confines *moral* ideals to those that involve the lessening of evils or harms—especially the relief of suffering—beyond the moral obligation or requirement of not causing them. Following these ideals, although not morally required, is nevertheless to be morally encouraged. The attitude taken to the moral ideals by an impartial rational person is "Everyone is encouraged to follow the ideal 'Prevent . . .,' except when a fully informed impartial rational person would not publicly allow following it" (249). Gert denies that any ideal that has to do with promoting benefits as distinct from reducing harms—what he calls utilitarian ideals—is a moral ideal. Now Gert has architectonic reasons—reasons tied to his theory of morality as a public system applying to all rational persons and having the lessening of evil as its goal—for not wanting to admit any ideals as *moral* ideals that do not fit this theory, and he could simply have stipulated, "I will call an ideal a *moral* ideal if and only if it aims at the lessening of harm or evil." But he doesn't do this. He admits that the attitude taken toward *utilitarian* ideals (promoting benefits) by an impartial rational person is identical to the attitude taken by such a person to moral ideals. But nevertheless he says, moral ideals must be carefully distinguished from all other ideals because "moral ideals can justify violations of the moral rules in situations where no other ideals can" (249), violations normally being justifiable only on the grounds that less evil will result from violating the rule in circumstances of the kind in question than from obeying it.[5] But given that the attitude of all impartial rational persons is the same in both cases, would this not tend to favor placing them together in the same category rather than making them separate and distinct? And would it not be more natural to say that the ability to justify violations of the moral rules regardless of any special relationship between the violator and the person(s) toward whom the rule is violated (231), is true of one subset in this category and no other, emphasizing the importance of this, rather than treating this ability as a defining characteristic of a moral as distinct from a nonmoral ideal?[6] Wouldn't it have been better, in order to keep the theory intact, simply to stipulate that nothing would be allowed to count as a *moral* ideal unless it were aimed at the lessening of evils? But then, of course, this distinction could not be defended as part of our common understanding of morality which is, of course, an important part of Gert's aim.

2. Gert confesses to a difficulty in distinguishing between moral and utilitarian ideals in the case of the two evils loss of freedom and loss of pleasure, saying that increasing the freedom and increasing the pleasure of deprived persons (as distinct from those who are not deprived) is not precisely distinguishable from preventing[7] their loss of freedom or their loss of pleasure, and indeed that in so acting we are following moral and not utilitarian ideals (253).[8] But this leads to a more general difficulty, for cannot the prevention of evils or harms (as well as the not causing of them which is required by the moral rules) be seen as a contribution to the maintenance of such well-being as there is, and hence a benefit,

and cannot the reducing or alleviating or eliminating of harms be seen as contributing to well-being's increase? While it is obvious that not every case of advancing or promoting or maintaining the good can be seen as a case of preventing or alleviating evil, it seems that the reverse does not hold—the preservation or advancement of well-being can be seen as the goal across the board: moral and "utilitarian" ideals, and the moral rules themselves, are ultimately directed toward (and grounded in) a single end which is the well-being of individuals in a social context, or *eudaimonia, even if* the moral rules and those ideals related to them are aimed at the lessening of evils or harms, which can be seen as a means to that end.

3. Not all the virtues that Gert recognizes as moral virtues are, as he maintains, tied to the moral rules and ideals (as he sees them) and hence exclusively to the goal of the lessening of evil. This is most obvious in the case of kindness, an undoubted moral virtue in the common understanding. Gert says that "a particular moral virtue involves following some part of the moral system [i.e. rules and ideals] significantly more than most people do" (283). Kindness he defines as "a disposition to follow the direct moral ideals, to act so as to relieve the suffering of others" (285). This would make a kind person someone who acts so as to relieve the suffering of others significantly more than most people do. (Mother Teresa comes immediately to mind, and possibly Princess Di.) But this is not an accurate account of kindness at all. A kind person *will* act so as to relieve the suffering of others, especially those close to her, but kindness can also consist in brightening someone's life, even where there is no suffering or other evil to relieve. To let a door slam in someone's face is certainly cruel or thoughtless, but it is also kind to hold a door open for someone or to yield in traffic even when this does not prevent or alleviate any pain or suffering, but confers a positive benefit—maybe just a little good feeling. "Be kind to animals" does not mean only that we should act to relieve their suffering! And consider the "random acts of kindness" ridiculed above. Kindness involves being willing, indeed disposed, to do things for others, but while it is highly unlikely that having a stuffed animal or a flower shoved at you in a shopping center is going to be a boon to you, that is how it is understood by the advocates of "random acts of kindness", and there is no *conceptual* error here. Kindness can probably best be conceived as doing things for the good of others, including the relief of suffering or distress, beyond what one is morally obliged to do (or refrain from doing).[9] It may consist in doing someone an unsolicited favor or in paying him or her a compliment. While primarily concerned with the relief of suffering, kindness is in no way *exclusively* concerned with it or with any other way of lessening evil. Yet it *is* a moral virtue. And there are other virtues (all with corresponding vices) which can be called moral virtues without conceptual strain, such as friendliness (coldness), generosity (stinginess), conviviality (closeness), modesty (immodesty), which are virtues because they contribute to a good and desirable social environment.

4. There are virtues, such as honesty, which I am in the habit of calling *deontic* virtues precisely because they do relate to the moral rules. Thus an honest person is one who has a strong motivation not to lie, cheat, or steal as a fixed state of character. Honesty is obviously related to Gert's virtues of truthfulness, dependability, and trustworthiness. (We can see that there is a great deal of overlap here.) Perhaps all these virtues can be summed up as probity or, perhaps (somewhat stiffer), rectitude. Gert seems to think that the word "justice" will do just

as well for this summary deontic virtue, taking his cue from Plato (in English translation) and from J. S. Mill, but this word has a much narrower sense in today's common speech.[10] Gert is right in saying that the possession of this summary deontic virtue—which I think should be defined as having a powerful and fixed motivation not to violate any valid moral rule—call it what you will, is not sufficient for moral goodness, saying: "Moral goodness requires not only justice but kindness" (285). Here kindness seems to be standing in for all the virtues tied to the moral ideals, where these are understood in terms of the prevention or alleviation or elimination of evils.[11] But moral goodness also requires more than kindness in this artificial sense. In addition to kindness as I have argued it is commonly understood, it requires such moral virtues as generosity and friendliness, which are tied not to lessening evil, but directly to advancing and preserving good.

My criticisms here have been directed to Gert's claim that morality, as it is commonly understood, is an informal public system *entirely concerned with the lessening of evil* and not with the promotion of goods or benefits. There is an element of truth in this, namely, that moral obligation or requirement or necessity (the system of *deontic* morality as exhibited in the moral rules), concerned as it is with the not causing of evils or harms (the avoidance of wrongdoing) *is* directed at their lessening and not at the increase or promotion of benefits. In respect to what Gert calls the moral ideals, all tied, as he puts it, to preventing[12] one or more of the evils, I have argued that, the end of following such ideals in this restricted sense (excluding the so-called "utilitarian" ideals), can be seen as contributing to the human good (*eudaimonia*) *through* the alleviation or remedying or elimination of evils, and to the *preservation* of such well-being as may exist through their prevention (as this word is normally understood). And similarly following the moral *rules* can legitimately be seen as contributing to the human good through the preservation of such well-being as may exist (the prevention of any further erosion). I have also argued that the so-called utilitarian ideals (aimed at the production of benefits or goods and not at the lessening of evil) should be bracketed with the moral ideals in Gert's restricted sense, since, on Gert's own account, the attitude of the disinterested rational person toward both kinds of ideal is identical. My argument takes a new turn at this point, for I am claiming here not merely (as before) that the not causing, preventing, alleviating, and eliminating of harms or evils can be seen as contributing to the human good, but that the so-called utilitarian ideals, which would add positive benefits rather than prevent, reduce, or eliminate evils, belong properly to the system of morality.[13]

Finally, concerning the virtues and vices, which Gert says are to be understood in terms of the moral rules or the moral ideals (in his sense): yes, there are many virtues, of which honesty is the most prominent, all collectable under the heading "probity" or "moral rectitude," which must be understood in terms of the moral rules (the powerful disinclination to violate them as an ingrained state of character). And true, rectitude is not the whole of moral goodness. One must possess other virtues, such as kindness, as well. But Gert's account of kindness is skewed in the direction of making it conform to the moral ideal of the relief of suffering, ignoring the common understanding that kindness may involve doing things for others in a quite positive way as well as the relief of suffering. And there are many virtues, generosity perhaps being the most evident, that have to do with benefiting others and not simply not harming them or preventing or relieving their suffering, misery, or distress.

Gert (15-17) objects to Mill's way (*Utilitarianism*, chapter 5) of distinguishing morality from expediency, which he does by connecting morality as a whole to punishment, while claiming that it is rights that distinguish "justice" (moral obligation) from the moral ideals, and there is no doubt at all that something *has* gone wrong here. *Contra* Mill, Gert claims that the moral is properly distinguished from the nonmoral (is defined) in terms of the lessening of evil, with only the moral rules being tied to punishment, which leaves the promotion of good on the nonmoral side of the ledger. Mill's chapter 5 account is certainly an improvement on the account given in the first four chapters, which can leave us with the impression that morality consists in the disinterested promotion of the general good (a view which appears to be contradicted in chapter 5), and Gert's account is certainly an improvement on Mill's. Nevertheless on Gert's account, the so-called "utilitarian" ideals (those that encourage the promotion of benefits or goods) are excluded from the realm of the moral where they are commonly understood to belong, and many of what are commonly acknowledged to be moral virtues, such as generosity, loyalty, and courage, also fall on the nonmoral side of the divide. If I were asked to produce a definition of the moral, as I understand it, and such as I believe to be in accord with the common understanding of the matter, it would be: a rule, ideal, or virtue is properly called moral if it is needed for or contributes to the well-being of individuals in the context of society or community.

One of Gert's main motives for keeping all promotion of benefits on the nonmoral side of the divide is clearly the fear that, if we allow it to cross over, we will be on the slippery slope descending into the cavern of consequentialism, where morality is falsely seen as the disinterested promotion of the good. (The Mill of chapters 1 through 4 of *Utilitarianism* has often been interpreted in this way.) But perhaps another source of Gert's (as it seems to me) misconstrual of the whole of morality as directed to the lessening of evil or harm is the fundamental individualism implicit in his view. Perhaps what I have called *deontic* morality (the ethics of moral requirement) to which impartiality is essential, an aspect of morality which is concerned only with the avoidance of wrongdoing (what, if allowed, would cause or lead to the increase of personal evils), can be understood in purely individualistic terms, as Kant's categorical imperative surely has to be. (His "kingdom of ends" is simply a set or collection of individual "legislators," and not in any sense a community or a *polis* having a common or communal good.) But deontic morality can also be seen as a necessary for the creation and maintenance of the social conditions under which people can satisfactorily live their own lives in the context of community with its relations of connectedness and dependence. And this is just as true of the moral ideals and virtues, even those (as I have claimed) that are directed to the increase of good as well as to the lessening of evil. The common good exists, and while it is part and parcel of the individual good of everyone in the community, it cannot be simply construed as the aggregate of private interests.

There is no danger, if we accept this view, of slipping into a form of consequentialism that requires individual persons to seek the general good, or as much good as possible, or the good of everyone indifferently. That outcome can only derive from taking deontic morality (moral obligation or requirement) to be an ethics of *general* requirement, whereas it is clearly an ethics of limitation that places restrictions on our freedom otherwise to do or not do as we please without moral transgression. This is the standard error of most forms of consequentialism, including utilitarianism. Obviously, the present view does not commit this error. It is desirable for the sake of the common good that the moral ideals be pursued, and it is good for anyone and for everyone to possess the moral virtues, again for communal and hence for individual well-being, but except in the political arena, impartiality, or attention to everyone indifferently, has no role to play in any ideal or virtue other than the summary deontic virtue of rectitude.

Speaking for myself, I would claim that adherence to the moral rules, encouragement of the moral ideals, and possession of the moral virtues—all of these desirable for everyone that everyone, including oneself, follow, encourage, or possess—create and maintain the good relations among people which enable individual persons to live rich and fulfilling self-directed lives in the social and institutional contexts in which they necessarily find themselves. Thus is resolved what I have elsewhere called "the central problem for ethics,"[14] namely, how to reconcile the unavoidable separateness of persons, each with his or her goods and ills, with their inherently social nature. On this account, the moral system is to be seen as both an enabling condition and an essential constituent of the *summum bonum*, which is individual and social *eudaimonia* or, in plain language, the good life for all.

Notes

1. As regards breaking the law it might be argued that sticking to the legal speed limit when everyone else is going faster would not only not decrease the probability of harms or evils but would even increase it, and it is true that someone going at the posted limit can be a real nuisance on the road and a possible *cause* of accidents. What we have to say here is that this is a justified *exception* to the rule, because violation in this kind of case is the cause of *less* evil than strict adherence to the law. *Any* violation of the law, however, tends to erode its authority and hence is the cause (or increases the probability of) some evil. (The real problem here is that some posted speed limits are absurdly low. In Ontario, for instance, you are not stopped for speeding on the highway unless you are more than 20 km/hr over the posted limit, and police officers are so instructed. If we want the law to be respected, what are effectively acknowledged as the *real* speed limits—those necessary for safety—should be posted and enforced. The present arrangement really does encourage a cavalier attitude toward strict adherence to the law which may spill over into other, more serious areas.)

2. Notice I am not stating (or attributing to Gert) the converse of these, hence I am not claiming equivalence. While to break a promise is always the failure to keep it, the failure to keep a promise need not be its breaking for one may be unable to keep it, and the failure to do one's duty need not be the neglect of that duty for one may be hindered or prevented from doing it. Nor can we say in such cases that the rule has been *violated*. These are not only not justified violations, they are not *excused* violations either. Because neither intention nor negligence is involved it would be a mistake to speak of violation in such cases at all.

3. I have long been advocating such a view myself. In 1968 I published a paper called "The Supreme Principle of Morality" (*Dialogue* 7 (1968): 167-79), by which I understood deontic morality, that is to say moral obligation, requirement, or necessity. I believe I can state this principle in a modified form that will yield Gert's ten moral rules. Supreme principle of morality: acts or omissions that are of a kind such that one cannot will, as a rational person (without wishing evil on oneself or those one cares about), that acts of that kind be done or omitted at will or at pleasure

(whenever a person feels like it), are morally wrong and hence forbidden to anyone (unless justified by special considerations that are publicly acceptable). All other acts and omissions are morally permissible. In a still unpublished paper which I wrote for the Raz-Griffin seminar at Oxford in 1990, called "Does Consequentialism as a Theory of Moral Requirement Rest on a Huge Mistake," I summarized my view by saying that consequentialists make the huge mistake of treating as an ethics of *general prescription* what is intelligible or defensible only as an ethics of *limitation.*

4. The only exception is to be found in the final chapter ("Morality and Society"), where Gert states (371): "Political judgments differ from *other moral judgments* in that promoting goods as well as causing, avoiding, and preventing evils is normally a relevant consideration."

5. Gert speaks (231) of violations permitted by utilitarian ideals in virtue of special relationships (parent-child, government-citizen). The first example is of a parent compelling his/her child to do his/her homework. It might look as if this were done *for the positive benefit* of the child, and thus be seen as the following of a utilitarian ideal, but it can just as easily come under the heading of preventing evil—the evil of being inadequately educated and so suffering in one's future life. The second example is of a government being justified in depriving a person of freedom where a private person is not. In the case of punishment, this is straightforwardly a justified violation of the rule on the grounds of preventing a greater evil. Gert, however, wants to include taxation by governments for the benefit of the people (parks, education, etc.) as a violation of the rules forbidding deprivation of freedom and deprivation of pleasure (367-68), and to claim that these violations are justified. He also wants to include parenting under the umbrella of government (253), and indeed to place all judgments based on the promotion of benefits as distinct from the prevention of evils in the realm of the political (253, 371), where it is confined to the actions of authorities of one kind or another (parents, governments). It should not occasion surprise when I remark that this seems strained to me and, let me add, dangerous as well, for I would argue that governments are never justified in violating the moral rules in order to promote benefits—one need only think of Lenin or—God help us—Pol Pot! Nevertheless taxation for the purposes of recreational facilities, education, health, etc., may, in a money economy, very well be justified, and this requires me to deny that it has to be construed as deprivation of freedom or pleasure to which no consent has been given.

6. Gert has told me that in speaking here of utilitarian ideals he had in mind governments (parents included) exclusively, but this is not clear from the passage in question. And surely acting so as to benefit other people over whom one has no authority (vs. governments, parents), and not just to prevent harm to them or to relieve them of distress, is a utilitarian ideal, hence to be encouraged, whether we call it "moral" or not. (See also note 8 below.)

7. I would say "alleviating" here, and I add it in this paragraph and elsewhere in paraphrasing Gert's accounts of the moral ideals and the moral virtues. We need "alleviating," "remedying," "eliminating" in addition to "preventing" in this theoretical context, for that concept will not bear so much weight. (Gert is in the habit of making things tidier—for the sake of theoretical simplicity—than they really can be made.)

8. In the passage claiming that only those in authority may use utilitarian ideals to justify the violation of a moral rule (253), Gert clearly implies that ideals encouraging the promotion of benefits or goods ("utilitarian" ideals) are not strictly the province of governments or those in authority. Thus: "Except for governments, utili-

tarian ideals, that is ideals that encourage the promotion of benefits or goods, do not normally justify the breaking of a moral rule." (But see notes 5 and 6 above.)

9. Kindness, in its positive aspect, here merges imperceptibly into generosity. Perhaps every act of generosity is an act of kindness, though not all positive acts of kindness are acts of generosity.

10. Mill uses "justice" in this sense in chapter 5 of *Utilitarianism* (ed. Roger Crisp (Oxford, Eng.: Oxford University Press, 1998)), a sense which is ultimately derived from the translation of *dikaiosúne* in Plato's *Republic* (ed. G. R. F. Ferrari, trans. Tom Griffith (Cambridge, Eng.: Cambridge University Press, 2000)) as "justice." Aristotle, however, is something else again. He does not, *contra* Gert, treat *dikaiosúne* as the sum of the moral virtues but as only one of many moral virtues, all seen as lying in a mean between excess and defect, and all necessitating *phronesis* or practical wisdom. Significantly, he has an impossible difficulty inserting *dikaiosúne* into this mold.

11. Another example of the tendency mentioned in note 7 above.

12. See note 7 above.

13. See notes 6 and 8 above.

14. E. J. Bond, *Ethics and Human Well-Being* (Cambridge, Mass.: Blackwell Publishers, 1996), 209-11.

Part V: Virtue and Character

14

Rules and Virtues

Julia Driver

Interest in virtues has continued to grow among ethicists, so it is surprising that there are very few recent examples of philosophers who have presented systematic accounts of the moral virtues. Bernard Gert is an exception. In his book *Morality*, he sets out an account of morality in which rules figure prominently and which attempts to systematize commonsense morality. Gert includes in his system an account of the moral virtues. Whatever one thinks of his overall strategy, there's no doubt he's accomplished an impressive task. In developing a moral system which systematically accounts for rules and virtues, he's done something many have talked of but few have actually attempted. His account deserves more critical attention.

One crucial requirement on his account is that it be universal, and another is that it be public. Thus, the rules which figure in his account are ones that are universal and would be publicly favored by all impartial rational persons. Gert presents himself as engaged in a project which is not at all revolutionary or revisionist. But Gert is more revisionist than he realizes. Certainly with respect to his account of the moral virtues, I will argue, he is departing from common sense or ordinary morality. His view of the moral virtues owes more to classic philosophical views, which hold that moral virtue requires rational belief, than to ordinary morality, which is more forgiving. Further, conditions which seem plausible for rules—i.e., that they be universal and public—don't translate as well for virtues and skew Gert's account away from commonsense morality. The fundamental mistake he makes is to come up with a moral system that accounts for our moral obligations, via the rules, and then tries to make evaluation, at least with respect to some crucial virtues, fit that model. This forces him to maintain that evaluative terms in morality share the features of the rules (or ideals). Here I am in agreement with virtue ethicists who would maintain that this is a mistaken approach to the virtues. My claim is not that the virtues should instead be viewed as theoretically primary; rather, the mistake is to view them as like rules, or guides to action. Instead, the approach I favor is one which accepts a consequentialist background theory which justifies certain guides for action, or rules, but also gives an account of why certain character traits as opposed to others are moral virtues. Both good rules and good character are accounted for by appeals to utility. But they don't function the same way, nor will they have the same features (aside from production of utility). The general strategy I will pursue in this paper will be to show that Gert's account runs into problems precisely because he tries to make evaluation conform to qualities we associate with good decision procedures.[1]

One great virtue of Gert's account is its clarity. Gert distinguishes character traits from personality traits, which he claims are often confused. Personality traits have more to do with feeling than with action. Thus, compassion is more properly viewed as a personality trait. Virtues are character traits since they have to do with action. He then distinguishes moral virtues from personal virtues. Personal virtues are those character traits that all rational persons want for themselves. (288)[2] A moral virtue, on the other hand, is defined as "any trait of character that all impartial rational persons favor all persons possessing." (285) Morally virtuous *actions* are those that all impartial rational persons would publicly favor. Personal and moral virtues differ not merely in terms of who the favored possessor of the trait is, oneself vs. everyone; they differ also in that personal virtues are those that all rational persons want for themselves, whereas moral virtues are those traits that all *impartial* rational persons want both themselves *and others* to have. Note also that personal vices then would be those traits that all rational persons want themselves not to have, whereas moral vices would be those traits that all impartial rational persons would want everyone else not to have. These categories seem to roughly correspond to what ordinary usage dubs "prudential" vs. "moral" virtues, or what some have called the self-regarding vs. other-regarding virtues. All rational persons want to have the self-regarding virtues of prudence and temperance for themselves.

Given his definition, Gert ends up with quite a short list of moral virtues. What are they? They mainly correspond to the last five of the moral rules:

Moral Rule	**Moral Virtue**
6. Do not deceive	Truthfulness
7. Keep your promises	Trustworthiness
8. Do not cheat	Fairness
9. Obey the law	Honesty
10. Do your duty	Dependability

There is also the moral virtue of justice which doesn't correspond to a specific rule.

However, some moral vices do not correspond to the last five rules. For example, the moral vice of cruelty is generally involved in a violation of one of the first five rules, particularly that rule which prohibits causing pain. There are no moral virtues corresponding to these first five rules. Kindness, which one normally thinks of as the opposite of cruelty, involves following an ideal to act to relieve the suffering of others. Ideals correspond to rendering aid, which one does not have a moral obligation to do. Thus, failure to be morally virtuous in these respects does not make one subject to punishment. Failure to be generous or kind, for example, is a failure of moral virtue, not of obligation. Other failures, however, are: failure to be honest does not violate an ideal, but a requirement, and would make one subject to punishment. Note that Gert's account of some moral ideals is negative in the sense that they do not concern elevating levels of happiness or creating positive good. Thus, kindness the moral virtue, for Gert, is restricted to alleviating suffering. What we would call a broader benevolence, or kindness, isn't considered a moral virtue by Gert. So, for example, the agent who creates more happiness for those who are not suffering is not exhibiting a moral virtue. This restriction on Gert's part (which follows from his negative account of the moral ideals) will strike many as wrong since the classic moral virtue of benevolence calls for improving and not just alleviating. One might possibly want to add further conditions to moral virtue, of course, to keep the account from becoming too broad (for example, there are many who would not regard wittiness as a moral virtue, though it certainly can produce happiness). Be that as it may, the broader point remains that Gert's account cannot handle a rather large class of cases involving the promotion of happiness as opposed to the alleviation of suffering.

Gert's claim is that his definition of moral virtue gives us a short list corresponding to these rules and to the ideals. Thus, we have a short, general list of the moral virtues. Not only that, we have a list which rules out certain traditional traits, such as courage. Courage may be a personal virtue, but it's not a moral one since all impartial rational persons couldn't want everyone to have this trait. After all, courageous thieves and enemies are not to be desired. So, the moral virtues will include only those traits with qualities that one associates with good moral rules or ideals: they will be general, and universal, and publicly favored or advocated.

In the remainder of this paper I will argue against the claim that these requirements are suitable for moral virtue, and will instead argue that Gert's moral system is inappropriate as a foundation for an evaluative system. The system he offers, while ambitious, is not a viable replacement for consequentialist accounts which also provide a unified account of morality.

Against Universality

The generality Gert considers crucial for the moral rules and ideals, and by extension the moral virtues, goes against ordinary usage, because we often talk of more narrowly defined virtue traits. For example, "He has the virtue of being a good father." Most would regard being a good father morally virtuous. Being a good father is not a moral virtue for Gert because it is not something which is universal—one wouldn't want everyone to be a good father since not everyone is or could be a father. One wouldn't even want everyone to be a good parent, since not everyone is or could be a parent. One might want everyone to be a good person—but that's at a high level of generality.

Note also that Gert elsewhere writes: "Any character trait that involves justifiably obeying the moral rules or justifiably following the moral ideals is a moral virtue." (285) This looks like a pretty strong universal claim about what counts as a moral virtue. Yet, it seems to conflict with the previous definition of moral virtues as traits of character that all impartial rational persons want all to have. On this definition being a good father is not a moral virtue. On the second definition being a good father would be a moral virtue, however, since being a good father is a trait which involves justifiably following the moral rules and moral ideals.

Gert would probably respond that this example, of being a good father, fits under the general moral virtue of dependability since being a good parent will involve essentially doing one's duty. While certainly it does involve doing one's duty toward one's children, one could plausibly argue, however, that this is not the only thing that is involved in being a good parent, and the very general trait of dependability doesn't come close to capturing it. Otherwise, there is little to distinguish being a good parent from being, for example, a dependable employee.

Gert's account doesn't seem to allow context specific traits to be moral virtues. This would not upset him, since his account is one which aims for universality. Context-specific traits are not universal, or, at least, they are not universal in the sense that Gert would endorse. Regarding the rules he writes, "the universality of the general moral rules requires that the rules must be such that rational persons in every society at any time in history might have acted upon them or broken them." (111)

This universality applies to the moral virtues as well. However, Gert *could* make a distinction between conditional universality and unconditional universality. There is a sense in which the norms which govern being a good father can be universal even though it is not the case that all rational persons are, or could be, fathers. One might call this sense "conditional" universality and oppose it to "unconditional" universality. So conditionally universal norms do apply to all (universally) who are in the relevant situation—in this case, fatherhood. Unconditional universality, on the other hand, would involve only norms governing those traits which would apply to all rational persons no matter their situation. One could argue for universality, but make it conditional universality, and avoid the problem mentioned above.

The problem with Gert's commitment to unconditional universality is that a trait which in some sense is good for everyone—regardless of his or her situation—will be extremely general in nature—so general that one has difficulty seeing how one would apply the account Gert offers. Is he giving an account of the moral virtues or merely listing traits that he intuitively finds to be morally virtuous?

Further, the definitions don't seem to always render the right result. Greed would not be a moral virtue, since it is not the case that all impartial rational persons would want all persons to have this trait; however, might it not, counterintuitively, come off as a personal virtue? Perhaps all rational persons would want to be greedy? I just don't know. Gert will claim that since all impartial rational persons wouldn't want to be greedy themselves it must follow that not all rational persons want to be greedy. The idea is that if *x* is impartial then *x* doesn't want to be greedy. But if one goes this route one will be severely limiting the scope of personal virtue. It also seems plausible to hold that if *x* is impartial, *x* would not want to be smarter than others. Thus, being extraordinarily intelligent would not be a personal virtue. Anything which gives one an advantage would go the same way. Yet, personal virtues are ones we consider to be personally advantageous (among other things).

Of course, if Gert decides to allow for context specific virtue traits by appealing to conditional universality, then he loses quite a bit. The account of the moral virtues is no longer in sync with his overall moral system, with its emphasis on rules and ideals that are unconditionally universal. Further, he would be forced to hold that certain traits *could*, in carefully specified circumstances, count as moral virtues. For example, the coldness of the physician may make him more dependable, or the viciousness of a politician may make her more effective, and so on.

There is the option of simply denying that being a good father is a moral virtue. True, the expression "John has the virtue of being a good father" seems to make sense, but Gert could argue that there is no disposition or character trait which corresponds to being a good father. Instead, being a good father is a hodgepodge of good making features, and as such does not qualify as a moral virtue. But this maneuver only works if one has the view that a moral virtue must be a single disposition, and not a disposition cluster. But it seems likely that many character traits we view to be moral virtues, or excellences of our character, are disposition clusters. That is, to have the fatherly virtue one must be disposed to, for example, care for one's children conscientiously, but must also, perhaps, be disposed to treat one's spouse with respect, and so on. What qualifies as making up this disposition cluster may be open to debate, but that's a debate about what is good. It can be generally agreed still that there is such a cluster of traits we take to mark the fatherly excellence, and that being in possession of this cluster is considered having a moral virtue.

Another interesting part of Gert's account is the view that the moral virtues require the agent to be extraordinarily diligent in adhering to the relevant rule: "a particular moral virtue involves following some part of the moral system significantly more than most people do; and a particular moral vice involves acting contrary to some part of the guide provided by morality significantly more than most people do." (283) Thus, the morally virtuous agent is more than morally adequate. This captures the intuition that there is something extraordinary about virtue—that it is an excellence, and, as such, not something which is run-of-the-mill or commonplace. I honestly find this feature of Gert's account odd, since he so closely ties most of the moral virtues to the last five moral rules. Thus, failure to adhere to the rule is a failure of obligation. Presumably, most people are pretty good about sticking to the rules. Most people, for example, will tell the truth most of the time. So I would want to call most people truthful, and thus most people have the moral virtue of truthfulness. There doesn't seem to be anything contradictory in saying, "She is truthful (i.e. she has the virtue of truthfulness), but less so than most people (who also have the virtue of truthfulness)." But on Gert's account this would be contradictory. Only those persons who are truthful to a greater extent than is normal would qualify as having the moral virtue of truthfulness. But note that the moral virtues are universal—they are not context dependent in any way according to Gert. This raises a problem regarding how one determines what counts as "normal" for everyone. Not just everyone here and now, but everyone who ever existed and ever will exist. How could I tell whether or not a given agent had the virtue, since I have no way of knowing what a normal level of truthfulness is for the entire history of humanity? This might mean that, for the agent here and now, or agents in the past, we have no answer until the entire history of humanity runs its course. What is normal for all of humanity *cannot* yet be determined.

This requirement also raises what Walter Sinnott-Armstrong terms the "Lake Woebegone" problem. If you combine this feature with Gert's stated definition, you get a serious problem. Gert defines the moral virtues as those character traits that all impartial rational persons favor everyone having. But how can all impartial rational persons favor everyone having dispositions to follow the rules to an extraordinary degree—that is, to a greater degree than normal or average? That isn't possible.

To get out of this problem and remain faithful to the core of his account Gert would have to jettison the condition that the moral virtues require rule obeying or ideal following to a remarkable degree. This, however, would seem to run counter to his stated goal of making his account as intuitive as possible. In addressing this issue Gert writes, "What impartial rational persons favor is everyone having a character trait that now corresponds to a moral virtue, although if everyone had it, it would not be called a virtue anymore." (308, n. 8) The intuition he is trying to capture is that when we use the words "moral virtue" we are talking about traits that we really would like everyone to have. In admiring Mother Teresa or Nelson Mandela one might remark, "I wish everyone had their moral qualities." If everyone did have those moral qualities, then they would no longer be extraordinary, but that's not the real world. We use the words "moral virtue" to pick out qualities we would like to see in everybody even though those qualities are currently quite rare. But the intuition that moral virtues are extraordinary isn't gripping; this condition could be eliminated with little violence to intuition, given some of the considerations brought out earlier. Further, in the account he offers Gert does seem to be engaged in more than mere linguistic analysis of how we use the words "moral virtue." He takes pains to distinguish these sorts of things from personality traits and other qualities, and he often explicitly makes claims about what the moral virtues are: "Any character trait that involves justifiably obeying the moral rules or justifiably following the moral ideals. . . ." (285)

Another difficulty with Gert's definition of "moral virtue" is that it seems to lend itself to a kind of unity of virtues thesis. This is the thesis, which Gert actually disavows, that the possessor of one virtue will necessarily possess them all. Consider the virtue of kindness or sensitivity—a disposition to avoid causing pain to others. Is this a trait that all impartial rational persons favor all persons possessing? It isn't clear because I could imagine not desiring that my doctor have a disposition to avoid causing distress in others if that interferes with the efficient delivery of medical services—that is, if the disposition is responsible for his squeamishness. I might want him to be tougher, and slightly hardened to the distress of others. Yet this doesn't make such a disposition a nonvirtue; it is simply a moral virtue that I wouldn't want *everyone* to have, since it may in some contexts interfere with other virtue traits or skills that I also value (e.g., being an efficient doctor less likely to make mistakes).

Kindness is clearly a paradigm moral virtue, yet it seems implausible to hold that it is because all impartial rational persons want everyone, in all contexts, to be kind. Suppose that Joe lives in a world dominated by an evil dictator who really ought to be killed. Suppose also that Joe is kind and sensitive, and that the kindness interferes with his ability to kill the dictator because he can't bring himself to act in a seemingly vicious way. An impartial rational person might not want Joe to be kind. Like the compassionate doctor, Joe is too inhibited by his kindness. Gert might respond by arguing that the impartial rational person would still want Joe to be kind—just not to exemplify kindness. Instead, good judgment would have him perform the ruthless act. But this doesn't successfully avoid the criticism—we often know of persons whose kindness makes them incapable of doing the ruthless act because the ruthless act type, so to speak, is so far out of their normal range, and it seems reasonable that in some contexts we might not want some persons to be kind, because ruthlessness is what is needed to bring about the best outcome for all persons.

But Gert points out that, on his view, moral virtue will require good judgment on the part of the virtuous agent:

> Having the moral virtues requires judgment because it involves obeying the rules and following the ideals in the way that an impartial rational person would, not simply always obeying the moral rules and following the moral ideals as much as possible. (278)

Gert believes that discernment is required in that the agent will not simply obey the rules, but obey them as the impartial rational person would. I take it that Gert wants to rule out persons being truthful, for example, as much as possible when the context is one in which kindness is called for instead and there is a conflict between the two. For example, there will be some situations in which no good end is served by hurting someone's feelings through telling him the plain unvarnished truth. The morally virtuous agent will learn to recognize when morality is better served by failing to be fully truthful. Thus, the good judgment would serve to give the morally virtuous agent flexibility, and could be construed as a response to the case of interfering kindness discussed earlier. Lacking judgment and strength of will to overcome his squeamishness, such a person would not be morally virtuous. Indeed, he would be morally vicious because the kindness would be a sort of blind kindness that all impartial rational persons would not favor for everyone. As I will argue in the next section, this requirement of judgment raises its own set of problems.

Against Publicity

The rule obeying aspect of Gert's view definitely goes against the trend in current virtue theory—much of which is spent trying to argue that rules are completely useless in morality. While this extreme approach seems incorrect, one could argue a middle ground. Moral virtue may or may not involve justifiably obeying rules and following ideals. Sometimes a person is morally virtuous who cannot clearly articulate why it is that she is behaving the way she behaves, and who thus would have some difficulty providing an accurate justification of her actions. Gert would not require the morally virtuous individual to be consciously aware of following rules and ideals. But allowing for clear mistakes seems foreign to his view. However, it seems quite possible that often people are mistaken about the moral status of what it is they are doing: villagers who risked their own lives and the lives of their families to save Jewish children sometimes viewed their actions as morally *obligatory* as opposed to supererogatory, even though those actions carried enormous risk:

> I must point out that the people of the village did not think of themselves as "successful," let alone as "good." From their point of view, they did not do anything that required elaborate explanation. When I asked them why they helped these dangerous guests, they invariably answered, "What do you mean, 'Why?' Where else could they go? How could you turn them away? What is so special about being ready to help (*prête à servir*)? There was nothing else to do." And some of them laughed in amazement when I told them that I thought they were "good people." They saw no alternative to their actions and to the way they acted, and therefore they saw what they did as necessary, not something to be picked out for praise.[3]

Perhaps they were mistaken and their actions should be picked out for praise. That doesn't make their behavior less courageous and generous, or less morally virtuous.

Not only should an account of moral virtue tolerate this sort of misjudgment of the moral status of what one is doing (since the villagers were doing something extraordinarily good), it should also tolerate outright ignorance and/or irrationality. Here I think my own views depart from Gert's in a very fundamental way. Agents can be habitually mistaken and still be morally virtuous. For example, Sandra might be charitable to others because she believes in the essential goodness of all human beings and thus fails to see the bad in others. She still has the moral virtue of charity, which is a form of kindness, though it is based on an irrationality—a failure to account for all the evidence.[4] Gert views a belief as irrational if it is an obviously false belief "held by a person who has sufficient relevant knowledge and intelligence to know that it is false" (34). The idea is that everyone else with similar knowledge and intelligence would know it to be false. I take it that believing against the evidence available to one (and to everyone else), then, would qualify as irrational. However, it might well be in Sandra's best interest to believe against the evidence. This sort of case points to a distinction between being irrational in one's beliefs, and being irrational in one's behavior. Sandra's avoidance of certain evidence might not be irrational, though it leads her to adopt obviously false beliefs, if the avoidance thereby leads to a good outcome for her.[5] Perhaps it allows her to form closer attachments to others or to be less critical, etc. But Gert has difficulty allowing such a distinction. Indeed, immediately after defining irrational belief he goes on to say that he favors this definition because persons who adopt false beliefs will be led to irrational *action:* "I call these beliefs irrational because holding them significantly increases the chances of a person acting irrationally" (34).

Moral virtues that involve irrationality *could* be accommodated by Gert, given that he softens the good judgment requirement, since his definition focuses on what the impartial rational person would want all others to have—and maybe all impartial rational persons would want everyone to be blindly charitable, or to be charitable and be blind to their faults where that is necessary to the charity, though this seems implausible. Still, it is certainly possible, and the account's indeterminacy in this regard constitutes a gap that should be filled.

The general problem has to do with identifying what the impartial rational person wants independent of the rules. Here Gert's account really has some difficulty—I have no idea whether all or any impartial rational persons would want all to be blindly charitable. Given Gert's short list of the virtues, I would imagine that he would simply respond by saying that they wouldn't, but this doesn't illuminate. Why wouldn't they? Gert could fall back on appealing to consequences—that is, perhaps it would be because the consequences of everyone having this trait would be terrible—think of all the evil that would be missed. But then what's doing the work is an appeal to consequences, and not an appeal to rationality per se, and this is something I believe Gert would repudiate.

Further, Gert's account does not allow for unknown virtues and vices, at least not in any straightforward way. This is because the moral virtues must be character traits which involve action that would be publicly allowed by an impartial rational person, and vices are character traits which involve action which would be publicly discouraged by an impartial rational person.[6] But suppose that the impartial rational person lacks crucial information, regarding, say, the consequences of a given trait? Indeed, on Gert's account for the agents to be impartial they must not make use of information that is inaccessible to any rational person. Suppose also that it turns out that particular acts of kindness undermine the characters of the beneficiaries, making them weak and dependent, but that these long-term consequences are not apparent. The impartial rational person wants everyone to be kind, but only because he can't see that kindness actually produces bad consequences in the long run. Thus, this would be a virtue, and a moral virtue, on Gert's account when the more natural response is to hold that it is a moral vice, just not recognized as such.

Gert could try to solve this problem by adding a condition that the impartial rational person be fully informed—in which case we'd have something like an ideal observer view—the moral virtues are those traits that the ideal agent wants everyone to have. Ideal observer views suffer from epistemic difficulties to a certain degree. Since we are not ideal observers it is difficult to try to figure out what the ideal observer would approve of.[7] However, this is a flaw that Gert's account would share with many accounts, including the standard consequentialist account. But it should be pointed out that for Gert this problem is particularly significant, because at least in spirit, he wants the moral virtues to meet a publicity requirement: "Moral virtues do require acting as an impartial rational person would publicly allow" (292). Technically, it might be a counterfactual publicity requirement since Gert specifies what the impartial rational person would publicly allow rather than what the impartial rational person allows under actual epistemic conditions. But if we move away from actual conditions to ideal ones, then we get the ideal observer interpretation, which Gert doesn't want. If we stick to actual epistemic conditions, then it becomes difficult to allow for mistakes about virtue. The impartial rational person would not be mistaken regarding what counted as virtue, and this seems counterintuitive since we want to maintain that improvements in information allow for changes in virtue judgments that are justified by the way the world is and not merely by what the impartial rational person is justified in believing. Further, Gert would be uncomfortable with the thought that there are moral virtues which are not known, and thus not actually encouraged. This runs against the spirit of requiring publicity.

A third option would be to hold that the impartial rational person must only use information available to all other impartial rational persons; thus, when Gert defines moral virtue holding it to require acting as the impartial rational person would publicly allow, it is understood that the impartial rational person is only working with information available to all. In the précis, this is more clearly specified as "rationally required belief." Moral virtues become those character traits approved of by all impartial rational persons using information accessible only to all (that is, using only rationally required beliefs). This is probably a pretty minimal amount of information.[8] This is the "dumbed-down" version.[9] On this third option we do not have an ideal observer, nor do we have an observer making use of what she actually knows. Rather she is restricted to what everyone else knows. This third option is the one actually endorsed by Gert, and makes the above problem even more severe. The impartial rational person might actually be forced to call something a moral virtue though he or she recognizes that it has disastrous effects (because she also recognizes that others do not know this). Indeed, recognition of the effects of traits is something which generally doesn't seem to be rationally required. Thus, if an agent realizes that generosity leads to terrible long-term consequences, this is not something that can be used to determine whether or not generosity is a virtue because it is not information accessible to all. It is not rationally required. When one asks what is a virtue, then, one is restricted to using a small set of beliefs—given what everyone knows or has good reason to believe, what traits would everyone favor everyone possessing?

Decision Procedures vs. Evaluative Criteria

Consequentialists standardly make a distinction between decision procedures and evaluative norms. This distinction allows them to avoid certain classic problems with their account. The Principle of Utility doesn't guide most morally proper action, but it can be used to evaluate action (or rules or motives). The appropriate decision procedures will be understood relative to the principle of utility—that is, they will themselves be judged good or bad, depending on whether or not following them maximizes utility. But the rules one is justified in following might vary enormously from context to context because the bottom justification is utility.

Rules, decision procedures, guide action and in this way are practical. Virtues guide action only in the derivative sense that they are simply dispositions to act a certain way and pick out evaluative criteria of a certain sort. Virtue terms may figure into rules such as "Don't be mean," but they are not themselves rules and do not guide action. On the consequentialist view what counts as a virtue will be a matter of what promotes utility (and there are a wide variety of ways one could go about spelling this out). But virtue judgments are used to evaluate character, not to provide decision procedures, so it's not surprising that they will have different qualities. While there may be good practical arguments for maintaining that rules must be universal and public, these arguments might not hold for virtues.

But for Gert all moral phenomena share the qualities discussed earlier—they must be universal and public. Virtues simply are dispositions to follow the rules to an extraordinary degree, and these are the traits that all impartial rational persons want everyone to have.

> Any character trait that involves justifiably obeying the moral rules or justifiably following the moral ideals is a moral virtue. However, moral virtues and vices can be characterized without mentioning the moral rules or ideals. They can be defined in terms of the attitudes of all impartial rational persons. A moral virtue is any trait of character that all impartial rational persons favor all persons possessing. . . . But regardless of how the moral virtues and vices are defined, they all have a direct conceptual relationship to moral rules and moral ideals. (285)

This makes the rules and ideals primary because we only know what counts as a moral virtue by knowing what the moral rules and ideals are. The moral virtues are defined in terms of them. As "moral" they share the same qualities which make the rules and ideals "moral." However, aside from problems discussed earlier about universality and publicity as requirements for moral virtue, the arguments Gert uses for these qualities with respect to the rules don't carry over with respect to the virtues, because they are different sorts of things and function differently in morality.

For example, Gert argues that the rules must be universal and public out of considerations of fairness and efficiency. It isn't fair to hold people accountable to standards they are unaware of, nor can such standards be effective as guides to action. Rather, they must be known, and they must apply to everyone; no one can opt out, so to speak. Like a game, the rules of morality must be known so that the participants can actually play, and within the scope of the game opting out of the rules isn't permitted.

But virtues need not function to guide behavior at all. They are used to evaluate our behavior, to praise or condemn it. Virtues may figure as terms within rules, but the virtues themselves simply work as evaluative terms. There is no virtue game, at least not analogous to the morality game. Someone can opt out of *some* of the virtues by simply not choosing to do anything falling under their scope. In deciding not to have children, one is deciding that one will not be a good parent in virtue of not being a parent at all. Of course, one will not be a bad or indifferent parent either. There is a situational sense, mentioned earlier, in which virtues are universal. The norms do apply to all in the relevant situations. While Gert does not consider this adequate, someone else who valued universality could argue that its demands are met by situational universality—it is fair to hold all parents to the same norms, though not fair to hold nonparents to norms that are not relevant to their lives.

Further, one of Gert's main arguments for publicity is that we do not hold animals responsible for their behavior, or make moral judgments about them, or about people we consider not responsible for their actions. If someone is unavoidably ignorant of the wrongness of his or her actions, then he or she is not responsible. But with respect to the moral virtues and vices we do make ascriptions of them even if the person is not responsible, so this argument will not work for moral virtues and vices.

Consider the case of Phineas Gage, a railway worker who suffered a head injury which resulted in the loss of a critical part of his brain. Mr. Gage, according to all of his acquaintances, was a trustworthy, friendly, and conscientious man before the accident. After the accident he became nasty, impulsive, and dishonest. The accident was not his fault, and he did not choose to become dishonest—yet he was. And this was a moral failing. Mr. Gage is a rather dramatic example of this phenomenon, but people are at least helped along in their goodness or badness by factors beyond their control all the time. We don't reserve moral evaluation for only those traits one has control over developing.

Further, as Hume noted, we tend to regard natural abilities and moral virtues in the same light—the distinction between them being merely verbal. Supposedly we are responsible for the former but not the latter since the former are voluntary while the latter are not. But this is an illusion:

> many of those qualities which all moralists . . . comprehend under the title of moral virtues are equally involuntary and necessary, with the qualities of judgment and imagination. Of this nature are constancy, fortitude, magnanimity; and, in short, all the qualities which form the *great* man.[10]

These labels aren't the same as those used by Gert for the moral virtues (though he would hold something like "constancy" to be a moral virtue on his account), but the point remains that a person's tendency to obey or violate the rules can be due as much to nature as anything else. The reason we focus on ones that are voluntarily acquired is that doing so produces a better outcome—if control works in those cases, bad traits can be jettisoned in favor of the good. Where the traits are not voluntarily acquired in the first place, this is not so clearly the case.

Conclusion

There may be some very good practical reasons for wanting rules to be universal and public, since fairness would dictate that we hold persons accountable to the same standards and, further, those standards should be ones the persons have access to. Yet in evaluating persons and their behavior there may also be an important function served by criticizing an agent's behavior or character, even if that agent had no access to the standards. I might evaluate Phineas Gage and his behavior or his character in a negative light, even though I realize that with his brain damage he had no way of internalizing the moral rules. Gert's response might be to claim that Gage, then, is like a vicious dog. One does not morally blame a vicious dog, though one certainly disapproves of its conduct. But this would be the wrong analogy to draw. Phineas Gage is no different from a person who, let's say, becomes bitter and blind to the claims of morality due to some personal tragedy. Both Gage and the misanthrope still perform voluntary and intentional actions; they still know what they're doing. They just don't care. I may not blame Gage for *becoming* dishonest, but this still allows me to view his character in a morally negative light. The connection between moral virtue and the voluntary has to do with the fact that we only ascribe moral virtue to beings who are capable of voluntary action.

The qualities that Gert requires the moral virtues to have seem ill-suited them. Gert's account, which ties them so closely to the moral rules and ideals of his broader moral theory, seems forced to maintain an account of moral virtues which is not faithful to ordinary views. This is in violation of the methodology of Gert's broader moral theory.

Notes

1. One could argue that the properties Gert views as necessary for good rules and ideals are not in fact necessary. I will leave aside this issue, arguing that even if they are appropriate for rules, they aren't for virtues.

2. All parenthetical page references are to Bernard Gert, *Morality* (New York: Oxford University Press, 1998).

3. Philip Hallie, "From Cruelty to Goodness," reprinted in *Vice and Virtue in Everyday Life*, ed. Christina Hoff Sommers (San Diego: Harcourt, Brace Jovanovich, 1985), 4-16, p. 16.

4. See my "The Virtues of Ignorance," *The Journal of Philosophy* 86 (July 1989): 373-84.

5. Gert defines an irrational action as one which, among other things, the agent performs believing it to lead to a bad outcome for himself (or significant risk thereof) and which he has no adequate reason for. (39) Sandra's action would not be irrational because it would lead to a good outcome, and at least in the objective sense she could arguably be said to have a good reason for engaging in such action.

6. Note that the publicity requirement is such that not all impartial rational persons must publicly advocate the specific virtuous action. Gert needs to make this move so that he can accommodate the fact that good people disagree on specific actions. As long as even one impartial rational person would publicly advocate the action, then presumably the condition is met.

7. See Geoffrey Sayre-McCord's article in this volume on why Gert is not offering an ideal observer view.

8. See Gert, 36-37, for details of what counts as rationally required. It's not very much.

9. See Sayre-McCord's paper in this volume.

10. David Hume, *A Treatise of Human Nature*, part III, section IV.

15

Character, Immorality, and Punishment*

Marcia Baron

My initial plan was to discuss Bernard Gert on impartiality. But I found that most of my disagreements with him are on foundational matters. So I shall focus instead on what seems to me to be wrongheaded about his theory. Actions are overemphasized; character gets short schrift, and when it is discussed, it is discussed primarily in terms of actions. His emphasis on actions is closely tied to his view that the notions of moral wrongness and punishment are conceptually linked, and I'll be challenging that view. Underlying each of these points is a disagreement I have with him concerning the nature of morality: "Morality," Gert claims, "is best conceived as a guide to behavior that rational persons put forward to govern the behavior of others, whether or not they plan to follow that guide themselves."[1] Throughout my paper I will be registering disagreements and indicating reasons for my disagreements. Insofar as it is possible, I will offer arguments against his views; but because my differences with him are so fundamental, often it won't be possible to do much more than point to some questionable assumptions and offer reasons for doubting them.

I

Gert's remarkably well worked out, remarkably systematic theory is in some respects an apotheosis of what Kantians are often expected to hold. In its emphasis on rules and on actions it fits a familiar but inaccurate picture of Kant's ethics. The approach that Gert takes to ethics is not at all the approach that I take, and when I explain why, I will sound rather similar to those who, with a false picture of Kant's ethics, criticize *it*. But although my criticisms are similar, what I favor will be Kantian.

There is a great deal in Gert's book with which I do agree, especially in the details, which I find very insightful (and in some instances, in fact, very Kantian). I am thinking, for example, of his remarks on kindness and compassion, in which he points out that it is a mistake to conflate the two, or to suppose that compassion invariably leads to kindness. "*To have compassion for others is to suffer because of their suffering*" (266). This may, but need not, lead to kindness.[2] To seek to relieve their suffering is only one way the compassionate person might respond. A different approach, as Gert observes, would be to seek to forget about those towards whom one feels compassion, resorting perhaps to drink or drugs or a search for excitement and adventure, or "even complete dedication to some intellectual pursuit" (266). "A person may be so overcome by his compassion that he completely avoids those whose suffering causes him to suffer" (266; see also 281).

Or, to cite other details on which I enthusiastically concur, Gert stresses the importance of distinguishing between pleasure and satisfying a desire, and between displeasure and failing to satisfy a desire, and observes that once we draw these distinctions, most of the plausibility of thinking that desires are reasons (in his sense of reasons) disappears.

> If it is clear that one will receive no pleasure from satisfying a desire and will not be bothered by not satisfying it, then the desire provides no reason for acting in any way that one knows will result in harm to oneself. This state of affairs is, in fact, quite common, and many people have desires that they forget about completely in a few moments. It is important not to confuse frustration of a desire that one is unsuccessfully trying to satisfy, and which almost invariably results in displeasure, with simply failing to satisfy a desire one happens to have. Indeed, as many ancient philosophers have pointed out, it is often rational to seek to rid oneself of some of one's desires. (63)

To note another point of agreement: I strongly endorse his remarks on loyalty and religious ideals, especially his point that "the harm done by . . . failure to distinguish universal moral ideals from ideals that depend essentially on belief in a particular religion cannot be overestimated" (257). Given the system of rules and ideals, I agree that "whenever the ideal that a religion supports rests essentially on a revelation, or scripture, or anything that is not known to all rational persons, impartial rational persons cannot publicly allow a violation of a moral rule in order to follow it" (257).

I said "given the system of rules and ideals"—and it is there that I part company. The basic elements of the theory, the basic structure of it, seem misguided to me. So rather than enumerate all the points on which I agree with Gert, I turn now to some fundamental disagreements, and challenge some of the premises at the foundation of his moral theory.

II

In his preface, Gert mentions that in earlier versions of his book he did not make it sufficiently clear that the moral rules were only one part of morality. "Morality consists, not merely of rules, but also of ideals, morally relevant features, and a two-step procedure for determining which violations of a rule are strongly justified, which are weakly justified, and which are unjustified" (ix). He seems to be suggesting that he has now addressed the problem. But I think that to some extent it remains. What is missing from his account is, in a word, character. I don't mean, of course, that he forgot to talk about it; he does talk about it (mainly in the chapter on virtues and vices), and his discussion teems with insightful observations. And although he does not do so in the passage I just quoted, he sometimes includes virtues when he enumerates the various things that morality consists in (13; 20). Nonetheless, character and virtues seem to be tacked on,[3] and the focus remains on actions.

Let me be more specific in indicating where I disagree. Gert holds that "emotions and feelings are morally important only insofar as they lead to morally good actions" (266). Whether he would say the same about attitudes, I cannot say for sure, but it seems likely. By contrast, I share with virtue ethicists the position that emotions, feelings, and attitudes are morally important even apart from their tendency to lead to certain sorts of actions. How one thinks about others, how one responds, affectively, when one hears that a colleague has just received a prestigious award, or when one hears of some grave injustice, does matter morally. It matters even if one does not exhibit one's sentiments in any way, or act accordingly. A desire to torture a child to death—even a mere fantasy of doing so—is of moral concern, even if the person in question would absolutely never act accordingly (and even if we are confident that this is the case).

To forestall misunderstanding, let me clarify that I would certainly not go so far as to say that it is *as* wrong to desire to do *x* as to do *x*. It is not. Moreover, when *x* isn't heinous, when "*x*" refers to, say, adultery rather than torturing someone to death, desiring to do *x* or fantasizing *x* is either not wrong at all or of marginal moral importance. I should also clarify that I am not taking the position that, as Michael Slote puts it, "the evaluation of actions is entirely derivative from and dependent on what we have to say ethically about (the inner life of) the agents who perform those actions." (Slote calls this position, or the theory whose core it is, an "agent-based virtue ethics."[4]) I am merely denying that emotions, feelings, and attitudes are morally important only insofar as they lead to morally good actions. My disagreement with Gert on this matter is, I believe, a difference in intuitions, so I cannot argue for the claim, but it clearly reflects differences in how we think about character. My view is that part of good character is that one responds affectively in certain ways (or at least doesn't respond in certain ways) and has certain attitudes (or at least doesn't have certain attitudes); and that claims that *x* and *y* are part of good character generally do not reduce to a claim that certain actions are likely to issue from these affective responses and attitudes.

When I say that attitudes and affective responses matter, or that they are of moral importance, I don't mean only that if we were scoring everyone's character, perhaps in the service of the gatekeepers of heaven, this is information that would figure into the score. It would. But I am not especially interested in determining the proper criteria for rating each other. How we think about others, how we respond, affectively, to news of a grave injustice, or to news of a neighbor's terminal illness matters in a more pragmatic way: recognition of the moral significance of sentiments should affect how we, both as parents and as a society, raise our children, and to the extent that it is possible to shape our own characters, it should affect how we do that, as well.[5] It should affect it not only because we think that our children will (as adults) be more likely to refrain from actions from which they should refrain (and perform those that they should perform) if they have these attitudes, desires, and affective responses, but because a person who has certain attitudes has, other things equal, a better character than a person who does not.

Gert would, I imagine, agree that it is important to raise children and shape our characters to have these feelings and attitudes and not to have certain other feelings and attitudes. However, he would say they are important not for their own sake, but only because they lead to morally good or right actions. This, however, would imply that as long as we could train ourselves to exercise perfect self-control so that the objectionable attitudes and feelings don't lead to immoral actions, it doesn't matter what our attitudes and feelings are. And on this I strongly disagree.

To make more vivid my claim that Gert overemphasizes action and attends too little to attitude and affect, let's take a look at his remarks on tolerance. This will also serve to bring out something else I take issue with, namely, the emphasis on rules, and on characterizing immorality as a violation of moral rules.

> Tolerance, properly understood, does not involve doing anything; rather, it consists in not doing certain things. To be intolerant is to violate any of the moral rules, particularly the first five, with regard to someone because of some morally indifferent characteristic he possesses. A tolerant person will not kill, cause pain to, disable, or deprive of freedom or pleasure any person because of the color of her skin, her place of birth, or her morally acceptable religious beliefs. An intolerant person is necessarily an immoral person, for he violates a moral rule unjustifiably. (263)

But surely it is possible to be intolerant without violating any of the moral rules. There are many intolerant people who would not kill, disable, and so on, but who feel disgust towards gays and lesbians, or perhaps towards interracial couples, or Jews. Most likely their disgust will be expressed in some actions—though the actions might just be those of avoiding such people, teaching their children to stay away from them and to find them repulsive, avoiding hiring anyone they believe to be gay, and so on, actions which do not violate any of Gert's moral rules. But even if it is not expressed in actions, their attitudes alone are morally objectionable. And if their disgust is expressed in morally objectionable actions, these actions need not involve violating any of the moral rules.

Of course, Gert does not limit moral judgments to judgments concerning violations of (or compliance with) the moral rules. Moral judgments can concern moral ideals. But I don't see that this will help address the problem regarding intolerance. For such judgments still concern actions (or omissions to act) and, moreover, they concern actions of a specific sort. They concern failure to act in accordance with a moral ideal. An example of the sort of action that does not violate a moral rule but which would be a proper subject of a negative moral judgment would be "failing to help someone avoid a significant harm when one is in a special position to do so and helping does not involve any significant personal sacrifice" (319). But the person who is intolerant has morally objectionable *attitudes*. Perhaps we could explain what is objectionable by saying that a person with these attitudes is likely not to help members of the group towards whom he feels disgust (or intense, unwarranted disapproval) in situations such as the one just described. But while it is probably true that such a person is less likely to help, the moral wrongness of the person's attitudes does not reduce to this. Even if he never helped anyone—in which case his failure to help *these* people would not be worse than his failure to help others—his intolerance is itself objectionable. It is objectionable both in itself and in the actions to which it gives rise. And only some of the objectionable actions to which it gives rise are objectionable for the reason that they violate a moral rule or fail to act in accordance with a moral ideal.

Some of the discussants at the Gert conference took issue with my claim that disgust towards gays and lesbians or interracial couples (etc.) is in itself morally objectionable. If someone feels disgust but makes an effort (and let us suppose it is a successful effort) to keep his disgust in check, should we say that because he has acted admirably in keeping his disgust in check, the disgust is not morally objectionable? (Suppose, for example, that he is a professor and succeeds in preventing his disgust from shaping his decisions about whom to hire and about whether or not to agree to direct a particular student's thesis.) The answer, in my view, is clearly *no*; but this seems to be a matter of intuition. The disgust, as I see it, remains objectionable, and not only because it is virtually sure to spill over into his conduct (e.g., in how he treats the thesis student and the people he hires despite his suspicion that they are gay).[6] It is morally objectionable in itself, as an instance of failing to respect persons as persons. To say that it is morally objectionable is not, of course, to say that the person who feels such disgust is responsible for feeling as he does; the question of responsibility is a separate question.[7]

III

Gert's emphasis on actions is prominent even in those sections of his book where he pays considerable attention to character and to judgments about persons. "A morally good person is one who does morally bad actions significantly less often than most and does morally good ones significantly more often than most" (319). He does soften this a little in the next paragraph, for he acknowledges that it is not only the action, but also the motive, that matters. "Good results, even if intentional, are not sufficient to make a person morally good; the appropriate motives are also important" (319-20). But that softens it only a little. The motives have to be appropriate for the action to count as morally good, and thus to reflect positively on the person, but this simply imposes a condition which actions have to meet to qualify as morally good. Actions are nonetheless the basic measure of the moral goodness of persons. We see this again in his discussion of moral standards, where he says that "the higher the moral standard, the more morally right and good actions are required for a person to be praised as moral or morally good" (321).

Why am I making a big deal out of this? Why would anyone object to Gert's claim about moral standards and the effect that they have on what is required for a person to be praised as morally good, or to his claim (quoted above) correlating a person's moral goodness to the frequency with which she performs morally good actions?

In each instance relevant considerations are ignored, for example, the obstacles that the person overcame in acting so impressively. Now Gert does mention obstacles, obstacles of one sort, anyway: temptations faced by the person in question. "Of two persons facing the same temptation," he writes, "we may praise the morally right action of the person who is tempted more than we praise the morally right action of the person who is not, but we admire the character of the latter more" (319). So we admire the character of the person who was less tempted more than that of the person who was more tempted.

I would argue that this depends on what sort of temptations we are picturing. It is true if the temptation in question is the temptation to embezzle, or to smash someone over the head when he has said something insulting. The really good person would not feel tempted. Of those who did feel tempted to embezzle or to smash someone over the head because of an insulting remark, certainly the better person is the one who is less tempted.

Gert's claim is less convincing if we imagine a different sort of temptation. Imagine a relief worker saying, "I was tempted to abandon the project; the heat, the stench, the sight of so much suffering were getting to me, and I longed for my air-conditioned office and the comfort and safety of my comparatively disease-free town." Or, "It was very difficult to be so far from my family, and I couldn't even be reached by phone, and just felt really lonely and desolate, so for a few days I was tempted to bail out." In these instances I don't think we admire the person who was tempted, and overcame the temptation, less than the person who wasn't tempted. We do not admire her less, since we do not judge it in any way a flaw that she was so tempted. We might even admire her more for having found it so hard to be away from her family, and in any case will admire her strength of character in overcoming the temptation to leave the project. If we consider other sorts of obstacles, obstacles less naturally described as temptations to be overcome, it is clear that the fact that the person had to overcome obstacles to persevere in her project makes us admire her character more. We admire more the character of the person who overcame shyness, or a fear of crowds or heights, in order to carry out important work; we also admire more the character of the person who overcame adverse circumstances (childhood poverty, for instance).[8]

The reason why Gert does not take such factors into account, I would venture to guess, is that he is thinking of character in terms of isolated actions rather than conduct viewed over a (considerable) stretch of time.[9] "A morally good person," he said (to repeat), "is one who does morally bad actions significantly less often than most and does morally good ones significantly more often than most." When we look at conduct, a great deal more enters in, including, crucially, the person's commitment to ongoing, demanding, and worthwhile projects. To tote up the number of good actions and compare that figure with the number of bad actions seems to be off the mark in the first place (even apart from the problem of how to individuate actions).[10]

IV

Gert's emphasis on actions is closely tied to the idea that to act wrongly is to violate a moral rule and to his position that an unjustified violation of a moral rule is punishable. Unjustified violations of the moral rules are punishable, he holds, and not just in some attenuated sense of "punishment." "Every civilized society enforces the moral rules. The criminal law is designed for precisely this purpose. In civilized societies the violation of every moral rule is punishable by the criminal law" (263).

What of those wrongs that do not deserve to be treated as crimes? Consider those who make malicious, biting remarks just to assert their own superiority and make others feel lousy; consider those who treat their friends or lovers badly, encouraging them to depend on them and leading them to expect an ongoing friendship when they have no such intention; consider those who divulge freely the confidences of friends who shared their secrets only after making sure that their confidantes would guard their secrets; consider parents who never read to their young children, and rarely talk with them, either, except to tell them what they must do, or reprimand them; consider Gert's example of José, who is standing on a street corner looking at the women who pass (but imagine, altering his example, that José isn't just looking, but ogling them, doing so conspicuously so as to get their attention). My view is that each of these actions or modes of conduct is morally wrong, but not deserving of punishment (at least not of punishment via criminal law).

Gert cannot take that position, for if the actions are morally wrong, they are punishable.[11] He must hold either that they are not morally wrong, or that they are, and are punishable. He can of course hold that they are punishable without holding that we ought to punish those who so act, and indeed he emphasizes that in saying that all unjustified violations of moral rules are punishable, he is saying that they *may* be punished, not that they *are* to be punished. "Situations may arise in which punishing [them] would cause significantly more evil than would result from failure to punish, for example, in political situations when attempting to punish might prevent the end of a civil war" (182). The point here is that sometimes actions are clearly illegal (and rightly so), but punishing those crimes is a bad idea because of the evil that is likely to result from carrying out the punishment. A different but related point is that criminalizing certain actions—i.e., having a law against these actions—itself has its costs. These include the increase in violence that often ensues when what is criminalized is a commodity for which there is an intense, often desperate, desire on the part of many people. (I am thinking here especially of the violence that attaches to the sale and distribution of illegal drugs.) Another cost, more relevant to our discussion, is the loss of freedom and privacy entailed by authorizing those who are encharged with enforcing the laws to investigate alleged violations of the laws in question. As Gert writes, "setting up a system that results in punishing all unjustified violations may cost more than it is worth. The potential for a significant loss of freedom may be considerably greater than the added protection against unjustified violations" (182).

It is thus open to Gert to say that actions of the sort I listed—malicious remarks aimed at putting someone down, failure to read to one's children, and so on—are moral wrongs, violations of some moral rule, and therefore punishable, but simply not worth punishing. As far as I can tell, he does not; he would, I think, say that (like José's annoying Maria by looking at her) these actions do not violate any rights. And although this would bar him from saying that the actions are morally wrong, he can at least classify them as morally bad. (To say that an action is morally bad, he explains in chapter 12, does not commit one to saying that it is punishable; to say that it is morally wrong does—with the exception noted in my endnote 11.)

Whether Gert considers the actions I listed to be morally wrong, and thus punishable, or instead holds that they are not morally wrong, I think they call into question the desirability of understanding "morally wrong" as conceptually tied to punishability.

That I find it far-fetched to say that something cannot be morally wrong unless it merits punishment is no doubt due in part to another difference I have with Gert, concerning the nature of morality: he holds that "morality is best conceived as a guide to behavior that rational persons put forward to govern the behavior of others, whether or not they plan to follow that guide themselves" (9). And: "morality is not primarily a guide for one's own behavior but rather is a guide to behavior that rational persons put forward to govern the behavior of others" (9-10). Now, if I have to choose between seeing morality as primarily a guide for one's own behavior, and seeing it as primarily a guide put forward to govern others' behavior, I will pick the former. In fact there are reasons to resist making this choice. Besides being concerned about my own conduct and about putting forward a guide to govern others' conduct (possibly, Gert emphasizes, without planning to follow that guide oneself), we have collective concerns. To improve ourselves as a society (as well as to improve and entertain ourselves as individuals) we support public radio and television, public funding for the arts, and subsidized adult education courses. We want to raise the next generation to be compassionate, creative, reflective, mindful of others' needs, and so on; and to this end we take various sorts of collective action, in the form of improving our schools, supporting tax increases that will provide better after-school programs, subsidized classes for children in art, music, and drama, well-directed youth soccer programs, and pleasant and safe neighborhood parks. In doing so we are neither focusing on our own individual conduct nor simply trying to get others to behave as they should. This is important to keep in mind. And we should note that it bears on Gert's emphasis on punishment, and on the link he sees between moral wrongness and punishment. One of the reasons for that link is that "only the infliction of an evil" will "discourage all rational persons from performing an unwanted act" (178). Be that as it may, surely the best way—the one that involves the least evil, at any rate—is to raise children in such a way that they will not be very tempted to act immorally, and to provide them with the judgment and self-control needed to overcome the temptations they do have.[12] But I digress. The point of the digression is to illustrate that the options he presents—morality is either primarily a guide for one's own behavior or primarily a guide to govern others' conduct—are more limited than they should be. (Moreover, the collective concerns that are not included in the picture he presents would, if addressed, have a bearing on the link he draws between immorality and punishment.) Having said that, I'll speak as if the options are as he presents them.

Choosing between his options, I see morality as primarily a guide for one's own behavior. This is not to deny that if I believe it is wrong for me to do *x*, I should hold that it is wrong for everyone who is similarly situated to do *x*; still, because it often is unclear what others' circumstances are, and thus unclear whether they are so situated that it is wrong for them to do *x*, it may happen that I do not make any judgments about them. If I do, they may be rather more tentative than my judgments to the effect that it is wrong for me to do *x*.[13] There is an additional reason, besides the difference between my knowledge of my circumstances and my knowledge of others' circumstances, for the primacy of my judgments that I should act in such-and-such a way over my judgments that others ought to: my behavior is clearly *my* responsibility. The behavior of others is generally not.[14]

Although I differ with Gert in his claim that "morality is not primarily a guide for one's own behavior," of course I agree that we make moral judgments about others (several a day, in fact; several a minute, on bad days). But I disagree with his claim that these judgments invariably entail a judgment that the party who acts morally wrongly deserves to be punished. And even when they do entail such a judgment, that judgment does not entail that it is appropriate for me or anyone else to punish the person. I can, for example, hold that a murderer deserves to die (a view which might be reflected in my thoughts, when I hear that he died an untimely death, that he got what he deserved) without thinking that capital punishment would be (or have been) morally appropriate.

Even before we get to the question of punishment, there is the question of whether we should interfere in any way at all, when we believe that someone is acting immorally. So in addition to denying that morality is mainly a guide put forward to govern the behavior of others, I am claiming that in those instances where we are concerned mainly about someone else's behavior, our judgment that they are acting immorally does not entail that we ought to try to get them to change their ways. The question of interference is a further question, separate from the question of whether they are acting immorally. That I think people ought, morally, to act in such and such a way does not entail that it is appropriate for me or anyone else to apply pressure on them to act accordingly. (And it certainly does not entail that it is appropriate for me or anyone else to compel them, by threat of punishment, to act accordingly.)

Let me offer some examples in support of my claim that judgments that someone acted morally wrongly do not entail a judgment that he deserves (if he has not already been punished) to be punished. Suppose I hear that one of my colleagues responded in the following way to a student's complaint about sexual harassment. To her complaint that another professor was repeatedly and insistently pressing her to have sex with him, my colleague responded by saying, "You're a very attractive woman; these things are going to happen to you, and you'll just have to get used to it." If I say that my colleague acted wrongly in responding in this way to the student, and mean *morally* wrongly, I need not hold that he deserves to be punished for having said this to her.

To take a different sort of example: I might judge, during a war, that Country X is acting wrongly in not joining in on peace talks, or that Country Y is morally wrong to provide weapons, or to refuse to join in on a condemnation of Country

Z's actions. In each of these cases I am making a moral judgment, saying that the country acted wrongly (morally wrongly), but I need not be saying that the country deserves to be punished.

Finally, before I quit offering reasons for questioning the conceptual link between wrongness and liability to punishment, I'd like to note the following problem. To claim, as Gert does, that an action is wrong only if it is punishable entails that we can only recognize the possibility of wrongs to oneself to the extent that we endorse legal paternalism.[15] Self-mutilation, a failure to take oneself seriously as a person, a failure to stand up for one's rights, a failure to take action to end one's addiction to alcohol or television—all of these can count as moral wrongs, if we accept Gert's position, only if they wrong someone other than the actor, or if the actor should be liable to punishment for the wrong she inflicts on herself (assuming, that is, that she does not act justifiably and does not have a legitimate excuse for acting as she does). I take this to be another reason to doubt the conceptual link he asserts between wrongness and liability to punishment. I realize, however, that this is not a consideration that would move Gert. Rather, it brings out deep differences in our views of morality. On Gert's view these are not moral wrongs (except insofar as they wrong others).[16]

V

The idea that punishability is conceptually tied to certain deontic concepts is not, of course, a new one. In *Utilitarianism*, Mill tied it to the notion of duty:

> It is a part of the notion of duty in every one of its forms that a person may rightfully be compelled to fulfill it. Duty is a thing which may be *exacted* from a person, as one exacts a debt. Unless we think that it may be exacted from him, we do not call it his duty. Reasons of prudence, or the interest of other people, may militate against actually exacting it, but the person himself, it is clearly understood, would not be entitled to complain. There are other things, on the contrary, which we wish that people should do, which we like or admire them for doing, perhaps dislike or despise them for not doing, but yet admit that they are not bound to do; it is not a case of moral obligation; we do not blame them, that is, we do not think that they are proper objects of punishment.[17]

Mill goes on to tie punishability to wrongness, as well:

> I think there is no doubt that this distinction lies at the bottom of right and wrong; that we call any conduct wrong, or employ, instead, some other term of dislike or disparagement, according as we think that the person ought, or ought not, to be punished for it; and we say it would be right to do so and so, or merely that it would be desirable or laudable, according as we would wish to see the person whom it concerns compelled, or only persuaded and exhorted, to act in that manner.[18]

We see in Mill, as in Gert, a fundamental division of morality into what is required, and what is merely encouraged. Gert is certainly not out on a limb in drawing such a division, nor in holding that if something is morally required, it is appropriate to demand compliance. Recall J. O. Urmson's influential article, "Saints and Heroes," which argued in favor of drawing a sharp distinction between what morality requires, and what he called "the higher flights of morality," which are beyond the call of duty. One of Urmson's arguments was that "it is part of the notion of a duty that we have a right to demand compliance from others."[19]

If you are happy with the Millian and Urmsonian picture, the only problem you might have with Gert's version of it is that there seems to be a gap that needs filling in, a gap, that is, between moral rules, unjustified violations of which are punishable via criminal law, and moral ideals. For that problem, we could look to Mill for a solution. What lies in between is the proper subject of exhortation, and, he suggests in *On Liberty*, might even call for a cold shoulder, or a chillier reception yet. We might choose to avoid people whose conduct we regard as, although not exactly wrong (for not punishable), disturbing enough to warrant our dislike, even perhaps to warrant being shunned by the rest of us. In response to the examples I gave earlier of conduct that I think of as wrong but not punishable, you might hold that the professor who responded to the student's report of sexual harassment by saying "You're very attractive; these things are going to happen, so you'd better get used to it" deserved a reprimand; that parents who don't read to their children deserve to be told by neighbors, relatives, teachers, or pediatricians that they are cheating their children; and that adults who make malicious remarks just to make themselves feel superior deserve to be shunned. (I find this forced, not mainly because I doubt that they deserve this, but because I don't see why a claim that the conduct is wrong or immoral entails it. Surely one can say that such actions are wrong without taking a stand regarding what sort of response from others the actors deserve.)

On Liberty offers considerable detail regarding appropriate behavior towards bad conduct Mill says in chapter 1 that if the conduct is not harmful to others, we may remonstrate with the actor, reason with him, persuade him, or entreat him, but may not compel him or visit him with any evil in case he doesn't heed our entreaties.[20] He adds in chapter 4 that unless conduct that is harmful to others injures any of those interests which "either by express legal provision or by tacit understanding, ought to be considered as rights," the offender may be "justly punished by opinion, though not by law."[21] So only those actions that harm (or threaten to harm) others entail a right on the part of others to interfere in such a way as to compel the person to alter his conduct, and of those actions, only those that violate others' rights merit punishment beyond punishment by opinion. Mill offers still more detail on what sort of reaction is appropriate towards those who in various ways are deficient in virtue. Even if the person does not harm others (or even himself),

> We have a right . . . to act upon our unfavorable opinion of anyone, not to the oppression of his individuality, but in the exercise of ours. We are not bound, for example, to seek his society; we have a right to avoid it (though not to parade the avoidance). . . . We have a right, and it may be our duty, to caution others against him if we think his example or conversation likely to have a pernicious effect on those with whom he associates. We may give others a preference over him in optional good offices, except those which tend to his improvement. In these various modes a person may suffer very severe penalties at the hands of others for faults which directly concern only himself; but he suffers these penalties only in so far as they are the natural, and, as it were, the spontaneous consequences of the faults themselves, not because they are purposely inflicted on him for the sake of punishment.[22]

Mill's thoughtful remarks are helpful if we think that Gert's basic approach is fine, but that a gap needs to be filled in. It is noteworthy that Gert talks about punishment and encouragement, but not about discouragement.[23] A modest revision would take care of that problem. Both Mill and Gert link the violation of duty to punishability; but Mill offers more options between punishment for clear wrongs and encouragement to follow moral ideals.

VI

This does not seem to me to be an optimal solution, mainly for reasons indicated above. I do not think it is a good idea to tie our basic moral concepts to the responses merited from those in a position to mete out punishment, scorn, discouragement, encouragement, or praise. I prefer to think about morality from the perspective of the agent thinking about how to conduct herself, what course of action to take, what projects to immerse herself in, rather than from the perspective of an onlooker judging others' conduct or (worse yet) trying to get others to behave as they should.[24] Clearly, this reflects a deep disagreement with Gert, who holds that "Anyone who takes the trouble to look at what is normally considered to be morality realizes that morality is not primarily a guide for one's own behavior but rather is a guide to behavior that rational persons put forward to govern the behavior of others" (9).[25]

The approach to deontic concepts that I favor—not surprisingly, a Kantian approach—decouples moral requirements from punishability or coercive intervention of any other sort (and even from gentle methods of trying to get others to act as they should). It recognizes a range of duties, some of which, the "juridical" duties, entail a right to exact compliance, while others, the "ethical" duties, do not. Moreover, the ethical duties themselves divide into the imperfect and the perfect duties—but to that shortly. I want first to emphasize that only juridical duties entail corresponding rights to exercise compulsion. Ethical duties do not. It is worth noting that one of Gert's criticisms of Kant turns on an assumption that all ethical duties do entail such rights. Gert claims:

> the categorical imperative permits far too many paternalistic actions to count as morally acceptable. A rational person, in Kant's sense, cannot only allow but can even will that everyone cause pain to a person in order to save that person's life, even if that action requires overruling that person's rational (in the normal sense) refusal. Kant explicitly claims that the categorical imperative rules out suicide because of pain, so that it seems quite likely that he would actually endorse the paternalistic overruling of competent patients' rational (in the normal sense) refusals of life-prolonging treatment. (242)

It would seem likely *if* Kant held that if it is wrong to do *x*, it is appropriate to interfere with others' conduct to stop them from doing *x*. But he emphatically does not hold this. Only if the wrong in question is a violation of a juridical duty would the inference hold. The duty not to commit suicide is an ethical, not a juridical, duty. (And whether Kant would regard a refusal of life-prolonging treatment as suicide is by no means clear.)

If we decouple the concept of duty from punishability, treating those duties the (unjustified) violation of which is punishable, as a special type of duty, it becomes easier to recognize the complexity of moral requirements. Morality encompasses both self-directed and other directed "oughts," and it encompasses duties that vary as to how much latitude they allow us. Here I am thinking of the division of ethical duties into perfect and imperfect duties. This is not a classification that wins Gert's praise. "Duties of imperfect obligation," he writes, "are not duties any more than false friends are friends. They share almost none of the features of real duties" (16). I think what he has in mind is what we have already discussed: they do not entail a right to exact compliance. (Nor, in most instances, do they entail other corresponding rights; my duty to perfect myself morally does not entail a right on the part of anyone that I act accordingly.)[26]

The distinction between perfect and imperfect duties is admittedly not the tidiest of distinctions and is more of a scalar notion than a clean division. If we envision a scale ranging from the narrowest duties to the widest, juridical duties are the narrowest and wide imperfect duties are the widest.[27] In addition, juridical duties are duties to perform certain sorts of actions (or, more typically, to refrain from performing certain sorts of actions), whereas ethical duties provide less direction with respect to what actions one should perform. Ethical duties are, first and foremost, duties to have certain ends, specifically, others' happiness and one's own perfection. (Once again, the distinction is more nearly scalar than a clear divide; perfect duties are, qua ethical duties, primarily duties to adopt an end, but they do give a fairly clear indication of how one ought to act. The indication is less definite when the ethical duties in question are imperfect, as are duties to promote others' happiness or to develop one's talents.)

One implication of this way of thinking about duty (and other deontic concepts) is that there is more continuity between what is strictly required and (as Gert would classify it) ideals (both moral ideals and nonmoral ones). Helping others is morally required. It is not merely an ideal, and never to help others would decidedly be wrong. (At the same time, it is by no means morally required to help others at all opportunities, or as much as one can. But the duty of benevolence should not be mistaken for a duty that says "Now and then, do help others, but it's fine to help only when it's really easy." Such a maxim would not be consistent with, much less reflect, a genuine commitment to the obligatory end of others' happiness.)

A related difference between Gert's theory and the Kantian approach that I favor is that virtue is quite separate, in Gert's theory, from what we are morally required to do, whereas in Kant's ethics, it is not. We have duties not to be arrogant[28] or contemptuous,[29] and to be forgiving.[30] Character has a more prominent place in Kantian ethics, and is not reduced to dispositions to act in certain ways.[31]

The Kantian approach stands in stark contrast to Gert's picture and to that of Urmson and others who favor a sharp division between what we are morally required to do and what it would be good (but not morally obligatory) to do. In Kantian ethics, perfecting oneself (both morally and in terms of natural talents) and helping others are obligatory, but these duties leave us more latitude than do perfect duties. This precludes the gap between moral rules and moral ideals that I, anyway, find problematic, and also shifts the focus away from isolated actions, onto conduct (viewed over a stretch of time), the agent's ends, and, more generally, character.

Notes

* I am grateful to discussants at the Dartmouth conference, May 13-16, 1999, for their helpful comments on my paper, and in particular to David Cummiskey. Thanks too to Walter Sinnott-Armstrong both for his excellent work in organizing the conference and for his comments on several drafts of this paper, and to Bernard Gert for his comments on the penultimate draft.

1. Bernard Gert, *Morality: Its Nature and Justification* (New York: Oxford Univer-

sity Press, 1998), 9. All references to Gert will be to this work and will be inserted parenthetically in the text.

2. In endorsing Gert's claim that these two must not be conflated, I do not mean to endorse all that he says in characterizing compassion and kindness. E. J. Bond rightly points out in his contribution to this conference that kindness is not exclusively (or even primarily) concerned with the relief of suffering.

3. Sometimes he includes "virtue" in his definition of morality, sometimes he doesn't; and at the start of his chapter "Virtues and Vices" he apparently remembers only the definitions that did not include it, for he says, "I have defined morality without even mentioning virtue or vice" (277). Thanks to Walter Sinnott-Armstrong for drawing my attention to that passage.

4. Michael Slote, "Virtue Ethics," in Marcia Baron, Philip Pettit, and Michael Slote, *Three Methods of Ethics: A Debate* (Malden, Mass.: Blackwell, 1997), 175-238.

5. I note here another point of agreement with Gert: I share his view that we are responsible to some considerable extent for our own characters (280), and I agree with him that a touchstone in thinking about ethics, especially about character, is how we should, and properly do, raise children (278).

6. Saying that it is objectionable in no way precludes the possibility of admiring them (even rightly admiring them) for having managed to keep the disgust in check, particularly if their success in this sets them off from their peers. Someone raised to be a racist might fail to extinguish some visceral racism—he might find it distasteful to shake hands with or share a dormitory room with a member of that race—but might merit some credit for having rejected the racist beliefs inculcated in him by his parents and teachers and partially overcome the racist attitudes. He might, in short, deserve credit for having overcome his racism to the extent that he has, and for his effort to overcome it further, while at the same time the racist sentiments that he hasn't overcome remain morally objectionable.

7. Some discussants at the Gert conference rightly questioned whether such disgust, even if it is objectionable, constitutes intolerance. Perhaps not. Someone who is disgusted by homosexuality but has a strong commitment to political liberalism (and abides by that commitment) might be tolerant—at least in a narrow sense of "tolerant."

8. See Elizabeth Pybus, "Saints and Heroes," *Philosophy* 57, no. 220 (1982): 193-99, for a good discussion of the relevance of such obstacles to what counts, and what should count, as heroism.

9. In correspondence (July 1999), Gert has told me that he does not think this is the reason. He writes, "Your examples of obstacles and temptations that I don't talk about is simply a lapse on my part and I agree with you that if the temptations are of the kind that you cite, I would not view them as a sign of a lesser character than someone who is not tempted. They are excellent examples, and I simply did not think of them when I was thinking of temptations."

10. I'm reminded here of R. M. Adams's discussion of Susan Wolf's "Moral Saints," specifically, of Wolf's characterization of moral saints. Wolf writes: "By *moral saint* I mean a person whose every action is as morally good as possible," and then adds "a person, that is, who is as morally worthy as can be." [Wolf, "Moral Saints," *Journal of Philosophy* 79, no. 9 (August 1982): 419-39. The quote is from page 419.] Adams comments, "Her words imply that these two characterizations amount to the same thing, but it seems to me that the first expresses at most a very questionable test for the satisfaction of the second. The idea that only a morally imperfect person would spend half an hour doing something morally indifferent, like taking a nap, when she could have done something morally praiseworthy instead, like spending the time in moral self-examination, is at odds with our usual judgments." [R. M. Adams, "Saints," *Journal of Philosophy* 81, no. 7 (July 1984): 392-401. The quote is from page 393.]

11. This needs to be qualified. On page 328 Gert refines his account of "morally wrong," observing that although a morally wrong action is usually an unjustified violation of the moral rules (and hence punishable), it can also be an instance of adhering to a moral rule when one should in fact violate the moral rule in order to follow a moral ideal. "An action that is in accordance with a moral rule when all impartial rational persons would publicly allow violating the rule in order to follow a moral ideal also counts as a morally wrong action." Yet only violations of moral rules (more specifically, unjustified violations of some moral rule) are punishable. "This class of morally wrong actions [i.e., adhering to a moral rule when one should instead follow a moral ideal] differs from unjustified violations of the moral rules in that only for the latter do all impartial rational persons favor liability to punishment." This exception to the rule that if an action is morally wrong, it is punishable, needs to be kept in mind, but I do not think that it bears on my argument, since none of my examples are instances of adhering to a moral rule when one should instead violate the moral rule in order to follow a moral ideal.

12. These reflections are prompted by discussions with David Cummiskey.

13. Not always, however. Sometimes I'll feel (with or without good reason) very sure indeed that it is wrong for them to do *x*, and I may be quite outraged over their conduct.

14. One exception is when those others are my children, and are minors, in which case their behavior is partially my responsibility (decreasingly, as they get older).

15. Or, if the wrong to self is not a harm, but a wrong in some other form, legal moralism.

16. While I am on the subject of punishment I'd like to register another disagreement, this one stemming from Gert's conception of "basic reasons." In discussing punishment, he seeks to show that he is not committed to saying that because "being punished involves being inflicted with an evil and no rational person wants to suffer an evil," it "is irrational for a person to voluntarily confess his crime and willingly submit to punishment" (102). There are, he explains, two reasons that people (who are not acting irrationally) have for wanting to be punished. "These reasons fall into two broad categories. One is psychological: some people feel extraordinarily uncomfortable when they know they are guilty of some crime and are not punished. They submit to punishment in order to relieve themselves of these unpleasant feelings. The other reason I shall call moral: some people seek to be punished because they believe that by confessing they are making it more likely that less evil will be suffered by others" (102). But what of the other kind of moral reason: suppose they believe that they deserve to be punished? Let's imagine that they do not think about the deterrent effect on others, and do not feel that they need to be deterred (for they are genuinely remorseful, they resolve never again to act as they did, and they are confident that they'll keep to their resolve). So their reason for confessing and submitting to punishment is not that they think that by doing so they make it more likely that less evil will be suffered by others. If asked, they might acknowledge that it will make some people happy to know that the perpetrator has confessed and is in jail, but they nonetheless are not confessing in order to confer this benefit. They are confessing because it is the right thing to do, and because they know that they deserve to be punished. It is noteworthy that, given Gert's conception of basic reasons, this would not make their action rational. It has to count as an irrational action. (Bear in mind that I am not claiming that it is common to confess and submit oneself to punishment because one believes that it is the right thing to do, and that one deserves to be punished; I am claiming, rather, that to do so would not be irrational.)

17. John Stuart Mill, *Utilitarianism* (Indianapolis: Hackett, 1979), 47.

18. Mill, *Utilitarianism*, 48. Earlier in the same paragraph Mill suggests a much

looser notion of what counts as punishment, so loose that if that were all that was meant by tying "wrong" to "deserves to be punished" or "ought to be punished," I would have little, if any, objection: "We do not call anything wrong unless we mean to imply that a person ought to be punished in some way or other for doing it—if not by law, by the opinion of his fellow creatures; if not by opinion, by the reproaches of his own conscience" (47). I have no quarrel with the notion that we don't call something wrong if we don't think that the person deserves the reproaches of his own conscience, though I wouldn't say that we "mean to imply" this. Not surprisingly, the addition that makes Mill's view more congenial to me makes it less congenial to Gert, who takes Mill to task for including "reproaches of his own conscience" (16). In any event Mill seems to be on Gert's side rather than mine; it seems clear that Mill doesn't mean for the addition to do much work. In the passage quoted above he ties "wrong" to "ought to be punished" in the fairly narrow sense of punishment that involves coercion by others, not merely the pangs of one's conscience.

19. J. O. Urmson, "Saints and Heroes," in *Moral Concepts*, ed. Joel Feinberg (London: Oxford University Press, 1969), 60-73, 71. Unlike Gert, Urmson doesn't claim that if we are unsuccessful in our demands for compliance, we have a right to punish by using the force of the law. (One might argue that Urmson intends this to be understood, but that is not evident to me.)

20. Mill, *On Liberty* (Indianapolis: Hackett, 1978), 9.

21. Mill, *On Liberty*, 73.

22. Mill, *On Liberty*, 75-76.

23. I am indebted to Walter Sinnott-Armstrong for this observation.

24. I am also happy to think about morality from the standpoint of a parent of a young child or an educator of young children, thinking about what sorts of qualities to foster in these children. And, as noted earlier, a collective standpoint is a very important one: we ask what, as a community, we can do to improve the quality of life, etc.

25. In his chapter on moral judgments, Gert stresses that a person making a genuine moral judgment "need not be motivated to act according to his own moral judgments." For it to be the case that he is making a genuine moral judgment, it has to be the case that he wants others to act on the judgment, but he need not be prepared to act on it himself (313). I don't see any reason for believing the latter—that he needn't be prepared to act on it himself—and very little reason for accepting the former—that he must want others to act on the judgment. If it is crucial to making a moral judgment that one have some particular attitude towards others' compliance with the judgment, it is not the attitude of *wanting* others to act in accordance with the judgment, but of believing that they *should* so act.

This bears on Gert's criticism of those who accept the overridingness thesis. He says that they deny that "there are any people who want others to act morally, but who do not care whether or not their own behavior is in accord with common morality" (314). But that is not what they deny. They are aware that some people want precisely that, but they—those who accept the overridingness thesis—deny that such people believe that those others morally *ought* to act in such and such a way. To make a moral judgment need not involve *wanting* others to act a certain way. It is to take a stand that people, in certain circumstances, and meeting a certain description, morally ought to act in such and such a way; and this applies to oneself as well as to others.

A comment is in order on Gert's characterization of the overridingness thesis. He characterizes it as follows: those who accept it hold that "what makes a judgment a moral judgment is that its maker regards it as one that cannot be overridden; that is, the maker is always prepared to act on his moral judgments regardless of any conflicting nonmoral judgments" (313). Gert says that this can be "softened" to allow for weakness of will—I'd say that it already allows for it, or else that it needs restating. I took it that "always prepared to act on his moral judgments" doesn't mean that one in fact always will act on one's moral judgments. If Gert intended it to mean that, his statement doesn't capture what those who accept the overridingness thesis accept. In any event, Gert says that "even if the overridingness thesis is softened by allowing for weakness of will and regret that one did not act as one judges people morally ought to act, it is still too strong. It denies that there are any people who want others to act morally, but who do not care whether or not their own behavior is in accord with common morality" (314). As I argued above, that is not the case.

26. Another reason why he thinks that duties of imperfect obligation are not real duties is that (with the exception of justified violations), moral rules must be obeyed all the time, and "with regard to everyone" (122). If it is not my duty to help everyone, and help all the time, then it cannot be the case that I have a general duty of beneficence, in Gert's view. Shelly Kagan's contribution to this volume brings out the importance of that position to Gert's rejection of a duty of beneficence, and provides an excellent critique of his rejection of positive duties.

27. I follow Thomas Hill, Jr. in using "wide imperfect duties" to refer to those imperfect duties that have the most latitude. See Hill, *Dignity and Practical Reason in Kant's Moral Theory* (Ithaca, N.Y.: Cornell University Press, 1992), ch. 8.

28. Immanuel Kant, *The Metaphysics of Morals*, trans. Mary Gregor (New York: Cambridge University Press, 1991), 465.

29. Kant, *The Metaphysics of Morals*, 463.

30. Kant, *The Metaphysics of Morals*, 461.

31. I discuss this more fully in my *Kantian Ethics Almost without Apology* (Ithaca, N.Y.: Cornell University Press, 1995) and in Baron, Pettit, and Slote, *Three Methods of Ethics*.

Part VI: Reply

16

Replies to My Critics

Bernard Gert

There is no way to do justice to the many excellent articles in this volume in the space allotted. Indeed, it is unlikely that I could do justice to them even if I had unlimited space. My replies to each of these articles shall focus on three areas: (1) explanations of the differences between my accounts of impartiality, rationality, and morality and the standard accounts of these concepts; (2) clarifications of the views that I have not changed; (3) revisions of some aspects of my accounts of morality and rationality. I hope these explanations, clarifications, and changes will satisfy those whose criticisms were responsible for them.

Reply to Tugendhat

Professor Tugendhat's close examination and comparison of two versions of my account of morality has taught me much, not least of which is that changes in what I say are subject to more interpretations than I had realized. Professor Tugendhat's central concern is with the primary task of the book, the justification of morality. As his paper makes clear, he originally thought that I had completely changed what I meant by justifying morality from *The Moral Rules* to *Morality,* but later realized that the change was "more subtle." He is correct that there was a change.

In *The Moral Rules* I thought that I could motivate all rational persons to endorse morality by showing that it was irrational for any person not to endorse it. Even then I realized that I was not providing a genuine motivation to actual people, for I regarded it as irrational not to endorse morality only if the beliefs that were used were limited to those shared by all other rational persons, i.e., to rationally required beliefs. Since no actual person is limited to rationally required beliefs, no actual rational person need be motivated by my justification of morality.

In the intervening years, I came to have a different view of philosophy, as well as to recognize that I had made some serious mistakes in that earliest justification of morality. My realization that I could not provide the kind of simple relationship between rationality and morality that I, Professor Tugendhat, and many others wanted, was accompanied by a realization that I had sometimes incorrectly taken "publicly advocating" as advocating out loud, or actually advocating to others. This mistaken understanding of "publicly advocate" is what led me to conclude falsely that all rational persons would publicly advocate the moral attitude toward the moral rules.

In *Morality* I eliminated the term "publicly advocate" completely, and concentrated on making explicit the conditions that were needed in order to guarantee that all rational persons would take the moral attitude toward the moral rules. I had always realized that a restriction to rationally required beliefs was necessary even to guarantee that all rational persons would take the egocentric attitude toward the moral rules. I came to realize that this restriction was not sufficient to guarantee that all rational persons would move from the egocentric attitude to the moral attitude and that a further condition was needed. All rational persons would move from the egocentric attitude toward the moral rules to the moral attitude toward them only if at least one of the following three further conditions were accepted: (1) they were seeking agreement among all rational persons, or (2) they were impartial with regard to all rational persons with respect to obeying the rules that I list as the basic moral rules, or (3) they viewed the rules as part of the moral system, which is a public system that applies to all rational persons.

I had not provided any motivation for a rational person to accept either the restriction to rationally required beliefs or to accept conditions (1), (2), or (3). This is why I said, "In a very important sense, this problem cannot be solved" (*Morality,* 167). By this problem, I meant the problem of convincing all rational persons to move from the egocentric attitude toward the moral rules to the moral attitude toward them. Philosophers can only show the conceptual relationship between different concepts; they cannot provide new beliefs that will motivate all rational persons. However, clearing up intellectual confusions that have led some people to doubt the rationality of morality may help those who have been brought up properly not only to endorse morality but also to act morally. Professor Tugendhat is correct that I no longer regard my more complex justification as providing motivating force to all rational persons.

Professor Tugendhat suggests that there is a fourth way to show that all rational persons would take the moral attitude toward the moral rules, namely, by adding the condition that "you want to arrive at a system of norms that is justifiable to the others (and, in the last resort, to everybody)" (28). However, as he recognizes, a rational person need not care about justifying his system of norms to others, let alone everybody. Thus his fourth way, which I consider as an important addition to my three ways, is equivalent to them in all essential respects. None of them provides motivation to all rational persons to endorse morality. It remains rationally allowed not only not to act morally, but also not to accept the conditions that require one to endorse morality.

Professor Tugendhat's proposal suggests another way that one could justify morality, one that resembles the way that I originally proposed in *The Moral Rules*. Start with the restriction to rationally required beliefs, then using Professor Tugendhat's proposal, add the condition that one is attempting to justify the moral rules (or the whole moral system) to a particular person. This new condition takes advantage of the fact that the restriction to rationally required beliefs includes knowing nothing about the person to whom one is attempting to justify morality except that he has all the rationally required beliefs. Confronted with this additional condition, all rational persons would put forward the moral attitude toward the moral rules as well as endorsing morality as an informal public system that applies to all.

This final way of justifying morality seems as elegant, if not more so, than any of the previous ways, and I must thank Professor Tugendhat for leading me to it. Nonetheless, my view that what I am doing is showing the conceptual relationship between rationality, impartiality, and morality is unchanged. I am specifying the conditions that need to be added to the restriction to rationally required beliefs to show that all rational persons would endorse morality. Although the condition that I have developed from Professor Tugendhat's proposal seems to provide motivation for endorsing morality to actual people, it does not, for no actual rational person is ever restricted to rationally required beliefs and people do not usually attempt to justify their attitude toward the moral rules or toward morality as a whole to anyone.

Professor Tugendhat is correct that it was my realization that one could favor a truncated version of morality, i.e., a system like morality except that it did not protect all rational persons, that made me realize that a rational person need not seek agreement among all rational persons. He is also correct that in the latest version of my theory I provide a more definitive account of morality. I do this in order to make sure that I am justifying what ordinary people normally regard as morality. I do not want to limit morality to what can be strongly justified to all actual rational persons. Rather, I want to retain the common sense of morality and then see what conditions are needed before one can conclude that all rational persons would endorse it.

Contrary to Professor Tugendhat's original speculation, I introduced the concept of impartiality because of my realization that my neglect of the concept of impartiality in *The Moral Rules*, whose index does is not even contain the term "impartiality," created some important problems in my moral theory. I also became aware that there was no adequate account of impartiality in the philosophical literature. Indeed, there were practically no accounts of it at all. Rather, as I had done in *The Moral Rules*, some new technical concept was used in place of that kind of impartiality required by morality, moral impartiality. I realized that other philosophers, e.g., Kant and Rawls, had made a similar error; they had replaced moral impartiality by their own special technical concepts, viz., the Categorical Imperative and the veil of ignorance. All three of these technical concepts, public advocacy, Rawls's veil of ignorance, and Kant's Categorical Imperative distort the concept of moral impartiality.

Professor Tugendhat is concerned about my claim that people are only encouraged to follow the moral ideals which involve preventing or relieving harm, whereas they are required to obey the moral rules which involve avoiding causing harm. This concern, which Kagan and Deigh also have, may be due, at least in part, to a misunderstanding of what I mean by saying that we are *required* to obey the moral rules. I do not mean that the motivation of the individual obeying the rule need be different from the motivation for following the ideal. I mean that all rational persons would favor liability to punishment only for failure to impartially obey the general moral rules, not for failure to impartially follow the general moral ideals. However, some rational persons might favor enforcing some more restricted moral ideals, that is, making them into duties.

Morality requires doing something only when all rational persons favor liability to punishment for not doing it. Not all rational persons agree that following the general moral ideals should be enforced. This does not mean that when a moral rule and a moral ideal conflict, all rational persons agree that the moral rule should always be followed. On the contrary, in some situations, all impartial rational persons may favor following the ideal, e.g., heroically rescuing a person from a burning building when this conflicts with keeping some non-critical promise. The essential difference between the general moral rules and the general moral ideals is that all rational persons favor liability to punishment for all significant violations of the former, but they do not all favor such liability for significant failures to follow the latter.

Taking seriously the consequences of making some action or nonaction liable to punishment involves giving a government the power to enforce the general moral ideals. That people are fallible and that they differ from one another in their estimates of the results of requiring people to act in various ways are rationally required beliefs. Given these beliefs, and that it is impossible to impartially follow any general moral ideal all of the time, some rational persons would not want to give any government the power to enforce following the general moral ideals. This argument may not convince all rational persons, but it is rational to be convinced by it. That all rational persons must favor enforcement before any act is morally required is all that is necessary to show that following the general moral ideals is not morally required.

Reply to Kettner

Matthias Kettner is correct that my account of common morality and its justification does not resolve those ethical questions that we most want to have resolved. Nonetheless, the framework that I provide can be used to limit the decisions reached to morally acceptable ones. Using my account of the moral system to provide such a limit guarantees that any consensus that is reached will be morally acceptable and, thus, solves an important problem for discourse ethics.

My account of moral reasoning can be adapted to deal with controversial moral issues. When making actual moral judgments, beliefs are not restricted to rationally required beliefs. They cannot be so restricted for actual moral judgments require knowledge about the particular situation to which they apply. It is only when formulating and justifying the basic moral system that people are restricted to rationally required beliefs. When making actual moral judgments or adopting norms, it is appropriate to use beliefs that are shared by all persons participating in the discussion and affected by the judgment or norm concerning the controversial moral issue. Further, even beliefs not yet shared by all of them, but which can be checked by some universally accepted procedure, are allowed. However, when making any moral judgments, no one participating in the discussion may use any beliefs which cannot be checked by such a procedure. This means that unless there is unanimity in religious beliefs among all those participating and affected by the judgment, no religious beliefs can be used as an essential part of the justification of any judgment or norm.

Using beliefs that are shared or that can be checked may result in the participants reaching agreement which they would not have reached if they limited themselves to rationally required beliefs. All the participants and those affected might also agree, or be close enough, in their rankings of all of the goods and evils involved, to enable them to reach an agreement which would not be possible when all rational persons are involved. It may even be that a shared history and experience may lead the participants to much closer estimations of the effects of publicly allowing a given kind of violation of a particular moral rule than would be arrived at if all rational persons were involved. Further, there may be more agreement on the scope of morality, that is, on who is impartially protected by morality, than would be in the larger group. People who agree that newborns and late term fetuses are in the impartially protected group, will agree about far more than those who have a wider disagreement about who is in this group. Thus, simply taking advantage of the greater agreement that a group smaller than that of all rational persons would have when making an actual moral judgment can result in the achieving of consensus concerning norms or policies that would not be reached in the larger group.

I have served for over two decades on the ethics committee of a hospital, and we have reached consensus on many issues that would not have been agreed to by all impartial rational persons. This group not only had greater agreement on facts, they tended to rank the goods and evils similarly, and their shared experience led them to estimate similarly the consequences of publicly allowing a kind of violation. Most of these cases did not involve the scope of morality, for there was not the same agreement on this matter that there was on the previous two sources of moral disagreement. I do not deny that the kind of communication supported by discourse ethics can actually achieve significant results. Some ethics committee discussions were discussions that came very close to embodying the requirements of discourse ethics, or of my variation, and resulted in achieving a consensus that was not present at the beginning of the discussion.

However, such reasoning will not be successful in resolving all controversial issues. Even though agreement on all of the relevant facts, including the beliefs about the probabilities of various outcomes, results in consensus surprisingly often, it does not always result in consensus. Although disagreement about the facts is by far the greatest source of moral disagreement, there are three other sources of disagreement: (1) different rankings of the harms (evils) and benefits (goods); (2) different estimates of the effects of a given kind of violation being publicly allowed; and (3) different views about the membership in the group that is impartially protected by morality. It is a serious mistake for discourse ethics to think that a consensus can be reached concerning all moral controversies.

Engaging in a discourse governed by the conditions specified by discourse ethics, or my variation, is an admirable way to attempt to resolve moral disagreement. But it is not only wrong but dangerous to assume that consensus would be reached if people continued talking and all were fully informed, impartial, and rational. Such an attitude may lead the participants to think that the failure to achieve consensus is due to the ignorance, partiality, or irrationality of those who fail to join the consensus. Of course, it is necessary that any conclusion "could be accepted by" all participants, in the sense that it would not be irrational for any of them to accept it. But it is important to recognize that equally informed, impartial, rational persons can continue to disagree forever. Acknowledging that, within limits, moral disagreement is not only legitimate but unavoidable, allows for more fruitful negotiation and compromise. It allows participants to accept the decision of those with whom they disagree without losing their moral integrity. This is extremely important if the same group of people, as on an ethics committee, must continue to work together to resolve moral dilemmas and formulate norms and policies.

When disagreements cannot be resolved, then it is morally acceptable to reach a decision by voting and acting in accordance with the will of the majority. If the moral framework sets the limits of the discussion, and the participants have determined all of the relevant facts, then the decision reached by the majority will be morally acceptable. It may be that Habermas requires a consensus, because he does not acknowledge a universally accepted moral framework that guarantees acceptable moral decisions. Thus he is unduly concerned that the majority might adopt an immoral policy. Of course, in real life, that is possible, but it is also possible that any actual consensus will result in an immoral decision being made. It is only the correct application of common morality to the problem that guarantees that no unacceptable moral decision will be made.

A critical feature of moral reasoning is that it requires a limitation on the use of beliefs to those beliefs that could be accepted as reasons by every moral agent. This means that even if the discussion is between members of the same religion, and only those who are members of that religion will be affected by the decision to adopt a given norm, the reasons offered will not be moral reasons and the norm will not be a moral norm, unless the reasons and the norm could be accepted by every moral agent. Discourse ethics does not clearly distinguish between moral reasoning and moral norms and the reasoning and norms of a group with regard to norms that affect only members of that group.

If all discussants and those affected by the norm share certain beliefs and count them as reasons, discourse ethics regards those reasons as an appropriate part of the moral reasoning leading to the decision and the norm involved as a moral norm. Such "reasons" may be appropriate for that discourse and the norm appropriate for that group, but they are not moral reasons, nor is that norm a moral norm. Although this may not create any practical limitation on decisions, it is important to recognize that, if acceptability is limited to any group smaller than all moral agents, then the reasons do not count as moral reasons and the norm is not a moral norm. This is important because at some later time other people may be affected, and it will be confusing or worse, if the original norms are regarded as moral norms.

Although reasons which are shared by all those who are discussants and who are affected by the decision may be appropriate for use in that limited group, e.g., a particular religious group, they are not appropriate for use in a larger and more diverse group. When the group includes those who are not members of the religious group in question, whether members of different religions, or members of no religion at all, no beliefs that would be counted as reasons only by those who are members of the religious group can be used in the discussion. The only kind of beliefs that can be used in all discussions are those beliefs that every rational person counts as a reason. For example, it is not a reason against some act, e.g., dressing in a certain way, that some sacred writing prohibits dressing in that way. However, it is a reason against dressing in that way that it greatly upsets members of the religion. This belief or fact does serve as a reason for prohibiting that kind of act, but it is a reason on a par with the desires and aversions of others. This may seem to trivialize religious beliefs, but there is no acceptable alternative. If members of a religion can claim their religious beliefs provide strong reasons even though others do not regard them as reasons at all, there will be no way to arrive at any mutually acceptable solution.

The acceptability of abortion is an excellent example of a controversial matter and, contrary to what is commonly accepted, need not involve the use of religious beliefs. Someone who is anti-abortion need not support her views with religious beliefs, for she is as entitled to regard all fetuses as deserving the impartial protection of morality as others are entitled not to so regard them. Discussions of the stage at which fetuses deserve impartial protection may not achieve any kind of consensus. Even if they did, this consensus would be limited to that group and would not have any weight in the discussions of other groups. The limitation to rationally required beliefs allows rational persons to hold either that fetuses are part of the impartially protected group or that they are not.

All of the standard arguments on both sides of the question are well known and no consensus has been reached. Nor will any amount of discussion lead to consensus, because, as mentioned earlier, the scope of morality is an unresolvable matter. Realizing that consensus is not attainable, discussants can concentrate on points about which everyone agrees. Abortions are not desirable activities but are engaged in because the pregnant woman regards the alternative as worse. It would be better if there were less unwanted pregnancies, including those pregnancies that often end in abortions. Those who are anti-abortion and those who are pro-choice are in agreement that it would be desirable to have less unwanted pregnancies.

Now the discussion can shift to what can be done to limit unwanted pregnancies. There are many things that can be done, including endorsing that kind of sex education that has proven to be effective in lessening unwanted pregnancies. Making contraception easily available is clearly another. Now the discussion switches from one about abortion to one about the pros and cons of sex education and easily available contraception. This discussion is more capable of resolution than that concerning abortion, for with the limitation to rationally required beliefs, the issues depends solely on the consequences of using these methods of reducing unwanted pregnancies.

Kettner is concerned with my proposal to count "any reason as adequate if any significant group of otherwise rational people regard that reason as adequate, that is, if they regard the harm avoided or benefit gained to compensate for the harm suffered" (*Morality,* 57). Unfortunately, Kettner puts the matter in a misleading way. He asks, "Why are good reasons indexed to groups of rational evaluators ?" (36) He goes on to talk of better and worse reasons, as if my talk of adequate reasons could be simply translated into talk of better and worse reasons, but the notion of a better or stronger reason is an objective matter. If a significant group of people rank a given amount of pain as worse than a specific disability, and another significant group of people rank that same specific disability as worse than that same given amount of pain, then the belief that one will avoid that amount of pain is neither a better nor a worse reason than the belief that one will avoid that specific disability.

The point of requiring a significant group of people to regard the reason as adequate is to rule out the rankings of a single otherwise rational person (or a small group of such people) who, e.g., because of some mental disorder, has a completely idiosyncratic ranking of reasons. Since reasons are limited to beliefs about universally acknowledged harms and benefits, there is no danger that any group of otherwise rational people will be able to tailor the ranking of reasons in some objectionable way. Kettner acknowledges that by defining an adequate reason in the way that I do, I rule out the kind of monological determination of what counts as an adequate reason that discourse ethics also wants to rule out.

Common morality provides a framework within which any dialogue which claims legitimacy for the particular moral norms it arrives at, must take place. My claim that most controversial matters cannot be resolved is extremely troubling to many readers who think that the whole point of a moral theory is to resolve controversial matters. But if the issue is genuinely controversial, in that no new factual information would lead to agreement among all impartial rational persons, then a theory that resolves that issue will result in those who think the issue has been resolved wrongly, rejecting the theory. Thus, there will be no common framework that all parties to the dispute accept and so the possibility of a fruitful and meaningful dialogue will be lost. By requiring consensus on every issue, Habermas and others make it impossible for discourse ethics to apply to any real dialogues about genuine controversial issues.

Kettner complains that my list of goods and evils "is an unconcrete (abstract, unsatisfied) common language: *esperanto* for expressing some universally intelligible axes of 'moral space'" (42). However, my list of goods and evils is not unconcrete and abstract, rather, it is dramatically concrete. I have been careful to include only those items which can usually be identified by everyone simply by looking at the situation as it develops. More work needs to be done to identify the criteria of pleasure and pain (unpleasant feelings), but generally people have no problem in picking out when someone is pleased or displeased (anxious, sad, or in pain). Similarly, it is usually clear when someone is dead, has suffered a loss of ability or a loss of freedom. Providing a universal language (Esperanto) for talking about those objective values that are relevant to moral dialogue is a major positive feature of my view.

Kettner complains that "In the face of real controversies, the test [of public allowability] is either so vague as to settle no disagreement at all or so generous as to leave all parties to the controversy 'weakly justified,' a normative label that is reassuring at best and devoid of any reflective disagreement at worst" (45). I sympathize with Kettner's lament, but it is not a criticism of my theory but a lament about the way the world is. All parties to a real controversy are very likely to be weakly justified in their position. That is the way the world is; my theory simply reflects this fact.

Reply to Sayre-McCord

Sayre-McCord claims that my justification of the moral rules, which depends upon limiting one's use of beliefs to those that are shared by all rational persons, does not really justify taking the moral attitude toward those rules to actual people who have far more beliefs than those that are included in my category of rationally required beliefs. Sayre-McCord characterizes the people who have only these rationally required beliefs as "extraordinarily ignorant" (54). However, talking about people who use only rationally required beliefs as if they were ignorant makes it sound as if it were possible for a person to have only rationally required beliefs. But it is a rationally required belief that no moral agent can have only rationally required beliefs. If he did, he could not know anything about the situation he was in and hence could never be held responsible for his actions. Rationally required beliefs are the beliefs that all moral agents share in common, but all moral agents have some beliefs, even some beliefs that it would be irrational for them not to have, that other moral agents do not have.

Sayre-McCord does not challenge my argument "that all who rely solely on rationally required beliefs and are concerned either with morality, or with impartiality, or with what all could favor, would favor the set of rules Gert advances" (55). Rather, he asks, "Why think that what they [those using only rationally required beliefs] might favor has any implications whatsoever for what people like us [who have far more beliefs] might rationally accept?" (55) He correctly notes that "reasoning in a practical sphere is nonmonotonic (i.e., defeasible)—adding premises to what was, initially, a good argument can undermine the conclusion" (56). He also correctly notes that some rationally permitted religious beliefs are such that they might make it irrational for the person holding those beliefs to take the moral attitude toward the set of rules I list as justified moral rules, namely, that they be obeyed impartially toward all rational beings. He does not note that some rationally permitted religious beliefs are such that they might even make it irrational for the person holding those beliefs to take the egocentric attitude toward the moral rules (see *Morality*, 167).

Although Sayre-McCord is correct that no strong justification of the moral rules is possible without limiting beliefs to rationally required beliefs, this limitation is supported by the fact that morality is a public system that applies to all rational persons. Moral judgments are never appropriately made about someone who is legitimately ignorant of what morality prohibits, requires, discourages, encourages, or allows, or who cannot rationally accept morality as a guide for his behavior as well as for the behavior of all other rational persons. This means that the moral rules cannot depend essentially on rationally allowed religious beliefs. Those who do not know about the religion in question would have no reason for accepting the resulting moral prohibitions or requirements, and since moral prohibitions and requirements limit one's freedom, it would be irrational to accept them for no reason.

No commonly accepted religious belief, perhaps no religious belief at all, conflicts with taking the moral attitude toward the moral rules. However, Sayre-McCord is not primarily worried about the fact that some rationally permitted religious beliefs may be incompatible with taking the moral attitude toward the ten listed rules. His major concern is that there might be some people who have beliefs, e.g., scientific beliefs, that it would be irrational for them not to have, which are incompatible with their taking the moral attitude toward the moral rules. He claims that it would be rational for these people to take the moral attitude toward the moral rules "only if a whole slew of rationally permissible beliefs are put aside—among them beliefs many people would be irrational to reject, given their evidence" (58).

It is logically possible that there could be such facts or beliefs; I cannot rule out *a priori* the existence of facts or knowledge such that someone knowing those facts would be irrational to take the moral attitude toward the moral rules. However, it is significant that Sayre-McCord does not provide a single example of such a belief. He does not even provide an example of a plausible scientific fact such that knowing it would make it irrational to take the moral attitude toward the moral rules. Sayre-McCord's objection is another example of philosophers putting form above content. It is logically possible that my account of morality is incorrect; however Sayre-McCord has provided no reason to think that it is.

Although Sayre-McCord notes that I explicitly state that many people have rationally allowed beliefs "such that it would not be irrational for them not to favor impartial obedience to these rules" (58; *Morality*, 167), he wants to go further. He says that people "might well find themselves with beliefs that would make it irrational for them to constrain themselves by the rules Gert proposes" (58). Again, however, he provides no examples. That is not due to negligence on his part. There are no plausible beliefs such that holding them would make it irrational to favor impartial obedience to the moral rules. There is an enormous difference between it not being irrational not to favor impartial obedience to the moral rules and it being irrational to favor impartial obedience to the moral rules. Sayre-McCord may be overlooking the importance of what is rationally allowed. Although it is not irrational not to be impartial, it is never irrational to be impartial with regard to all moral agents with respect to the moral rules.

Sayre-McCord points out that consequentialists may disagree with my account of the moral rules in two kinds of cases (57-58). First, they might claim that it is morally required to follow what I call the general moral ideals, and perhaps even the general utilitarian ideals, thus enlarging what is morally required. I address this question in my replies to Sinnott-Armstrong, Kagan, and Deigh. Like these others, Sayre-McCord may not appreciate that when I claim that acting in a certain way is morally required, I mean that all impartial rational persons favor making one liable to punishment for not doing it. No plausible view, including contemporary consequentialism, holds that liability to punishment is appropriate for failure to act on either general moral or utilitarian ideals.

Second, consequentialism, as indicated by Sinnott-Armstrong's defense of act consequentialism, might not require that all justified exceptions to the rules be publicly allowed. This is the view of act consequentialism, and it results in some consequentialists allowing cheating in circumstances where everyone would regard such cheating as morally wrong. It does not, however, follow from my criticism of act consequentialism that I think that people who accept it are irrational, as Sayre-McCord claims (57). All that follows is that they have a mistaken account of the nature of morality. Morality is not, as some consequentialists like Driver take it to be, a system of evaluation independent of the public guide to behavior that moral agents use in making their moral decisions and judgments. Just as the grammar of a language systematizes the way competent speakers of the language talk, so an account of morality systematizes the way competent moral agents act and judge in moral situations.

Sayre-McCord says,

> Any plausible moral theory, it seems, will need to include a prohibition (at least under normal conditions) on blaming, punishing, and holding people responsible for violating norms they justifiably didn't know about. Still, such a prohibition does not constitute a constraint on what might count as a moral system. Instead, it serves as a constraint, within the moral system, on various ways of reacting to violations of the system's requirements. (66)

It may seem that Sayre-McCord is saying the same thing that I say in the first chapter (4) of *Morality*, "It is, however, an essential feature of morality in all of its variations that everyone who is judged by it, knows what morality prohibits, requires, encourages, and allows." However, he is disagreeing with my statement. He maintains only that any plausible moral system must prohibit blaming, punishing, and holding people responsible for violating norms they justifiably didn't know about. I claim that one cannot make any moral judgments on people who are legitimately ignorant of what morality prohibits, requires, discourages, encourages, and allows.

Although Sayre-McCord's substantive moral constraint might be justified by a consequentialist account of morality, it does not seem that there is a consequentialist justification for not crediting, rewarding, and giving people responsibility for following norms they justifiably did not know about. But not only do we not give people moral credit for following norms they justifiably didn't know about, we do not even give them moral credit for following norms they should have known about, but didn't. However, we do morally blame people for violating norms they should have known about, but didn't. This asymmetry in assigning moral credit and blame may have several explanations, but on all of them it is clear that assigning moral credit is always closely related to a judgment about the character of a person, whereas assigning moral blame often is related to possible punishment for the particular bad consequence. Sayre-McCord's claim that the knowability requirement is "a substantive moral constraint" rather than "a constraint on what counts as morality" does not explain at all why the knowability requirement applies to assigning moral credit.

Only the view that morality, the moral system that is the basis of our moral judgments, requires knowability explains that any judgment, positive or negative, on people's actions when they are totally and justifiably ignorant of what they are doing, does not count as a moral judgment. According to Sayre-McCord, by "recognizing it [the knowability requirement] as a constraint on praise and blame, etc. *in the face of violations of morality's standards*, one is implicitly recognizing the standards as genuine despite their being unknown by at least some to whom they apply" (66). Unfortunately, Sayre-McCord talks about "praise and blame" as if there were also a substantive constraint within morality against moral judgments of praise. Sayre-McCord correctly takes it for granted that we do not make moral judgments of praise on those who do not deserve it, but he never even tries to make it plausible that this is a substantive constraint within the moral system.

Sayre-McCord presents no arguments for holding that knowability is a constraint on all moral judgments, not just negative ones. He also does not seem to realize that no judgment made about anyone who cannot even be expected to know that he has violated some moral standard counts as a moral judgment. No judgment about a baby who cries and irritates everyone and hence violates a moral standard against irritating people counts as a moral judgment. Similarly, no judgment about some adult who violates a law, a taboo, or what some religion takes as a moral requirement that he could not even be expected to know, counts as a moral judgment.

This is what distinguishes morality from law and religion; moral judgments are never made about someone that who is justifiably ignorant of the standard that applies to him. If any plausible moral system must have constraints on moral judgments about matters which are unknowable to a person, then we would not count something as a plausible moral system unless it had such a constraint. Since my remarks about morality are limited to moralities that are not only plausible but also justifiable, Sayre-McCord has not provided any arguments against taking knowability as a necessary feature for any judgment to count as a moral judgment, i.e., as a necessary feature of morality.

Just as one can speak prose without knowing that it is called prose, or speak grammatically without knowing that there is a grammatical system, so one can act morally without knowing that there is some moral system on the basis of which one decides how to act or to judge the acts of others in moral situations. In claiming that knowability is a necessary feature of morality, I am not claiming that anyone can explicitly state the features of morality. I am not even claiming that anyone consciously thinks about morality in a systematic way. I am claiming that we count a judgment as a moral judgment only if we believe that the person about whom the judgment is made is not completely and legitimately ignorant of what morality prohibits, requires, discourages, encourages, and allows.

Sayre-McCord is disturbed by my claim that when there is unresolvable disagreement about whether something morally ought to be allowed, e.g., abortion, neither position is wrong (63-65). But I make it clear (*Morality*, 334) that I am using terms in an "idealized" way, and not attempting to capture the ordinary flexibility of terms like "right" and "wrong." This more precise use of the term "wrong" does not, however, have the practical implications that Sayre-McCord suggests. For I do not limit liability to punishment to acts that are morally wrong in my strict sense. Any violation of a moral rule that is not strongly justified may be liable to punishment. Otherwise one could not enforce laws about which there was legitimate moral disagreement. Thus, although nothing is morally wrong unless there is agreement among all qualified persons, it is morally permissible to have laws which make it punishable to perform some actions about which there is unresolvable moral disagreement.

It is disturbing to many philosophers that my account of morality does not settle genuinely controversial moral questions. But only such an account provides a moral framework that all parties to the controversy can accept. This is far more valuable than having an account of morality that settles controversial questions, but is then rejected by all those who are on the other side of the controversy.

Reply to Audi

Robert Audi has tried to show how I might benefit from taking into account some of the traditional philosophical distinctions and how they might benefit from some of my insights. However, I believe that almost all of the standard philosophical accounts of rationality are so seriously flawed that I have avoided the standard ways of expressing my views about reasons and rationality. The standard view mistakenly holds that the fact that there are better reasons for *A-ing* than for *B-ing* makes it more rational to *A* than to *B*. This implies a much closer relationship between reasons and rationality than they actually have. Audi wants this closer relationship, for he thinks it odd to claim that "there is no difference in the action's degree of rationality but only in the degree of its grounding in reasons" (83).

If the reason for *A-ing* involves only the interests of others and the reason for *B-ing* is a reason of self-interest, then even if the reason for *A-ing* is better, it is not more rational to *A* than to *B*. That one way of acting is supported by better reasons than another does not entail that the former is more rational than the other. Rather, both may merely be rationally allowed. Otherwise, in a conflict between self-interest and morality, it would almost always be more rational to act morally. Second, if *A-ing* simply results in more goods than *B-ing* when one already has enough, then it is not clear that it is more rational to *A* than to *B*, even if there is a better reason to *A* than to *B*. To hold otherwise is to hold that it is always more rational to maximize. When (1) the reason of self-interest for *A-ing* is stronger than the reason of self-interest for *B-ing*, (2) both of these reasons involve avoiding significant harms, and (3) there are no other reasons involved, then the claim that it is more rational to *A* than to *B* is true. However, to say this is extremely misleading, for it is irrational to *B* in these circumstances. Audi is committed to the mistaken position that when comparing two rationally allowed actions, the one that is supported by better reasons is more rational than the other.

That there is an objective way to rank reasons and irrational actions does not entail that one can rank rational actions. However, Audi accepts the standard view of the relationship between reasons and rationality and approvingly mentions philosophers who hold that "even without being *ir*rational, suboptimal actions can fail to be rational or can be less rational than alternatives" (75). He does not appreciate that this way of talking trivializes the category of rationally allowed actions and so leads almost inevitably to a maximizing view of rationality (as indicated by Audi's use of the term "suboptimal"). The lack of a significant category of genuinely rationally allowed actions is a crucial flaw in almost all of the standard philosophical accounts of rationality. Both Copp and

Smith (to be discussed later) recognize that this is a flaw, and their accounts of rationality try to avoid it, but neither are successful in doing so.

When talking about the rationality of persons the comparative use of rationality does not raise problems, for everyone agrees that being more rational means doing fewer or less significant irrational actions. Audi is mistaken in holding that "the overall rationality of a person is in part determined by the proportion of the person's actions that are well-grounded in reasons" (83). A rational person who rarely does anything that causes or risks harm to himself, has less need of reasons than another person who often risks harms to himself and thus has many more of his actions well grounded in reasons, but the former is not less rational. Holding such a close relationship between reasons and rationality is likely to lead to either rational egoism or the view that rationality requires acting on the best reasons, which are usually taken to be reasons supporting acting morally. On both of these views the category of rationally allowed actions loses its significance, and the false and dangerous view that rationality provides unique answers to controversial questions returns.

Audi's talk about good and bad reasons is also misleading (74). Although some reasons are better than others, e.g., that one will avoid ten years in prison is a better reason than that one will avoid five, there is no general category of good and bad reasons. Good and bad reasons are not equivalent to adequate and inadequate reasons. The later kinds of reasons require reference to a particular kind of action, talk of good and bad reasons does not require such reference. On the contrary, talk of good and bad reasons suggests that bad reasons are beliefs that are motives but are not really reasons as all, thus reinforcing the confusion between reasons and motives.

Audi has an interesting suggestion that I make use of a type-token distinction in order to distinguish between an act type that is rationally allowed, but the particular token of which is supported by a "bad" reason (motive that is not a reason at all). He says that acting for a bad reason would "produce a nonrational action-token" (74). He suggests that a person may have a belief (reason) that would make rational an action type that would be irrational without a reason, but when that belief is not the person's motive, the action token may be irrational. For example, a man may kill himself while having the belief that the money from his life insurance will help save the lives of several of his children, but that belief is not his motive for acting. Rather his motive is the belief that this will cause his wife and children to feel terrible guilt. Although the action is rational in the basic advisory sense, that is, a rational person having these beliefs might advocate that it be done, it is irrational in a parasitic personal sense, that is, it counts against the rationality of the person acting. However, as Joshua Gert has continually pointed out to me, I was not clear about the distinction between the basic advisory sense and parasitic personal senses of an irrational act. My unclarity about this distinction may have prompted Audi to try to clarify my view by making his type-token distinction (80). But when this distinction is made clear, the type-token distinction is not needed.

My definition of an irrational action not only contains elements of both the basic and parasitic senses of an irrational act, it is also ambiguous in another way. Audi catches this ambiguity. When I said "An action is irrational in the basic sense if and only if it is an intentional action . . . that one knows or should know will cause harm to oneself and one does not have an adequate reason for the action," I did not mean that only actions intentionally done in order to cause oneself harm are irrational. Rather, I meant that any intentional action, regardless of why it is intentional, that one knows or should know will cause harm to oneself is an irrational action in the basic sense. Audi correctly notes that such an action should be counted as a basic irrational action, and I am pleased to note that I intended precisely this. Audi also clarifies some other ambiguities. For example, he is certainly right that in talking about concern, I am talking about "intrinsic" concern, not "instrumental" concern.

Audi is also completely correct in pointing out that irrationality cannot be completely egocentric, (81) for whether some action is irrational depends upon whether the agent has an adequate reason for the action, and I state clearly that reasons need not be egocentric. I should have been more careful and thanks to Audi, in my précis I state my view more carefully, viz., that an action is regarded as irrational in the basic sense only if it is taken to cause or to significantly increase the risk of some harm to oneself or those for whom one cares.

Other criticisms by Audi such as his claim that I hold that there is an important difference between a loss of pleasure on the one hand and a loss of ability or a loss of freedom on the other, may be due to misleading examples on my part. He says, "Gert apparently thinks of losing ability and freedom as changes in one's *present* condition. . . . But this does not seem to be Gert's main conception of loss of pleasure" (77). However, I did not intend to make such a distinction. I am as concerned with the loss of future abilities and freedom as with the loss of future pleasure. Absent reasons, it is not only irrational to do something that causes an immediate loss of ability, e.g., cut off one's arm, but also to do something that will cause the loss of an ability in the future, e.g., inject one's arm with a toxin that will result in a loss of ability in the future. Similarly, it is irrational both to do something that causes one to lose freedom now, e.g., lock oneself in a room and throw away the key, and to do something that will cause the loss of freedom in the future, e.g., do something that one knows will result in imprisonment in the future. Finally, unless one has an adequate reason, it is irrational to do something that causes one to lose some pleasure immediately, e.g., turn off a record that one is enjoying listening to now, or to do something that causes one to lose that pleasure in the future, e.g., destroy that record so that one will not have that pleasure later. There is no significant difference in the irrationality of any of these different cases.

Contrary to Audi's suggestion, it is not irrational for a happy person not to seek further pleasure, even though he has a reason to seek more pleasure (77). Similarly, as will be apparent from my reply to Copp, unless a person is disabled or deprived, it is not irrational not to seek further ability or freedom. People who are appropriately satisfied with what they have are not normally judged irrational for not trying to get more. They are, however, judged irrational to positively seek to avoid present or future pleasure, just as it is irrational to seek to avoid any good without an adequate reason. When replying to Copp, I acknowledge that it is difficult to make a precise distinction between avoiding a good and not seeking one. However, it is important to make this distinction. Otherwise one will end up holding either that it is not irrational to avoid goods for no reason at all, or else be committed to a maximizing theory of rationality.

Audi is concerned that my basic sense of irrational may be too limited. He thinks that a desire for something that is clearly unattainable, e.g., "to fly to the moon on gossamer wings" (78) should be regarded as an irrational desire. He is aware that such a desire, if taken seriously, might lead one to do irrational actions in the basic sense, that is, to do things which cause an evil or a loss of some good without a compensating benefit. However, he wants the desire to be irrational independent of any effects it might have on one's actions. He claims that "we certainly try to eliminate desires of this sort in ourselves or those we care about, and we would do so even if we thought the action in question would do no harm" (79). The truth of his claim depends on who "we" are. Parents would not necessarily try to eliminate such unattainable desires in their children, especially if they thought such desires were evidence of admirable character, e.g., the desire of a small child to cure his mother of her serious disease. Thus, Audi has not provided a kind of basic irrational desire that all rational persons would agree is irrational independent of its relationship to actions. An objective account of rationality cannot count any action or desire as irrational unless no significant group of people would regard it as rational.

Of course, an action can be irrational in a parasitic sense if it is based on an irrational belief, but that is because such actions normally cause harm. Since desires and actions are very closely related, there is no problem in regarding desires based on irrational beliefs as irrational in the same parasitic sense. However, if all irrational actions, beliefs, and desires can be accounted for without adding any other basic categories, nothing is gained by adding additional categories of basic irrational desires.

I do not reduce theoretical rationality to practical rationality, or vice versa, but I do explain why we sometimes use the same term "irrational" to characterize both beliefs and actions or desires. An irrational belief (delusion) is a belief that is in conflict with what is believed by almost everyone with similar knowledge and intelligence. Such beliefs are called irrational because, in normal circumstances, they, like irrational desires and irrational actions, are beliefs that all rational persons want to avoid. Although some claim that people want to avoid irrational beliefs simply because they are another basic harm, I relate irrational beliefs to irrational actions. Irrational beliefs often result in one's suffering some harm without any compensating benefit, that is, irrational beliefs often lead to irrational actions. The primacy of action is shown by those unusual cases where holding an irrational belief (delusion) results in preventing a person from suffering some serious harms. People may not want that irrational belief to be avoided. This does not show that irrational beliefs are not basic harms, but I prefer not to expand the list of basic harms if it is not necessary to do so.

Audi raises a common objection to my account of rationality, asking why beliefs about preventing harm to others can be strong enough to make it rational to harm oneself but never strong enough to rationally require one to act (82). This essential element in my account of rationality is one that philosophers find it most difficult to understand, let alone accept, at least in the abstract. However, examples make it clear to most people, including most philosophers, that although rescuing people from a burning house makes it rational for me to risk serious injuries, it is still not irrational for me to refuse to risk these injuries. Many philosophers, perhaps influenced by Kant, have trouble accepting that it is not rationally required to help others when I can do so at no cost to myself. But, if I do not care for the person who needs help, if, in fact, I do not like people of that kind, my not helping them, even my hurting them, although morally bad, is not irrational in any ordinary use of that term.

Audi presents a more unusual example, one in which a person, with no reason not to help, believes that it would be morally good to help the person and yet does not do so (82). Audi's example includes the person being surprised at his failure to act, so that it is difficult to know whether to characterize the failure to act as intentional. But the person need not be surprised at his failure to act; many people fail to do what they believe to be morally good actions. People are not rationally required to do what they believe to be morally good. There is no inconsistency in believing both that an action would be morally good and that there is no reason not to do it, and still not do it. Such behavior is not even unusual. The number of people who know that it would be morally good to send (more) money to various charities and who believe that sending this money will not harm them in any way, and yet do not send (more) money is extremely large. Although the lack of actions by such people can be criticized as callous, they are not judged to be behaving irrationally.

Audi tries to show that acting contrary to one's beliefs can by itself make an action irrational by expanding on the example cited above. He says it may be irrational not to help someone if "I believe that I have nothing to lose by being moral and also believe that I ought to be" (85). Audi's disagreement with my view is based on my failure to make clear that when I talk about beliefs, I mean empirical and quasi-empirical beliefs (including religious and mathematical beliefs). I do not mean moral beliefs or beliefs about what I ought to do. On my analysis of "ought," to believe that you ought to be moral is equivalent to advocating to yourself to be moral. If you advocate to yourself to be morally good, then you desire to be morally good and feel bad when you realize that you are not acting in the way that you advocate acting. Having these beliefs, desires, and feelings, you may be acting irrationally by failing to act. But failing to act in ways that will frustrate your desires and will cause you to feel bad is acting irrationally in the basic sense. There is no need to bring in some new category of basic irrational action.

Audi is right in pointing out that my definition of an adequate reason as a reason that "makes the otherwise irrational action for which it is a reason, rational" needs revision. I was too concerned with contrasting adequate reasons which normally make the otherwise irrational actions for which they are reasons, rational, with reasons in general, which *can* make some otherwise irrational actions rational. Thus, I substituted "makes" for "can make." I did not appreciate that the important contrast was between "the otherwise irrational action for which it is a reason" and "some irrational action." I should have kept the "can make" for adequate reasons as well, for as Audi correctly notes, the present formulation rules out having two adequate reasons for the same action (83). The problem that Audi raises about this revised formulation (88, n. 17), viz., that there may be two reasons, each inadequate, but which together are adequate, is a problem only if one does not allow complex or compound beliefs. The belief that *A-ing* will help José avoid a given amount of harm may not be an adequate reason for *A-ing* and the same may be true of the belief that *A-ing* will help Maria avoid a given amount of harm. Yet, the compound belief that *A-ing* will help both José and Maria each avoid a given amount of harm may be an adequate reason for *A-ing*.

Audi's other problem with my account of an adequate reason, viz., that a reason is adequate "if any significant group of moral agents regard the harm avoided or benefit gained as compensating for the harm suffered" (quoted on page 76) is due to a distinction that he makes "between a *preferential* and a *permissional* notion of adequacy" (84). He uses the preferential notion of an adequate reason to make the action for which it is an adequate reason "rationally preferable to one or more alternatives" (84). but I have already pointed out the problems involved in talking of one rationally allowed action as rationally preferable to another. Given that one can already say that there are stronger reasons for *A-ing* than for *B-ing*, saying that *A-ing* is rationally preferable to *B-ing* provides no advantage. On the contrary, it has the disadvantage of leading to the troubling result that some rational people, e.g., egoists, very often prefer not to do what is rationally preferable. That rational egoists prefer not to do what is supported by the best reasons is not troubling in the same way. It is neither irrational nor uncommon to know that there are better reasons for giving to one charity rather than to another, but give to the latter because of some personal connection with it.

Audi's remarks have also led me to realize that some of my statements about adequate reasons need to be clarified. For example, when I say that "any significant group of moral agents regard the harm avoided or benefit gained as compensating for the harm suffered," I should have been explicit that I was not talking about tokens of harm, but rather of types. My claim is that whether a given kind (including intensity) of harm or benefit compensates for another kind (including intensity) of harm depends on whether a significant group of moral agents regard it as so compensating. That one person thinks it is an adequate reason for killing himself that he will thereby avoid a very short but intense pain does not make it an adequate reason. But if a significant group of moral agents (people whom we hold responsible for their actions) regard avoiding a certain kind of pain, e.g., long-term intense shame, as an adequate reason for killing oneself, then it is an adequate reason. Since I am using irrationality as the fundamental normative concept, I have adopted the methodological principle of not calling any action irrational that any significant group of moral agents would regard as rational. Irrationality could not be the fundamental normative concept if a significant group of moral agents would choose to do an action that is classified as irrational.

Audi has led me to see that sometimes I did not say exactly what I meant, indeed that sometimes I was not even clear what I meant. In several instances, I have changed what I said in the direction that Audi suggested. Even in those instances where I did not accept the suggestions that he made, I clarified my point of view and explained more clearly why I do not want to make what I regard as a significant change in my view. I think that these clarifications may be as useful as the revisions, so I am equally grateful to Audi for the suggestions that I have not taken as for those that I have.

Reply to Copp

Copp supports most of the distinctive features of my accounts of irrationality, rationality, and reasons. However, like Audi and most other philosophers, he finds it puzzling that in considering the Baby Rescue Case, rescuing the baby can justify, that is, make rational, what would otherwise count as the irrational action of risking one's life, but that it is never irrational not to rescue the baby even if one can do so with no risk to oneself (93). Copp and Audi share the standard philosophical view that a reason which is strong enough to justify an otherwise irrational act must also rationally require an action when there are no countervailing reasons. The standard philosophical account of rationality does not distinguish between reasons of self-interest and reasons related to the interests of others, so it is impossible for it to account for the fact that some reasons that a rational person is not required to act on may nonetheless justify an otherwise irrational act. My hybrid account of rationality acknowledges that although irrationality is primarily egocentric, reasons need not be egocentric.

Consider a woman who is not concerned at all with people, even babies, of a certain ethnic or racial group. Suppose an Albanian Kosovar sees a Serbian baby drowning. It is rationally allowed for her not to rescue the baby, but although she is unlikely to do so, it would also be rational for the woman to risk her life to save that baby. If the situation changes so that she can rescue the baby with no risk at all, it may be immoral for her not to do so, but it is still not irrational. As the concept of rationality is ordinarily used, it would be rationally allowed for the woman to risk her life to save the baby, but also rationally allowed for her not to rescue the baby even when there is no risk. Philosophers who define acting rationally in terms of acting on reasons may claim this to be counterintuitive, but considering a real example such as an Albanian Kosovar decision not to rescue a Serbian baby makes it clear that such a decision is not irrational, even though it may be immoral. Copp, like most people, including most philosophers, correctly holds that it is not irrational to be immoral.

Copp, like Smith, also objects to the fact that I define irrationality in terms of a list. He realizes that I categorize all the items on the list as evils or harms, but he correctly notes that I do not regard this as explaining the list or providing any justification for the list (93-95). Copp wants to take harm as the primitive undefined concept that unifies my list, although he admits that it would have to be taught by means of the items on the list that I provide. I agree with his claim that taking harm as fundamental has an aesthetic advantage. It also has the advantage of being more traditional. But his claim that the concept of harm "*explains* why the items on the list belong there" (95) involves the same kind of mistake as the view that "being contrary to one's self-interest" explains why the items on the list belong there. Of course, all rational persons would avoid all of the items on the list unless they had a reason, but the lists help explain what is meant by harm and self-interest, not vice versa.

No one, including Audi, Copp, Smith, or Kagan, disagrees with my claim that no person acting rationally would seek any of the items on this list just because he felt like doing so. However, Copp and Smith think that there may be other unrelated items (or categories) that it would also be irrational for any person to seek just because he felt like doing so. If there is any other unrelated item which everyone would agree it would be irrational for any person to seek just because he felt like doing so, then that item should be added to the list. It is certainly possible that I have omitted something. In a sense, the list is unified by the attitude that rational persons have toward the items on it. However, we would not regard a person as rational if he did not have the appropriate attitude toward the items on the list. I define "harm" (*Morality*, 90), which Copp regards as a fundamental but undefined term, by relating it to the attitudes of rational persons. I do not know if Copp or Smith would accept this close relationship between the attitudes of rational persons and harms as unifying the list, and providing explanatory and epistemic advantages. If they do, then we have no serious disagreement, only a verbal one.

Philosophers do not like using lists in defining important concepts, but it may be instructive to note that in the last two editions of *The Diagnostic and Statistical Manual of Mental Disorders*, an official publication of the American Psychiatric Association, a similar list is used as part of the definition of a mental disorder. This list is easy to understand, clear, and precise, and is used to teach the concepts of mental disorder, irrationality, and harm. However, Copp claims that even though the concept of harm cannot conflict with any of the items on the list, one might be able to use this undefined concept to add items to the list. Of course, I have not proved that the list is complete, but I have provided some evidence that it is. The items on the list exhaust the list of harms traditionally used in the definitions of both punishment and malady (disorder, disease). Since most of the items are themselves categories, e.g., loss of freedom, it is quite likely that all proposed additions that have universal support will fit into one of these categories. All additions to the original list must be supported by universal agreement that it would be irrational for any person to seek that thing just because he felt like doing so. Postulating harm as an undefined term to provide some aesthetic unity to the list provides no epistemic or explanatory advantage, rather it makes it more likely that something will be slipped in as a harm without a thorough examination.

Some evidence for the greater likelihood of error is offered by Copp when he complains, "Gert does not give the kind of status to avoiding harms to *projects* that we care about that he gives to avoiding harms to *people* that we care about," (96) as if it were clear what was meant by harm to projects. With regard to irrationality the status of avoiding harms to *projects* that we care about is not significantly different from the status of avoiding harms to *people* we care about. As Copp recognizes later, "the irrationality of bringing about harm to those we care about is derivative, not fundamental" (97). Only if harm to a project that we care about causes us to suffer harm is it irrational to cause harm to that project. The difference between the status of causing harms to people and causing harms to projects is that causing harms to people counts as a reason against the action whether or not one cares about those people, whereas causing harm to projects only counts as a reason against doing it if doing so results in causing harms to people, ourselves or others. Does Copp want to grant avoiding or preventing harm to projects the same kind of independent reason providing status as avoiding or preventing harm to people?

Copp correctly claims that I hold that (1) desires are not a source of reasons, (2) the reason for rescuing someone one does care about is not better or stronger than the reason for rescuing someone one does not care about, and (3) whereas it cannot be irrational not to rescue someone one does not care about, it can be irrational not to rescue someone one does care about. But he finds it "difficult to make sense of this combination of ideas" (96). Copp may find it difficult because he does not take into account that (3) is true because rescuing someone for whom one cares always involves avoiding harm to oneself. Copp should be aware that saying that one reason is better or stronger than another means only that it can justify all irrational actions the other can justify and more besides. It has nothing to do with whether the reason requires any action.

We just do care about other people, not for any gain we get from them, so our caring is not egoistic, though it is egocentric. Yet the fact that we care does make it irrational to harm them, for we suffer when they are harmed. This common kind of irrational action occurs when a person is angry with a loved one and hurts her and suffers because of it. Failing to rescue a person for whom one cares, when one has no reason not to rescue that person, is to fail to avoid a harm to oneself for no reason, and that is irrational. The hybrid account of rationality captures what Smith calls "the grain of truth that lies in Kantianism" (111), that helping others provides reasons that can justify harming oneself. But at the same time it recognizes that Kantianism is incorrect in holding that helping others is rationally required.

Copp, like many others, is also concerned with another asymmetry in my account of rationality, that between avoiding harms and gaining goods. Although I hold that there is such an asymmetry, as Copp presents his example of someone refusing a cost-free, risk-free operation to restore the sight in his blinded eye, I would regard refusing the operation as irrational. Refusing a cost-free, risk-free operation is as much or more like giving up or avoiding a good than not seeking it, and though I do not regard the latter as irrational, I do so regard the former. It may be significant that it is so difficult to find a clear counterexample to my claim about the difference between seeking goods on the one hand and avoiding goods and not avoiding or relieving evils on the other. The asymmetry between goods and evils is that it is irrational not to make some effort to avoid any significant evil, but, when one has enough, it is not irrational not to make an effort to gain additional significant goods.

Although there is a significant distinction between "avoiding or giving up a good" and "not seeking a good," there is not a clear line between them. When the line is clear we always regard it as irrational to avoid or give up a good without an adequate reason, but we do not always regard it as irrational to fail to seek a good without an adequate reason. The claim that one is rationally required to seek goods leads to the maximizing view of rationality. A person who has enough is rationally allowed to say, "I've got enough, I'm not interested in trying to get any more," and act accordingly. It is not irrational for him not to seek additional goods, even if he has no reason for not wanting more. However, with no reason for not wanting what he has, it is irrational for a person to say, "I've got more than enough, I'm going to destroy some of my present goods," and act accordingly. It is irrational to destroy one's own goods when no one benefits.

Copp is correct that it would be irrational for a person who has not lost his interest in his manuscript, which gives him intellectual stimulation by discussing it with others, reading it, working on it, etc., to burn it when he has no reason to do so. But he is incorrect that burning the manuscript will not result in any of the harms on my list and so, on my account of irrationality, it is not irrational (100). Burning the manuscript causes the person to lose the opportunity to discuss it with others, read it, work on it, etc. Not only does he lose all of these goods, but losing the intellectual stimulation that the manuscript provides creates a greater risk of boredom. Copp admits that intellectual stimulation can prevent unpleasant boredom, but still claims that neither this nor any other risk of harm account for the irrationality of the act; that it is simply irrational for a person "to destroy the fruits of his life project" when he has no reason to do so (101). But if, contrary to fact, he could be certain that there is not even a risk that he will suffer any of the harms on my list, or lose any good, then it is not irrational to burn his manuscript. Of course, in real life it is irrational to believe that he can know this kind of complex fact about the future with certainty, so it is irrational for him to destroy his manuscript.

It seems so obvious that a person risks suffering any number of harms on my list, e.g., loss of opportunities and pleasures, as well as psychological harms, by burning the manuscript that this example of Copp's, like the case of refusing a risk-free, cost-free sight restoring operation, is not a counterexample to my view. On a normal reading of my account of rationality, when one has absolutely no reason for doing so, it is irrational to burn a manuscript from which one still receives intellectual stimulation. Copp is committed to the view that one can value something which is completely unrelated to any harm or benefit on my list, and that this value can make it rational for one to harm oneself, but it is significant that none of his examples are clear cases of this kind of value. Indeed, the plausibility of taking values as a source of reasons is that all of the values that Copp cites, particularly intellectual stimulation, are clearly related to items on my lists.

Copp recognizes that our views are similar. His proposed counterexamples designed to show that his account of rationality is superior are not really counter-examples to my account. Copp complains that my view does not explain why it is irrational to risk those items on my list of harms without an adequate reason (102-3). But there is no need to explain to anyone why it is irrational to kill himself, cause himself pain, disable himself, or cause himself a loss of freedom or pleasure when no one will benefit from his doing so. Copp disagrees more with the form of my view than with its substance. He includes as irrational most of what I call irrational, but he wants to embed my view in what he claims to be a more unified and comprehensive view (103), which is a sophisticated desire satisfaction account of rationality.

His account requires "a person . . . to have a coherent set of values and to govern her behavior so as to best serve these values, as assessed in light of her own epistemic situation, except that, in 'emergency situations,' she may act instead to secure her ability so to govern her behavior" (104). He calls this an "autonomy standard" of rationality and summarizes it by saying "it calls on us to manifest or to secure our ability to be self-governing" (104). He then offers his alternative account of irrationality. "*Irrationality* is a kind of failure to serve our *autonomy*" (104). Copp admits that his account includes only three of my harms: death (permanent unconsciousness), loss of ability, and loss of freedom. In brief, Copp has put forward an account of rationality such that it is irrational not to act so as to best satisfy one's stable values or desires, except that one may refuse to satisfy one's values in order to protect one's ability to satisfy one's values or desires in the future.

Copp's view resembles Rawls's in not giving any basic status to pleasure and pain. He holds that it is just a matter of fact that most people value pleasure and the avoidance of pain (105). But there is no doubt that if someone caused himself to suffer great pain for no reason, we would consider him to be acting irrationally. Nor would we change our mind about this if he reported that he valued suffering that pain; not valued it for the insight it gave him into the suffering of others, etc., but simply valued it for its own sake. The status of pleasure and pain with regard to rationality is not derivative, although there is still a need for an adequate account of pleasure and pain.

Although still inadequate, Copp's proposal is an improvement over Rawls's account of rationality which requires one to follow one's values without limiting those values at all. (See chapter 12 of *Morality: A New Justification of the Moral Rules* for a more detailed criticism of Rawls's view.) Although Copp's view also imposes no limitations on a person's values, it does allow her not to follow her values if doing so limits her ability to be self-governing in the future. On Rawls's account, if one values dying in the most painful possible way more than everything else, it is irrational not to act so as to achieve this goal, whereas on Copp's account it is rationally allowed not to act to achieve it. But, unfortunately on Copp's account it is also rationally allowed for a person to act so as to achieve it. Copp acknowledges this problem when he states that on his account one may value not only pain and loss of pleasure, a person can even value death, loss of ability, and loss of freedom for no reason (107, n. 14).

Copp's account is an excellent example of what happens when a desire for unity becomes overriding. Copp's sophisticated desire satisfaction view is an attempt to incorporate as much of my view as he can while still maintaining the aesthetic character and unity of a desire satisfaction view. (Smith's view, as we shall see, is similar.) Copp's view is complex enough to allow that, at least in emergency situations, reason may allow either of two or more alternative courses of action. However, to keep the desire satisfaction view intact, he must allow it to be rational to pursue what even he calls "irrational" values (107, n. 14). Thus, all of the counterexamples that have been offered to the original desire satisfaction views count as counterexamples to Copp's view. Further, on Copp's view, "It would be a clear failure of self-government if a person ignored her values on a whim or momentary impulse" (104). Thus, if a person does not value the life of another, as in the Baby Rescue case, acting on a momentary impulse to rescue that other at any risk to herself is positively irrational.

Allowing for "irrational values" results in Copp making a troubling statement when talking about one's children. Copp says, "We can be critical of their values. But, on the conception of rationality that I am proposing, insofar as we want them to be rational, we want them in ordinary situations to govern their lives on the basis of their values" (105, note omitted). The phrase "insofar as we want them to be rational" is particularly troubling. On any adequate account of rationality, parents always want their children to be rational; it counts against any account of the concept of rationality that normal parents do not always want their children always to act rationally. However, if the children have "irrational values," as some children with mental disorders do have, Copp implies that parents might sometimes not want their children to act rationally. However, any account of rationality that allows parents ever to want their children not to act rationally, fails the basic test of any adequate account of rationality. Even parents who are religious fanatics do not want their children to act irrationally; they just believe that avoiding displeasing God is a stronger reason than avoiding harm to oneself.

Copp's view has the counterintuitive conclusion that it is irrational to help others at some risk to oneself if one does not value their lives or interests. It suffers, though less obviously, all of the flaws of the desire satisfaction or cool moment theories, because it allows all values or desires to determine the rationality of actions. That someone with the insight of Copp into the complexities of rationality still comes up with a clearly inadequate account is strong evidence that no desire satisfaction account of rationality, no matter how sophisticated, provides an adequate account of rationality.

Reply to Smith

Smith, like Copp, claims a close connection between reasons and rationality. He says, "In determining the rationality of an agent's actions, the commonsense conception of practical rationality . . . [asks] whether they act . . . as they believe that they have reason to" (110). Thus, he accepts a view which I claim to be incorrect, namely, that the concept of rationality is the same as the concept as acting on what one believes one has reasons to do. Smith admits, "if I am wrong that the conception of practical rationality just described is commonsensical, then my objections to Gert's complex hybrid conception will simply fail" (110).

Smith's formulation of the commonsense conception of practical rationality is wrong. On the commonsense concept, as long as a person determines that she will suffer no harm by doing a given action, she can simply act on a whim and still be acting rationally. A person need not have any reason for doing something in order to be acting rationally, e.g., if a person correctly believes that there are no reasons either for or against her sitting in the green chair rather than the red one, no one would classify her sitting in either one of them as irrational. Yet on Smith's account of the commonsense conception of practical rationality, if a person does either of these actions without believing that she has any reason for doing it, her action is irrational. Indeed, on Smith's view, in a normal case, it is irrational for a person to do something because the coin came up heads rather than tails, unless his view allows a coin coming up heads as a reason for doing the action.

Although I do not claim that all reasons are nonegocentric, I do argue that the strength of a reason does not depend on whether it is egocentric or non-egocentric. I give an argument and some examples to support this point (see *Morality*, 76-79). Contrary to Smith, the strength of a reason is not correlated with the strength of the motive it provides to any given person, even to an idealized fully rational person. The strength of a reason depends solely on what otherwise irrational actions it can make rational.

Smith quotes the following sentence from my definition of a rational action: "A reason is adequate if any significant group of moral agents regard the harm avoided or benefit gained as compensating for the harm suffered" (*Morality*, 84). But his concern with motivation leads him to misunderstand this passage. He claims that since "some significant group of moral agents would each give more weight to their making it less likely that they will suffer greater harm themselves than they would give to their making it less likely that just someone will suffer greater harm, then it surely follows that, even by Gert's own criterion, the reasons have different weights" (112). But once one distinguishes clearly between reasons and motives, it is clear that this conclusion does not follow.

Suppose that a significant group of moral agents regards curing oneself of a disability as being an adequate reason for undergoing two weeks of pain, and they are motivated to undergo that pain in order to cure that disability. Suppose also, with Smith, that they would not be motivated to undergo that pain to cure another person's disability, that is, they would not regard curing another person of a disability as being an adequate reason for undergoing that pain. But note that in the preceding sentence, the clause that follows the "that is" is not the same as the clause preceding it. What is at issue is not whether a significant group of moral agents would be motivated to undergo that pain to cure some other person's disability, but whether a significant group of moral agents would regard undergoing that pain to cure some other person's disability as irrational. But even if they did regard undergoing that pain to cure some other person's disability as irrational, that would not be sufficient to make the egocentric reason stronger or better than the nonegocentric one. This is because there is another significant group of moral agents, those who are impartial, who do regard it as rational to act so as to decrease the overall amount of harm suffered, regardless of who is suffering the harm.

Reason *A* is not better or stronger than reason *B* if any significant group of moral agents would regard reason *B* as an adequate reason for every harm that reason *A* is an adequate reason for. Impartial moral agents think it rationally allowed to act so as to decrease the overall amount of harm suffered, regardless of who is suffering the harm. People who donate a kidney to an unknown recipient are not regarded as acting irrationally. Since they regard curing a disability for someone else as an adequate reason for suffering as much pain as curing a disability for themselves, it follows that the strength of a reason is independent of who avoids the harm. (This is quite distinct from Kagan's view that it is rationally required to act in this way.) Smith's talk of the weight of reasons is the result of his tying reasons too closely to motives, even if the motives are the motives of idealized fully rational persons.

Smith is correct that my official definition of an irrational action and my discussion of the relationship between internal and external reasons are in need of revision. For example, as quoted by Smith, I say, "If one has internal reasons to do something, then one believes that there are external reasons to do it" (114). This sentence should be revised as follows: "if one has internal reasons to do something, then one believes that there are empirical facts that correspond to these beliefs. These corresponding empirical facts are external reasons for doing the action." It should be noted, however, that Smith's facts are not standard empirical facts at all, but rather what he calls "idealized psychological facts" (116).

I have now accepted Joshua Gert's point that objective rationality (what I called external rationality) is the fundamental normative concept of rationality and that personal rationality (what I called internal rationality) is parasitic. Thus I accept Smith's point that basic reasons should be thought of as what I called external reasons, which are facts rather than internal reasons which are beliefs. However, Smith holds that it is one's beliefs about the reasons that determine the rationality of a person's actions, so that he also regards beliefs, not facts, as relevant to personal rationality. However, Smith's later comments show that his primary interest is with objective rationality, not personal rationality (117-18).

Unlike Copp, Smith does not even try to offer any counterexamples to my view. He not only does not argue against my substantive views, he accepts most of them. He says that any adequate theory of rationality must include all of the important elements of my account of rationality, its hybrid character, that some desires are intrinsically irrational, and that rational actions come in two forms, rationally required and rationally allowed. He even creates desires with "disjunctive content" (121) so that he can incorporate the category of rationally allowed actions. However, like Copp, he prefers a formal account of rationality to a substantive one.

Because he has no specific arguments against any item on my list of irrational desires, Smith provides the following general hypothetical argument. He claims, "no matter how high our confidence that the desires for death, pain, disability, loss of freedom, and loss of pleasure are irrational, provided that our confidence isn't 100 percent, the bottom line is that we *do* thereby grant that it is at least possible, even if only barely, that that confidence could be undermined by further reflection" (119). Smith then states, "If the premises and the steps in the argument, taken together, are something about which we could be more confident than we are that the desires for death, pain, disability, loss of freedom, and loss of pleasure are irrational, then it is our confidence that these desires are irrational that would be undermined, not the former, and rightly so" (119).

Smith's hypothetical conclusion seems to be an analytic statement, however, there are no relevant premises and steps of an argument, that taken together, are something about which we should be more confident than that desires for death, pain, etc. are irrational. It is significant that Smith does not even try to provide the premises and the steps of such an argument. Unless "could be" means merely that it is logically possible, there could not be such premises and steps in an argument. Smith's argument against my view seems to come down to saying that it is logically possible that I could be wrong. As confident as I am, I admit that it is logically possible that I could be wrong.

Despite Smith's attempt to incorporate the distinctive features of my account of rationality into his version of the cool moment satisfaction of desires theory, there are serious problems with his theory. The primary problem is with his account of a reason. It is very complex, so I shall quote it in its entirety. Smith says, "To be a little more precise, in my view the fact that an agent *A* can perform an action of a certain kind *K* in certain circumstances *C* by performing an act of kind *K** in those circumstances constitutes a reason for him to perform an act of kind *K** in *C* if and only if everyone, *A* included, would want that they themselves perform an act of kind *K* in *C* by performing an act of kind *K** in those circumstances if they were fully rational" (117). His example, that the fact that a person can save his own life is a reason for his cutting off his own arm, does seem to satisfy his definition of a reason.

However, that his definition fits one example does not mean that it fits all examples. Since Smith admits that benefits to others also count as reasons, his definition needs to fit an example where the fact that *A* will save a foreigner's life is a reason for *A*'s cutting off his own arm. Unless Smith denies that a rational egoist or nationalist can be fully rational, his definition does not fit this example. For, on Smith's account, something is a reason "if and only if everyone, *A* included, would want that they themselves perform an act of kind *K** in those circumstances if they were fully rational." A rational egoist or nationalist would not want himself to perform an act of kind *K** in those circumstances, i.e., cutting off his own arm in order to save a foreigner's life, even if he were fully rational. On Smith's view, this entails that the fact that *A*'s action will save a foreigner's life is not a reason.

Smith thinks of reasons, or rather the strongest reasons, as requiring actions, that is, if one does not act on the strongest reasons one is acting irrationally. But what makes facts reasons is not that they can make it irrational not to act on them, but rather that they can make it rational to do some otherwise irrational action. The unifying character of reasons is that they can justify otherwise irrational actions. Only some reasons require one to act, those that if not acted on would result in the action being an irrational one. The only reasons that do this are reasons that involve suffering some harm oneself. If an action will harm oneself, then and only then is it an irrational action if one has no reason for doing it. But one can have strong reasons for harming oneself, reasons that are strong enough to justify suffering the greatest harm, death, but if these reasons involve the interests of others, it is never rationally required to act on them.

Smith's view, like all cool moment views, links reasons too closely to motives. He falsely holds that all reasons must serve as motives for all fully rational persons. Smith's view not only has the consequence that rational egoists cannot be fully rational; it also has the consequence that all those who care only for a limited group of people, such as family, friends, or fellow citizens, because they are not motivated to help just any moral agent, cannot be fully rational. He also has to hold that all those who are not motivated to help nonhuman sentient beings are not fully rational, or else he has to hold that avoiding harm to nonhuman sentient beings that one does not care about is not a reason at all. The former position seems to be even more extreme than a Kantian view of rationality, which only requires one to help other moral agents. His position has the consequence that Smith himself correctly does not want: it allows the question "Why should I be fully rational?" to be a sensible question.

That avoiding or preventing harm for others is not a reason at all is not a consequence that Smith or anyone other than a rational egoist would like. That someone's life will be saved is a reason whether or not it is a motive for all "fully rational" persons; all that is required for it to be a reason is that saving someone's life can justify suffering some harm to oneself. Some rational persons would be motivated by the fact that their actions would save the life of someone they didn't even know, even though they would suffer some harm themselves, but some rational persons would not be so motivated. Claiming that all rational persons must share any motivation in addition to that of avoiding harm to themselves has consequences that Smith cannot and should not accept.

Smith realizes that his official definition has problems, and he puts forward on my behalf two horns of a dilemma concerning the meaning of the phrase "fully rational" (117). Either fully rational is not defined in terms of my list of irrational desires, in which case there may be clear counterexamples, e.g., someone wanting to kill himself without any compensating benefit, or fully rational is defined in terms of my list of irrational desires in which case my theory has in fact been adopted. Smith claims that he can provide a unifying feature that is not defined in terms of my list but which would "underwrite our confidence [in Gert's list], rather than undermine it" (119).

Thus Smith agrees that if the list of irrational desires comes into conflict with any formal definition, the list wins, but he does challenge my account of rationality, by claiming that my account of reasons might possibly be wrong. On my account of rationality one must not merely not have any of the five irrational desires, one must also accept that the facts that I list as reasons are the only reasons. Smith thinks it is logically possible that there could be reasons beyond those that I list. He asks how likely it is that one could desire something on my list of harms "in circumstances in which the loss enables the preservation of a work of art, or area of rain forest." His answer is, "Certainly, it doesn't seem impossible" (123, n. 9). I agree it doesn't seem impossible, but his examples do not support his criticism. It would be irrational for any person to suffer any significant evil to preserve a work of art or an area of rain forest unless he believed that it were possible that some sentient beings, not necessarily persons, would benefit from that work of art or that area of rain forest.

It is quite remarkable that all of the formal accounts of rationality have clear counterexamples, whereas my account, which is substantive, has none. This is partly due to their attempt to take rationality rather than irrationality as the fundamental concept and to provide a positive definition of it. Smith realizes the need for the concept of rationally allowed actions, but does not see that the importance of this category comes from taking irrationality rather than rationality as basic, and that talk of a "fully rational" person still creates problems. He thinks that he can incorporate all of my substantive points into a formal account which satisfies other traditional philosophical constraints. He has not done so, nor can he do so. Either his theory will coincide with my lists, in which case it is unnecessary, or it will conflict with my lists, in which case it is mistaken. It is, of course, still logically possible that my theory of rationality might be mistaken, but I do not think that confidence in my theory should be lessened by my admission that it is logically possible that it might be wrong.

Smith acknowledges that I am "right to insist that some of the so-called conflicts between morality and self-interest are . . . [such that one is] not rationally required to act in one way or in the other. Moreover, I think [Gert] is right that a theory of rational action that suggested otherwise would be flawed in a quite decisive way" (121). Thus, Smith agrees with my criticism of Kagan's view of rationality as being decisively flawed. But Smith holds that I am "wrong that [my] hybrid conception of rationality is unique in making room for the category of acts that are rationally allowed, as opposed to rationally required" (121). Note that Smith does not deny that my hybrid theory does account for rationally allowed actions, he simply claims that my theory is not unique in this respect.

However, in order to account for this category of action Smith has to invoke the concept of a disjunctive desire, e.g., "either to buy himself a holiday or to give his money to charity" (121). But for this disjunctive desire to do what Smith wants it to do, the person cannot have a desire for each of the disjuncts, that is he cannot have a desire to buy himself a holiday and another desire to give his money to charity. For if he has both of these desires and they are not of equal weight, then for Smith he is not rationally allowed to act on the desire of lesser weight. Thus, Smith's theory requires either disjunctive desires with no independent desires for either of the disjuncts or desires of equal weight for both of the disjuncts. The latter reduces the importance of the category of rationally allowed desires to the status that any consequentialist can give it, namely, to break ties. The former requires an incomprehensible psychological state.

Contrary to expectations, all formal theories, including Smith's, need many implausible ad hoc adjustments in order to avoid conflicting with the common-sense conception of practical rationality. Since Smith accepts almost all of the substantive features of my theory, it seems that it is primarily the power of philosophical tradition that leads him to reject that theory in favor of a formal one. I understand the pull of a formal theory, one that is not committed to any particular content. Indeed, my initial goal was to have a formal theory myself. But my greater goal was to have a theory that accurately accounted for the common-sense conception of practical rationality, and I came to realize that no purely formal theory could do that. I am pleased that Smith acknowledges the power of my theory and I appreciate that he has pointed out places where the theory needs to be stated more carefully, and even slightly revised.

Reply to Kagan

Kagan is one of the few philosophers at the conference who claims to have serious substantive disagreements with my account of rationality. He says, "I believe that morality actually requires us to do as much good as we possibly can do—and I believe that reason requires the same thing" (127). Although Kagan does not attempt to defend these claims in this bold form in his paper, it is important to remember that he does hold them, for these claims involve such distortions of our ordinary understanding of rationality and of morality that it is quite likely that other distortions of these concepts will be involved in his criticisms of my account of them. Kagan's view of rationality entails that in our world in which we can often do more good by helping people for whom we are not concerned, it is irrational to act selfishly or to act so as to help those for whom one is concerned, such as family, friends, countrymen, etc. Indeed, Kagan holds an even stronger position with regard to rationality than Kant, who also holds that rationality coincides with morality, but who does not hold that either "requires us to do as much good as we possibly can do."

Kagan admits that most people do not hold his very extreme view, and offers many more modest versions of this view, including various deontological constraints and constraints of self-interest, but he is clear that he himself holds the claim about rationality in its boldest form. This reinforces the claim that if Kagan means what I mean by "rationally required," he is holding an incredible position. His position entails that people who act only on these more modest claims are regularly acting irrationally. If he is using "irrational" in the way that I do, he must hold none of these people are responsible for their actions. Kagan either is not using "reason requires" such that acting contrary to the way reason requires is acting irrationally or is not using "irrational" in any ordinary sense. Kagan can make up any technical sense of "reason requires" that he wants, but if he is using "reason requires" as equivalent to what I mean by "rationally required," and is using "irrational" in its ordinary sense, what he is saying is clearly false. If he is not using these words and phrases in this way, what he says has no relevance to the positions that I put forward.

I use the term "irrational" such that no person who is held responsible for his actions, would ever advocate to anyone for whom he is concerned, including himself, that he act irrationally. Kagan criticizes me for simply claiming that it is not rationally required to aid others. He wants an argument for my not holding that "one can be irrational for failure to act on reasons even when those reasons are concerned only with the interests of *others*" (130). And by "others," Kagan means any others, not others that are related to one in some way. But many people whom no competent speaker of the language would regard as acting irrationally advocate to those for whom they are concerned that they act only on reasons related to the interests of their friends and family, their race or ethnic group, or their countrymen or religious group. Kagan has to know this, so if he is concerned with the ordinary use of the concept of irrationality, it is not clear what kind of argument he wants.

It seems surprising that Kagan never mentions the category of rationally allowed actions, until one realizes that on Kagan's view there are no rationally allowed actions, except for the rare situations where there are two or more alternatives which will result in our doing as much good as we possibly can. Kagan never explicitly argues against there being such a category. Kagan also never explicitly argues against the hybrid account of rationality that I offer. He suggests that since I hold that "mere change of person affected cannot affect the force of a reason, then perhaps mere change of person affected cannot affect other aspects of what is rational as well" (134). Perhaps, but in fact on the ordinary concepts of reasons and rationality, change of person does not effect the strength of a reason, but does affect whether an action is irrational. As Smith acknowledges, my hybrid theory accounts for the sliver of truth in both rational egoism and in Kant's view about the relationship of rationality to acting morally. Kagan obviously rejects my hybrid theory of rationality, but he offers no argument against it at all. Both Smith and Copp acknowledge that the category of rationally allowed actions is part of our normal concept of rationality. Although Kagan does not accept it. he gives no argument for rejecting the category or for rejecting the hybrid theory that makes that category possible.

I criticize standard philosophical views about rationality like Kagan's because they result in a distortion of the ordinary use of that concept. Given Kagan's claim that I have a mistaken account of rationality, it does seem appropriate to cite authorities. Kagan account of rationality entails that not only I, but all of those philosophers who talk about rational egoism, including Henry Sidgwick, do not use the term "rational" correctly. It is a mark of a genuine philosophical temperament to claim that people who are regarded by almost everyone as competent speakers of the language, nonetheless consistently misuse terms that they regularly use. Some skeptics claim that no one knows anything, that on the basis of the correct account of knowledge, everyone who claims to know something is misusing the word "know." Perhaps Kagan is claiming that almost everyone is misusing the terms "rational" and "irrational."

Kagan's account of morality suffers many of the same faults as his account of rationality, for he holds that "morality actually requires us to do as much good as we possibly can do" (127). Parallel to his account of rationality, his account of morality results in everyone acting immorally almost all of the time. To act contrary to the way morality requires not only entails that one is acting immorally, but also that everyone agrees that doing this kind of action should make one liable to punishment. Unless the phrase is being used simply as a rhetorical device, to hold that a kind of action is morally required is to hold that all impartial rational persons agree that there ought to be a law requiring that kind of act be done. If Kagan is using "morality requires" in this ordinary sense of the phrase, then he holds that almost everyone should be liable to punishment whenever they do not do as much good as they can possibly do.

Given that it is fallible and biased human beings who decide about whether one should actually be punished, it is easy to see why at least some impartial rational persons would not endorse an account of morality which requires everyone to do as much good as they can possibly do. Morality requires people to do only those kinds of acts that all impartial rational persons would agree that their not doing should make them liable to punishment. If Kagan is using the phrase "morality requires" in the same sense I am, he is probably unique in holding that we should be liable to punishment any time that we do not "do as much good as we possibly can do." If he is not using it in my sense, then he is not objecting to my view at all.

Kagan's failure to appreciate the relevant distinctions is apparent from the following quote: "in at least many cases, all impartial rational people would oppose failing to aid others. Which is to say, such failure to aid would be morally wrong. But this, in turn, is equivalent to saying that aiding others is often morally required" (134). But saying failing to aid is morally wrong is not equivalent to saying "aiding others is morally required." I state,

> In that earlier account I said that a morally wrong action is usually an unjustified violation of the moral rules. Now it can be seen that an action that is in accordance with a moral rule when all impartial rational persons would publicly allow violating the rule in order to follow a moral ideal also counts as a morally wrong action. This class of morally wrong actions differs from unjustified violations of moral rules in that only for the latter do all impartial rational persons favor liability to punishment. (*Morality*, 328)

This last sentence makes it clear that it is incorrect to go from "it is sometimes morally wrong not to violate a moral rule" to "an act can be morally required even though it is not required by any moral rule."

After considering several interpretations of my view, Kagan correctly concludes that the key issue between us is whether "Aid the needy" is a moral rule (138-39). He realizes that the key issue is the correctness of my argument that not all impartial rational persons would favor liability for punishment for unjustified violations of this general rule. Kagan admits that I am clearly "right about at least one thing: given human limitations, and widespread need, I literally cannot give aid to all who need it" (139). He suggests, however, that this inability is not important, because "if the agent literally cannot aid anyone else, this will simply be recognized as a valid justification for his failure to aid anyone further" (138). Kagan here seems to confuse justification and excuse.

However, the kind of situation that is relevant to the discussion is not that in which "some agent literally cannot aid anyone else." Rather it is about the more common situation in which a person has the ability and opportunity to aid the needy, but he is tired or is writing a paper rebutting arguments showing that there is not a moral rule requiring one to aid the needy. (I assume that Kagan does not think that doing this is doing "as much good as we possibly can do.") If "Aid the needy" were a moral rule, any time that one spent time doing philosophy, crossword puzzles, or almost any other recreational activity would not count as following that rule and hence should be liable to punishment. These kinds of situations occur every day, but Kagan does not consider them.

Morality is concerned with real human beings, who are fallible and vulnerable. At least some impartial rational persons would not favor having a law requiring everyone to "Aid the needy," for that would require giving fallible persons the authority to punish everyone who unjustifiably violates that rule. Giving any fallible person that much authority might risk more harm being caused than harm prevented. This is even more obvious if one accepts Kagan's view that one is violating the rule "Aid the needy" if one helps those for whom one cares rather than helping the needy when the latter would be doing more good. Just authorizing someone to punish unjustified violations of a moral rule is enough to make some impartial rational persons reject "aid the needy" as a moral rule. Thus, contrary to Kagan, that violating a moral rule only makes one liable to punishment rather than requiring that one actually be punished is sufficient to make at least some impartial rational persons quite worried. Kagan, like many consequentialists, simply ignores the practical implications of morality as a guide to actions for fallible vulnerable human beings. He does not even consider the implications of making almost all of one's behavior liable to punishment.

Despite these misunderstandings, Kagan has pointed out a problem in the way that I talk about the duty to aid others. He, along with others, has led me to realize that the rule "Do your duty" should not be interpreted simply as a more informal version of the preceding rule "Obey the law." On that understanding of the rule, I claimed that the only duties were those that were recognized as duties in the society to which one belonged. This seemed completely parallel to the understanding of "Obey the law" in which it was clear that one is only required to obey actual laws, not laws that some impartial rational persons might put forward. On this understanding, it seemed as if the duty to rescue when one is in a unique or close to unique position, the cost is minimal, and the evil otherwise suffered great, is limited to those societies which actually have such a duty, that is, which make one liable to punishment for not performing that duty.

I had said that "In civilized societies one had a duty to help" in the specified circumstances (*Morality*, 210) because I was concerned that some societies, e.g., those which were suffering serious food problems, might not actually have such duties, and thus would not hold liable to punishment someone who failed to rescue in the situation described. But I have come to realize that some societies also might not hold liable to punishment someone who violates one of the first eight moral rules. This does not count against the view that these rules are moral rules, i.e., rules toward which all impartial rational persons would take the moral attitude, an attitude that involves favoring liability to punishment for violations that were not strongly justified. Kagan's criticisms have made me realize that the duty to rescue in the kind of situation described above resembles the moral rules in this respect, even though it resembles societally recognized duties in most other respects.

I now realize that all impartial rational persons would favor everyone having the duty to rescue in such situations, just as all impartial rational persons would favor everyone being liable for punishment if they unjustifiably disobey any of the moral rules. Just as there need not be an actual law that requires punishment for failure to obey any of the first eight moral rules for them to count as moral rules, so there need not be a societally recognized duty in order for all impartial rational persons to regard aiding someone in the circumstances described above to be a duty. If rational persons are limited to rationally required beliefs, they would take the same attitude toward this duty as they would toward the each of the moral rules.

Thus the question arises, why not simply add another moral rule requiring one to rescue? One answer is that all of the moral rules require one to do or refrain from a kind of action in all situations, whereas duties require one to do or refrain from a kind of action only in specified circumstances. A person is morally required to aid only in fairly well-defined situations. There is no general duty to aid or rescue in situations which are not like the one under discussion, (1) being in a unique or close to unique position, (2) being almost cost-free, and (3) preventing serious evils or harms. However, if a person is in such a situation, he has a duty to rescue. Because it is a duty, it falls under the rule, "Do your duty," and thus it is morally required for one to aid in this kind of situation.

Because a person has a duty to aid only in special circumstances, the kind of circumstances in which most people will never be, it is misleading to regard the duty to aid as another general moral rule. Rather it is more appropriate to regard it as a duty, thereby bringing it under an already existing moral rule. How can it be a duty if it is not recognized as a duty in a given society? It can be by the same argument that the moral rules can be moral rules even if some society does not have a liability to punishment for breaking that rule. Every rational person in every society knows or should know that every rational person wants this duty to be enforced. This results in a universal duty to rescue in these special kinds of situations. Limiting this duty to people in civilized societies, where I assumed it was socially recognized, was a mistake. Impartial rational persons would favor people being liable to punishment for failing to rescue in this kind of situation even when there is no explicit duty in that society.

Regarding the duty to rescue as a duty even in societies where it is not recognized as such is slightly troubling, for it seems to be using "duty" as philosophers have commonly misused it, simply as a synonym for "morally required." However, even the ordinary use of the term "duty" seems to be sufficiently flexible that it is not a misuse of "duty" to hold that there are the kinds of duties which are so universally acknowledged that there is no need for official societal recognition. There may even be other such duties, although I do not know of any other with the same kind of universality as this duty to rescue in the specified circumstances. There is no general duty to help those in need and all of the arguments against this general moral ideal being morally required still have the same force. Of course, it is morally good to help those in need even when one is not in the special circumstances that make it a duty, but there is no general moral requirement to aid the needy.

People who favor a general duty to aid the needy usually focus on the wealthy and claim that they have a duty to give some of that money to the needy; the amount and percentage differs with different philosophers. This makes everything seem quite straightforward and easy. Some people have more money than they need, it would not hurt them to give some of that to the poor and so they should be morally required to do so. But it seems arbitrary to pick on the wealthy to give money and not to require time and effort from those who do not need that time and effort to support themselves in a comfortable situation. Imagine twins, one of whom works hard to make money, and the other spends his time vacationing, making only enough money to live comfortably. Why should the one who works hard be required to give up some of that money and the other twin not be required to give up some of his vacation time?

Once one has considered these kinds of problems, it is clear that making aiding the needy a general moral rule would involve a fantastic interference with people's freedom. There may be some impartial rational people who would claim, contrary to Rawls, that freedom is not more important than welfare, at least until the level of welfare has reached a certain minimal point. However, there may be others who rank freedom so high that they are prepared to risk being the worst off rather than have everyone but the worst off having their freedom so significantly limited. Further, given the fallibility of people, including the people who have the authority to punish, it is doubtful that more will be gained by making aiding the needy a general moral rule than will be gained by recognizing that it is a moral ideal and encouraging people to follow it. No argument has been given to show that all impartial rational persons would favor making aiding the needy a general moral rule that applies all of the time, and hence that makes one liable to punishment almost all of the time.

I thank Kagan for leading me to recognize that there are circumstances in which one has a duty to aid even in a society that does not explicitly recognize such a duty. This account of duties allows some duties that resemble the moral rules, in that there need not be societal recognition of a duty in order for it to be a duty, just as there need not be a law enforcing the kind of conduct required by a moral rule in order for it to be a moral rule. A moral rule applies to people even if they live in a society which does not explicitly have a law prohibiting violating that rule. The duty to rescue applies to people even if they live in a society which does not explicitly recognize that duty. Recognizing that the duty to rescue in specified circumstances is a universal duty, not restricted to societies that actually recognize such a duty, is in no way the first step on the way to making the general moral ideal of aiding the needy into a general moral rule. On the contrary, by removing the most plausible counterexamples, it actually strengthens the distinction between the moral rules and the moral ideals.

Reply to Sinnott-Armstrong

Sinnott-Armstrong is correct that I am a consequentialist with regard to basic reasons, for I hold that all basic reasons for acting involve the consequences (the goods and evils) that result from the action. But I am not a consequentialist with regard to rationality. Although I hold that the only actions that are irrational are those in which one harms oneself (or risks such harm) without some compensating benefit for someone, I do not hold that acting rationally requires acting to achieve the best balance of goods over harms. My hybrid account of rationality explicitly denies that rationality requires this.

A rational egoist holds that rationality requires acting so as to achieve the best balance of goods over harms for himself, whereas a universal act consequentialist like Kagan holds that rationality requires acting so as to achieve the best balance of goods over harms for everyone. My hybrid account of rationality claims that it is rationally allowed not to act on the best reasons, or not to act on any reasons at all. The ordinary concept of rationality, which my hybrid account describes, recognizes that a person can act rationally without acting either to bring about the best consequences for herself or to bring about the best consequences for everyone. Although I hold that it is only the consequences, that is, harms and benefits, or risks of harms and benefits, that determine the rationality of an act, I am not a standard consequentialist.

With regard to morality, my account of the moral system seems as if it could be interpreted as the form of rule consequentialism that Sinnott-

Armstrong describes as "a sophisticated form of negative objective universal public rule consequentialism" (147). I even agree that the point of morality is to lessen the amount of evil, which can be taken as a consequentialist justification of morality. Thus, there may be no point in denying that I am some form of consequentialist. Nonetheless, I think it is important to point out the differences between my view and even the sophisticated and persuasive form of rule consequentialism that Sinnott-Armstrong provides.

Part of that difference stems from my objection to Sinnott-Armstrong's phrase "Gert's own moral system." I am not creating some new moral system, rather I am describing and justifying common morality. I accept the view that ignorance of morality never counts as an excuse for any moral agent, those whom we hold responsible for their actions. No rule counts as a moral rule unless every moral agent knows that the kinds of actions that it prohibits are immoral unless the agent has adequate justification for doing them. No form of rule consequentialism accepts this.

Rule consequentialism is an attempt to formulate rules that do, or would, have the best consequences if adopted, or publicly adopted, or followed, etc. Contemporary rule consequentialism is not an attempt to describe or justify the rules of common morality, rather it is an attempt to create rules for a new morality, rules that if adopted etc., would have the best consequences. All versions of rule consequentialism not only allow for the discovery of entirely new moral rules, they try to provide procedures for discovering these new rules. My account of morality does not allow for the discovery of entirely new moral rules, nor, as Julia Driver points out in her paper, for the discovery of entirely new moral virtues. Some may count this as a difference in favor of rule consequentialism, but I regard natural law theorists as correct in holding that it is an essential feature of morality that all those responsible for their actions know what kinds of behavior morality prohibits, requires, discourages, encourages, and allows.

Rule consequentialists seem not to fully appreciate the fact that according to their theories what rules are moral rules is an empirical matter in a full-blooded sense, that is, it requires real empirical investigation. It is the job of anthropologists, psychologists, and sociologists, not philosophers, to determine what rules would have the best consequences for all. These rules could change over time, be different in different societies, different ethnic groups, different religious groups, etc. Many rules that are not now regarded as moral rules, e.g., rules requiring ways of dressing that are most pleasing to others, could become moral rules. In common morality, the moral rules are not concerned with promoting pleasure or any other goods, but rather with avoiding causing, or increasing the risk of causing, harm to others. Since neither the basic harms, e.g., pain and loss of freedom, nor the basic ways of behaving that cause these harms, e.g., deceiving and cheating, have changed, the moral rules have not changed. However, the findings of anthropologists, psychologists, and sociologists, as well as other empirical facts, are relevant in deciding what exceptions should be publicly allowed.

The discovery that there would be a reduction in harmful consequences if a given rule were publicly adopted, may lead a country to make that rule a law. According to rule consequentialism, the discovery that a rule would have the best consequences if adopted, etc., is the discovery of a new moral rule. Although a reduction in harmful consequences does morally justify making a rule into a law, it does not make that rule into a moral rule. If new moral rules could be discovered, then morality would not be a public system that applies to all rational persons; some moral agents would legitimately be completely ignorant of this rule and so the rule would not apply to them at all. There already is a moral rule requiring one to obey the law, so that making the rule a law is sufficient to make it morally required to obey that law unless one has an adequate justification.

Consequentialists disagree with each other about which consequences are relevant in determining what the moral rules are. Some, like the classic utilitarians think that only pleasure and pain are relevant, others hold that everything on my lists of basic goods and evils are relevant consequences, and some even hold that moral properties such as fairness are relevant consequences. It is clear from this disagreement that none of them holds that every moral agent knows what morality requires them to do. Since consequentialists hold that consequentialism is correct even though they disagree on what consequences are relevant in determining whether an act is morally right or wrong, they cannot hold that every moral agent knows what morality requires them to do. If morality does require every moral agent to know what kinds of acts need moral justification, no form of rule consequentialism provides an adequate description of morality.

If justifying the moral system by looking at the consequences of publicly adopting that system were sufficient for a theory to be consequentialist, I would be a consequentialist. However, this is not normally thought sufficient to classify a theory as a form of rule consequentialism. Further, most consequentialists claim that the moral system itself is consequentialist, whereas on my account, the moral system itself is clearly not a consequentialist system, even though consequences are an important feature of the moral system. No consequentialist view has anything like my morally relevant features, or the two-step procedure for determining when it is justified to violate a moral rule. Rule consequentialists generally concentrate on particular rules, sometimes developing quite complex rules, but they do not consider morality as a complete system, of which the moral rules are only one part.

Sinnott-Armstrong agrees that act consequentialism is not an accurate description of common morality and admits, "If you want universal public rules as practical guides, then . . . Gert's system might seem to have advantages over the most sophisticated act consequentialism" (161). But he holds that act consequentialism can still be the correct account of the "conditions of moral rightness" (156). The conditions of moral rightness, which act consequentialists claim are the actual consequences of the act, are actually those conditions that are put forward by the justified common moral system. There is no "possibility of radical moral progress" if moral progress means discovering new moral rules (161). Radical moral progress is possible only in the sense that many more people may come to be motivated not only to avoid unjustified violations of the moral rules, but also to be motivated to justifiably follow the moral ideals far more often. There is not any "deeper justification" (161) than that by which common morality is justified. The elitist view of act consequentialism, that the best and the brightest could be doing what is morally right by doing those "acts that are forbidden by the best public guide," (160) if "those acts have the best consequences," (161) shows that act consequentialism does not recognize the moral significance of humility.

Act consequentialists do not recognize that the only information that it is appropriate to use when making a moral judgment about an act is information that was available at the time the act is done. Act consequentialists seem to hold the odd view that moral rightness, wrongness, goodness, and badness are best determined by knowledge gained retrospectively, as if a completely unknowable future happening could change the correctness of a moral judgment that all fully informed impartial rational persons had agreed upon at the time of acting. The act consequentialist rationale for distinguishing between holding that an act is morally wrong and holding that the agent should be blamed for doing that act has some plausibility. Blaming a person makes him liable to punishment, and this may cause unnecessary harm. But what is the act consequentialist rationale for distinguishing between holding that an act is morally good and holding that the agent should be praised for doing that act? No unnecessary harm is caused by someone receiving praise.

Act consequentialists hold that consequences determine both whether an action is right or wrong, and whether it is morally right or morally wrong. Of course, the kinds of consequences may be different in the two cases, but in their total reliance on consequences consequentialism claims that moral judgments about right and wrong are no different than judgments about the stock market (156). Sinnott-Armstrong's version of act consequentialism, which uses actual consequences, considers the following two sentences as equally correct ways of talking: "it was extraordinarily bad luck that a meteor fell on the factory and so your decision to buy the stock of that company a month ago turned out to be wrong," and "It was extraordinarily bad luck that a meteor fell on the playground and so your decision to donate and build the playground in that place a month ago turned out to be morally wrong."

Act consequentialism's distinction between holding that an act is morally wrong and holding that the agent should be blamed for doing that act is necessary to avoid total absurdity. But to call an act that has bad consequences only because of a completely random and unknowable happening, e.g., a meteor falling from the sky, "moral wrong" is absurd. Failure to appreciate this inappropriateness makes it completely arbitrary that we do not make moral judgments about the actions of nonhuman animals, infants, small children, and the severely retarded, or indeed about the actions of anyone who is legitimately ignorant of the consequences of his action. Everyone is legitimately ignorant of the complete actual consequences of his actions.

Sinnott-Armstrong's distinction between (1) justifying morality as a public system which should be taught to children, etc., and (2) specifying "conditions of moral rightness" (156) cannot be sustained. He admits that the morality that is and should be taught is a justified public system. It follows that the phrases "morally right," "morally wrong," "morally good," and "morally bad" are and should be learned on the basis of this justified common morality. It seems that act consequentialists hold a linguistic version of Plato's noble lie, where everyone is taught to use "morally right" and "morally wrong" in a certain way, but only act consequentialists know what "morally right" and "morally wrong" really mean. There is no parallel to the use of scientific terms like "mammal" where the term is ordinarily taught in a somewhat simplified way, but biologists realize that a more complex account is more accurate. In this case, biologists have additional empirical information, and the difference almost never makes any difference outside of the work of specialists. Philosophers have no additional empirical information, and unless they thought that their different definition might make some difference in the life of nonphilosophers, there would be no point whatsoever in proposing it.

The view of moral theory as being concerned more with specifying the conditions of moral rightness or evaluation than with decision making is most prominent in the work of G. E. Moore. In his book *Principia Ethica* he even has a chapter with the odd title of "Ethics in Relation to Conduct" as if conduct just happened to be one of the matters that ethics was related to. Surprisingly, Moore, who is an act consequentialist, held that due to the fallibility of people and their inability to know the complete consequences of their actions, they should never violate the traditional moral rules in order to produce the best consequences. Most act consequentialists have not followed Moore in this respect, but claim that people should decide what to do based upon their evaluation of the consequences of the alternatives actions open to them. Thus, for most act consequentialists, decisions follow upon evaluations. Acceptance of this kind of act consequentialism may lead to both linguistic and moral arrogance.

In order to deny my claim that act consequentialism sometimes favors cheating, Sinnott-Armstrong is forced to hold that "Cheating seems to have the best foreseeable consequences in Gert's case only because the student knows more than any real student could ever really know or justifiably believe" (160). Sinnott-Armstrong has to hold that it is quite rare for cheaters to know that they will not be caught and that no one else will be hurt by their particular act of cheating in order to make it plausible that the counterintuitive conclusions of act consequentialism do not refute it (159). But all surveys indicate that far more than half of all students have cheated, and, contrary to what is suggested by Sinnott-Armstrong (160), only the smallest fraction of these have been caught. If students do not commonly know that they can safely cheat, then in what situation can anyone possibly know that the best consequences will result from doing those "acts that are forbidden by the best public guide"?

When considering a couple who enters into an "open marriage," Sinnott-Armstrong tells us that "each does have sex with others and tells the spouse. This does not bother either of them" (157). Given this scenario, Sinnott-Armstrong concludes that their adultery is morally right. But if, as may very well happen, one of them is bothered, has the previous adultery become morally wrong? How can Sinnott-Armstrong be so confident about the harmlessness of adultery when he was so doubtful that anyone could know that they could safely cheat on a single test? There is no point in specifying "conditions of what morally ought to be done in particular situations that could ground a distinct practical public guide" when these conditions cannot be known at the time of acting.

Nonetheless, act consequentialists are right that morality has a point, and that this point is concerned solely with the consequences of the moral system. However, it is false to conclude from this correct observation that the moral judgments that are made on the basis of the moral system are therefore to be made solely on the basis of consequences. Act consequentialism holds that each action, rule consequentialism holds that each rule, and virtue consequentialism holds that each virtue, should be directly morally evaluated or judged solely by its consequences. Consequences do count in the moral evaluation of acts, rules, and virtues, but not only consequences count. Moral judgments, like moral decisions, must be made on the basis of all of the relevant features of the complete moral system. These include far more morally relevant features than simply the consequences of the particular act. It is the whole moral system, that informal public guide which applies to all moral agents, not merely the consequences of a particular action, that determines the conditions of moral rightness.

Sinnott-Armstrong provides an extremely powerful account of my theory as a form of rule consequentialism. He very generously states that my view is "more sophisticated than most versions of rule consequentialism" (146-47). Indeed, he regards "rule consequentialism" as a misleading phrase, and holds that rule consequentialists should be "system consequentialists," that is, they should be concerned with the consequences of the moral system as a whole, not with the consequences of each moral rule on its own. By incorporating almost all of the distinctive features of my account of morality into both rule and act consequentialism, he brings out the essential differences between these two forms of consequentialism. His very fair comparison of these two forms shows that they have different goals. I agree that my goal is the same as that of rule consequentialism, providing a practical guide to conduct that should be publicly taught. However, I regard the goal of act consequentialism as misguided. There is no way to specify the conditions of moral rightness and wrongness other than by using the public moral system that is common morality.

Reply to Wolf

Susan Wolf correctly points out that, although in the titles of the succeeding editions of my moral theory I have "increasingly retreated from a description of [my] theory that highlights the role of rules," (165) I continue to assign to rules a very important place in my theory. She even regards her paper as "a defense of the role rules play in Bernard Gert's moral theory" (166). But as she points out, "By far the biggest problem philosophers have with rules involves the thought that rules are objectionably rigid" (166). It was in response to this problem that I de-emphasized rules in favor of talking about the moral system, of which the moral rules are only one part. The other parts include the moral ideals, the morally relevant features, and the two-step procedure for determining whether violations are justified.

Wolf agrees that it is a mistake to think of the rules as absolute; she realizes that even the rule against killing can have justified exceptions. She also sees that trying to build specific exceptions into the rules, as rule utilitarians often do, only makes the rules more complex, and still encourages thinking of the rules as absolute. As she notes, it is very unlikely that one will ever be able to specify every exception to the rule. She realizes, but does not explicitly point out, that my way of allowing rules to have exceptions does not have this problem. As a further objection to rules she notes that it is intellectually unsatisfying to have rules as the foundation of morality, for it makes sense to ask "what makes it plausible, commendable, desirable that these rules be followed" (167). She sees that, contrary to this understanding of rules, "One may take rules seriously and assign them a central place without either taking them to give absolute moral guidance or to be rationally foundational" (167). She correctly states that "Gert's use of rules is a prime example of this: Gert's list of rules occupies a central place in his theory—it comprises, at the least, a first answer to the question of what morality requires one to do—but it does not govern conduct absolutely nor does it constitute the end of the moral justificatory line" (168).

After noting that Kantian theories take moral rules more seriously than most forms of consequentialism, she says that for Kantians, "abiding by the rules that one expects and relies on others to obey implicitly acknowledges that one is on an equal plane with them" (172). In this context, Wolf could mention that I identify humility as the virtue that involves recognizing that one is subject to the same constraints of morality as everyone else. She could also mention the significance of impartiality with respect to the moral rules; that morality requires impartiality whenever one is considering violation of a moral rule. Impartiality in this context is what requires the use of the two-step procedure in order to determine if one would publicly allow this kind of violation. As I point out in my reply to Kamm, that morality is a public system is what guarantees that acting morally expresses respect for other persons. It does this because a public system, as I define it, necessarily involves the appropriate kind of impartiality, an impartiality that is closely associated with humility.

It should be clear that this discussion of Wolf is in no way a reply to her paper. Her paper does not call for a reply by me, for it may offer a better reply to a Kantian like Baron, or a consequentialist like Kagan, than I did in defending my account of the special status of the moral rules. She points out that my rules "for many people constitute the paradigm or the core of morality" (176). She makes clear that by emphasizing the moral rules I provide an answer to "an important and distinct question . . . what ought we to *require* of each other in order to live peaceably and well in a common world?" (177) As one of the leading contributors to the discussion of how one should live, her general agreement with my view that "morality has a distinct and specific subject matter, much narrower than the question 'How should one live?'" (174) carries considerable weight. It is also significant that she regards this view of morality as involving rules that involve requirements "that it would be legitimate to punish people for failing to meet" (175).

I am grateful to Wolf for defending in a subtle and nuanced fashion the view that obedience to the moral rules, and only to the moral rules, is morally required. I hope that those who are unpersuaded by my replies will read her paper.

Reply to Deigh

Deigh points out that there are at least two different distinctions that I make between moral rules and moral ideals. The first is what he calls a functional distinction, that moral rules prohibit or require, whereas moral ideals only encourage. The second is what he calls a substantive distinction. He claims that this second distinction between avoiding causing harm and preventing harm (187) is not clear because many cases of preventing harm are cases of avoiding causing harm. But Deigh's own example, "the signs 'Prevent Forest Fires' . . . are meant to be a call to avoid causing forest fires" (183) shows that he is quite clear about what is meant by my distinction between preventing and avoiding causing.

Although he sometimes suggests that I make the substantive distinction between the rules and ideals by contrasting negative actions (omissions) and positive actions (acts), Deigh correctly concludes that I do not use such a distinction and that I regard many positive actions to be required by a moral rule, e.g., keeping a promise (183-84). Indeed, I co-authored a number of papers showing that the traditional way of distinguishing between killing and letting die cannot be made by distinguishing between acts and omissions.

Deigh comes up with a clear account of why I distinguish between moral rules and moral ideals by noting that "one cannot follow [an] ideal all of the time" (185) and that "unlike moral rules, one can sensibly ask how much time one should devote to following [the moral ideals]" (185). "Ideals prescribe ends" (185) whereas "rules do not prescribe ends. Rather they set constraints on the pursuit of whatever ends people adopt, and everyone can be expected always to live within these constraints" (185). Deigh's way of putting the matter is a clear way to make what he calls my substantive distinction; I accept it completely.

Deigh's primary concern is whether what he calls the functional distinction yields the same distinction as what he calls the substantive distinction, i.e., that the moral ideals have the goal of lessening evil, whereas the moral rules set constraints on the pursuit of whatever ends people adopt (185-86). He correctly notes that some philosophers, e.g., Mill and Kant, claim that we have a duty to aid others, which involves adopting an end. He claims that this means that for them adopting an end can be morally required. Deigh then concentrates on what he calls the Gert-contra-Kant argument that "there are no moral requirements to adopt certain ends" (186).

Deigh acknowledges that I am clear that a person can promise to adopt some end, and if she does, then she can be morally required to adopt that end. I am also clear that some jobs have duties which involve adopting ends, e.g., nurses have duties the involve preventing and relieving the pain of their patients. I am equally clear that the law can require a person to adopt certain ends, e.g., reduce the amount of pollution his factory puts out. Indeed, Deigh, unlike Kagan, recognizes that having a duty to rescue in the special circumstances I describe does not entail that one has a duty to contribute to saving starving children overseas (190). Deigh's discussion enables me to clarify what I mean when I say that morality never requires adopting an end. I mean that morality never requires adopting an end unless adopting that end is also required by some moral rule. I deny that people are morally required to follow any general moral ideal when none of the rules, including the rule, "Do your duty," requires them to follow it.

A moral theory should construct a system of morality that describes and explains the moral decisions and judgments of competent moral agents. There are two classes of moral decisions and judgments, those that are best explained by the moral rules and those that are best explained by the moral ideals. People are generally praised for justifiably following moral ideals, trying to achieve certain ends when they are not required to do so by the moral rules. People are generally condemned for unjustifiably violating moral rules. Moral rules are rules that impartial rational persons would favor being enforced by laws. To say that a kind of action is morally required means that impartial rational persons favor liability to punishment for failing to do that kind of act. Whether it is appropriate to actually punish every action that is morally prohibited, or every failure to do what is morally required, depends on the circumstances.

The question may now seem to arise, "Why should we accept what you say rather than what Kant and Mill say, namely, that we do have imperfect duties to follow general moral ideals?" But Kant and Mill do not disagree; they do not use the term "imperfect duty" in such a way that it entails favoring liability to punishment if one does not act on an imperfect duty. That is why I object to their use of the phrase "imperfect duty"; it trivializes the term "duty." Imperfect duties are no more duties than rubber ducks are ducks; genuine duties should make one liable to punishment for failing to do them. Respect for common morality leads me to take seriously the fact that common morality does not regard people as liable to punishment for failing to act on general moral ideals.

I justify the functional distinction between moral rules and moral ideals by showing that impartial rational persons would make the same distinction. People know that it is generally not difficult to avoid committing unjustified violations of the moral rules, but they also know that it would be a great burden to be morally required to act on moral ideals whenever it is not unjustified to do so. The realization that everyone would have a significant risk of being punished if acting on the general moral ideals were morally required, supports common morality's functional distinction between moral rules and moral ideals. Impartial rational persons can always propose laws which require following more specific moral ideals, so that no practical advantage would be gained by making following general moral ideals morally required, and quite a bit would be lost.

One of the major flaws of most philosophical accounts of morality is that they omit any consideration of punishment in describing the moral system. (Rawls does this intentionally.) But without consideration of punishment, it is impossible to distinguish between those acts that are morally encouraged or discouraged and those that are morally required or prohibited. Impartial rational persons may prefer to live in a society where acting on moral ideals is only encouraged rather than to live in a society where someone whom they do not know decides whether or not to punish people for failing to do what everyone will fail to do for most of the times of their life. Impartial rational persons do not assume that whomever makes the decision to punish those actions that are liable to punishment will do so as they would. They know that all persons are fallible. They also know that not all persons are impartial rational persons.

Further, even if the punishment would be decided by an impartial rational person, such people can differ significantly in their ranking of the evils and their ideology, in particular, their estimates of the harms involved in not punishing failures to do morally required actions. An impartial rational person might not be willing, even for another impartial rational person to have the power to decide at almost any time, that he can be punished for failing to act on the general moral ideals. With regard to the general moral rules, even those that require positive actions, a person can usually easily avoid doing what is morally prohibited or avoid failing to do what is morally required. This would not be true if failing to act on the general moral ideals were morally required.

Deigh says, "Why Gert should deny that morality ever directly requires the promotion of some end when at the same time he allows that it can indirectly require the promotion of ends in virtue of these moral rules and the possibility of duties and promises to promote certain ends is a puzzle in itself" (187-88). He notes that when ends are adopted as a result of duties or promises, "one does not need to be engaged in an action promotive of some end to be in compliance with a requirement to promote it" (188). Thus, Deigh does not think that taking the general moral ideals as moral requirements means that one must be constantly acting on these ideals, whereas I regard taking the general moral ideals as moral requirements to mean that one is required to be acting on these ideals unless one has an adequate justification or excuse. That is why I do not want to regard them as moral requirements. The ends that are adopted indirectly as a result of promises, duties, or laws are limited by the proper understanding of these moral requirements. To take the general moral ideals as moral requirements eliminates these limitations.

Further, even on Deigh's account of what is involved in adopting an end, if one does nothing at all to promote that end, then if adopting that end is a moral requirement, one has violated that moral requirement. Thus, scholars who obsessively pursue their scholarship without following the general moral ideals would be liable to punishment. But no one would hold that a person who never acts on the general moral ideals should be liable to punishment, whereas everyone holds that a person who does nothing to act on a moral ideal that is required by some moral rule should be liable to punishment. "If I promise to take care of your ten children for a day," (188-89) I must do something that counts as taking care of them. I cannot simply go off to the library that whole day and leave them alone. To do so makes me liable to punishment. A scholar is not liable to punishment for spending all of his time in the library.

In the end, Deigh does not disagree with my attempting to distinguish moral ideals from moral rules, rather he thinks I go wrong by not distinguishing between them enough. He criticizes me for taking "moral ideals to be precepts" and putting them in "the same category of standards as moral rules" (193). He wants them, instead, to be viewed as "models of conduct" (193). Deigh recognizes that there are many other ideals and suggests that those ideals that "function in people's lives by enlarging their understanding of the significance and value of compliance with moral requirements and moral prohibitions and thus strengthening their disposition to comply . . . is for that person a moral ideal" (194). I understand and appreciate Deigh's use of the phrase, "moral ideal," but it is not my use. I am not claiming that my use is better than Deigh's, only that it is different for, unlike the phrase "moral rule," I do not think that there is a standard use of the phrase "moral ideal."

I use moral ideals as part of the public system that describes and explains the considered moral decisions and judgments that are made by competent moral agents. I formulate them as precepts in order to facilitate that description and explanation. If Deigh does not include my moral ideals in the moral system, he has no way to deal with the question of when following what I call a moral ideal justifies breaking a moral rule. He admits that, for he holds, "Moral ideals, then, do not come into the study of morality as an integral part of the system of rules and principles that, in contemporary philosophy, is seen as the proper object of that study" (195-96). But a moral theory is supposed to describe, explain, and justify the moral decisions and judgments of thoughtful people. Without moral ideals in my sense Deigh cannot explain our judgments about those actions that are called morally good, that is, those judgments in which we praise people for doing more than they are morally required to do.

Deigh wants his moral ideals to "answer directly a common uncertainty about the meaningfulness of one type of conduct" (195). That type of conduct, "Compliance with the demands of morality, its requirements and prohibitions, is commonly a source in people of uncertainty about whether it serves any of their own purposes" (195). I agree with Deigh that it is important to meet that uncertainty. Indeed, my whole moral theory can be taken as addressing itself to that uncertainty. I address this question most directly in my chapter concerning why one should be moral. My disagreement with Deigh is about the nature of morality. I do not think that it consists entirely of requirements and prohibitions, the domain of the moral rules; rather it includes actions that go beyond what is required, following what I call the moral ideals.

Deigh has pointed out many places where I did not express the distinction between moral rules and moral ideals clearly enough. He has forced me to be more explicit and detailed in my explanation of why not all impartial rational persons would favor making following general moral ideals morally required. My functional distinction gains some confirmation by accounting for the fact that people are not held liable to punishment for failing to justifiably follow general moral ideals, whereas they are held liable to punishment for failing to justifiably obey general moral rules. By recognizing the importance of being liable to punishment—and not just the importance of actually being punished—my theory is able to explain why impartial rational persons would not make following general moral ideals morally required. Thus, Deigh has helped me to strengthen the force of the distinction between moral rules and moral ideals and has led to a clearer justification of this distinction.

Reply to MacLean

MacLean says, "some moral theorists give accounts of morality that are not restricted to prohibiting and reducing harms, and they also claim to start from and remain consistent with common morality" (207). He uses this fact to argue that common morality does include positive aspects. He agrees with Bond who claims that, although deontic morality is restricted to rules, there is a broader view of morality in which fashioning ideals for individual lives and societies is an important part. "Morality" is used in many ways; I claim only to be providing an account of the central concept, one that systematizes people's thoughtful and coherent moral decisions and judgments. This concept of morality is also what most of the great moral philosophers of past were primarily concerned with. Even John Stuart Mill, whom MacLean cites as one of the primary proponents of the positive account of morality, says the following: "The moral rules which forbid mankind to hurt one another (in which we must never forget to include a wrongful interference with each other's freedom) are more vital to human well-being than any maxims, however important, which only point out the best mode of managing some department of human affairs. . . . [A] person may possibly not need the benefits of others, but he always needs that they not do him hurt" (*Utilitarianism*, chapter 5, par. 31, quoted on page 247 of *Morality*).

Susan Wolf in her paper has pointed out, "It is fashionable these days to say that moral philosophy asks, or should ask 'How should one live?' (173)" MacLean takes this fashionable view. Common morality is concerned with a much narrower question. Although moral judgments are not always distinguished from nonmoral judgments, there is a set of judgments about actions, character, motives, and persons that form a complete and coherent whole and can be distinguished from other judgments. These are the judgments that I try to account for by describing the moral system that is common morality. MacLean recognizes that avoiding and preventing harm has greater importance than producing positive goods with regard to morality (206). However, he does not seem to appreciate how important this is. As I point out in my reply to Bond, when concerned with individuals, absent consent, only preventing harms can justify violating a moral rule; promoting goods cannot. Given the central role that everyone assigns to the moral rules, this explains why the moral ideals are essential to morality, whereas the utilitarian ideals are marginal.

Although MacLean holds that my claim that morality is concerned with lessening the amount of suffering is too strongly stated, he agrees that "the case for moral philosophy accentuating the negative is a strong one" (211). He thinks that there is still some point in including the promotion of social goods in the field of moral philosophy. At this point, our disagreement may be almost completely verbal. I agree that political philosophy does involve the promotion of goods such as education, and even parks and playgrounds. Since political philosophy can be viewed as a part of moral philosophy, moral philosophy is concerned with promoting goods. But when one is concerned with the behavior of individuals toward one another, the promotion of goods is not part of morality. MacLean makes this point himself in contrasting the "moral admiration [we might have] for someone who devoted considerable time and energy looking around for occasions to relieve suffering and acting to relieve it wherever he could" (208) with "someone [who] spent time and energy instead looking for occasions to bring pleasure to people" (208). Of this second person, MacLean says, "we would not admire such a person at all. We would regard him as a busybody whose interest in the welfare of others was inappropriate" (208). Goods and evils play different roles in morality. A bribe, no matter how large, does not excuse or justify a player cheating; a threat of harm, if sufficiently large, does.

However, I do not agree with all of MacLean's points about the asymmetry of pleasure and pain or goods and harms. I think that Bentham was correct in saying that, other things being equal, a pleasure that lasts longer is better than one that is shorter. The same is true about the badness of pain; other things being equal, a pain that lasts longer is worse than one that is shorter. The same is true of intensity of pains and pleasures. The world may be a better place "if there is less suffering in it" (208), that is, if each person suffers less, but it is not a *morally* better place if the actions of moral agents have nothing to do with there being less suffering. MacLean is correct that "There is no reason to think . . . the world would be better if there were more people in it than are alive today, even if each additional person were living a happy life" (209). But there is also no reason to think the world would be worse if there were more people in it than are alive today, even if each additional person were living a unhappy life.

MacLean sometimes seems to equate value and moral value. He suggests "that happiness or pleasure is good only on condition that people desire it, and that without this desire, additions of pleasure or happiness have no positive moral value at all" (209). He even goes so far as to say that "pleasure itself has no intrinsic value" (209). But part of the criterion for saying that an activity or a sensation provides pleasure is the same as the criterion for desiring to have it continue, and part of the criterion for saying that an activity or a sensation is painful is the same as the criterion for desiring to have it stop. The criterion for desiring a sensation to continue is not the sole criterion that it is pleasant, and the criterion for desiring a sensation to stop is not the sole criterion that it is painful. There are natural expressions of pleasure and pain that also serve as part of their criteria. Nonetheless, understanding what "pleasure" and "pain" mean requires knowing their conceptual relationship to desires.

This does not mean, as MacLean seems to think, that the badness of pain depends on a desire to avoid it. That, absent an adequate justification, it is morally wrong to inflict pain and that, absent reasons to the contrary, it is morally good to relieve pain are views that are almost universally accepted. Normally, that a person simply wants to have pain inflicted on himself is not an adequate reason for inflicting that pain, for such a person may be suffering from a mental disorder. However, that a person does not want his pain relieved does provide a reason for not relieving it, but that is because to relieve his pain without his consent is to deprive him of freedom.

MacLean cites the interesting research of Daniel Kahneman and his colleagues that shows "that preferences for the relief of pain do not fit the model that more pain is worse than less" (209). Supposedly people "process these episodes cognitively as a function only of the experience at its peak and at the end. We tend, in other words, to ignore the duration of the painful episode" (209). But clearly that is only when the difference of the duration is measured in minutes, not in days or months. Although MacLean is correct that it should be left to the fully informed competent patient to decide whether he wants a shorter pain with an end that is just as painful or a longer pain with a less painful end, it not clear how this affects the moral relevance of relieving pain. But this is because one needs a very strong reason to deprive a person of freedom.

Kahneman's explanation of why a person prefers the longer pain which decreases in intensity to the shorter one that retains the same intensity may be correct, but it is not the only explanation. Many people find that the experience of pain decreasing in intensity as itself pleasurable. It is not irrational for people to undergo some pain to increase their pleasure. People often do so by remaining hungry for a long time in order to make their eating experience more enjoyable. No one holds that it would be morally good to make them eat earlier so as to relieve their hunger pangs. Thus, there seems to be nothing morally troubling in the discoveries of Kahneman and his colleagues.

MacLean agrees with Bond on the greater importance of avoiding causing harm and preventing harm to promoting goods. He also agrees with Bond that there is more to morality than simply avoiding causing harm and preventing harm. When morality is regarded as including politics, then they are correct. When, however, morality is regarded as a guide to behavior for individuals with regard to other individuals, then morality is more restricted. All three of us agree that whether morality is completely restricted to the avoiding and preventing of harm or also includes the promotion of good, the former goals so far outweigh the latter that if the harm is serious, no amount of good promoted justifies causing that harm.

Reply to Kamm

I am pleased that Kamm finds my account of morality to be in accord with common morality, but I am disturbed that she does not find Hobbes' account to be similarly in accord with common morality. This is not the place to discuss Hobbes, but it may be relevant to point out that, unlike Kamm, who writes as if morality is concerned primarily with particular acts, Hobbes views morality as being primarily concerned with virtues and vices. This means that Hobbes does not try to decide what morally ought to be done by looking at the probable consequences of a particular act, but rather discovers which traits of character are most conducive to peace, and then recommends acting to exemplify those traits of character. This point is significant. Although Hobbes holds that the point of morality is to achieve peace, and hence to lessen everyone's chances of being harmed, he strongly recommends that individual citizens act as the sovereign commands (obey the laws) rather than act in the ways that they believe will result in a greater lessening of harm. Hobbes holds that, except in very rare cases, people should obey the law even if they do not agree with it.

I agree with Hobbes that the point of morality is to lessen the suffering of harm, and I also agree with him that this does not mean that in any particular situation one morally ought to act in the way which one believes, even justifiably believes, will lessen overall harm. Both Hobbes and I recognize the importance of fallibility in morality. Kamm says, "If Gert really believed that common morality were concerned with reducing evil, he should, for example, think it permits killing one person in order to save two from death (or from being killed) or maiming one to save another from death" (217). I do not agree. I do believe "that common morality [is] concerned with reducing evil," but I do not believe that this should lead me to hold that it is permitted to kill one person to save two. Kamm mistakenly seems to think that the fact that morality is concerned with reducing evil entails that morality requires or encourages any act that reduces evil. Just as Kamm does not appreciate that Hobbes regards morality as applying primarily to virtues and vices and not to particular acts, she may not appreciate that I regard morality as a public system that is primarily concerned with kinds of acts, not particular acts.

It is a mistake to say that if the point of a game is to test one's athletic abilities, every move in the game should be determined by which move best tests one's athletic abilities. The same is true of Kamm's claim that if the point of morality is to lessen evil, then every act that is governed by morality should be the one that most lessens evil, a kind of negative act consequentialism.

Common morality presupposes the fallibility of persons. Recognition of this presupposition shows that negative act consequentialism, which requires each act to be the one that (one justifiably believes) results in the least overall harmful consequences is a mistaken account of morality.

Since morality is a public guide to conduct, rather than considering the consequences of each particular act, there is an explicit decision procedure for determining when it is morally justified to violate a moral rule. If one is considering violating the rule against killing in order to save two lives (217), the two-step procedure involves more than merely looking at the consequences of that particular act, although this is part of the first step, namely, describing the act using only morally relevant features. This description, in addition to including the consequences of the particular act, also includes other features as well, including whether a violation of a moral rule is being prevented. (By the way, that I list this last feature as a morally relevant feature indicates that Kamm is mistaken in holding that I do not distinguish between breaking rules in order to prevent "evil that is not caused by human interference" and "evil that is caused by human interference" [216].)

After describing the act using only the morally relevant features, the consequences of that kind of violation being publicly allowed must be estimated and compared to the estimate of that kind of violation not being publicly allowed. This is how an impartial rational person determines whether she will publicly allow that violation. If all impartial rational persons would publicly allow the violation, then it is strongly justified and all impartial rational persons would favor doing it. If no impartial rational person would publicly allow the violation, then it is unjustified and no impartial rational person would favor doing it. If only some impartial rational person would publicly allow the violation, then it is weakly justified and impartial rational persons would disagree on whether it should be done. Notice that the consequences of the particular act play no more than a small role in determining whether the violation of the rule is morally justified. Realizing that people are fallible and that the impartiality required by common morality takes this fallibility into account, it becomes clear that everyone knowing that everyone is allowed to kill one in order to save two would result in far more people being killed than if people knew that they were prohibited from killing unless the number of people to be saved were so great that an impartial rational person could publicly allow that kind of violation.

That morality is a public system that applies to all rational persons is what results in respect for the separateness of persons. Thus I disagree with Kamm's conclusion "that Gert and the common morality he seeks to describe and justify are more concerned with respect for the separateness of persons than with the avoidance of evils" (218). Rather, both Gert and common morality recognize that common morality is a public guide to conduct for fallible persons. Such a public guide must, by its very nature, require respect for the separateness of persons. A public guide must be one that it would be rational for everyone to whom it applies to follow. Following such a guide results in far less evil than a guide to conduct that requires a person to do the act that (she justifiably believes) will result in the lesser evil. There is no incompatibility between holding that the goal of morality is to lessen the suffering of evil and that morality requires respect for the separateness of persons because both follow from the fact that morality is a public system that applies to all rational persons.

Reply to Bond

Whereas Kagan and Deigh criticize my distinction between moral rules and moral ideals, Bond accepts that distinction but criticizes my distinction between moral ideals and utilitarian ideals. He agrees completely with my view that it is morally required to obey the moral rules and that these rules prohibit causing harm. He says, "Gert has correctly seen that *deontic* morality (the ethics of moral requirement) has to do with the avoidance of wrongdoing (causing or contributing to evil) and not with the disinterested promotion of good" (219) and "Gert is absolutely right in seeing moral *obligation* or requirement . . . as entirely concerned with the not causing of evils or harms" (219).

Bond claims that since I admit that impartial rational persons take the same attitude toward the utilitarian ideals as toward the moral ideals, namely, encouraging justified following of them, this would "tend to favor placing them together in the same category rather than making them separate and distinct" (221). The moral system, that system that thoughtful people use, generally unconsciously, to make their moral decisions and judgments consists of the moral rules, the moral ideals, the morally relevant features, and the two-step procedure for determining if a violation of a moral rule is justified. Moral ideals can sometimes justify violating moral rules, even without the consent of the person toward whom one is breaking the moral rule. Except for special circumstances, the utilitarian ideals cannot. That is why moral ideals, but not utilitarian ideals, are included in the moral system. That impartial rational persons take the same attitude toward the utilitarian ideals as toward the moral ideals is an interesting feature of the moral theory, but it has limited relevance to morality. Bond may not sufficiently appreciate the distinction between morality and the moral theory that is used to describe, explain, and justify it.

Bond does not disagree with me about any matter of substance regarding common morality, that is, he does not disagree with any of the moral decisions or judgments that result from my account of morality. Rather, like most others, he prefers a more positive characterization of morality rather than the negative characterization that I provide. Bond thinks that the virtues show that my negative characterization is inadequate. In particular, he thinks that I provide an inadequate account of "kindness" by limiting it to the following of the moral ideals. According to Bond, "kindness can probably best be conceived as doing things for the good of others" (222). He admits that kindness is "primarily concerned with the relief of suffering," (222) but he claims that "kindness is in no way *exclusively* concerned with it or with any other way of lessening evil" (222).

I do use terms somewhat more precisely than they are ordinarily used (see *Morality,* 322), but I do not think that I distort the ordinary sense of terms. It is interesting and it may be important that almost all of the examples of kindness that Bond presents as concerned with the promotion of good, e.g., "to hold a door open for someone or to yield in traffic" (222) can equally well be described as preventing or avoiding harm. It is not unknown for failure to yield in traffic to cause road rage, and although that is extreme, being upset by someone failing to yield is extremely common. Thus, yielding in traffic can be seen as trying to avoid causing another person being upset. Similarly, to hold a door open not only makes someone feel good, it also prevents their feeling bad. A salesperson who is helpful is often described as kind, but that is because the person who needs help is often relieved of an unpleasant confusion about where to go. Imagine someone simply promoting good for someone when they do not think that person needs cheering up; "kind" is not the term that we are likely to use. To make someone who is obviously having a good time have an even better time is not the kind of action that anyone would use to teach the word "kind".

This examination of kindness indicates that limiting moral virtues to those that involve preventing or relieving harm is more in accord with our ordinary understanding than Bond acknowledges. More important, Bond agrees that acting on those virtues that do not involve preventing or relieving harms or evils never justifies violating a moral rule. Thus, it is appropriate not to classify these virtues as moral virtues. Some of the virtues that Bond puts forward as moral virtues (with the corresponding vice in parentheses), "such as friendliness (coldness), generosity (stinginess), conviviality (closeness), [and] modesty (immodesty)" (222), seem to me to be best characterized as social virtues, for the very reason that Bond calls them moral virtues, "because they contribute to a good and desirable social environment" (222). However, all would agree that exemplifying a social virtue never, by itself, justifies violating a moral rule. You are never justified in deceiving someone just in order to be friendly.

This new category of social virtues, seems to me to be a useful one, for the virtues that Bond cites are neither moral or personal virtues. Unlike personal virtues, social virtues are not traits that primarily aid their possessors in carrying out their plans, regardless of whether these plans are egoistic or moral. Unlike the moral virtues, the social virtues are not based on the moral rules and ideals. They are traits of character that make for more pleasant interaction between people. However, unlike the moral vices, the corresponding social vices do not seem to involve being morally bad. I admit that people do not ordinarily distinguish between different categories of character traits that they dislike, so that the distinction between moral and social virtues is not one that is ordinarily made. Further, I am not now endorsing the particular list that Bond puts forward, for I think that there may be some problem in distinguishing some of these virtues and vices from personality traits. Nonetheless I do think that he is right to regard traits of character that "contribute to a good and desirable social environment" to be virtues. However, it does not follow that they should be regarded as moral virtues.

According to Bond, however, "a rule, ideal, or virtue is properly called moral if it is needed for or contributes to the well-being of individuals in the context of society or community" (224). He regards what I take as the goal of morality, "the lessening of evils or harms" (220) as only the most important part of "morality's ultimate purpose . . . namely, the social good" (220). On the other hand, as noted earlier, he says: "Gert is absolutely right in seeing moral *obligation* or requirement (what I have called *deontic* morality) as entirely concerned with the not causing of evils or harms" (219). Bond's error is that his account of deontic morality is too restricted, it fails to include those elements of the moral system that affect one's moral requirements, namely, the moral ideals, the morally relevant features, and the two-step procedure. Were he to have included those features, he would have seen that what I call morality is simply a more complete account of what he calls deontic morality.

Although my use of the term "morality" is not the only correct use of that term, it is a correct use. It captures the concept of morality that almost all of the great moral philosophers, e.g., Kant and Mill, were trying to justify. It is a concept of morality that has great unity and consistency. It has the kind of power and universality that explains why everyone, including all of the great religious leaders, regard morality as so important. There might be no great harm done if a few additional ideals and virtues were included within morality, but there is no benefit in doing so. Morality is not all of life, it is not even all of the good life.

There are rational ideals and virtues outside of morality; there is no point in trying to push them all inside, especially when doing so requires distinguishing between those moral ideals and moral virtues that are directly related to the moral system and those that are not.

I want to thank Bond for helping me to appreciate the category of social virtues. These virtues—friendliness, generosity, conviviality, and modesty—are important virtues. They deserve more investigation than I have given them.

Reply to Driver

Driver argues that my view of moral virtues "owes more to classic philosophical views, which hold that moral virtue requires rational belief, than to ordinary morality, which is more forgiving" and that I depart "from common sense or ordinary morality" (231). However, Driver may come to this conclusion because she falsely equates my distinction between the personal and the moral virtues with the distinction between "'prudential' vs. 'moral' virtues, or . . . self-regarding vs. other-regarding virtues" (232). I do not view the personal virtues as being self-regarding. As Driver notes, I call them personal, because all rational persons want to have them personally, but they want them regardless of whether they want to aid others or to benefit themselves. Driver's acceptance of the standard philosophical distinctions may lead her to misunderstand my views.

Driver criticizes me for omitting "the classic moral virtue of benevolence," (233) but as she defines "benevolence," it is exhibited by an "agent who creates more happiness for those who are not suffering" (232). So defined, benevolence is not a moral virtue, rather it is what, in my reply to Bond, I called a social virtue. A moral virtue is one whose exemplification sometimes would, even without the consent of the person toward whom the moral rule is broken, justify violating that moral rule. Without such consent, it is never justified to break a moral rule in order to exhibit the social virtue of benevolence as Driver describes it. Although I use terms in a more precise way than they are used in everyday language, the distinction between a social virtue and a moral virtue is embodied in ordinary language as well. A philanthropist who gives generously to fund the opera, concerts, and museums, but gives nothing to hospitals, might be praised for his civic virtue, but not for his moral virtue.

Driver also criticizes me for ruling out "certain traditional traits, such as courage" as a moral virtue (233). Driver notes that I consider courage a personal virtue, but she does not mention that I explain that courage is sometimes thought to be a moral virtue because it is "often required in order to follow the moral ideals" (*Morality*, 298). Moreover, she admits that there can be "courageous thieves" (233) so that it seems clear that courage *per se* is not a moral virtue, although it may be necessary for the expression of some moral virtues. These examples show that Driver is not criticizing me on the basis of any deviation from ordinary usage, but rather from a consequentialist account of the virtues. This is important to note, for otherwise it is hard to find a unified basis for her criticisms.

Driver's use of ordinary language to criticize my account sometimes seems slightly out of focus. From the fact that we say, "He has the virtue of being a good father" (233), she concludes that "being a good father is a moral virtue" (234), and so some moral virtues are not universal. I admit that it is a virtue to be a good father, but that simply means that it is praiseworthy to be a good father, it does not mean that there is some specific trait of character that is the good father virtue. The question, "What virtues must a good father have?" not only makes sense, it is commonly asked. It can and should be answered by naming all of the moral virtues that I list—kindness, honesty, fairness, etc.—not just "dependability" as Driver suggests (233). Indeed, Driver explicitly says that "being a good father is a trait which involves justifiably following the moral rules and moral ideals" (234). Driver simply creates a new moral virtue, the moral virtue of being a good father, without realizing that being a good father simply involves having all the moral virtues. Driver may be claiming that my account of moral virtues is only an account of the basic moral virtues, and that there are complex moral virtues, such as being a good father, that do not fit my analysis. The concept of complex moral virtues is an interesting one, but it is not one that has much support in ordinary language.

Driver realizes that "greed would not be a moral virtue, since it is not the case that all impartial rational persons would want all persons to have this trait" (234). But then she goes on to say, "however, might it not, counter-intuitively, come off as a personal virtue? Perhaps all rational persons would want to be greedy? I just don't know" (234). This statement is odd because Driver has already stated that "it is not the case that all impartial rational persons would want all persons to have this trait" (234). Since they are impartial, that means that they would not want themselves to have this trait. Since they are rational that shows that not all rational persons would want to be greedy, so it is absolutely clear that greed is not a personal virtue. Driver objects to this reply by claiming that it will severely limit "the scope of personal virtue" (234). However, what she claims is an example of an unacceptable limitation, is that it rules out being "extraordinarily intelligent" as a "moral virtue" (234).

Driver makes two mistakes here. First, and least important, is that she seems to forget that personal virtues are virtues of character, such at courage, prudence, and temperance. Intelligence is not a virtue of character at all. However, it is a virtue in that it is a trait that all rational persons would want for themselves. Driver's second mistake trades on the ambiguity of the phrase "being extraordinarily intelligent." When this means being "smarter than others" it is true that not all rational persons would want this trait, because impartial rational persons would not want it. However, if "extraordinary intelligence" means a trait that involves having the high degree of knowledge and other intellectual abilities that are now had by only a few people, then all rational persons would want this trait.

It is true that when we talk about someone having a virtue, e.g., courage, we imply that he is better than others in that regard, e.g., he is more courageous than others. However, when a person wants a personal virtue, what he wants is a trait of character that will enable him to act appropriately in the relevant circumstances, that is, to act as a courageous person in situations of danger. Insofar as he wants a personal virtue, he does not want to be better than others, for he does not even have to be thinking about others at all. He simply wants to act in the appropriate way for the appropriate reason, etc., as Aristotle describes the virtues. Neither moral virtues, personal virtues, nor virtues like intelligence are traits that are essentially comparative, even though when we say that someone has a virtue we are making a comparative judgment. This point is more complex than I had realized and perhaps Driver was misled by my not being as clear about it as I should have been.

Driver says, "One great virtue of Gert's account is its clarity" (232), and cites my distinction between character traits and personality traits as an example of that clarity. Yet she seems to confuse the two in several criticisms of my view, e.g., claiming that "the coldness of the physician," a personality trait, "may make him more dependable" (234). Later she talks about not wanting a doctor to be "squeamish" and wanting "him to be tougher, and slightly hardened to the distress of others" (236). These comments show that Driver thinks that it may interfere with doctors doing what they should do if they are too compassionate. I agree with this, but it does not count in the slightest against my account of the virtues. Her use of the phrase "the virtue of kindness or sensitivity" (236) suggests that she does not distinguish between personality and character traits. Her failure to distinguish between kindness, a character trait, and compassion, a personality trait, comes out clearly in the following sentence. "Like the compassionate doctor, Joe is too inhibited by his kindness" (236). But on my account of kindness, it would never inhibit doing what is morally right or morally good. I explicitly state that confusing kindness with compassion involves the confusion between personality traits and character traits and may lead to mistaken moral judgments (*Morality*, 281). Driver realizes that I regard kindness as involving good judgments and even realizes that I regard her criticism to be based on a confusion.

Driver lists as "an irrationality—a failure to account for all the evidence" (237), but that is not my fundamental sense of irrational. Rather, as I continually emphasize, my account of rationality is based almost completely on consequences. An irrational action is one that causes the agent some harm without a compensating benefit for anyone. Thus, it follows that an impartial rational person would never favor doing something that makes the overall consequences worse. However, Driver claims that I "could fall back on appealing to consequences . . . then what's doing the work is an appeal to consequences, and not an appeal to rationality per se, and this is something I believe Gert would repudiate" (238). As Sinnott-Armstrong has pointed out, I have a consequentialist account of reasons, and my general account of rationality relies on consequences, so Driver must have some other concept of rationality in mind when she thinks I would repudiate an appeal to consequences and contrasts "an appeal to consequences" with "an appeal to rationality per se."

Driver is correct that my "account does not allow for unknown [moral] virtues and vices, at least not in any straightforward way" (238). Although she regards this as a criticism, it is not a criticism based on the ordinary view of moral virtues; it is quite clear that this criticism only makes sense if one accepts a consequentialist account of the virtues. I reject virtue consequentialism for the same kind of reason that I reject rule consequentialism. Just as the latter allows for the discovery of previously completely unknown moral rules, the former allows for the discovery of previously completely unknown moral virtues. Both are incompatible with an essential feature of morality, that everyone to whom morality applies knows what it prohibits, requires, discourages, encourages, and allows.

Driver claims that on my account "for agents to be impartial they must not make use of information that is inaccessible to any rational person" (238). However, that is not my account of impartiality. It is only when setting up the moral system that agents cannot "make use of information that is inaccessible to any rational person." When making particular judgments, impartial persons can and should make use of all the available facts. Her misunderstanding of my account of impartiality may be responsible for her claims about what I would say about "particular acts of kindness [that] undermine the character of the beneficiaries, making them weak and dependent, but that these long-term consequences are not apparent" (238). I would say that given all the information available at the time, if everyone believes that acting in a certain way is helpful, not harmful, then someone acting in that way is exhibiting a moral virtue. Of course, once one knew about the consequences it would no longer be exhibiting kindness, or any other moral virtue to act in that way. Moral judgments about virtues, like all other moral judgments, must be made on all the information foreseeable to people at the time of the action. But Driver maintains that even when the facts were completely unknowable at that time, "the more natural response is to hold that it [a person acting in that way] is [exhibiting] a moral vice, just not recognized as such" (238).

Only a radical consequentialist who thinks that moral evaluations are properly made on the basis of completely unknowable consequences could hold such a view. All ordinary people make their moral evaluations based upon the justified following of the public moral guide given all of the information foreseeable at the time. However, once it is discovered that certain acts that were formerly regarded as kind acts had bad consequences, those actions would come to be regarded as acts of misplaced kindness, i.e., not as acts of kindness at all. Indeed, something like this has actually happened in medicine. Doctors used to believe that it was kind to withhold the unpleasant truth from their patients; when it became known that this had more bad consequences than good ones, it was no longer regarded as kind for a doctor to withhold the truth. It was at most misplaced kindness, or compassion, and generally became criticized as paternalistic behavior. Kindness remains the same virtue; new knowledge simply tells us that what we used to think was a kind act is not really so.

Not surprisingly, Driver cites with approval Hume's view that "we tend to regard natural abilities and moral virtues in the same light—the distinction between them being merely verbal" (241). This is another example of the tendency of consequentialists to hold that there is no essential difference in the criteria for saying that something is "good" or "bad" and saying that it is "morally good" or "morally bad." In both cases, it is only the consequences that count. In my reply to Sinnott-Armstrong I have already shown that this is a mistaken view. Driver explicitly claims that "We don't reserve moral evaluation for only those traits one has control over developing" (241). Perhaps, like Hume, she holds that since we call some dogs "vicious," the judgments we make about dogs differ from moral judgments about the character of persons only in a verbal way. Indeed, since, according to Driver, the judgments we make about Phineas Gage, someone suffering from a serious mental disorder, are straightforward moral judgments, it does seem that judgments about the character of dogs do differ only in a verbal way from moral judgments about the character of persons. It seems paradoxical that someone who holds this kind of extreme consequentialism should claim that my account, which contains all of the standard moral virtues, "is not faithful to ordinary views" (242).

Driver wants to provide an account of virtues and vices in which the distinction between moral and nonmoral virtues and vices is not important. Further, she is concerned with traits of character that will be virtues in some contexts and vices in others. This is a possible topic, but it is not the topic with which I am concerned, nor is it a topic with which those philosophers who attempt to provide a moral guide to conduct are concerned. Hume is not attempting to provide such a guide, he is merely describing what he takes to be the causes of our judgments, including our moral judgments. My account of moral virtue and vice is such that all rational persons who adopt the moral system as a guide for their own behavior would not only regard the virtues and vices that I list as moral virtues and vices, they would all want to have these virtues and avoid these vices. That this list comes so close to what is regarded by both philosophers and ordinary people as moral virtues and vices seems to me to be a confirmation of my account of the moral system.

Since Driver is a consequentialist, it is not surprising that she is more concerned with evaluation than with decision making. She admits that "The Principle of Utility doesn't guide most morally proper action, but it can be used to evaluate action" (239). However, as I pointed out in my reply to Sinnott-Armstrong, moral evaluation must be made on the basis of the public moral system that does guide action, not on some completely independent criteria that considers consequences that no one could have known about at the time of acting. Driver admits that "Rules . . . guide action and in this way are practical" (240). "But virtues need not function to guide behavior at all. They are used to evaluate our behavior, to praise or condemn it. Virtues may figure as terms within rules, but the virtues themselves simply work as evaluative terms" (240). But this is to confuse virtues which are praiseworthy traits of character with virtue terms which are used to praise those traits of character. Moral virtues are those traits of character that involve justified obedience to the moral rules and justified following of the moral ideals. Our evaluation of these traits of character is based on their conformity to the moral system. To think otherwise is to make it purely accidental that trustworthy people keep their promises and kind people try to relieve pain and suffering.

Reply to Baron

Baron disagrees with my view that "Morality is best conceived as a guide to behavior that rational persons put forward to govern the behavior of others, whether or not they plan to follow that guide themselves" (243). However, looking at those rules that are most commonly put forward as moral rules, Do not kill, Do not cause pain, Do not deceive, Keep your promises, etc., it is obvious that these rules are best explained by thinking of morality in the way that I characterize it. Further, even the moral judgments that are made about people depend ultimately on the way that they act with regard to the moral rules and moral ideals. Normally, people who unjustifiably violate the moral rules significantly more than most people do are judged morally bad, and those who, with the appropriate motives, justifiably follow the moral ideals significantly more than most people do are judged morally good. Baron agrees with me about these judgments. My moral theory accounts for all of them.

Baron claims, "what is missing from [my] account is, in a word, character" (244). She holds that I do not provide an adequate account of these virtues and vices and disagrees with my claim that "emotions and feelings are morally important only insofar as they lead to morally good actions" (244). She holds,

> How one thinks about others, how one responds, affectively, when one hears that a colleague has just received a prestigious award, or when one hears of some grave injustice, does matter morally. It matters even if one does not exhibit one's sentiments in any way, or act accordingly. A desire to torture a child to death—even a mere fantasy of doing so—is of moral concern, even if the person would absolutely never act accordingly (and even if we are confident that this is the case). (245)

Baron does not say exactly what she means by "moral," but it is clear she would not accept my view that the philosophically significant use of the term "moral" must be based, directly or indirectly, on that informal public system that is morality. She claims that her difference with me is "a difference in intuitions," but I think it is more a matter of what is meant by "moral."

Baron correctly notes that parents would prefer that their children not have bad attitudes, even apart from the effect of those attitudes on the children's actions, (245) but mistakenly thinks that this confers on these attitudes some moral character independent of their effect on the children's actions. Baron is clear that I view the raising of children as morally very significant, but thinks that I hold that we want our children to have certain affective responses and attitudes "only because they lead to morally good or right actions" (245). I hold that we want our children not only to act morally, but to enjoy acting in that way, that is, to have the appropriate affective responses and attitudes. As parents, even if we could guarantee that our children would act morally by exercising "perfect self-control" (245), we would still prefer that they enjoy acting in that way rather than not enjoy it. This is true even if we would still count it as a moral virtue if a person always acted in the appropriate way regardless of her affective responses and attitudes. There is not much difference between Baron and myself on the general issue of the importance of affective responses and attitudes independent of their affect on actions, we differ only in whether to use the term "moral" to refer to those affective responses and attitudes.

The same is true about our disagreement regarding tolerance. For Baron, "the person who is intolerant has morally objectionable *attitudes*," (246) but she admits that there is at least "a narrow sense of 'tolerant'" in which it is actions, not affective responses and attitudes, that determine whether one is tolerant (255, n. 7). She claims it is a difference in intuitions, but again it seems to me to be a difference in the use of the terms, this time "tolerant." Especially, given that Baron presents her views as Kantian, it seems quite odd to me that she can write, "To say that it [disgust at gays] is morally objectionable is not, of course, to say that the person who feels such disgust is responsible for feeling as he does; the question of responsibility is a separate question" (246). Kant would not regard anything as morally objectionable that was not the responsibility of some moral agent. I agree with Kant that moral judgments are not appropriate about anything for which a person is not at least partly responsible. Baron herself says that she shares my view "that we are responsible to some considerable extent for our own characters" (255, n. 5).

Baron may be using the term "moral" in a traditional sense, such that "moral" simply refers to matters related to character. But unless character is closely related to actions, then I do not think that she can account for the use of phrases like "morally wrong." I am trying to provide a systematic account of morality that accounts for all of our moral decisions and judgments. Such an account must take actions as central. As I mentioned earlier, it does not follow from the fact that parents want their children to enjoy acting morally that enjoying acting morally is itself a moral matter. Morally speaking, that is, from the perspective of the moral system, it makes no difference if a person acts morally because she enjoys acting that way or because she has some religious belief that leads her to act that way. What makes a moral difference is the reliability of the motivation, especially in those circumstances when one can act undetected by other persons, or when acting morally conflicts with acting in some other way, e.g., acting as one's country or religion requires.

Baron is correct that my claim that "we admire the character of the person who was less tempted more than that of the person who was more tempted" does depend on what temptations we are picturing (247). I was thinking of temptations to act immorally, that is, to violate a moral rule, when the temptations are those normally considered by philosophers, fame, status, and wealth, that is, egoistic temptations. But when the temptation to act immorally involves compassion, e.g., lying to prevent someone from suffering a deserved punishment, I admit that we might sometimes admire the character of the person who is tempted more than the character of one who is not. It makes perfect sense to morally condemn an action of a person while at the same time morally praising the motivation that made him act in that way. But that happens only when that kind of motivation generally leads to morally right or good actions.

Interestingly, Baron's cases do not involve temptations to act immorally, but rather to give up acting in a morally good way, that is, to stop following some moral ideal (247-48). These cases are complex, for acting on a moral ideal when one is tempted to give it up already shows a good moral character. She is right that in the cases she presents we do not admire the character of the person who is tempted less than the character of one who is not, but might even admire her more. But her basis for saying this is that "we do not judge it in any way a flaw that she was so tempted" (247). All of this is perfectly consistent with my view that actions are fundamental in making moral judgments. Overcoming a temptation of a kind that, in itself, does not lead to morally bad actions, in order to continue doing morally good actions, is even a stronger indication of a good moral character. When it is not clear whether the temptation to act immorally makes one more or less likely to act in moral or morally good ways, then it is not clear whether we admire the person who is tempted more or less than the person who is not. It is one's view about the normal effect on a person's actions of having these kinds of motivations that determines our judgments about the person's character.

Returning to her initial difference with me, Baron says, "Now, if I have to choose between seeing morality as primarily a guide for one's own behavior and seeing it primarily as a guide put forward to govern others' behavior, I will pick the former" (249). In making this choice, Baron sides with the vast majority of moral philosophers. But any unbiased look at what are ordinarily considered to be moral rules, like the ten that I list, or the moral ideals, reveals that the most natural way to look at them is as a guide that rational persons want others to follow with regard to themselves and those for whom they are concerned, no matter how they feel about following them themselves. Showing that morality is best conceived in the way that I conceive it is in no way incompatible with having "collective concerns" (249). Indeed, Hobbes, whom I hold in the highest regard, conceives of all of the moral virtues as those virtues that lead to peace, that is, to the institution and preservation of a stable society. Also, I do not know why she thinks that the strong connection I make between morally wrong actions and being liable to punishment is somehow incompatible with the view that the best way to get people to act morally is to bring up children in the right way (249). I make this point myself (see *Morality*, 277-78), and Hobbes, who regards sovereign power as essential for reliable moral behavior, still regards education as the best way to get people to act morally.

Although Baron is bothered about the close connection I make between moral wrongness and punishment, she notes that many actions which might be classified as morally wrong, I classify as morally bad (249). She disagrees with what she takes to be my claim that judgments that someone unjustifiably violated a moral rule "entail a judgment that the party who acts morally wrongly deserves to be punished" (250). I never say this. I say only that if a person's action is morally wrong, then it is of a kind that makes him liable to punishment, a much weaker claim. If the particular action is trivial, i.e., if publicly allowing it would not result in much harm, then it may be that punishing that kind of action would result in more harm than not punishing it. In such a case, impartial rational persons would not want anyone to punish that kind of action.

What I mean by a morally wrong action is more closely related to what I understand Kant to mean by a violation of a juridical duty than to what he means by a violation of an ethical duty. Baron, on the other hand, may identify morality with ethical duties. The violation of a juridical duty concerns the action itself, rather than as with an ethical duty, with the maxim on the basis of which one acts. I hold that motives are irrelevant to the moral rightness or wrongness of our actions, just as Kant holds that motives are irrelevant to the juridical rightness or wrongness of our actions. However, Kant, like many rule utilitarians, tries to formulate duties, including juridical duties, in such a way that they never conflict, and it is never justified to violate any juridical duty. Thus, Kant never deals with the question of how one might justify the violation of a juridical duty. Whereas for me, the critical question generally is whether a violation of a moral rule is justified, either weakly or strongly.

I agree with Baron's claim about people who do morally wrong actions that "our judgment that they are acting immorally does not entail that we ought to try to get them to change their ways" (250). From the fact that I hold that it is only appropriate for authorized parties to interfere with those who do morally wrong actions, it should be obvious that I agree that one's judgment about the immorality of someone's action does not entail that one ought to interfere with them. To do so in any serious way is to act as a kind of vigilante, and that would not be publicly allowed by any impartial rational person. Publicly allowing this kind of violation would result in more harm than not publicly allowing it. Further, Baron notes that I recognize that "morally wrong" is not always related to punishment (255-56, n. 11). But Baron and I do seem to disagree about whether judging that someone has done a serious morally wrong act does entail that one judges that it is appropriate for an authorized someone to "compel them, by threat of punishment, to act accordingly" (250). She says it does not, I say it does. However, even here our seeming disagreement may simply be a matter of terminology; what I mean by morally wrong actions in this context are unjustified violations of moral rules, closely related to Kant's violations of juridical duties, whereas her morally wrong actions seem to be violations of what Kant calls ethical duties.

I continue to think that there is less substantive disagreement between Baron's view and mine than there seems to be. This is clearly the case when Baron talks about moral wrongs to oneself (251). Here she is clearly talking about Kant's ethical rather than his juridical duties. I acknowledge in the first chapter of my book that there is a broad view of morality, stemming from religion, that includes harm to self as immoral. (This seems to be the German concept of morality.) However, I am not concerned with this purely personal sense of morality. If being immoral is only violating ethical duties, that is, not acting on the appropriate maxims, and does not affect others at all, then I agree with Baron that, except for special relationships, it is inappropriate for anyone to interfere with them. With regard to public morality, harming oneself is only morally wrong when it affects one's ability or motivation not to harm or to help others, e.g., drinking too much when this interferes with performing one's duties appropriately. If Baron holds that harming oneself can be morally wrong even when this has no connection at all with my behavior toward anyone else, then we are clearly using the phrase "morally wrong" in different ways. I would regard such behavior as irrational, not as immoral, not so much as a judgment about a person's character, as about her mental health.

Baron's paper shows that "morality" is used in different senses. It is an empirical question how the term "moral" is most commonly used by English speakers. I do not deny that it is sometimes used as Baron uses it. Contrary to both of our uses, it may even be used most frequently to characterize sexual behavior. Indeed, many would disagree with Baron and view disgust toward gays as morally appropriate rather than morally wrong. But if one is interested in a coherent concept of morality that accounts for the vast majority of moral judgments made by thoughtful people, then the account that I provide does this better than any alternative account, including that of Kant. Further, this concept of morality fits together with our ordinary concepts of rationality and impartiality such that it shows that this concept of morality is justified, that is, that with appropriate qualifications it would be endorsed by all rational persons, and acted on by all rational persons who were impartial in the way that morality requires.

Baron has saved me from some clear misinterpretations of Kant. However, it is quite likely that, despite her help, I have persisted in some mistaken interpretations. My primary aim in contrasting my view of morality to what I take to be Kant's account of morality, is to clarify my account of morality. I do not make any claims about the accuracy of my interpretations of Kant.

Index

About the Contributors

Robert Audi is Charles J. Mach University Professor of Philosophy at University of Nebraska, Lincoln.

Marcia Baron is Professor of Philosophy at Indiana University.

E. J. Bond is Professor Emeritus of Philosophy at Queen's University, Kingston, Ontario.

David Copp is Professor of Philosophy at Bowling Green State University and a Senior Research Fellow at the Social Philosophy and Policy Center at Bowling Green State University.

John Deigh is Professor of Philosophy at Northwestern University and Editor of *Ethics*.

Julia Driver is Professor of Philosophy at Dartmouth College.

Bernard Gert is the Stone Professor of Intellectual and Moral Philosophy at Dartmouth College and Adjunct Professor of Psychiatry at Dartmouth Medical School.

Shelly Kagan is Henry R. Luce Professor of Social Thought and Ethics at Yale University.

Frances Kamm is Professor of Philosophy, Professor of Medicine (Bioethics), Law School Affiliated Faculty, New York University.

Matthias Kettner is Assistant Professor at Frankfurt University and Fellow at the Institute of Advanced Cultural Studies at Essen, Germany.

Douglas MacLean is Professor of Philosophy at University of North Carolina, Chapel Hill.

Geoffrey Sayre-McCord is the Bowman and Gordon Gray Professor of Philosophy at University of North Carolina, Chapel Hill.

Walter Sinnott-Armstrong is Professor of Philosophy at Dartmouth College.

Michael Smith is Professor of Philosophy at the Research School of Social Sciences, Australian National University.

Ernst Tugendhat is Professor Emeritus of Philosophy at Freie Universität, Berlin.

Susan Wolf is Edna J. Koury Distinguished Professor of Philosophy at University of North Carolina, Chapel Hill.